THE BEGINNING AFTER THE END

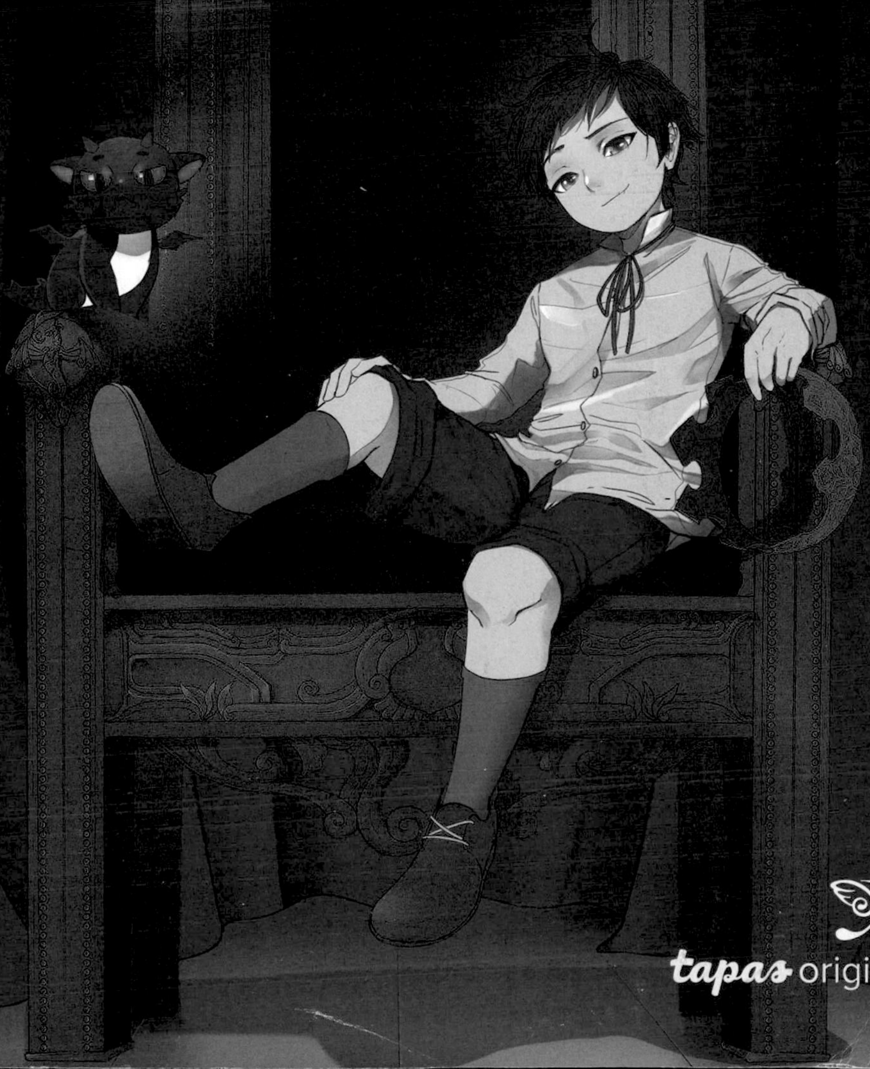

Yen Press
tapas original

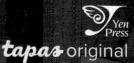

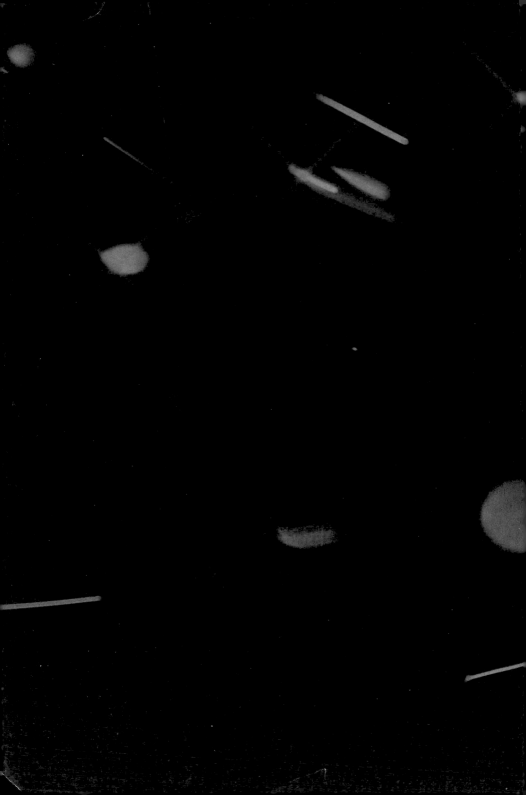

THE BEGINNING AFTER THE END

1

STORY BY TURTLEME
ART BY FUYUKI23

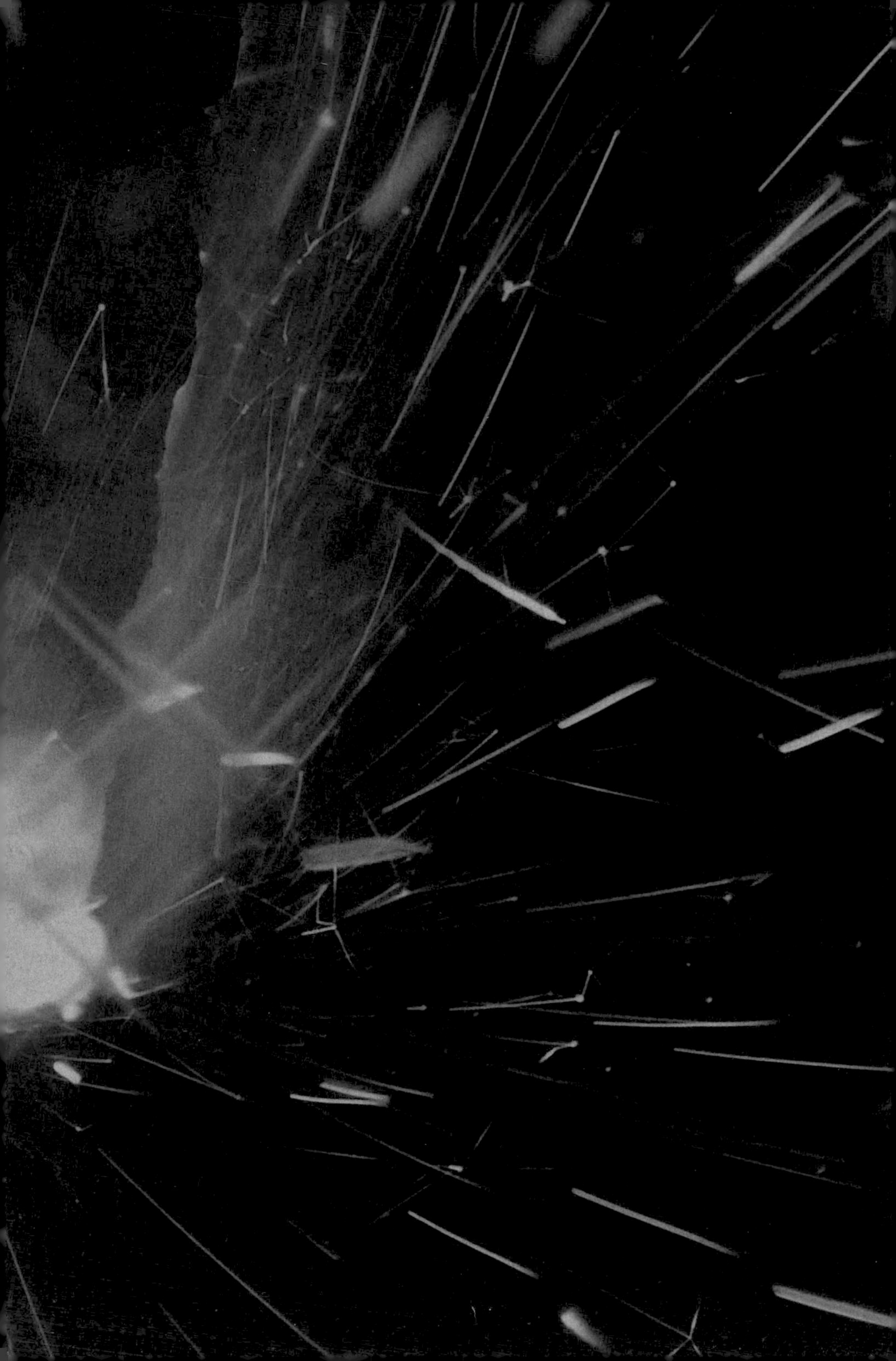

TABLE OF CONTENTS

CHAPTER 1—The End of the Tunnel

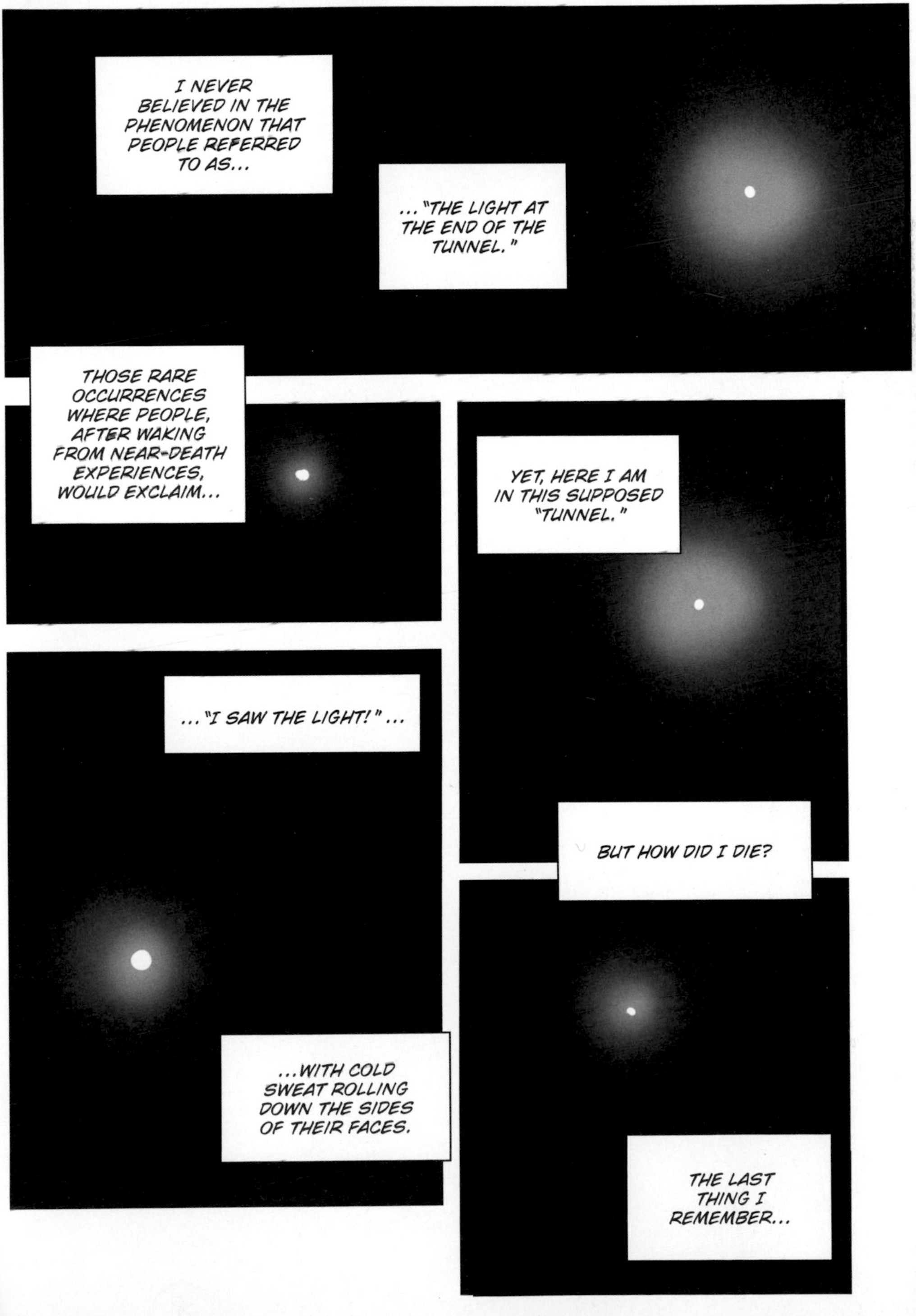
I NEVER BELIEVED IN THE PHENOMENON THAT PEOPLE REFERRED TO AS...
..."THE LIGHT AT THE END OF THE TUNNEL."
THOSE RARE OCCURRENCES WHERE PEOPLE, AFTER WAKING FROM NEAR-DEATH EXPERIENCES, WOULD EXCLAIM...
..."I SAW THE LIGHT!"...
...WITH COLD SWEAT ROLLING DOWN THE SIDES OF THEIR FACES.
YET, HERE I AM IN THIS SUPPOSED "TUNNEL."
BUT HOW DID I DIE?
THE LAST THING I REMEMBER...

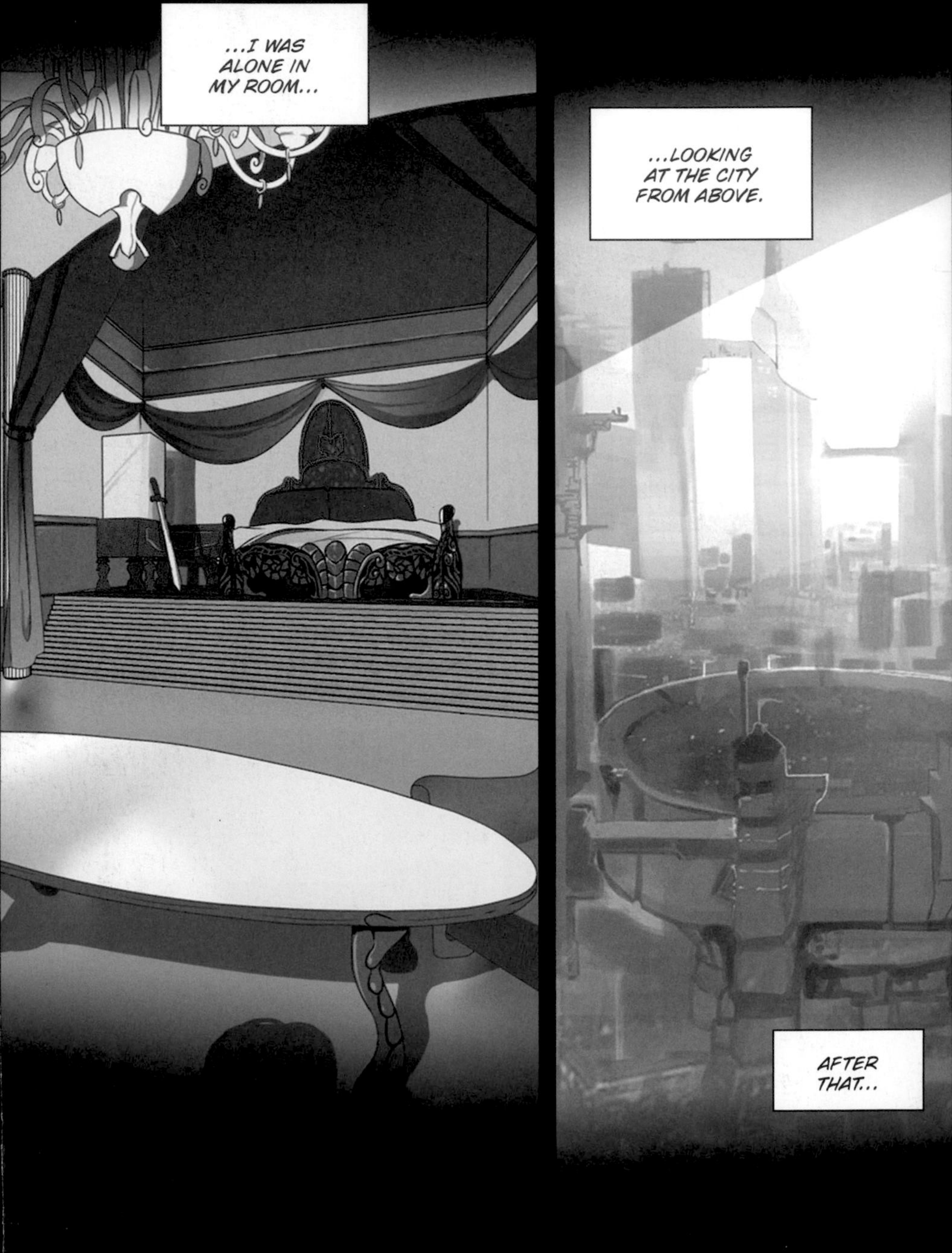
...I WAS ALONE IN MY ROOM...
...LOOKING AT THE CITY FROM ABOVE.
AFTER THAT...

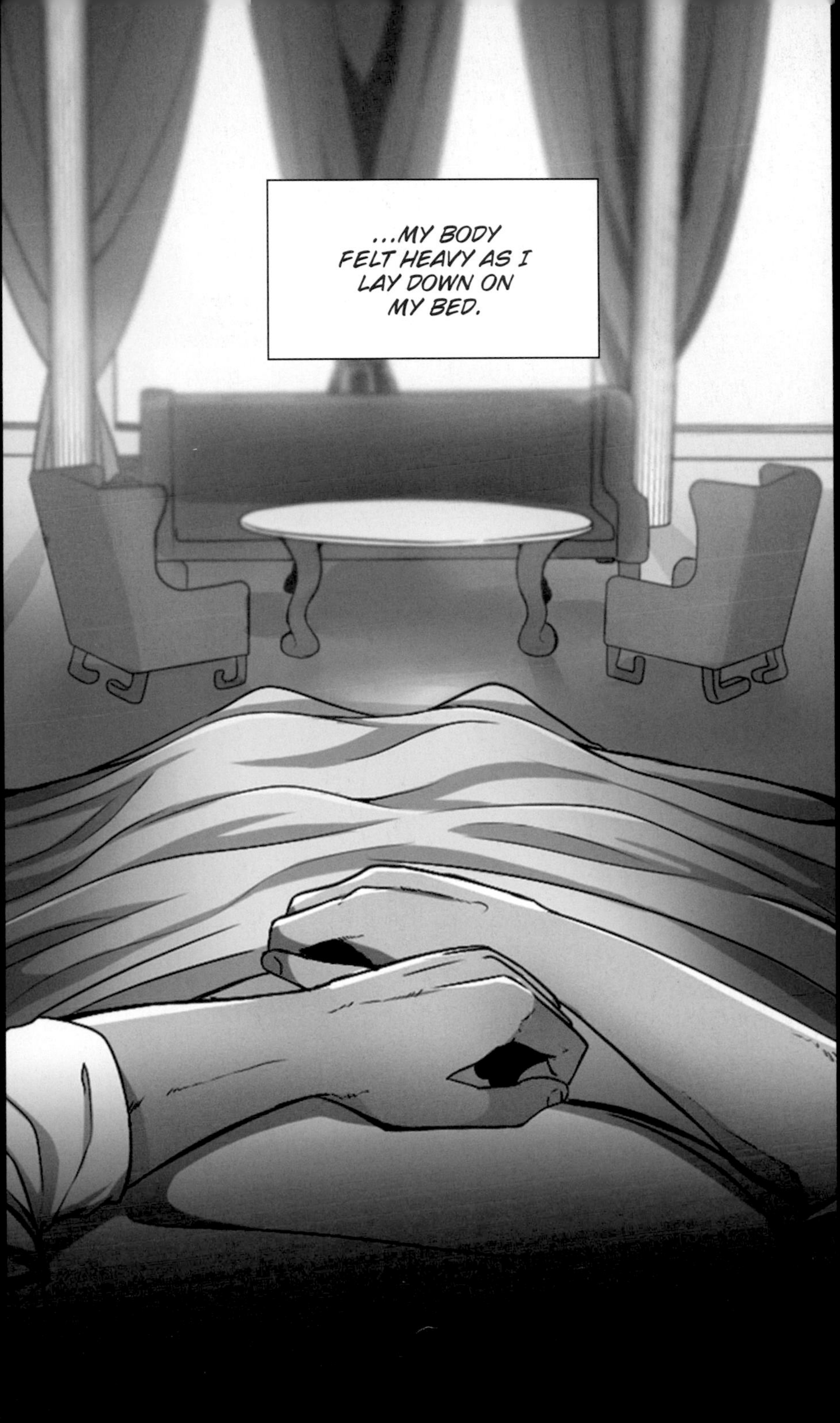
...MY BODY FELT HEAVY AS I LAY DOWN ON MY BED.

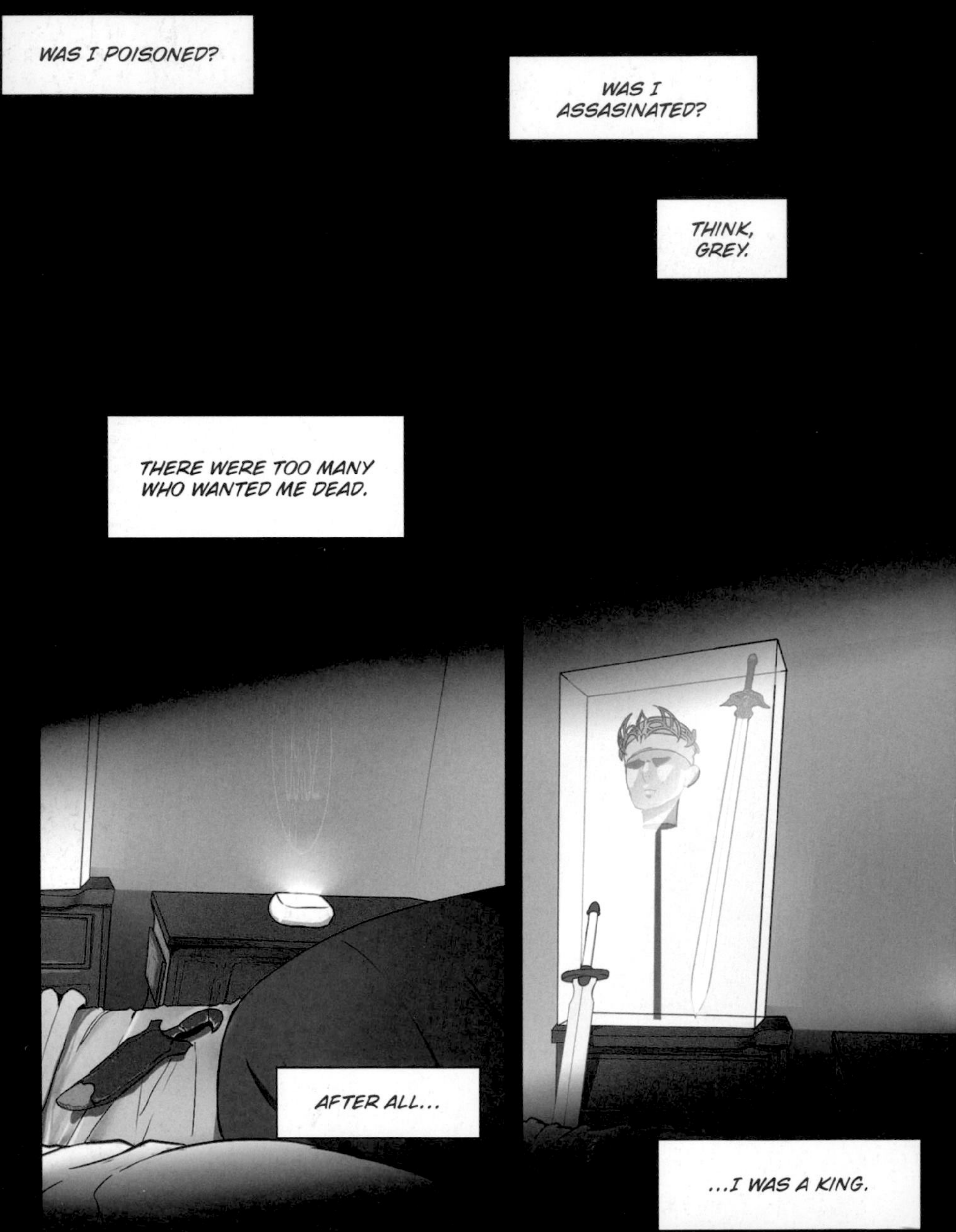
WAS I POISONED?
WAS I ASSASINATED?
THINK, GREY.
THERE WERE TOO MANY WHO WANTED ME DEAD.
AFTER ALL...
...I WAS A KING.

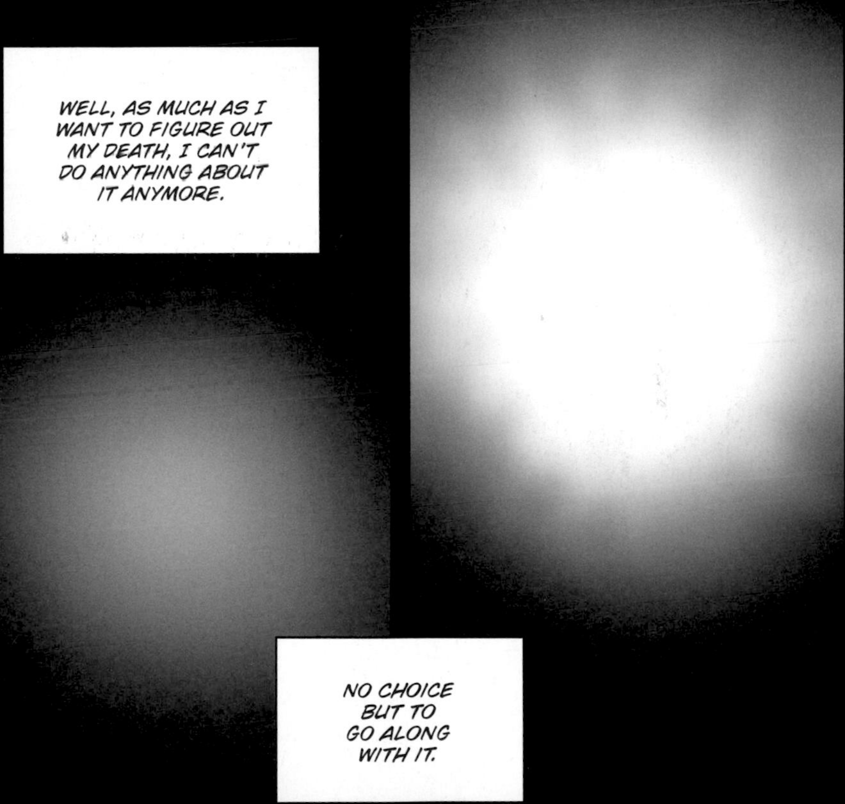
WELL, AS MUCH AS I WANT TO FIGURE OUT MY DEATH, I CAN'T DO ANYTHING ABOUT IT ANYMORE.
NO CHOICE BUT TO GO ALONG WITH IT.

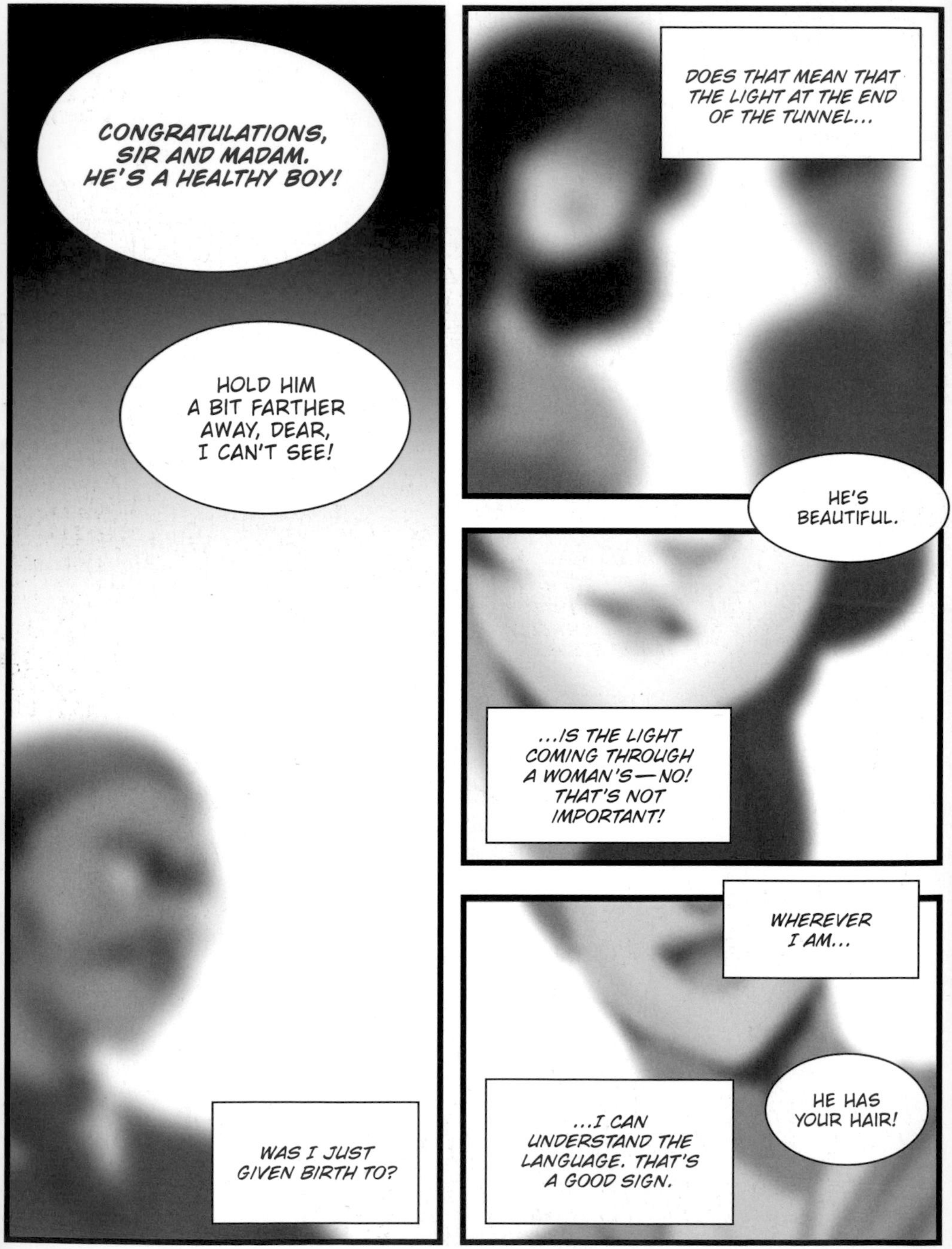
CONGRATULATIONS, SIR AND MADAM. HE'S A HEALTHY BOY!
HOLD HIM A BIT FARTHER AWAY, DEAR, I CAN'T SEE!
WAS I JUST GIVEN BIRTH TO?
DOES THAT MEAN THAT THE LIGHT AT THE END OF THE TUNNEL...
HE'S BEAUTIFUL.
...IS THE LIGHT COMING THROUGH A WOMAN'S—NO! THAT'S NOT IMPORTANT!
WHEREVER I AM...
...I CAN UNDERSTAND THE LANGUAGE. THAT'S A GOOD SIGN.
HE HAS YOUR HAIR!

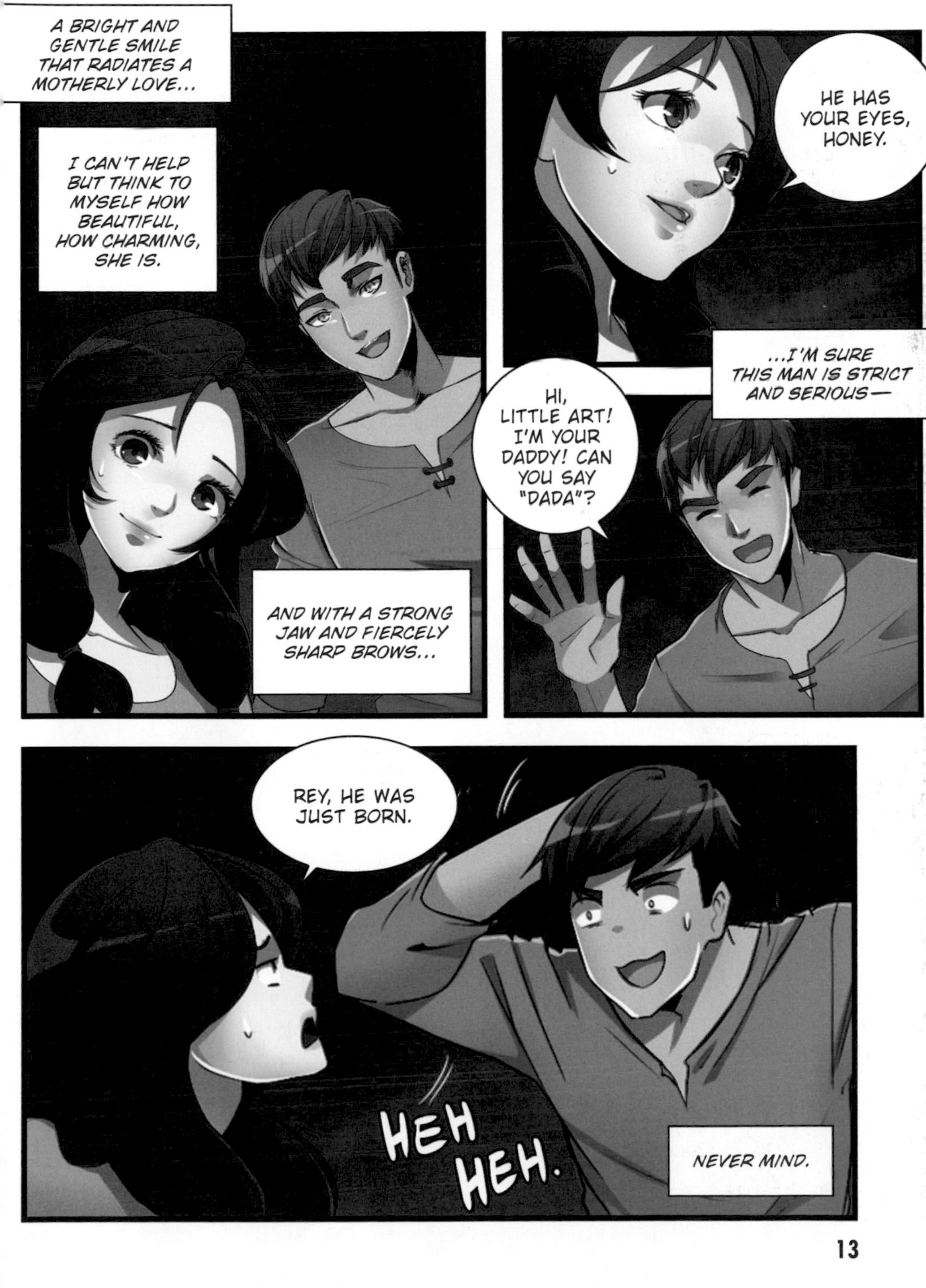
A BRIGHT AND GENTLE SMILE THAT RADIATES A MOTHERLY LOVE...
I CAN'T HELP BUT THINK TO MYSELF HOW BEAUTIFUL, HOW CHARMING, SHE IS.
AND WITH A STRONG JAW AND FIERCELY SHARP BROWS...
HE HAS YOUR EYES, HONEY.
...I'M SURE THIS MAN IS STRICT AND SERIOUS—
HI, LITTLE ART! I'M YOUR DADDY! CAN YOU SAY "DADA"?
REY, HE WAS JUST BORN.
HEH HEH.
NEVER MIND.

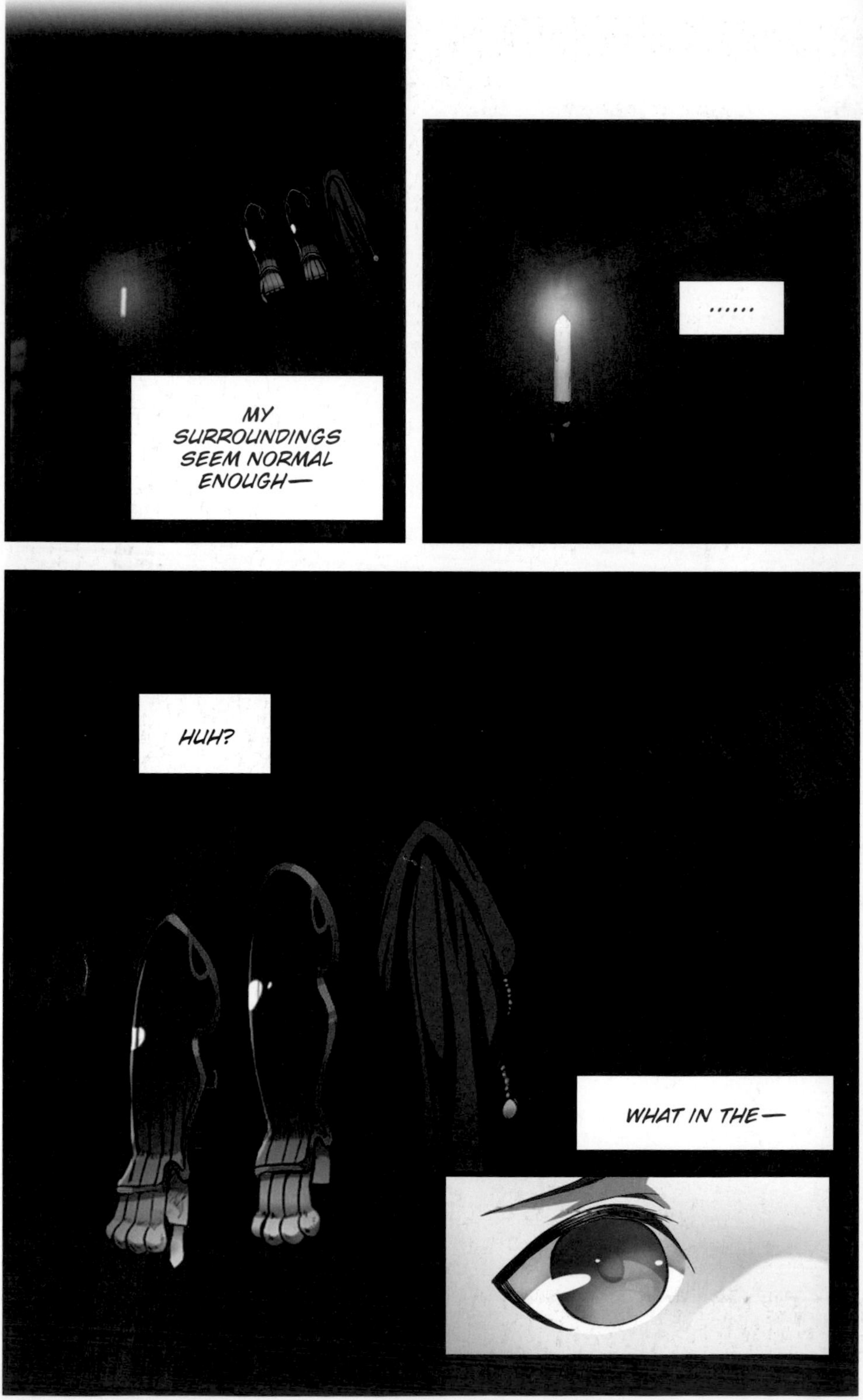
MY SURROUNDINGS SEEM NORMAL ENOUGH—
......
HUH?
WHAT IN THE—

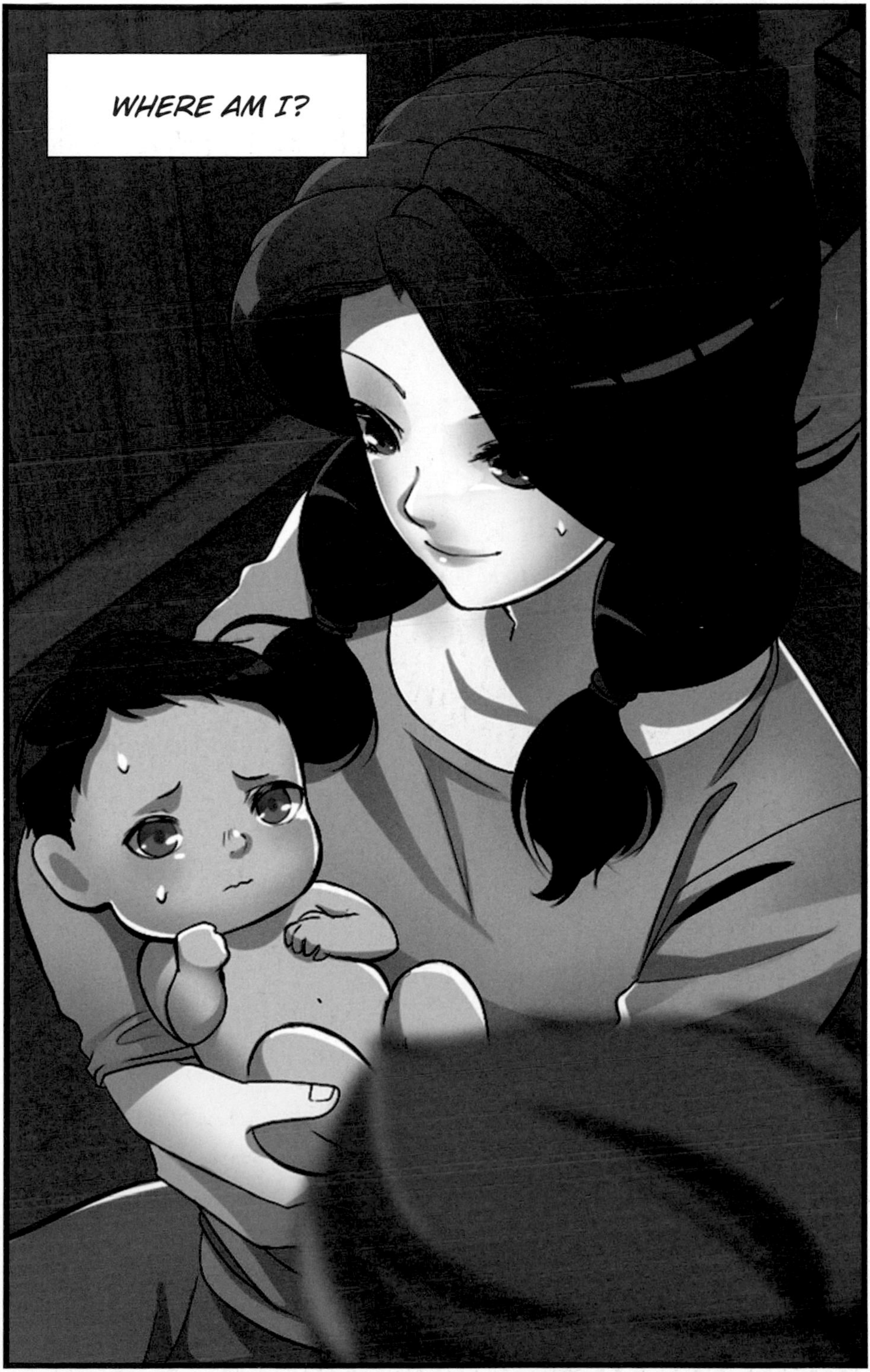
WHERE AM I?

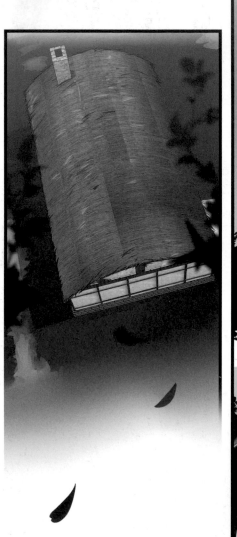

WEEKS SLOWLY
TRICKLED BY.

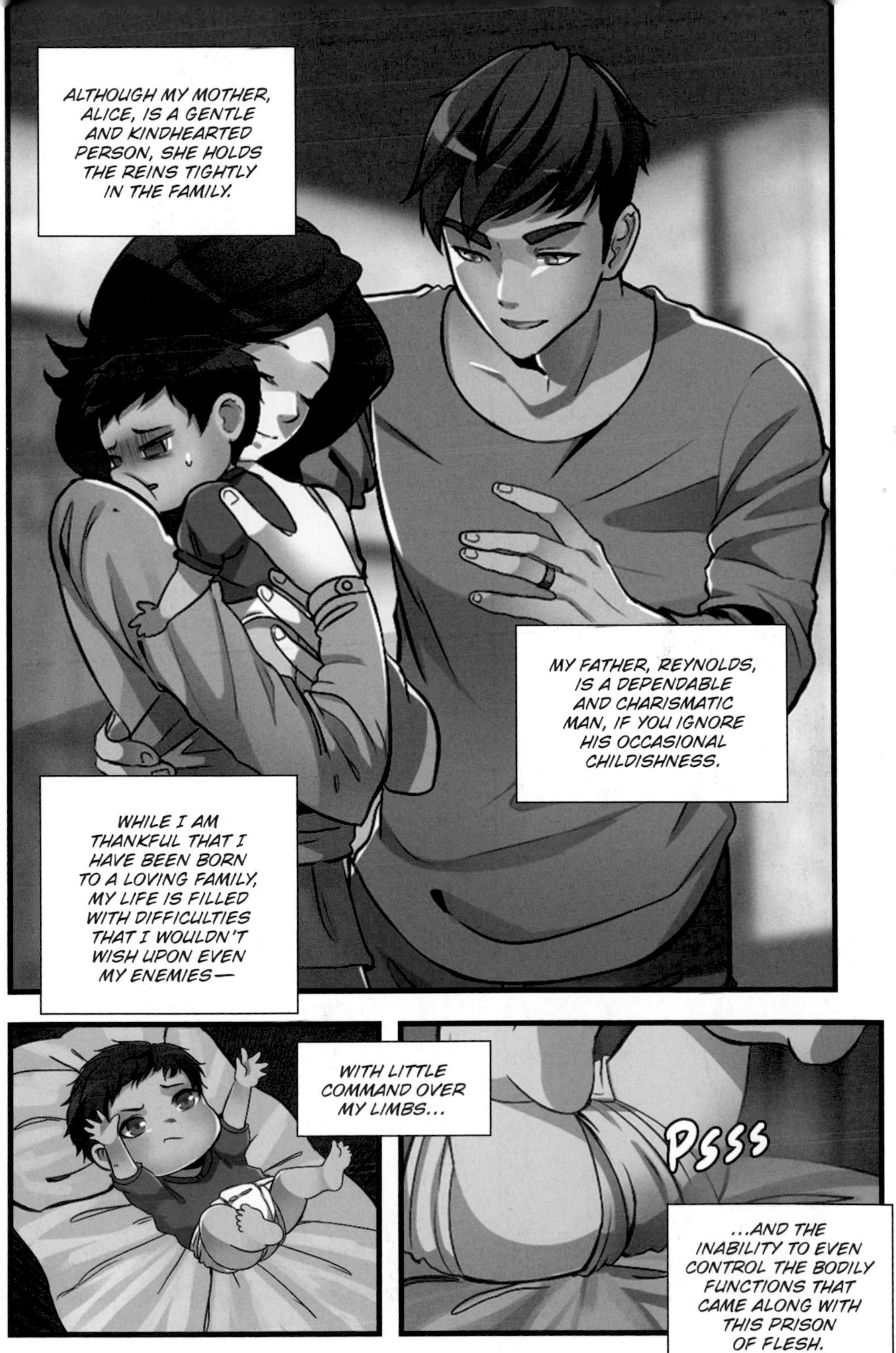
ALTHOUGH MY MOTHER, ALICE, IS A GENTLE AND KINDHEARTED PERSON, SHE HOLDS THE REINS TIGHTLY IN THE FAMILY.
MY FATHER, REYNOLDS, IS A DEPENDABLE AND CHARISMATIC MAN, IF YOU IGNORE HIS OCCASIONAL CHILDISHNESS.
WHILE I AM THANKFUL THAT I HAVE BEEN BORN TO A LOVING FAMILY, MY LIFE IS FILLED WITH DIFFICULTIES THAT I WOULDN'T WISH UPON EVEN MY ENEMIES—
WITH LITTLE COMMAND OVER MY LIMBS...
PSSS
...AND THE INABILITY TO EVEN CONTROL THE BODILY FUNCTIONS THAT CAME ALONG WITH THIS PRISON OF FLESH.

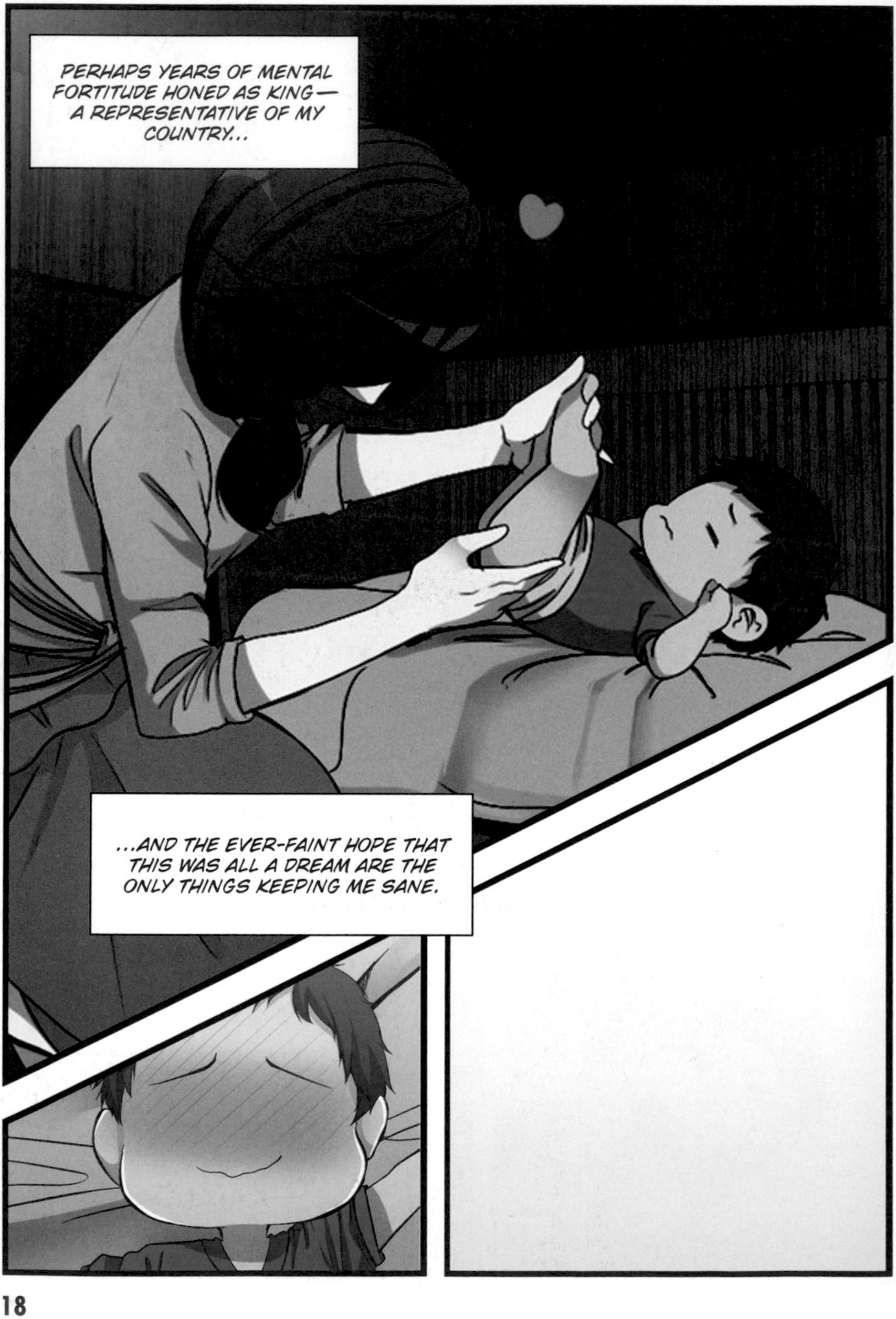
PERHAPS YEARS OF MENTAL FORTITUDE HONED AS KING— A REPRESENTATIVE OF MY COUNTRY...
...AND THE EVER-FAINT HOPE THAT THIS WAS ALL A DREAM ARE THE ONLY THINGS KEEPING ME SANE.

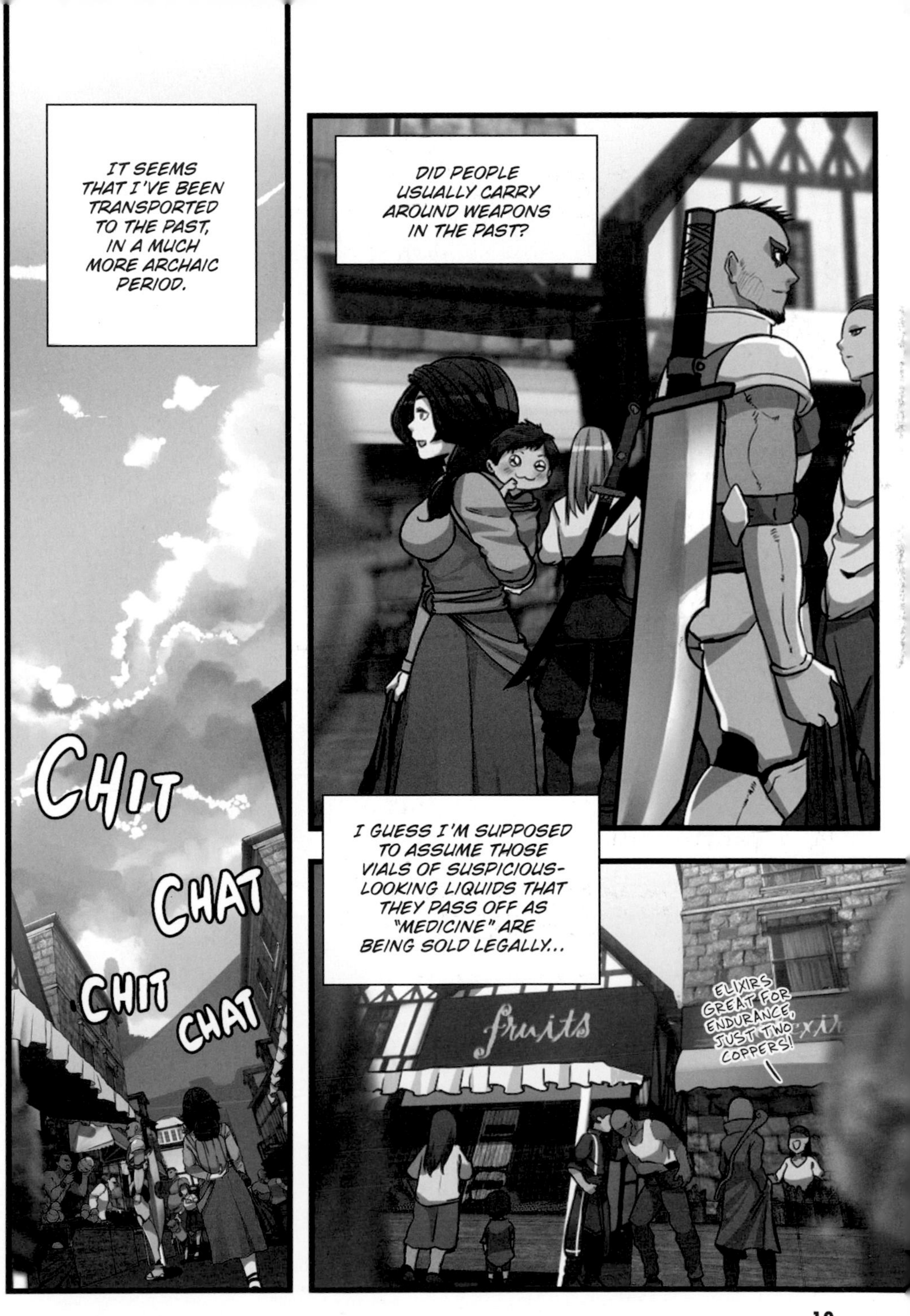
IT SEEMS THAT I'VE BEEN TRANSPORTED TO THE PAST, IN A MUCH MORE ARCHAIC PERIOD.
CHIT
CHAT
CHIT
CHAT
DID PEOPLE USUALLY CARRY AROUND WEAPONS IN THE PAST?
I GUESS I'M SUPPOSED TO ASSUME THOSE VIALS OF SUSPICIOUS-LOOKING LIQUIDS THAT THEY PASS OFF AS "MEDICINE" ARE BEING SOLD LEGALLY...
fruits
ELIXIRS GREAT FOR ENDURANCE, JUST TWO COPPERS!

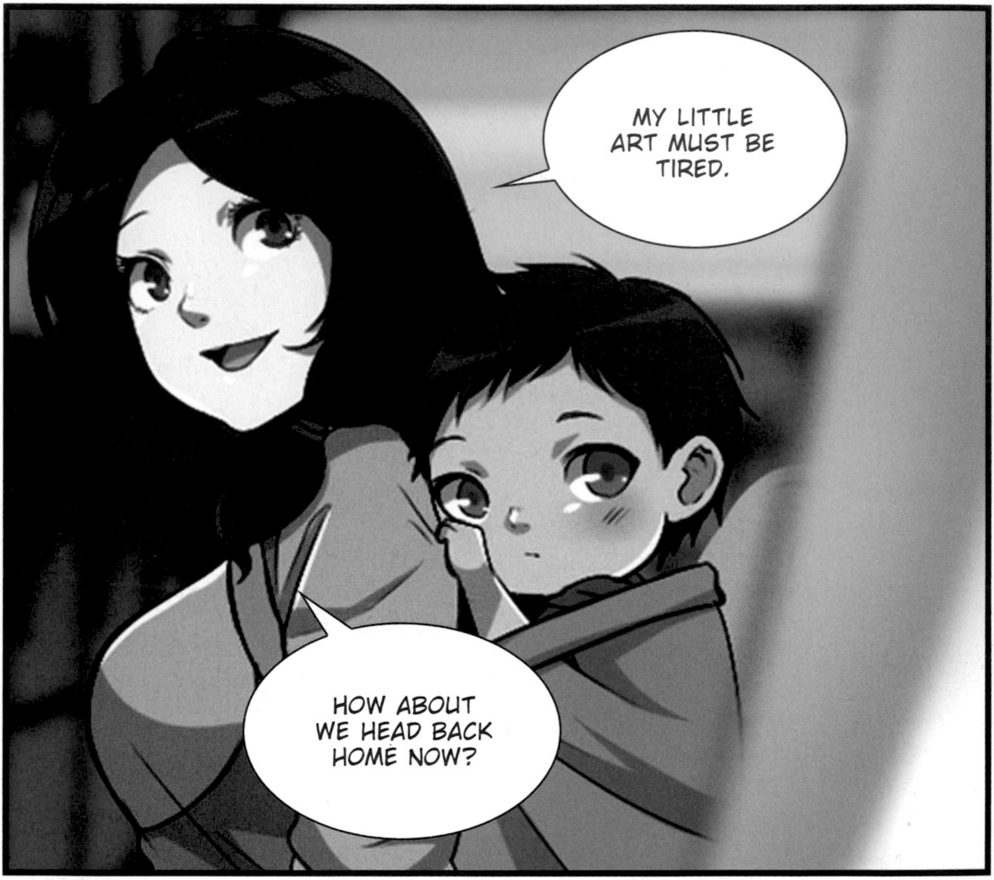
MY LITTLE ART MUST BE TIRED.
HOW ABOUT WE HEAD BACK HOME NOW?

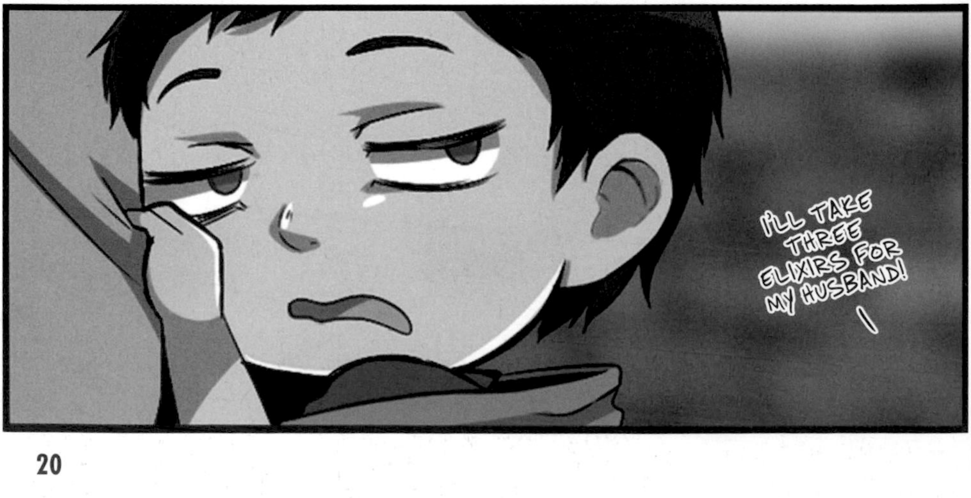
I'LL TAKE THREE ELIXIRS FOR MY HUSBAND!

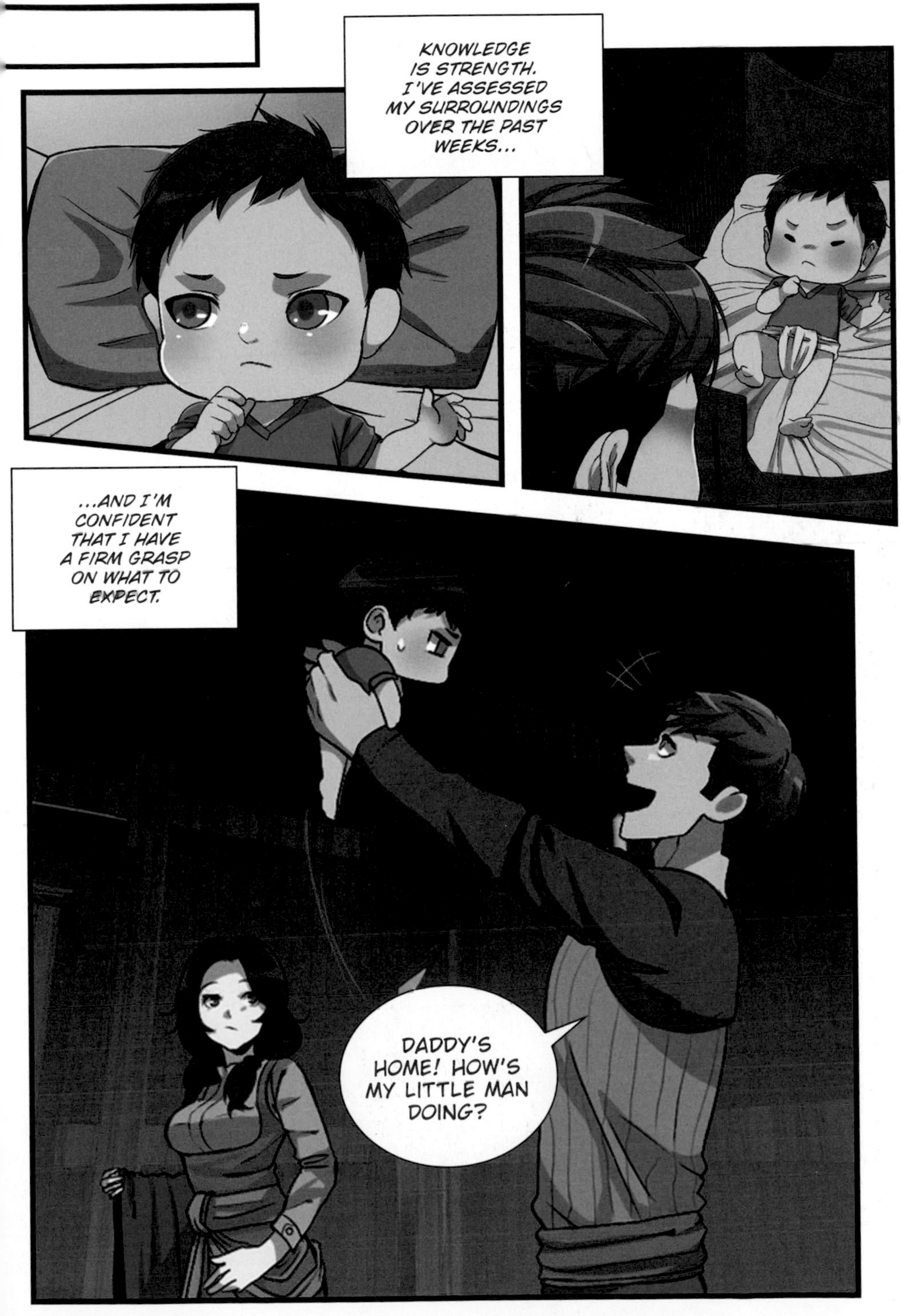
KNOWLEDGE IS STRENGTH. I'VE ASSESSED MY SURROUNDINGS OVER THE PAST WEEKS...
...AND I'M CONFIDENT THAT I HAVE A FIRM GRASP ON WHAT TO EXPECT.
DADDY'S HOME! HOW'S MY LITTLE MAN DOING?

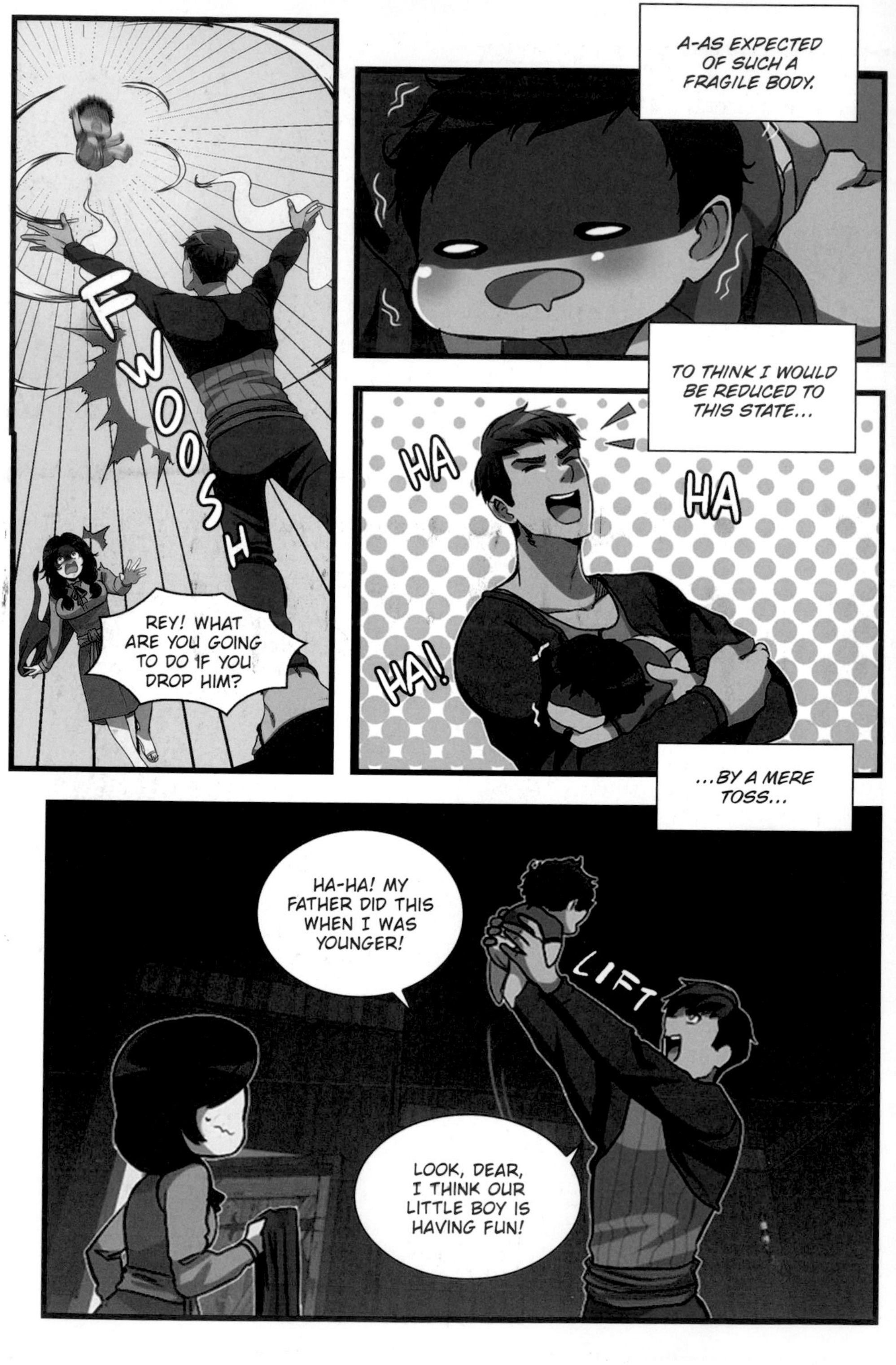
FWOOSH
REY! WHAT ARE YOU GOING TO DO IF YOU DROP HIM?
A-AS EXPECTED OF SUCH A FRAGILE BODY.
TO THINK I WOULD BE REDUCED TO THIS STATE...
HA
HA
HA!
...BY A MERE TOSS...
HA-HA! MY FATHER DID THIS WHEN I WAS YOUNGER!
LIFT
LOOK, DEAR, I THINK OUR LITTLE BOY IS HAVING FUN!

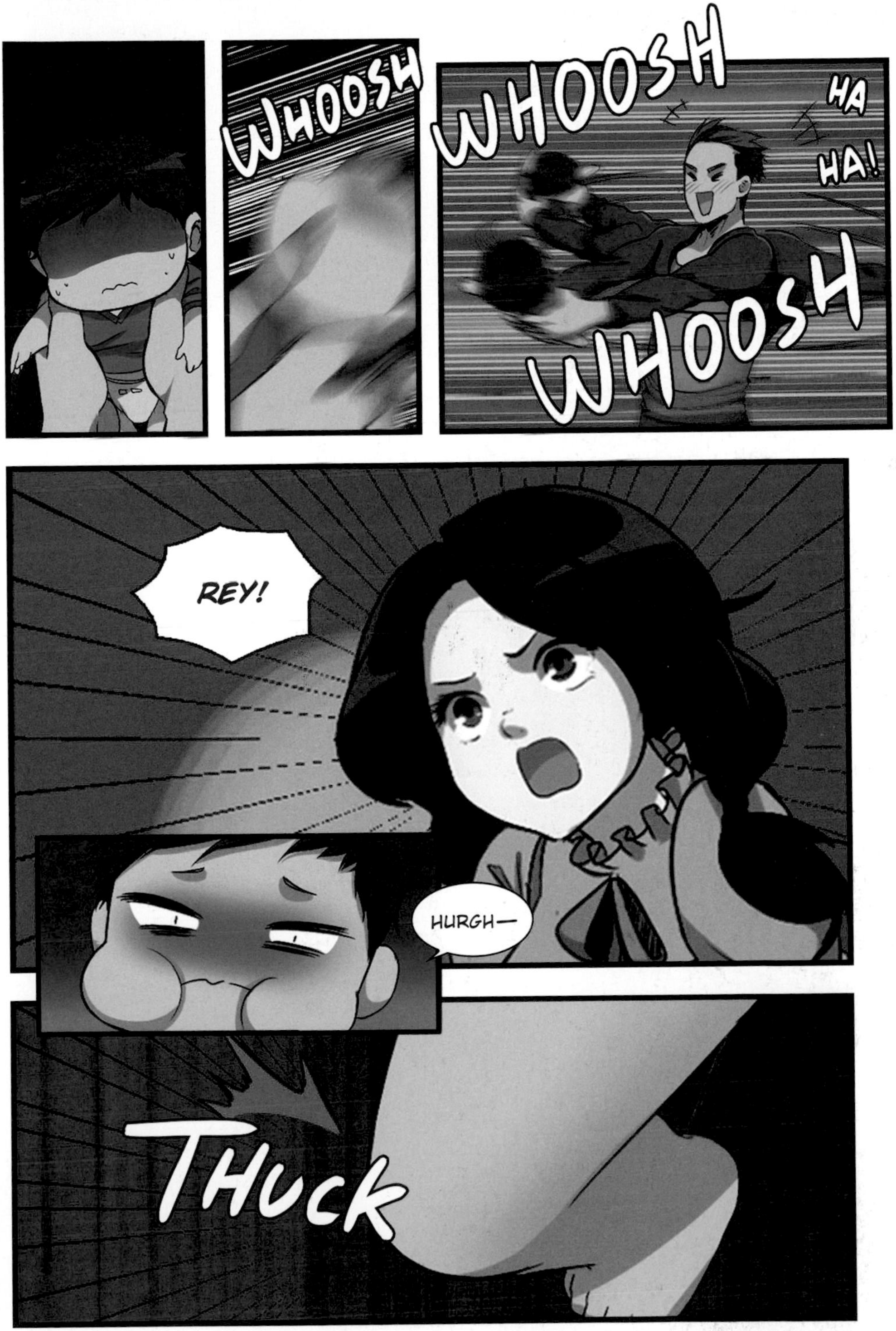
WHOOSH
WHOOSH
HA
HA!
WHOOSH
REY!
HURGH—
THUCK

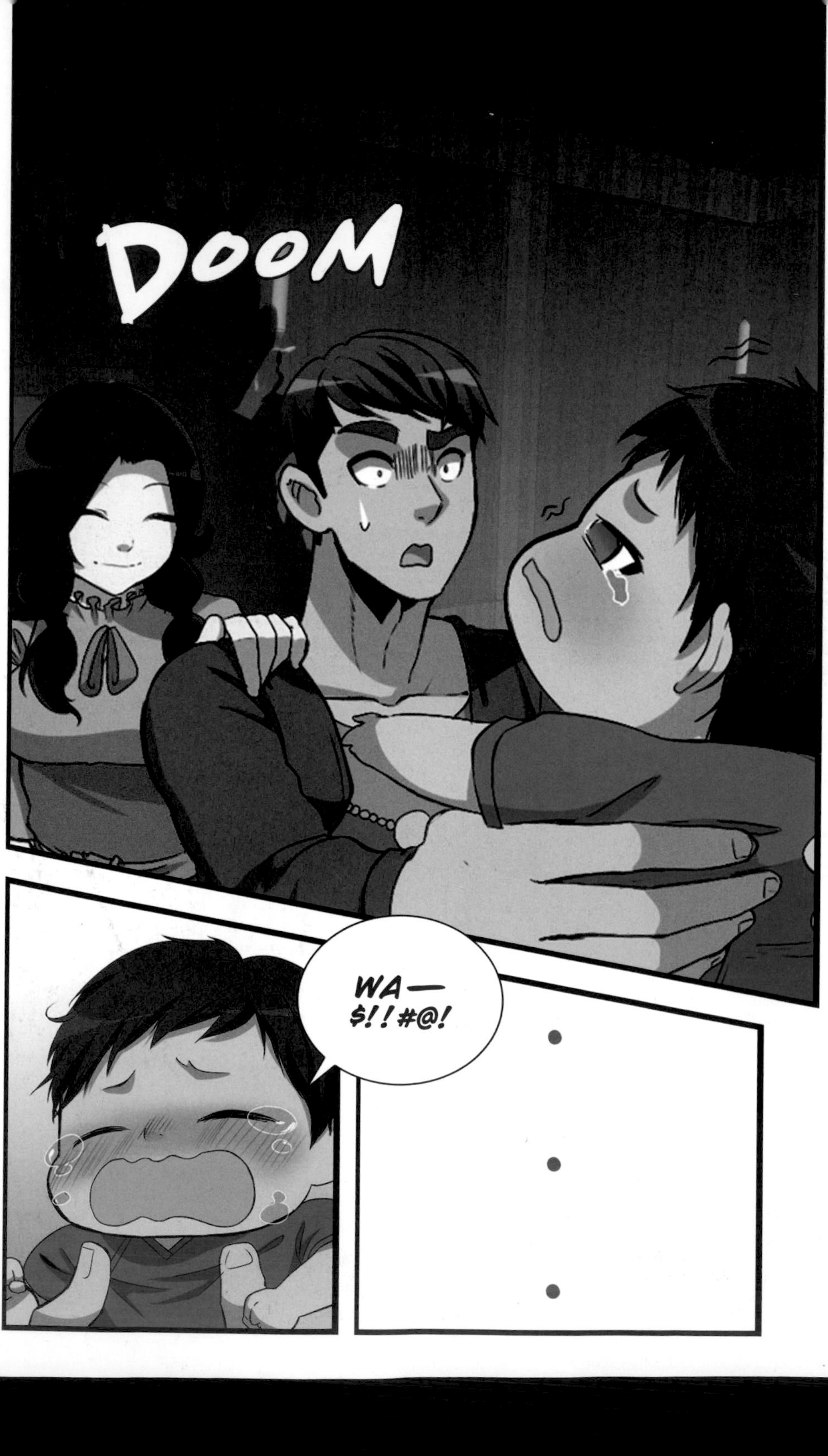
DOOM
WA—
$!!#@!

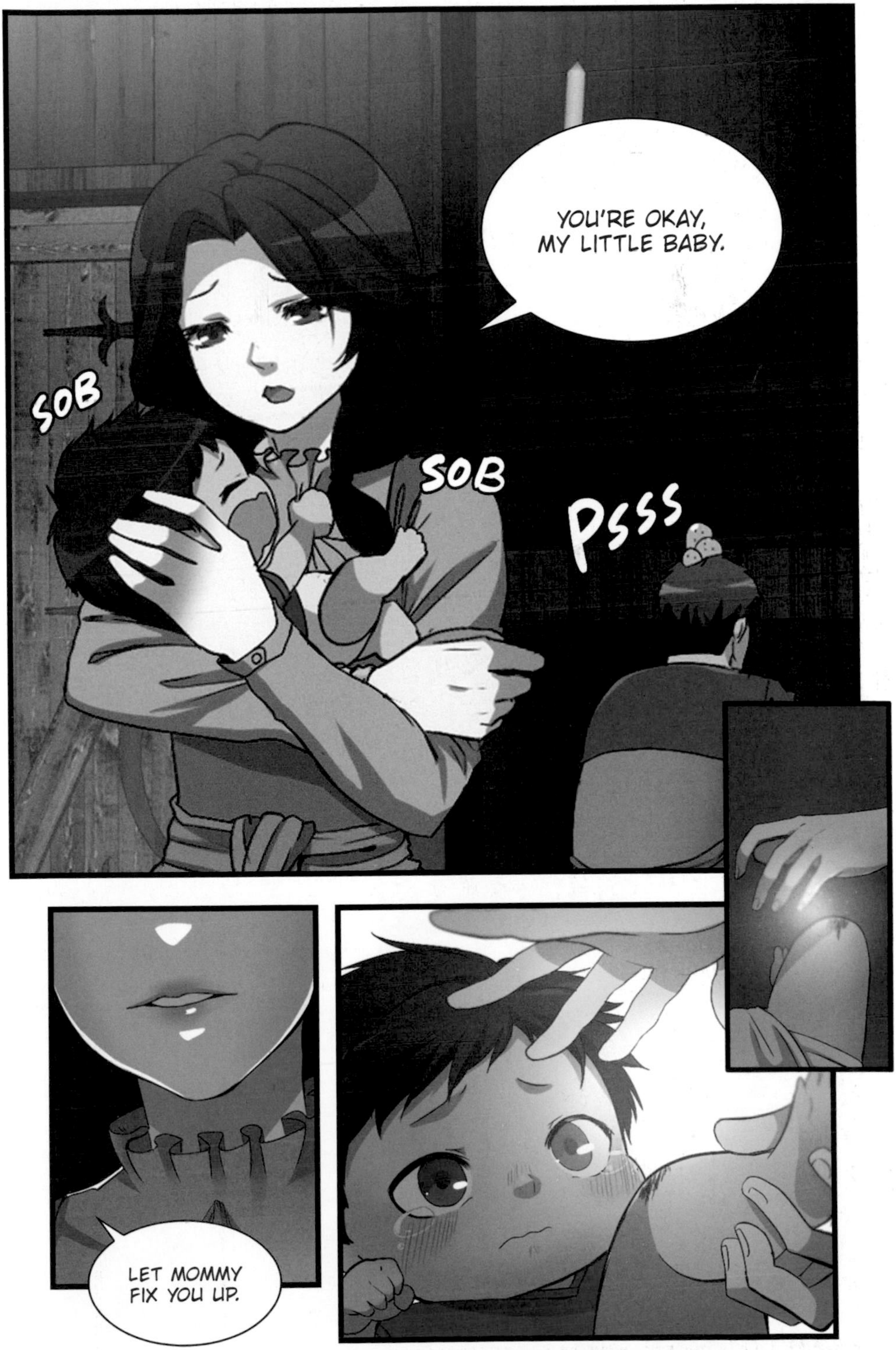
YOU'RE OKAY, MY LITTLE BABY.
SOB
SOB
PSSS
LET MOMMY FIX YOU UP.

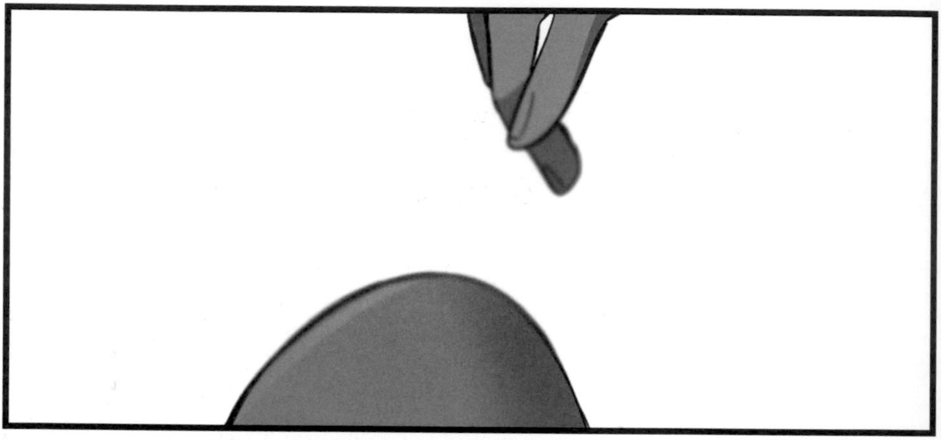

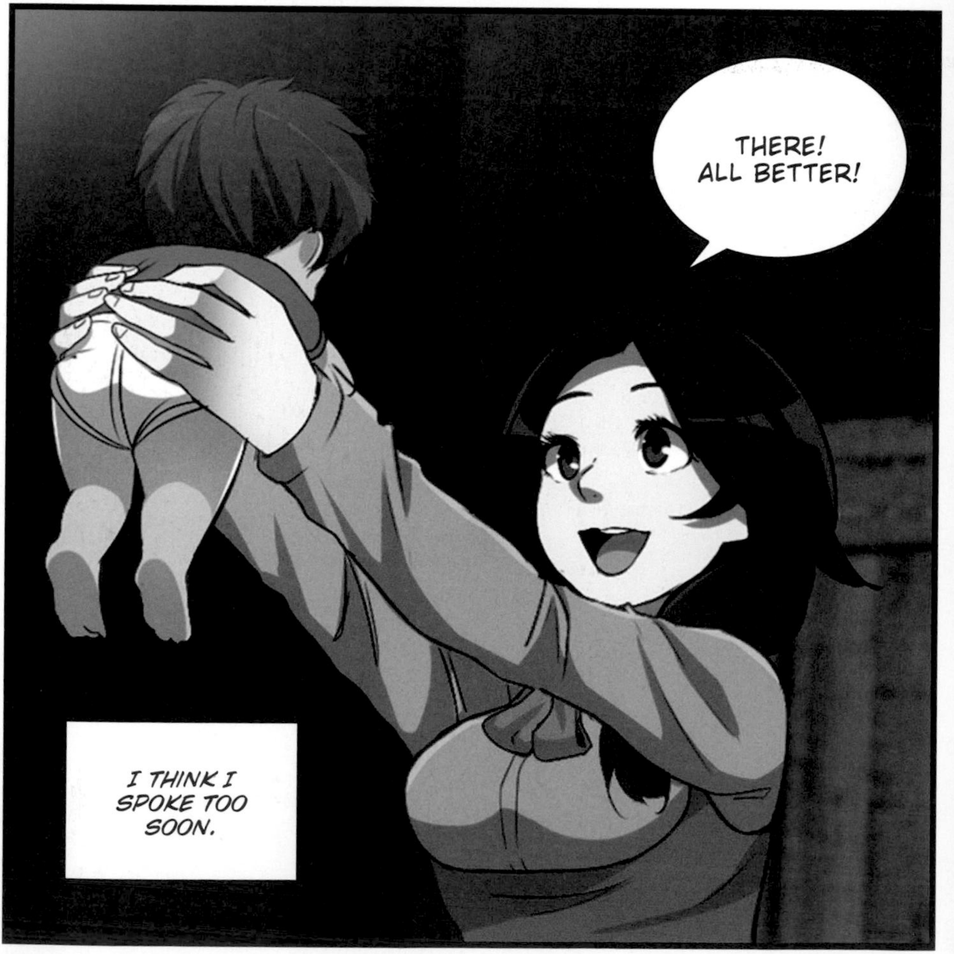
THERE!
ALL BETTER!
I THINK I
SPOKE TOO
SOON.

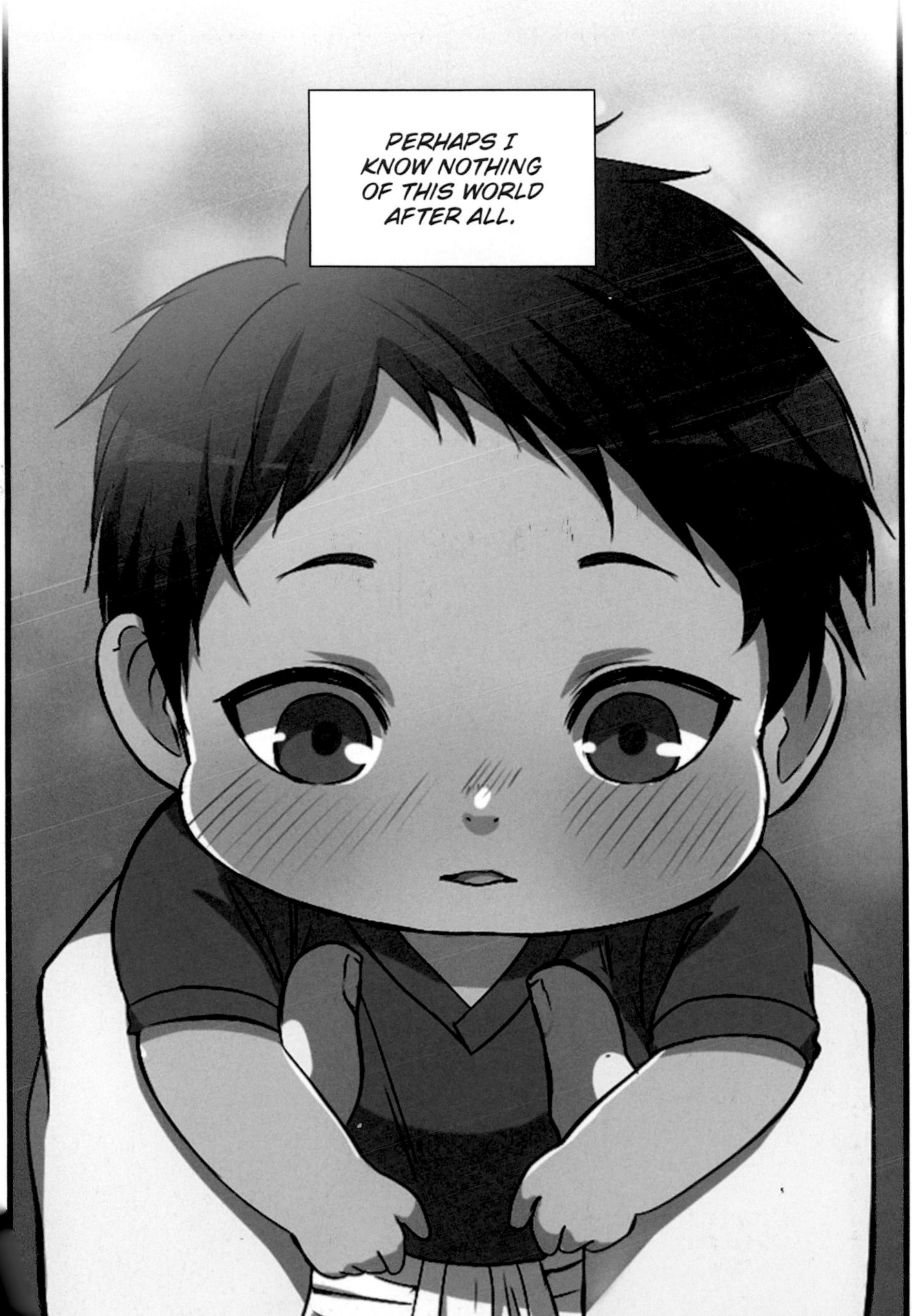
PERHAPS I KNOW NOTHING OF THIS WORLD AFTER ALL.

CHAPTER 2—My Life Now

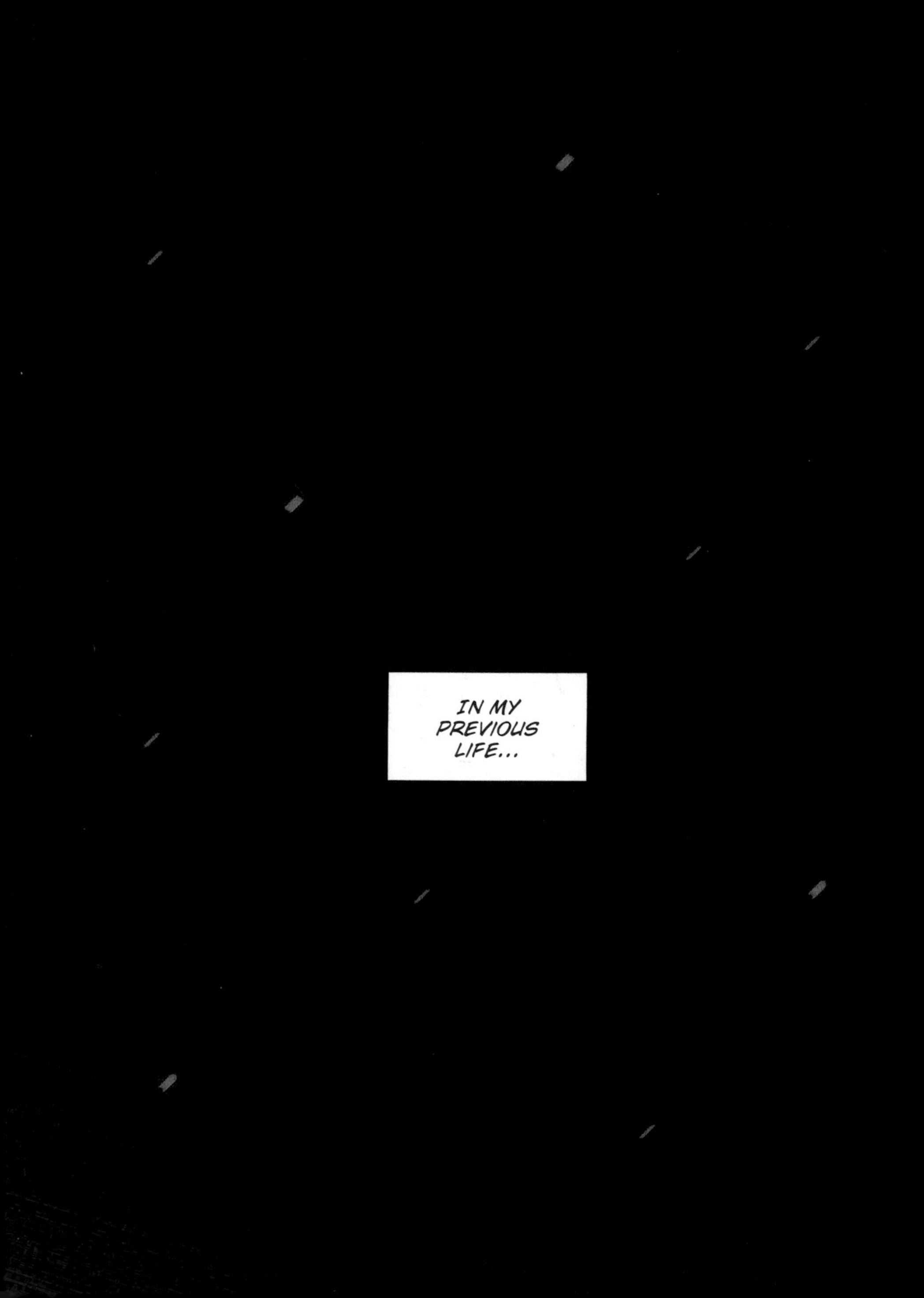
IN MY PREVIOUS LIFE...

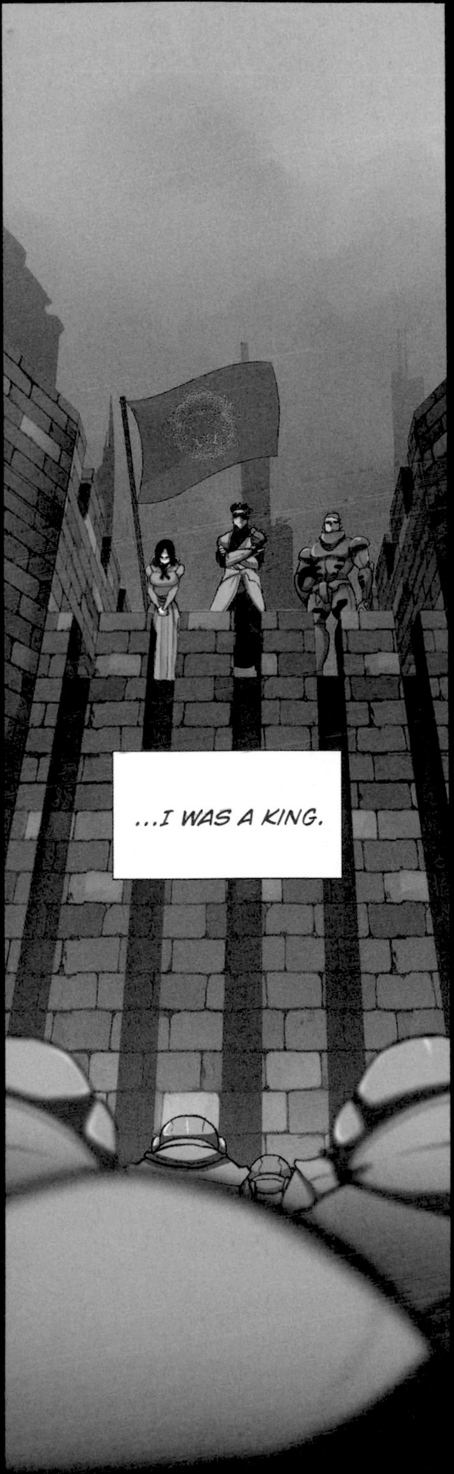
...I WAS A KING.

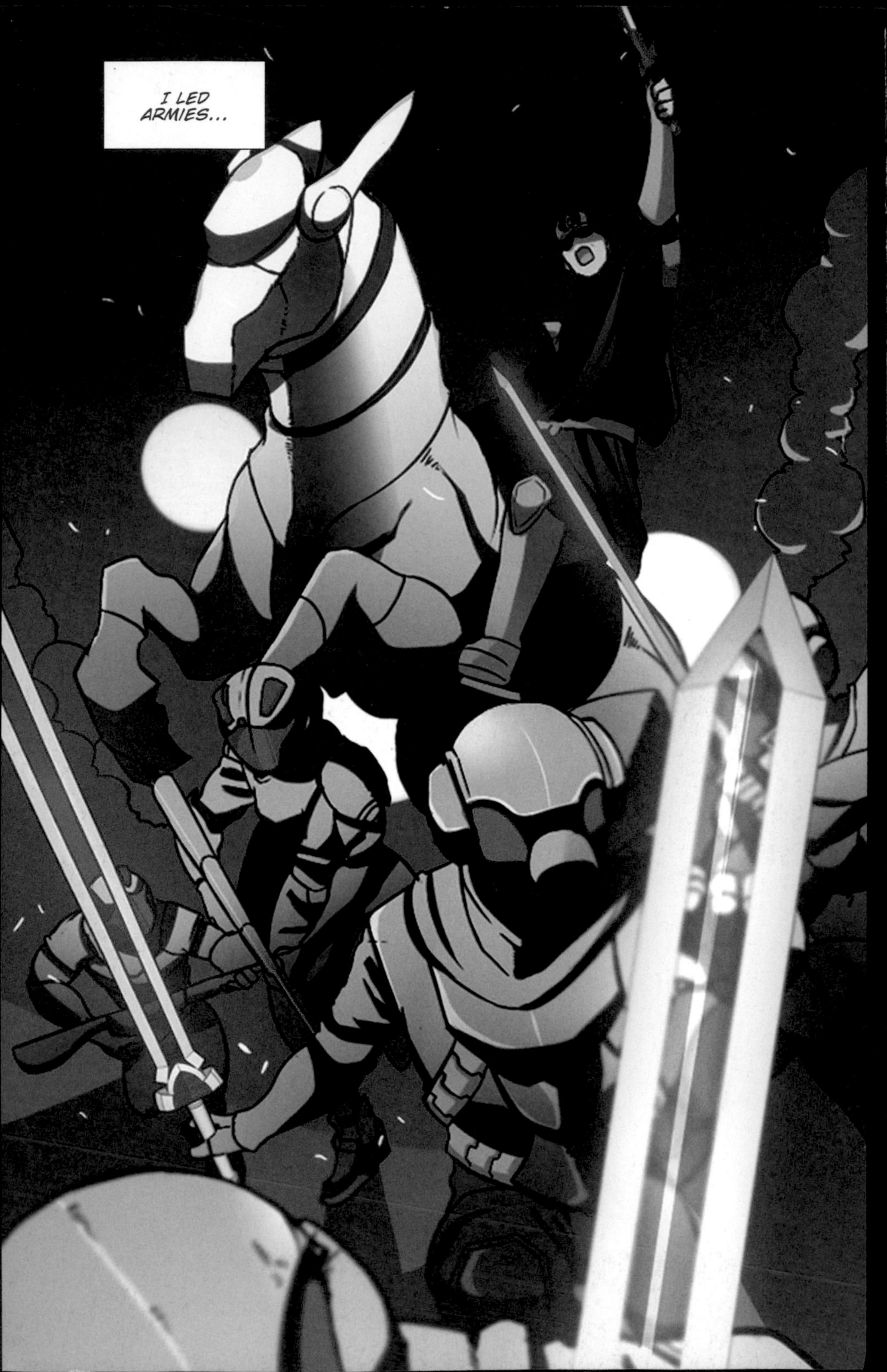
I LED ARMIES...

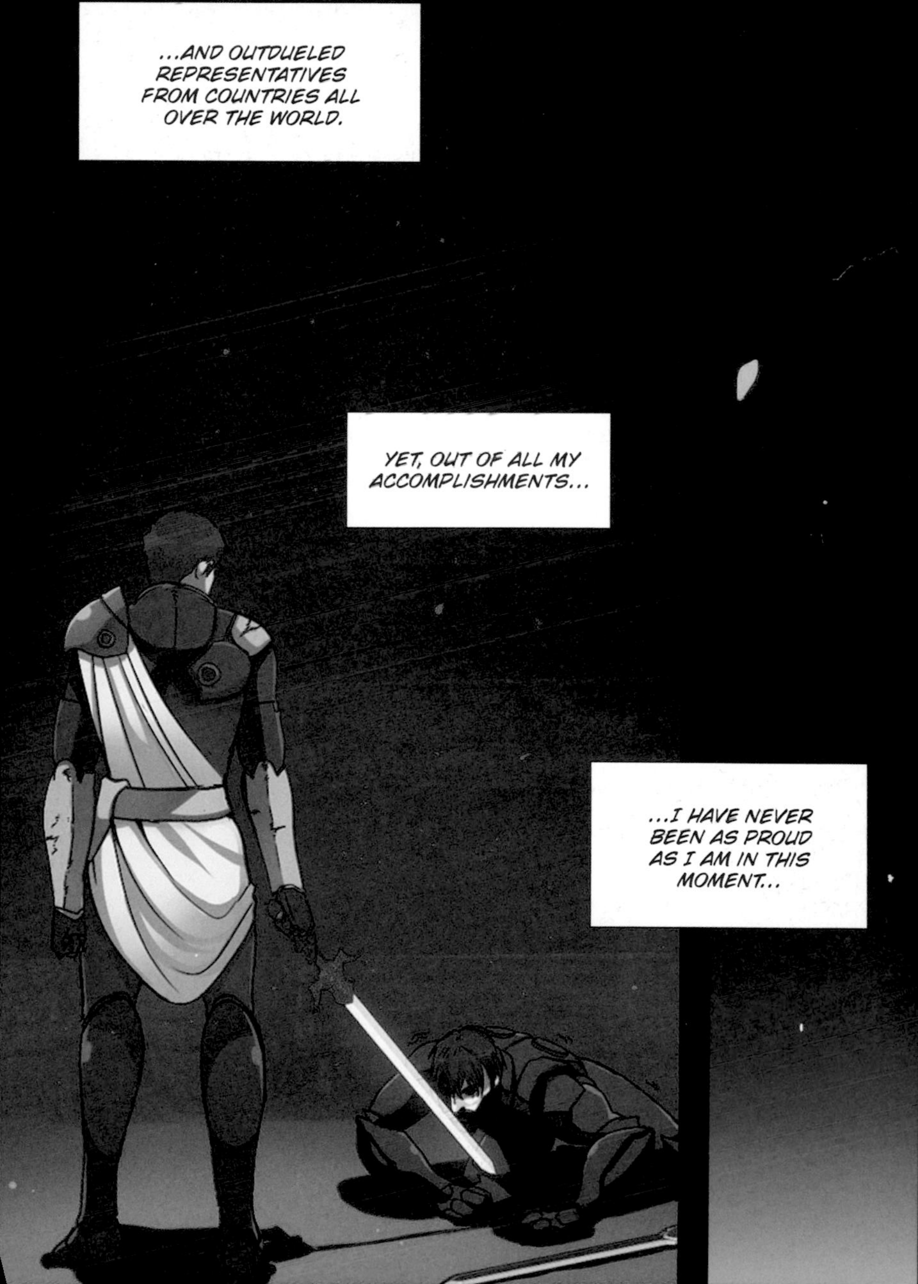
...AND OUTDUELED REPRESENTATIVES FROM COUNTRIES ALL OVER THE WORLD.
YET, OUT OF ALL MY ACCOMPLISHMENTS...
...I HAVE NEVER BEEN AS PROUD AS I AM IN THIS MOMENT...

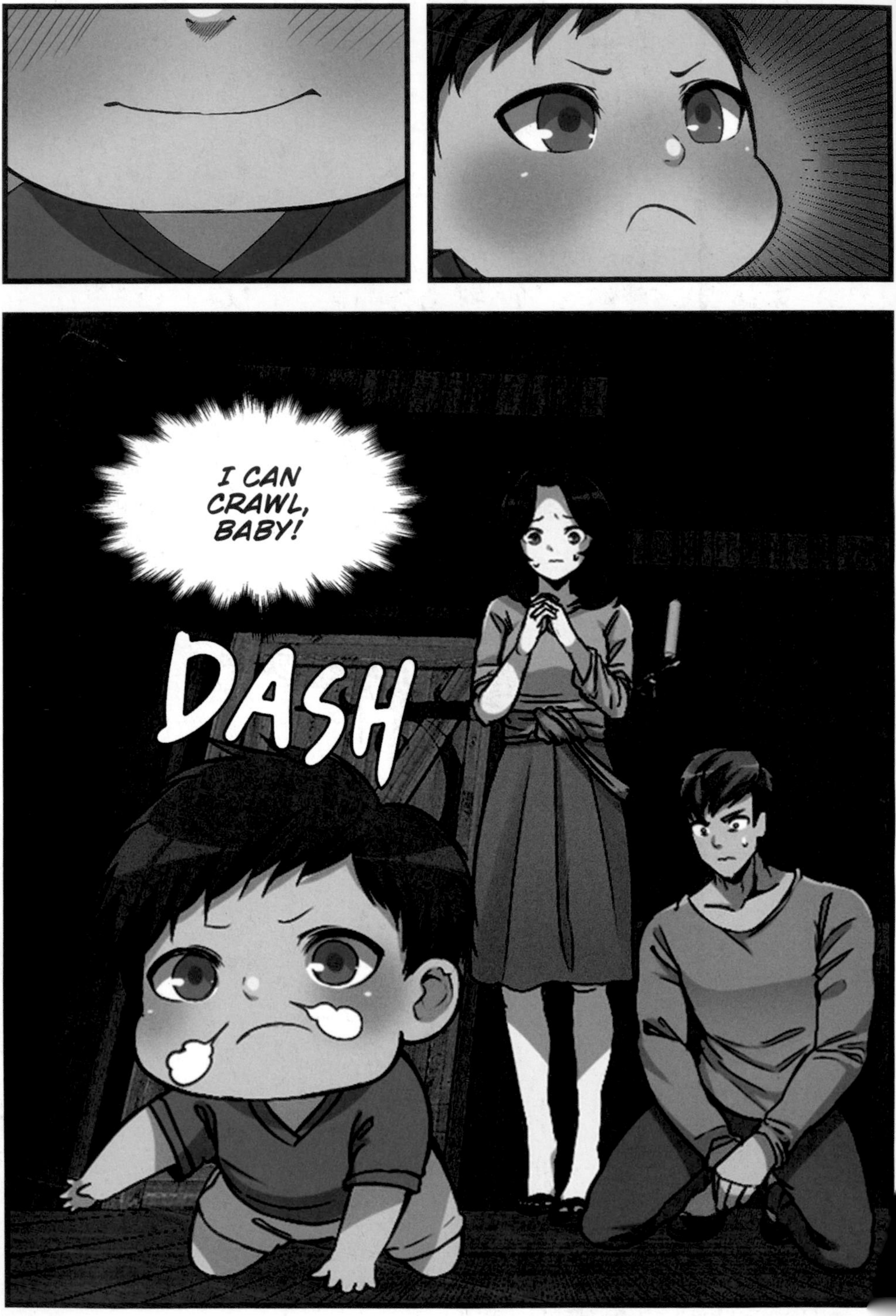
I CAN CRAWL, BABY!
DASH

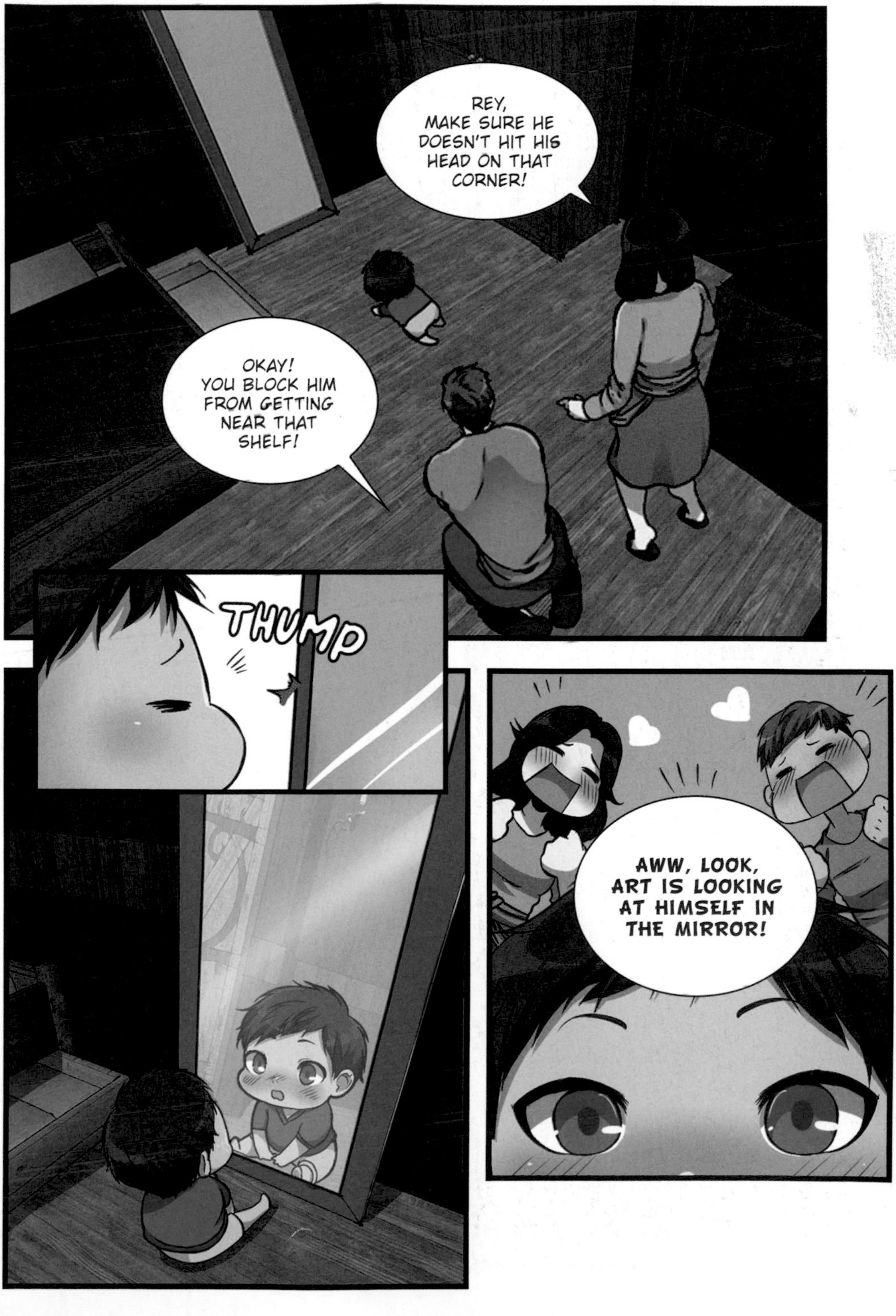
REY, MAKE SURE HE DOESN'T HIT HIS HEAD ON THAT CORNER!
OKAY! YOU BLOCK HIM FROM GETTING NEAR THAT SHELF!
THUMP
AWW, LOOK, ART IS LOOKING AT HIMSELF IN THE MIRROR!

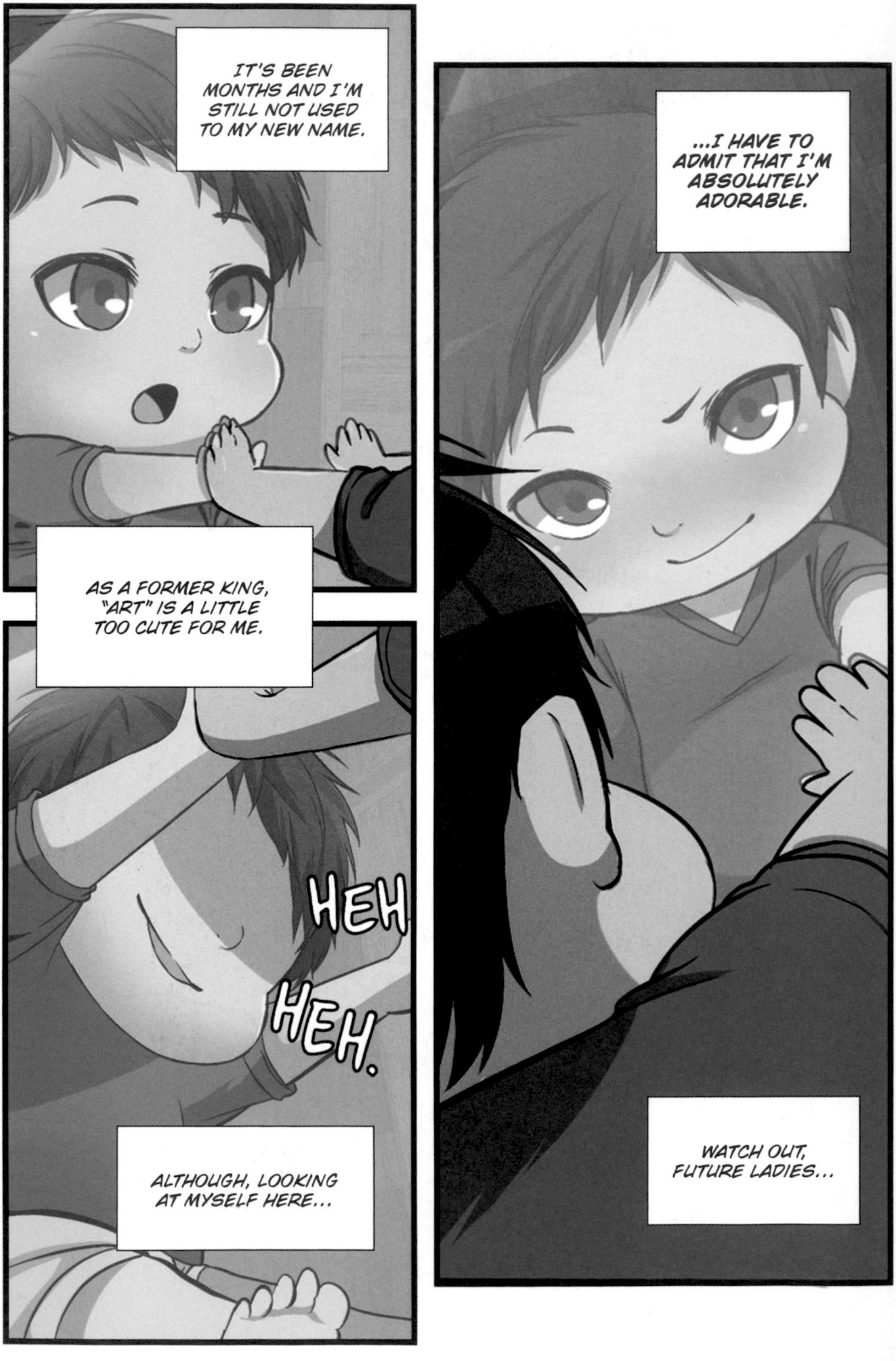
IT'S BEEN MONTHS AND I'M STILL NOT USED TO MY NEW NAME.
AS A FORMER KING, "ART" IS A LITTLE TOO CUTE FOR ME.
HEH
HEH.
ALTHOUGH, LOOKING AT MYSELF HERE...
...I HAVE TO ADMIT THAT I'M ABSOLUTELY ADORABLE.
WATCH OUT, FUTURE LADIES...

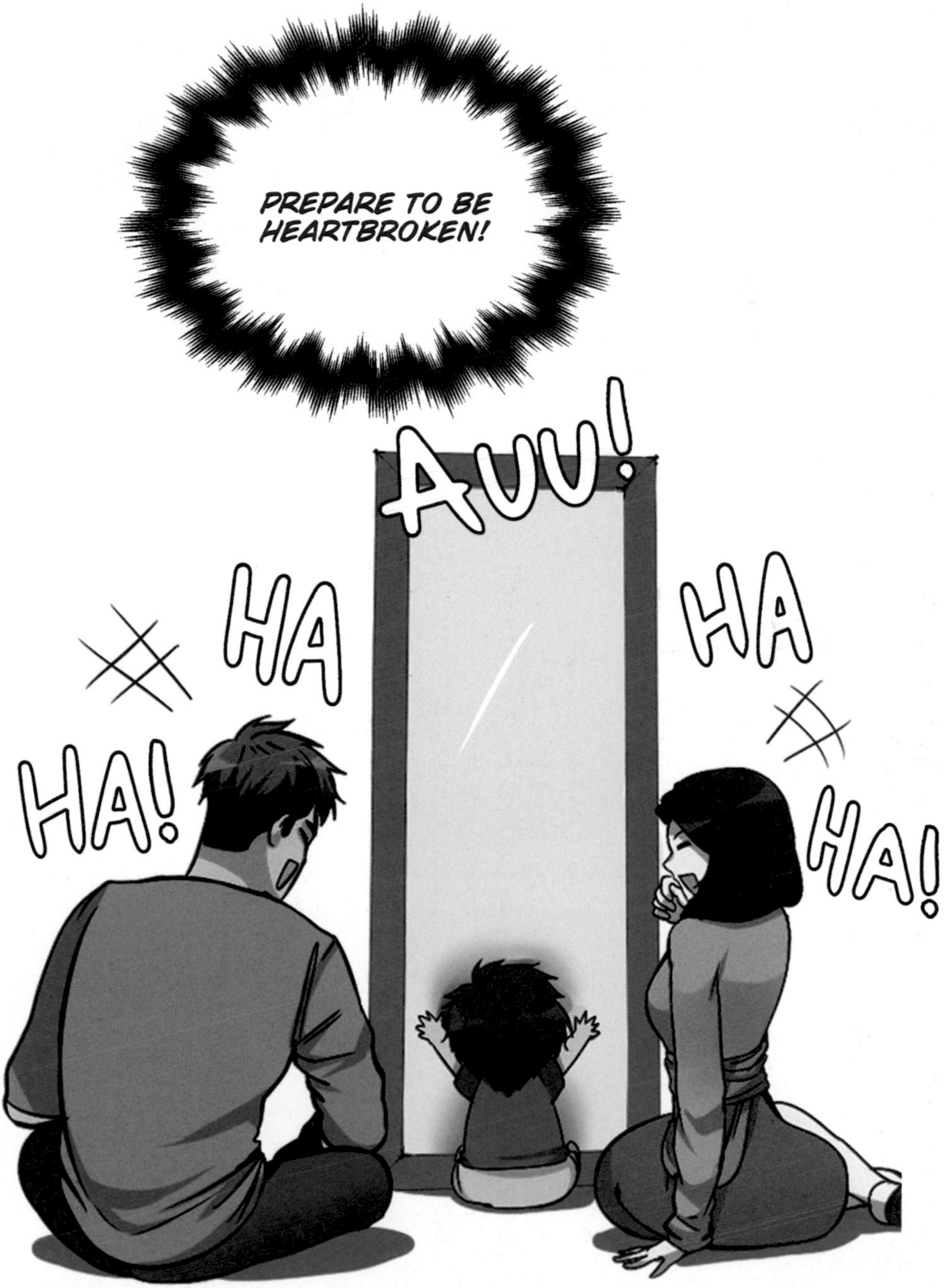
PREPARE TO BE HEARTBROKEN!
AUU!
HA
HA!
HA
HA!

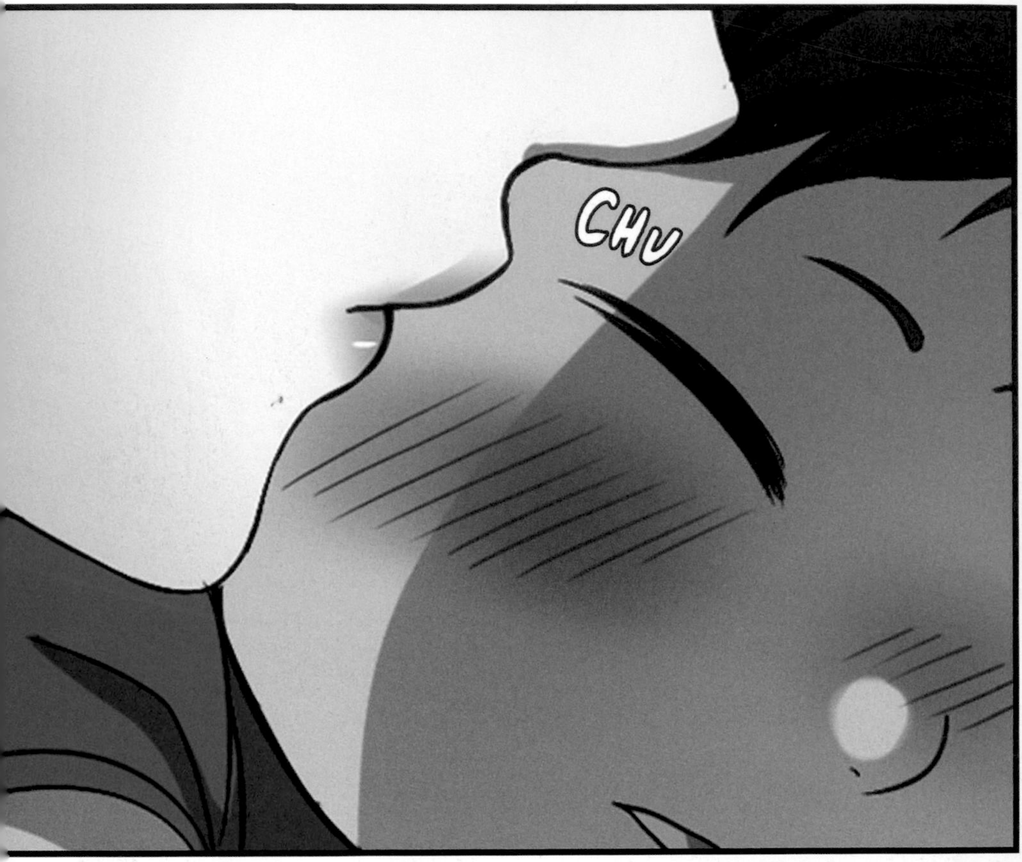
CHU

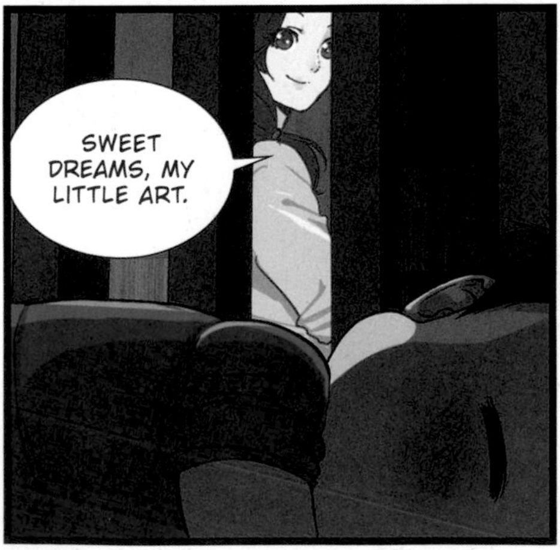
SWEET DREAMS, MY LITTLE ART.

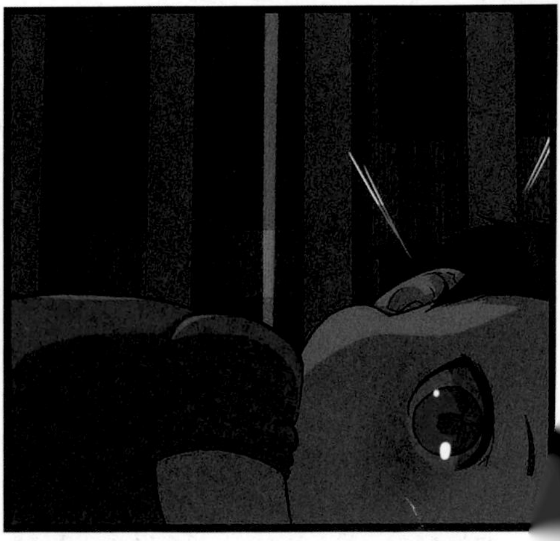

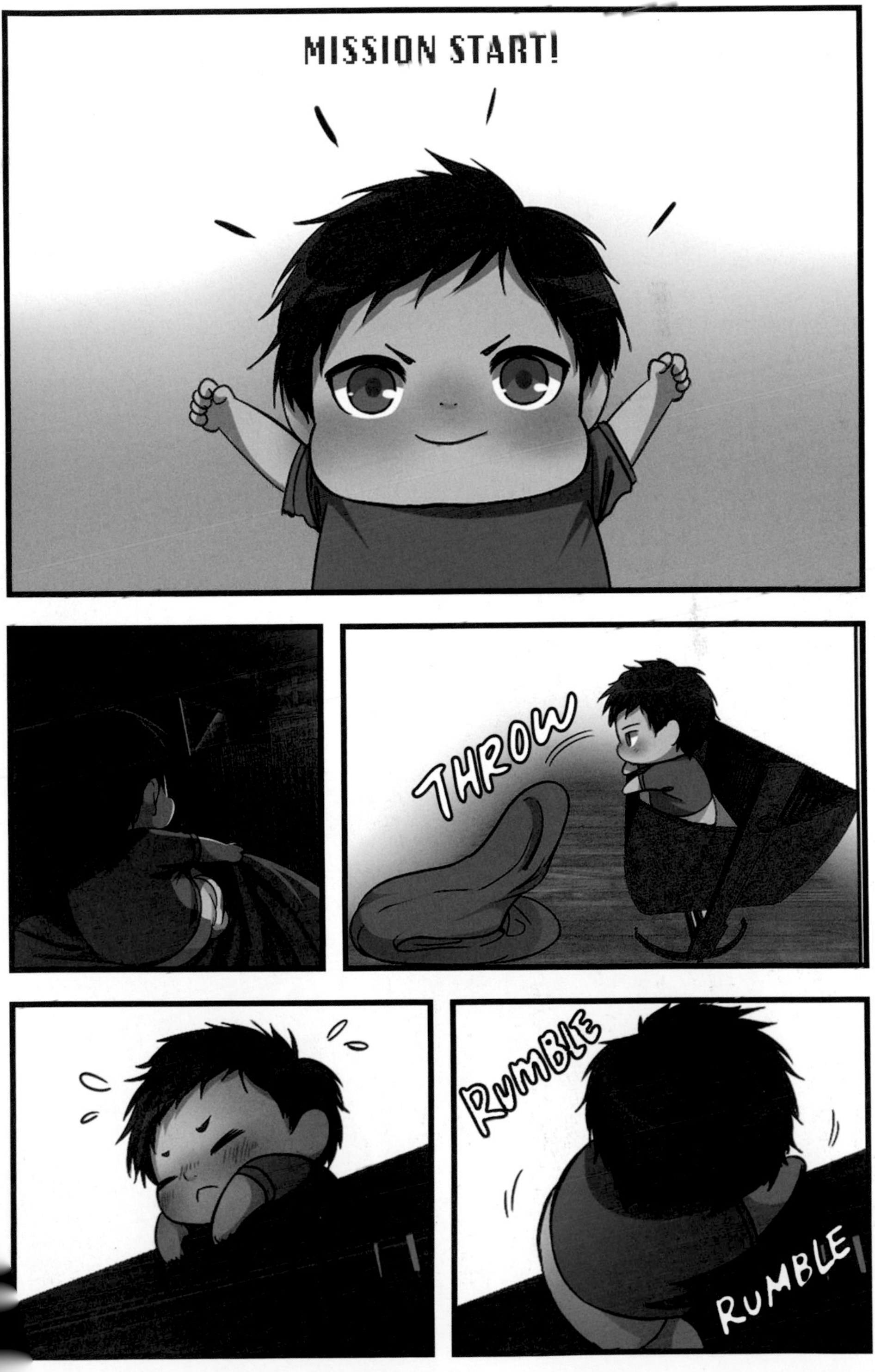
MISSION START!
THROW
RUMBLE
RUMBLE

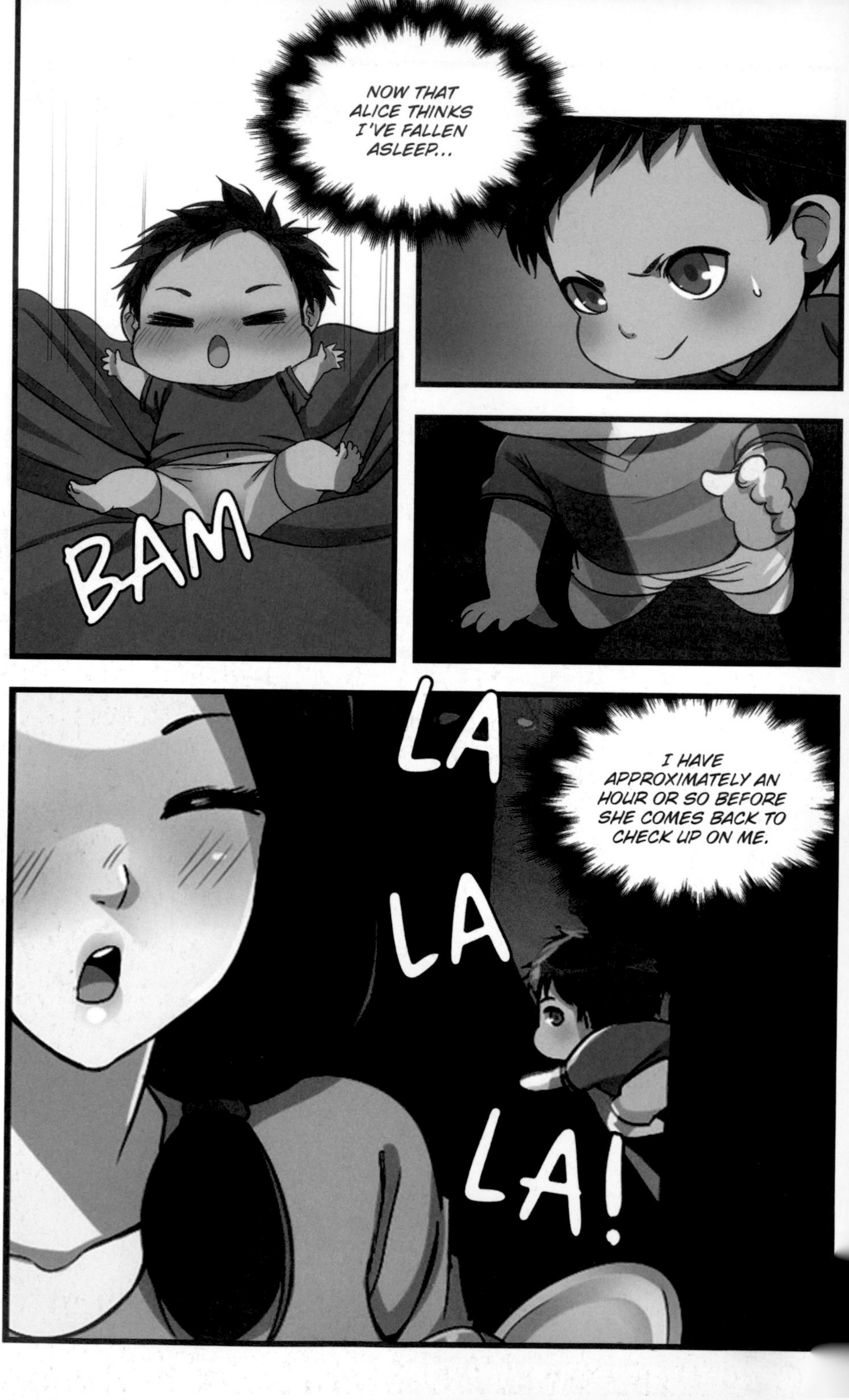
NOW THAT ALICE THINKS I'VE FALLEN ASLEEP...
BAM
LA
LA
LA!
I HAVE APPROXIMATELY AN HOUR OR SO BEFORE SHE COMES BACK TO CHECK UP ON ME.

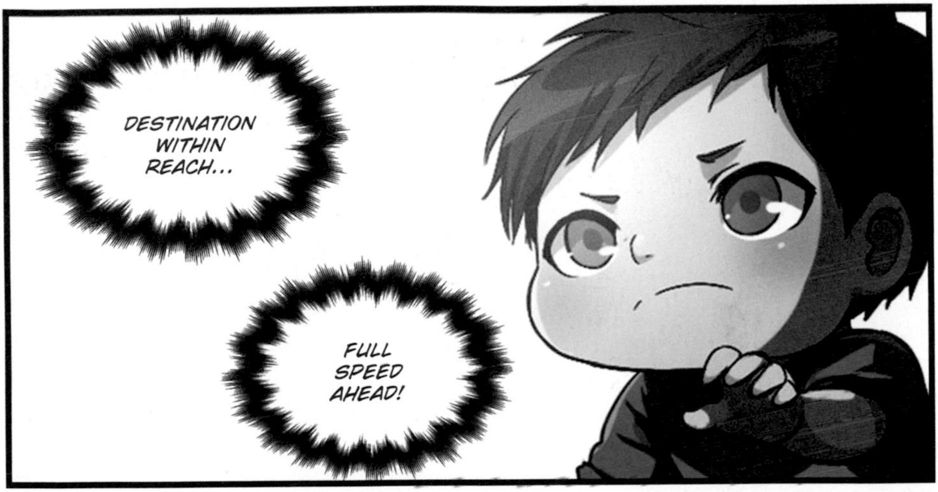
DESTINATION WITHIN REACH...
FULL SPEED AHEAD!
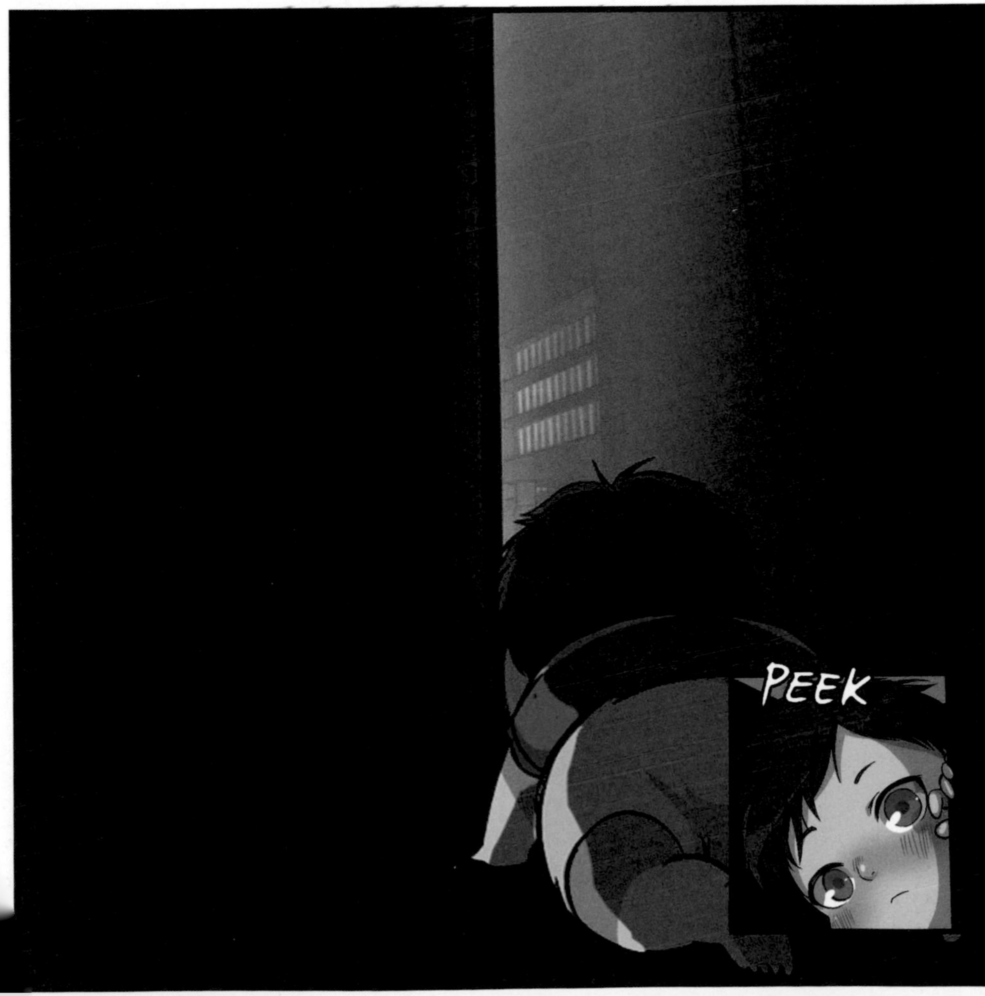
PEEK

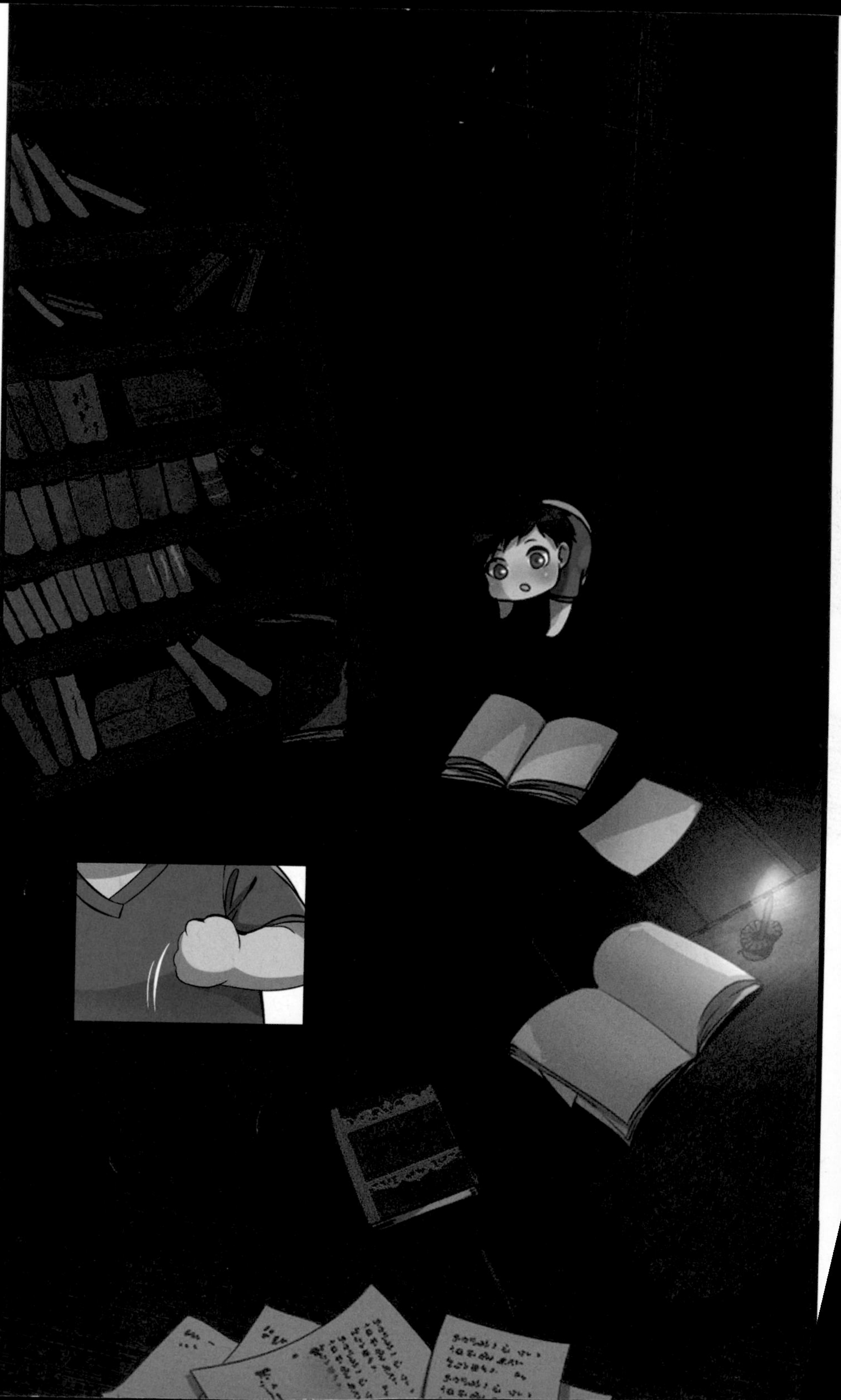

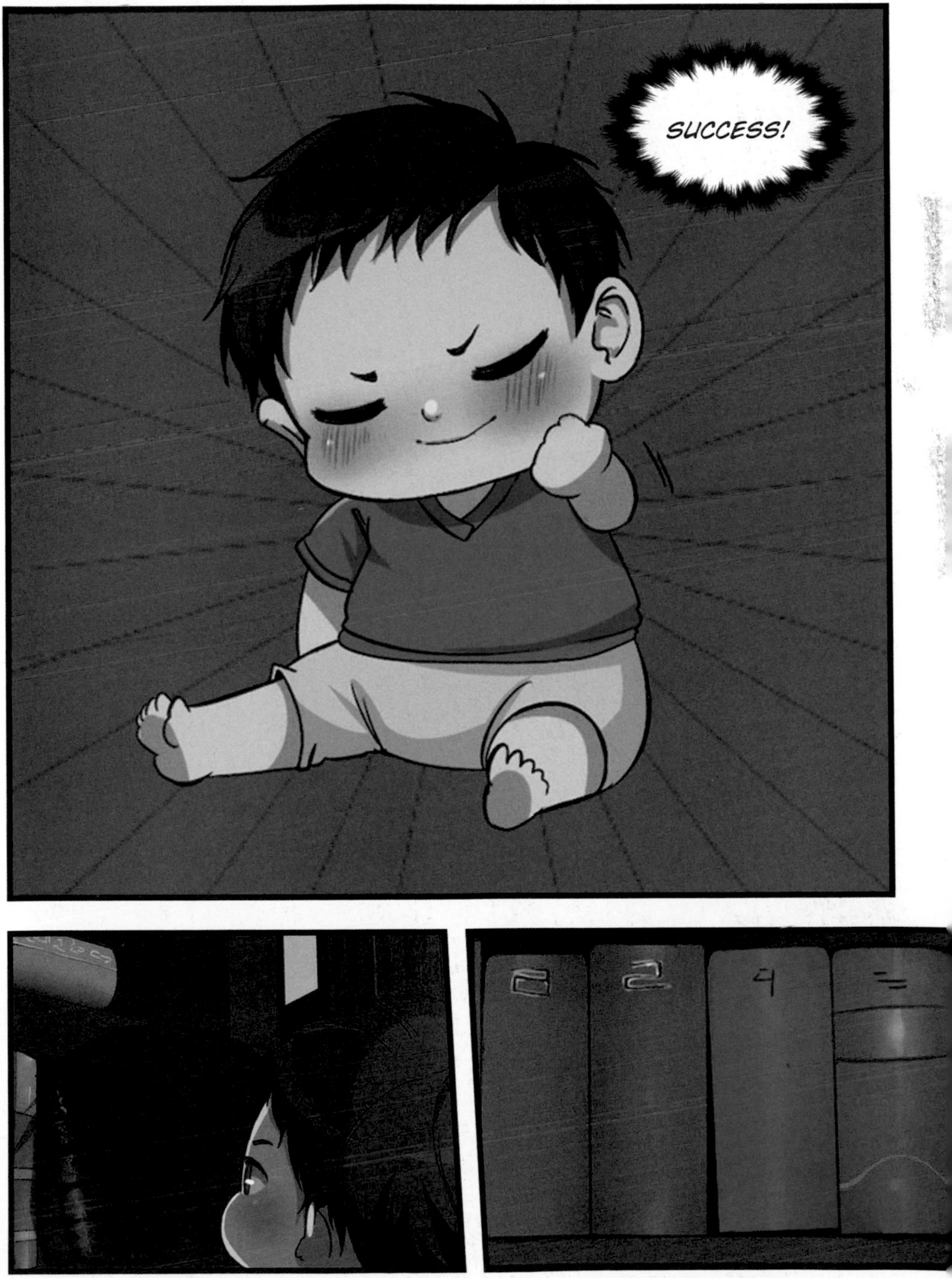
SUCCESS!

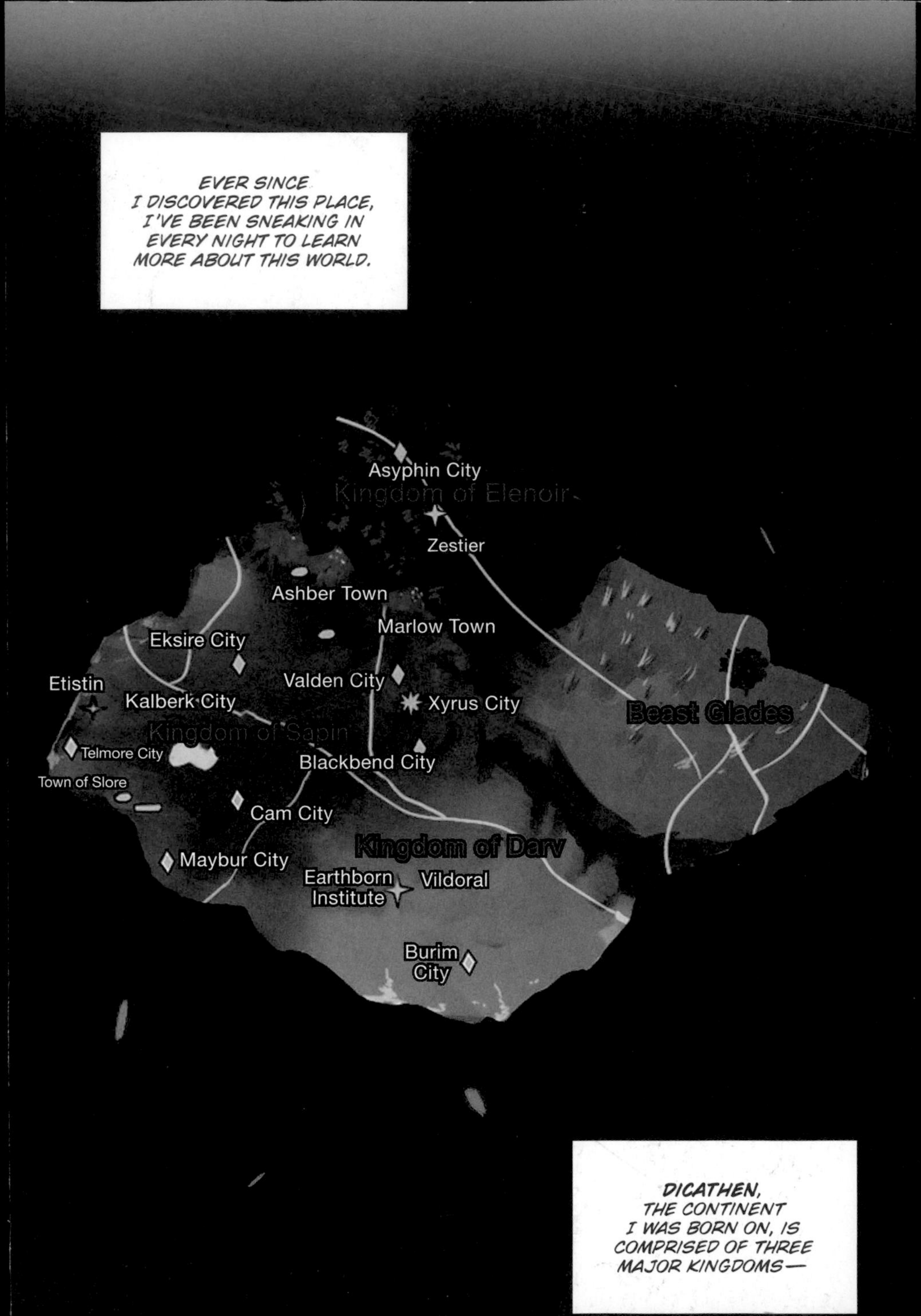
EVER SINCE I DISCOVERED THIS PLACE, I'VE BEEN SNEAKING IN EVERY NIGHT TO LEARN MORE ABOUT THIS WORLD.
Asyphin City
Kingdom of Elenoir
Zestier
Ashber Town
Marlow Town
Eksire City
Valden City
Etistin
Kalberk City
Xyrus City
Beast Glades
Kingdom of Sapin
Telmore City
Blackbend City
Town of Slore
Cam City
Kingdom of Darv
Maybur City
Earthborn Institute
Vildoral
Burim City
DICATHEN, THE CONTINENT I WAS BORN ON, IS COMPRISED OF THREE MAJOR KINGDOMS—

ELENOIR

SAPIN

ELENOIR, THE
ELVEN KINGDOM
DEEP IN THE
FOREST.

AND **SAPIN**,
THE HUMAN KINGDOM
AND EASILY THE MOST
POPULATED REGION.

DARV, THE VAST
UNDERGROUND
KINGDOM AND HOME
OF THE DWARVES.

DARV

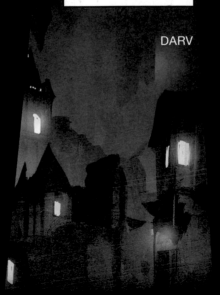

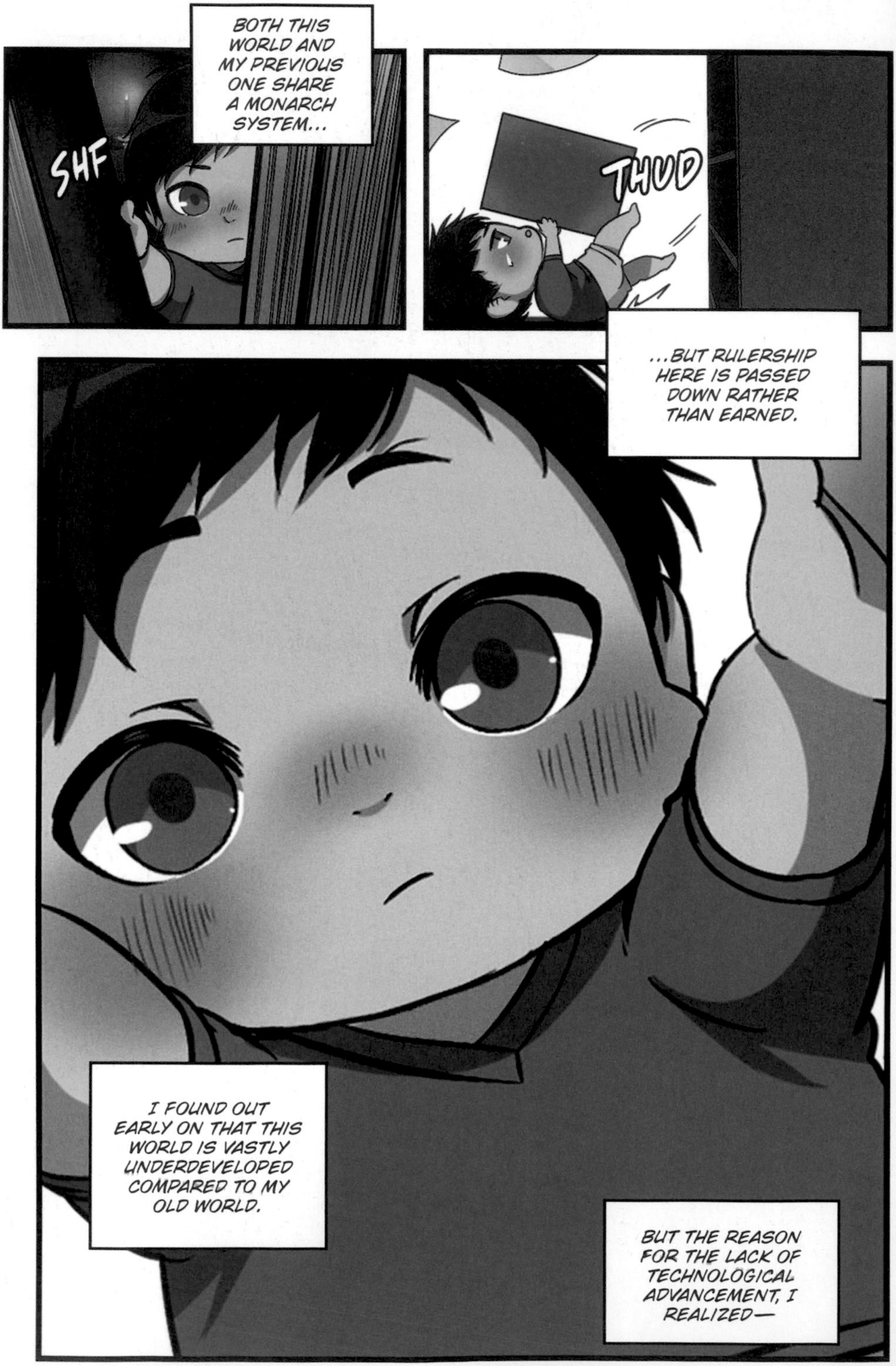
BOTH THIS WORLD AND MY PREVIOUS ONE SHARE A MONARCH SYSTEM...
SHF
THUD
...BUT RULERSHIP HERE IS PASSED DOWN RATHER THAN EARNED.
I FOUND OUT EARLY ON THAT THIS WORLD IS VASTLY UNDERDEVELOPED COMPARED TO MY OLD WORLD.
BUT THE REASON FOR THE LACK OF TECHNOLOGICAL ADVANCEMENT, I REALIZED—

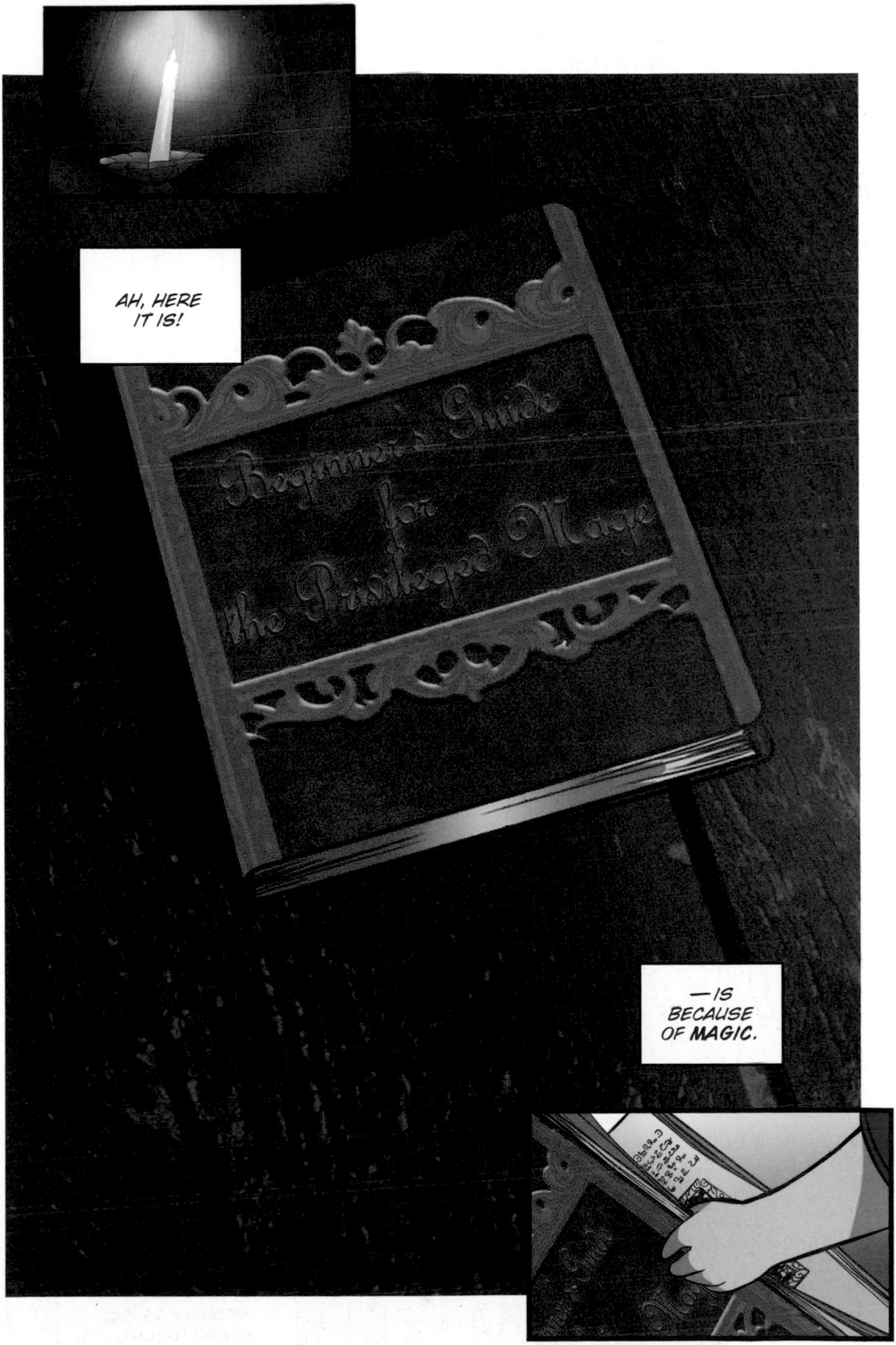
AH, HERE IT IS!
Beginner's Guide for the Privileged Mage
—IS BECAUSE OF **MAGIC**.

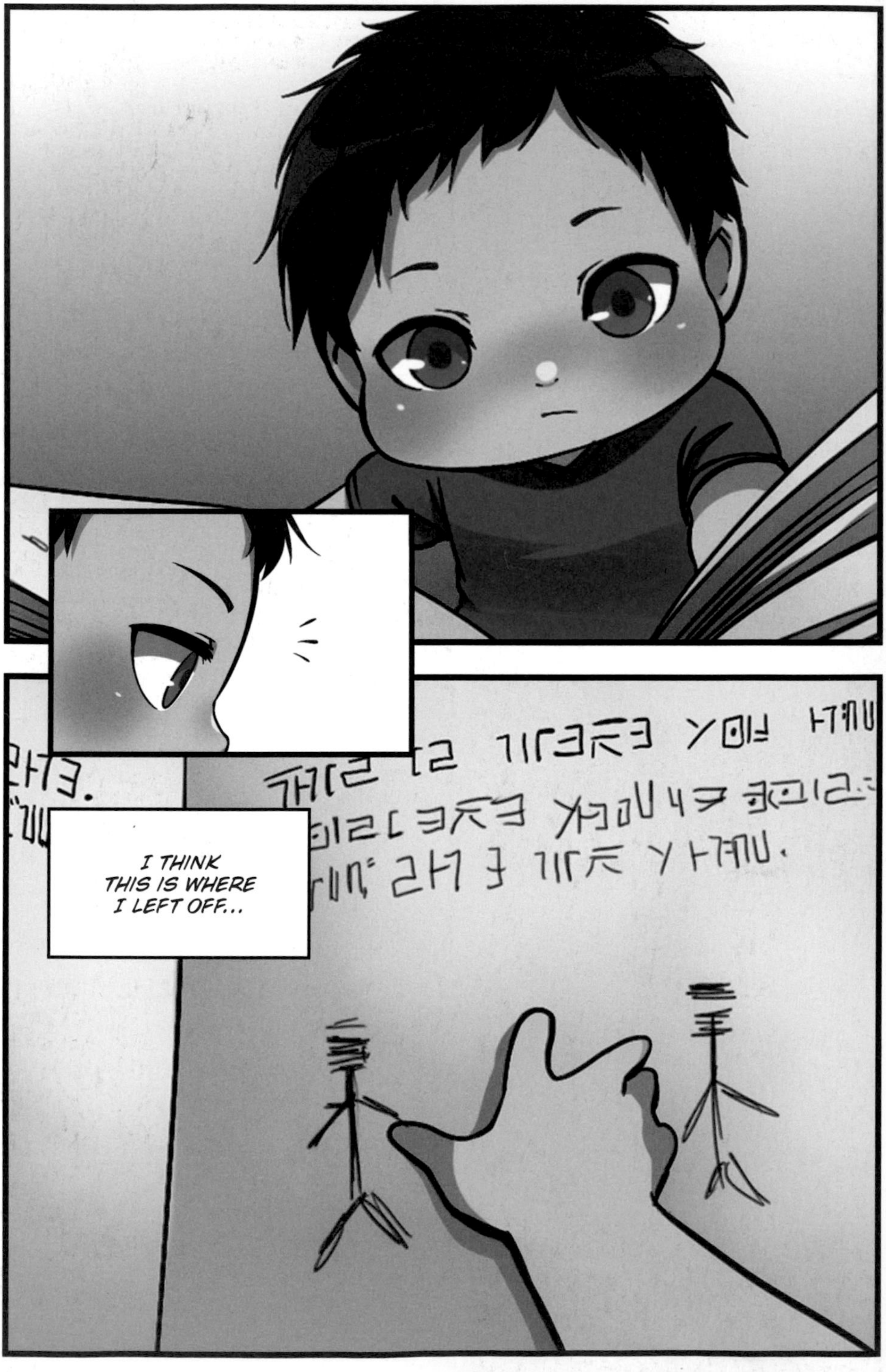
I THINK THIS IS WHERE I LEFT OFF...

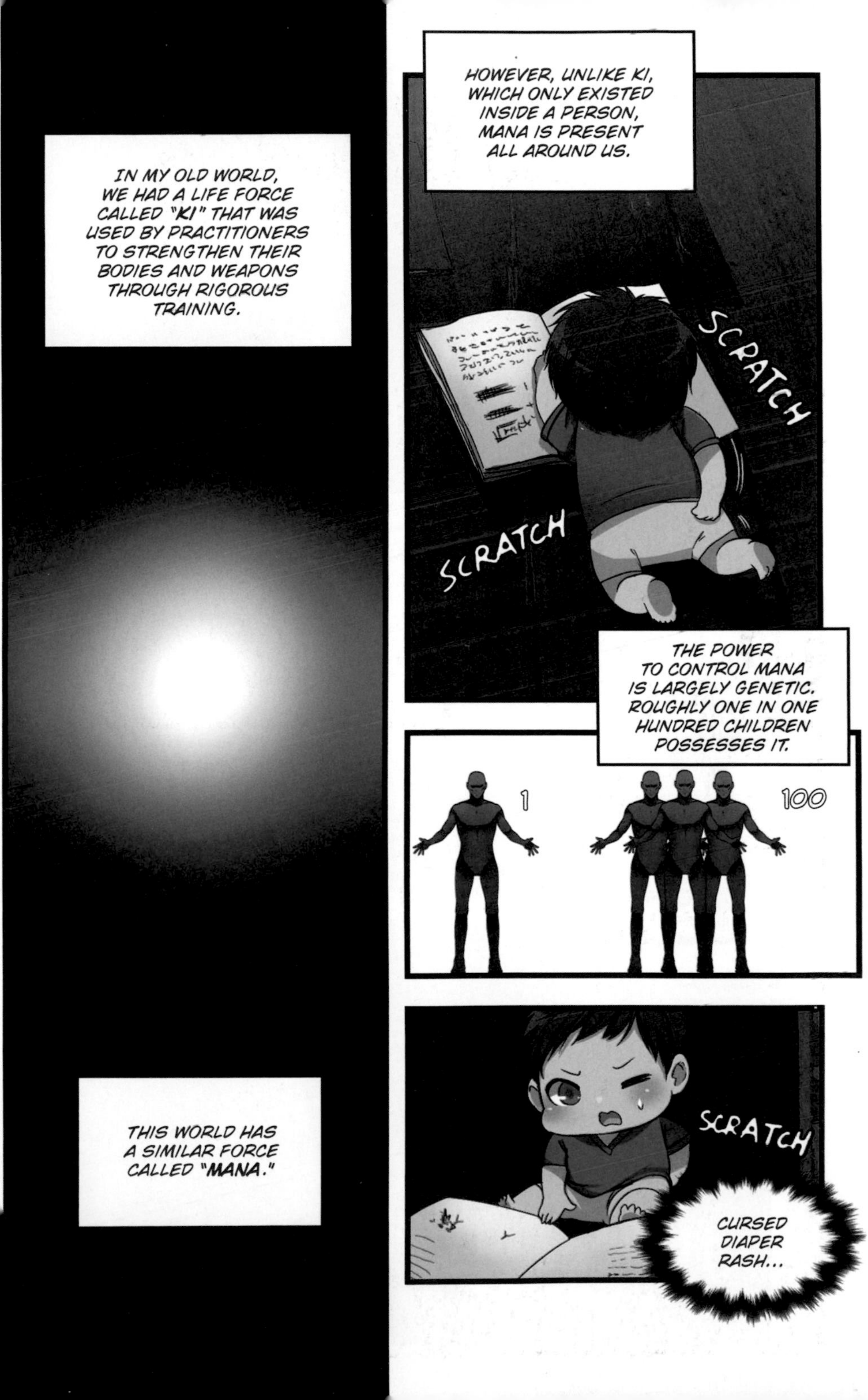
IN MY OLD WORLD, WE HAD A LIFE FORCE CALLED "KI" THAT WAS USED BY PRACTITIONERS TO STRENGTHEN THEIR BODIES AND WEAPONS THROUGH RIGOROUS TRAINING.
THIS WORLD HAS A SIMILAR FORCE CALLED "MANA."
HOWEVER, UNLIKE KI, WHICH ONLY EXISTED INSIDE A PERSON, MANA IS PRESENT ALL AROUND US.
SCRATCH
SCRATCH
THE POWER TO CONTROL MANA IS LARGELY GENETIC. ROUGHLY ONE IN ONE HUNDRED CHILDREN POSSESSES IT.
1
100
SCRATCH
CURSED DIAPER RASH...

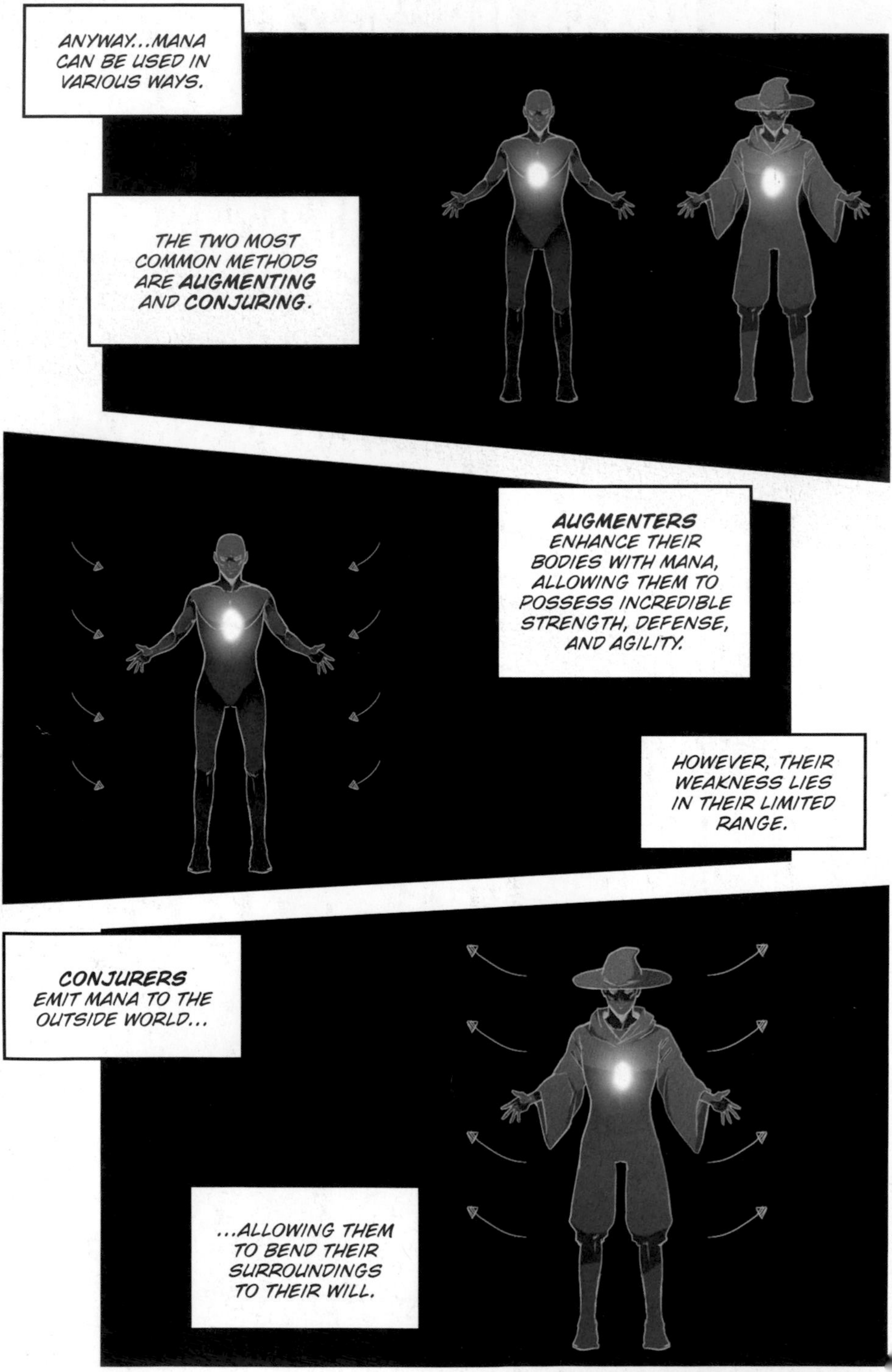

ANYWAY...MANA CAN BE USED IN VARIOUS WAYS.

THE TWO MOST COMMON METHODS ARE **AUGMENTING** AND **CONJURING**.

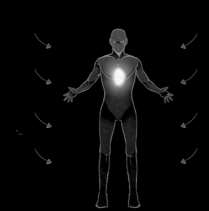

AUGMENTERS ENHANCE THEIR BODIES WITH MANA, ALLOWING THEM TO POSSESS INCREDIBLE STRENGTH, DEFENSE, AND AGILITY.

HOWEVER, THEIR WEAKNESS LIES IN THEIR LIMITED RANGE.

CONJURERS EMIT MANA TO THE OUTSIDE WORLD...

...ALLOWING THEM TO BEND THEIR SURROUNDINGS TO THEIR WILL.

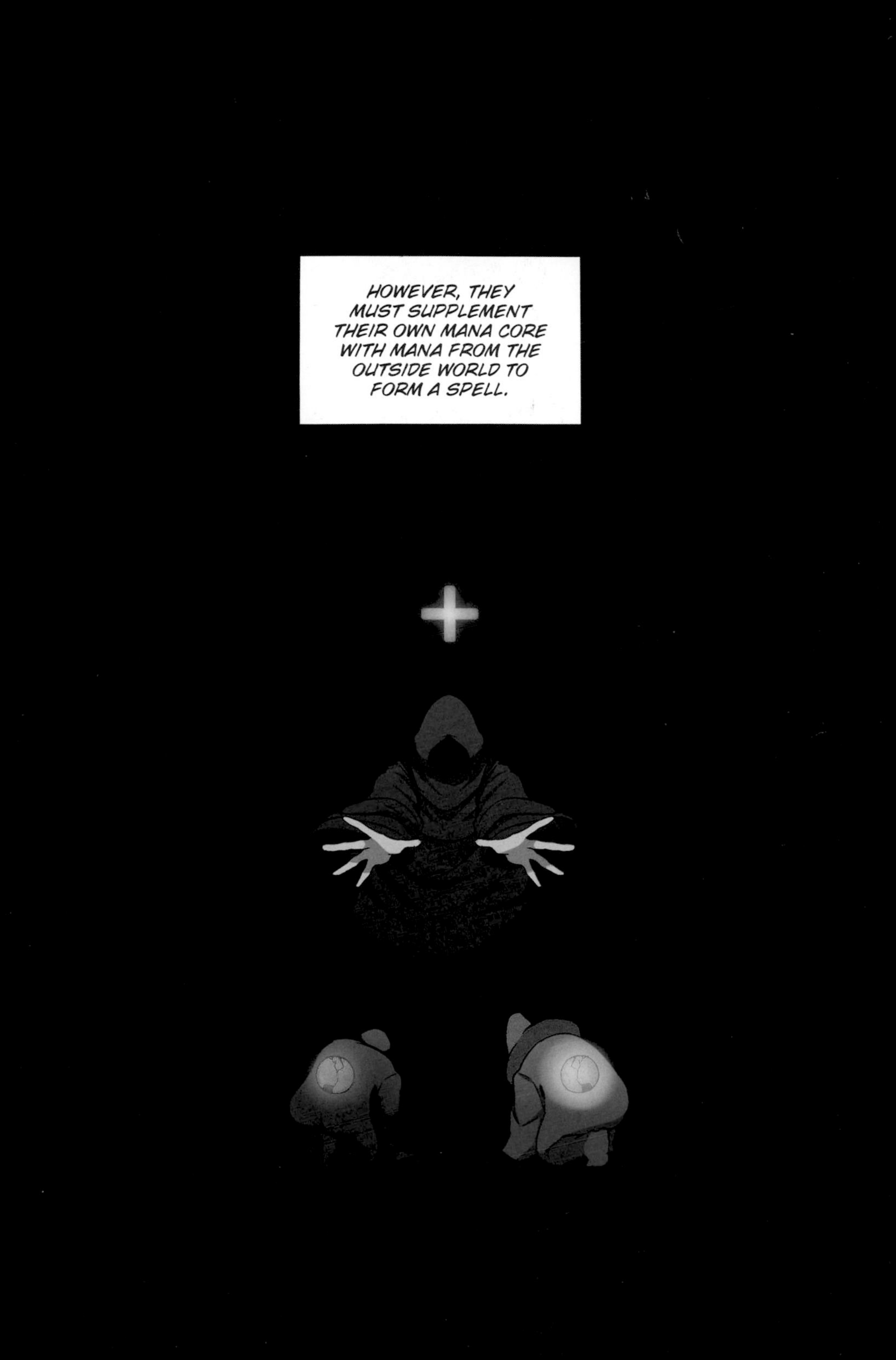
HOWEVER, THEY MUST SUPPLEMENT THEIR OWN MANA CORE WITH MANA FROM THE OUTSIDE WORLD TO FORM A SPELL.

MY MOTHER IS WHAT THEY CALL A *"DEVIANT."* MORE SPECIFICALLY, AN *EMITTER.*

THEY ARE A RARE TYPE OF MAGE ABLE TO CAST UNIQUE RESTORATIVE MANA.

ACCORDING TO THIS BOOK...

THE MANA CORE SOUNDS UNCANNILY SIMILAR TO THE *KI CENTER* FROM MY PREVIOUS LIFE.

...A MAGE'S FIRST AWAKENING HAPPENS BETWEEN EARLY ADOLESCENCE TO LATE TEENAGE YEARS WHEN THEIR *MANA CORE* MANIFESTS.

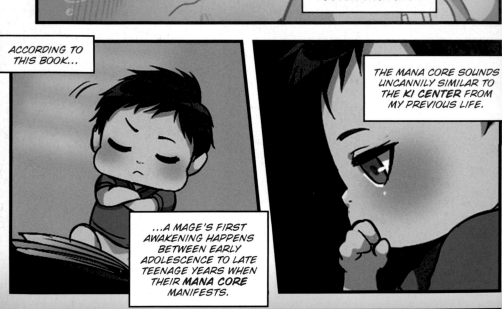

TO FORM A KI CENTER, CHILDREN WERE TAUGHT TO MEDITATE...

...SENSE THE FRAGMENTS OF KI SCATTERED INSIDE THEIR BODIES, AND GATHER THEM INTO A SINGLE PLACE.

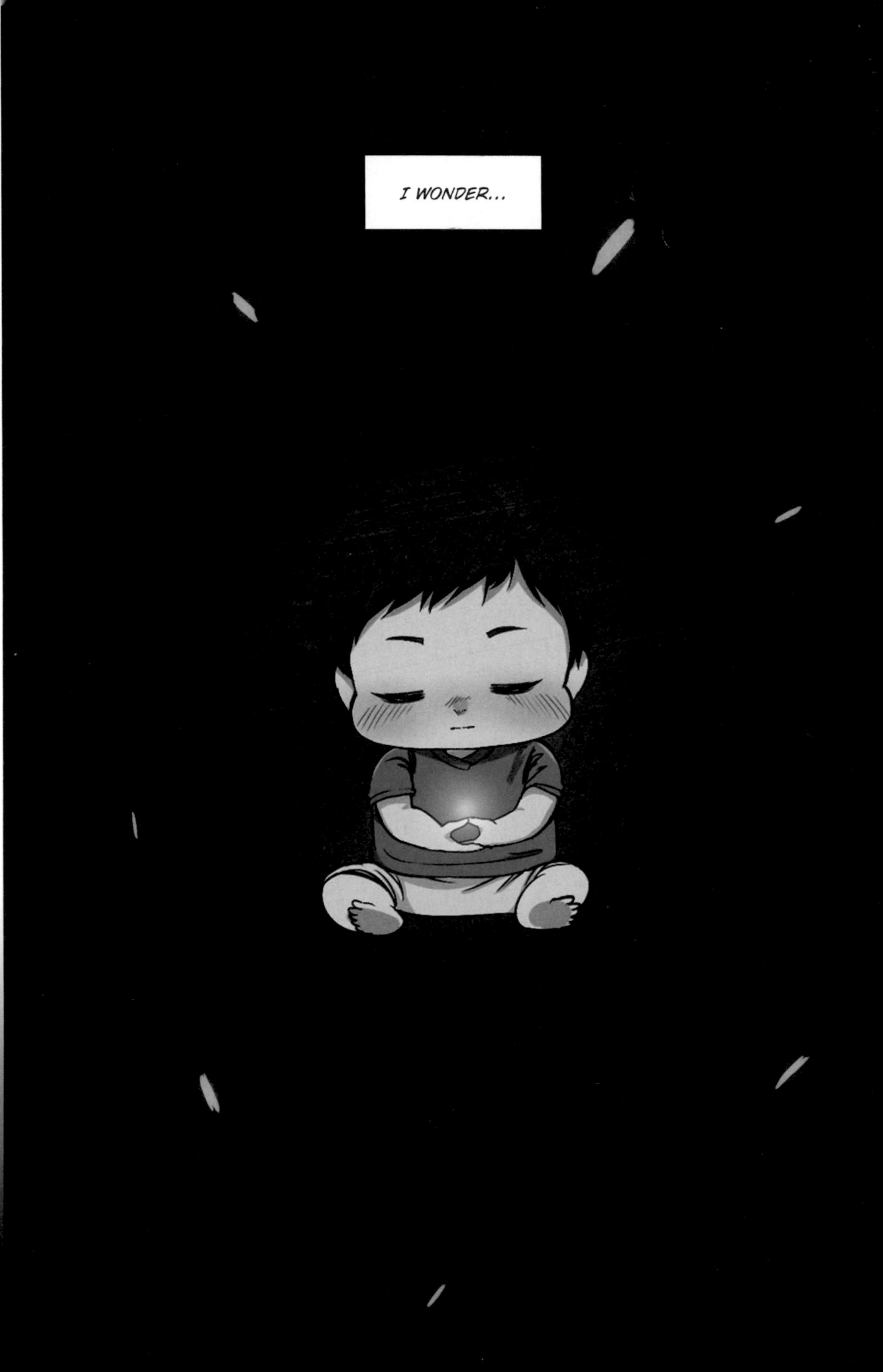
I WONDER...

IT'S WORKING!
IT'S WOR—

GRAB

THERE
YOU ARE, ART!
WORRYING ME
LIKE THA—

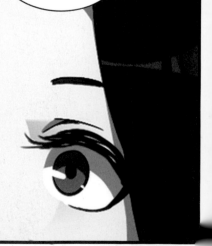

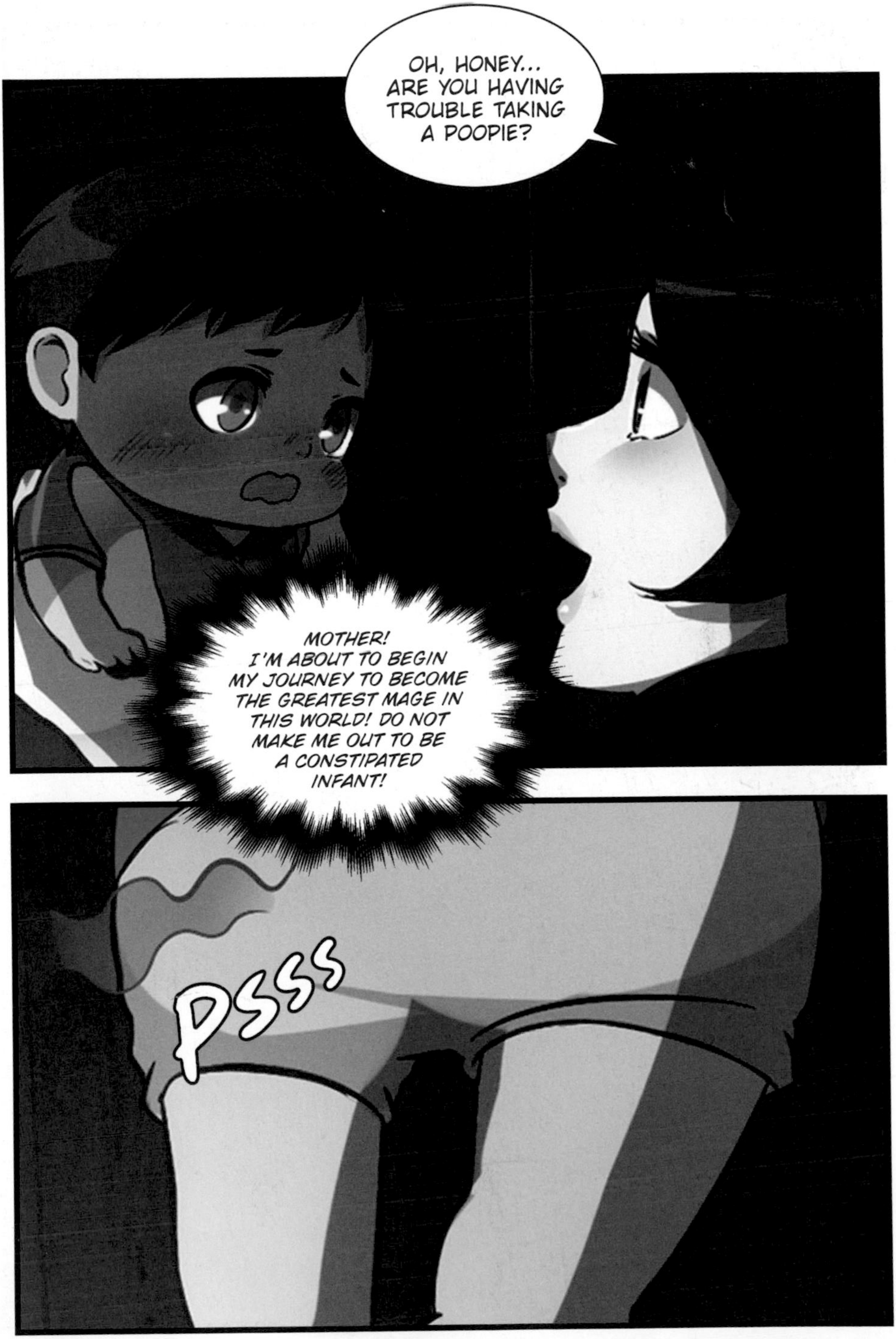
OH, HONEY... ARE YOU HAVING TROUBLE TAKING A POOPIE?
MOTHER! I'M ABOUT TO BEGIN MY JOURNEY TO BECOME THE GREATEST MAGE IN THIS WORLD! DO NOT MAKE ME OUT TO BE A CONSTIPATED INFANT!
PSSS

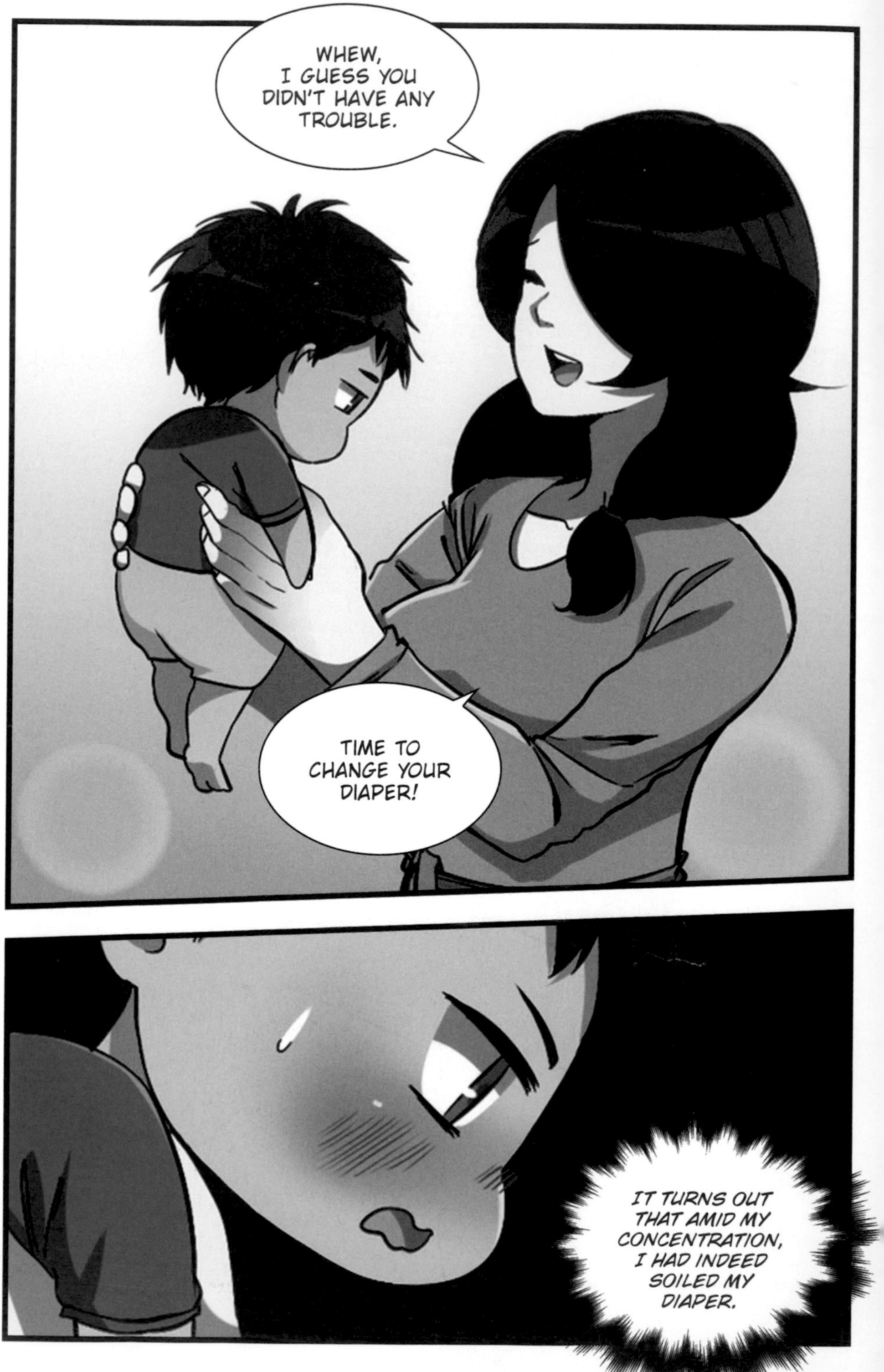
WHEW, I GUESS YOU DIDN'T HAVE ANY TROUBLE.
TIME TO CHANGE YOUR DIAPER!
IT TURNS OUT THAT AMID MY CONCENTRATION, I HAD INDEED SOILED MY DIAPER.

THE
BEGINNING
AFTER
THE END

CHAPTER 3—(Not) a Doting Mother

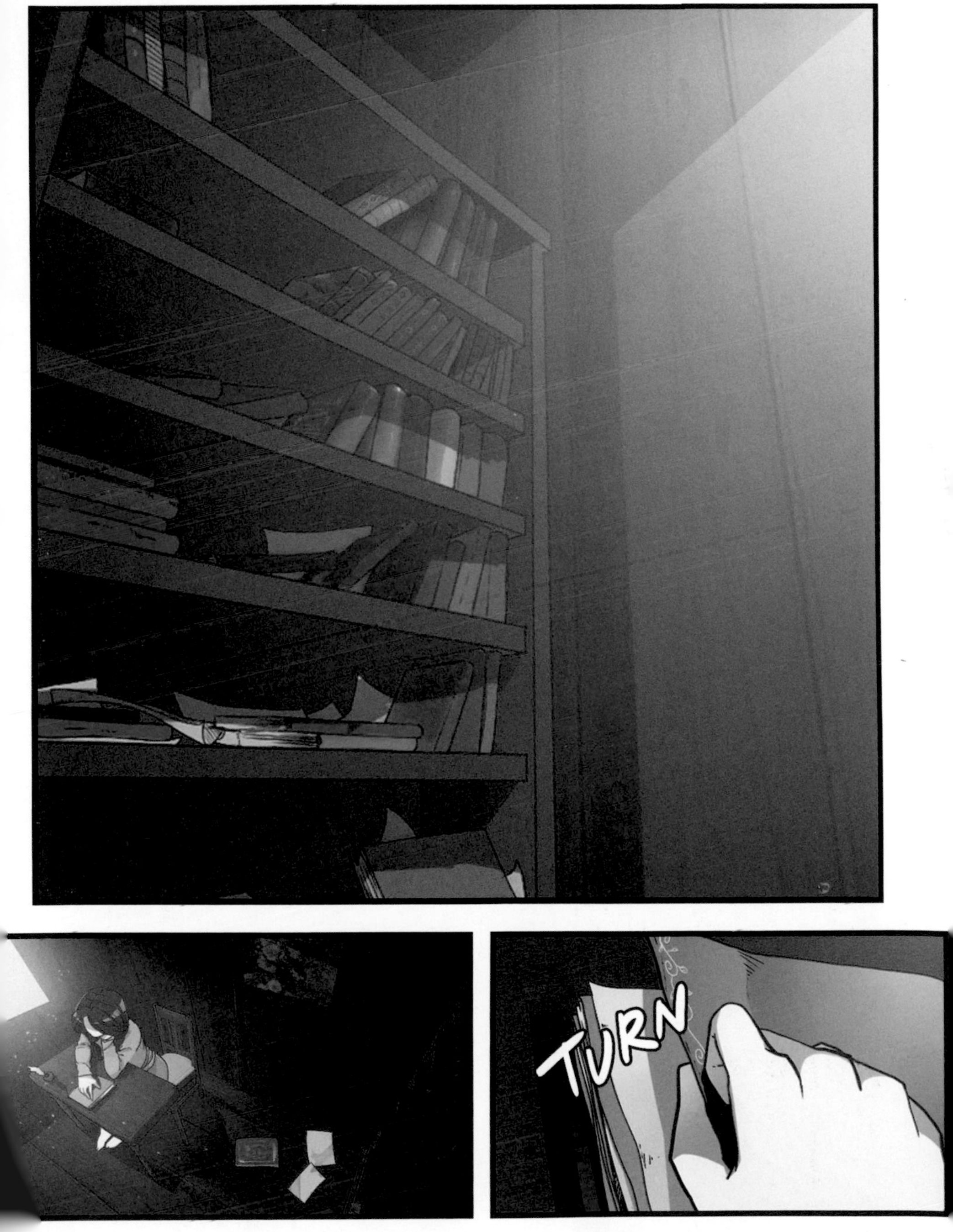
TURN

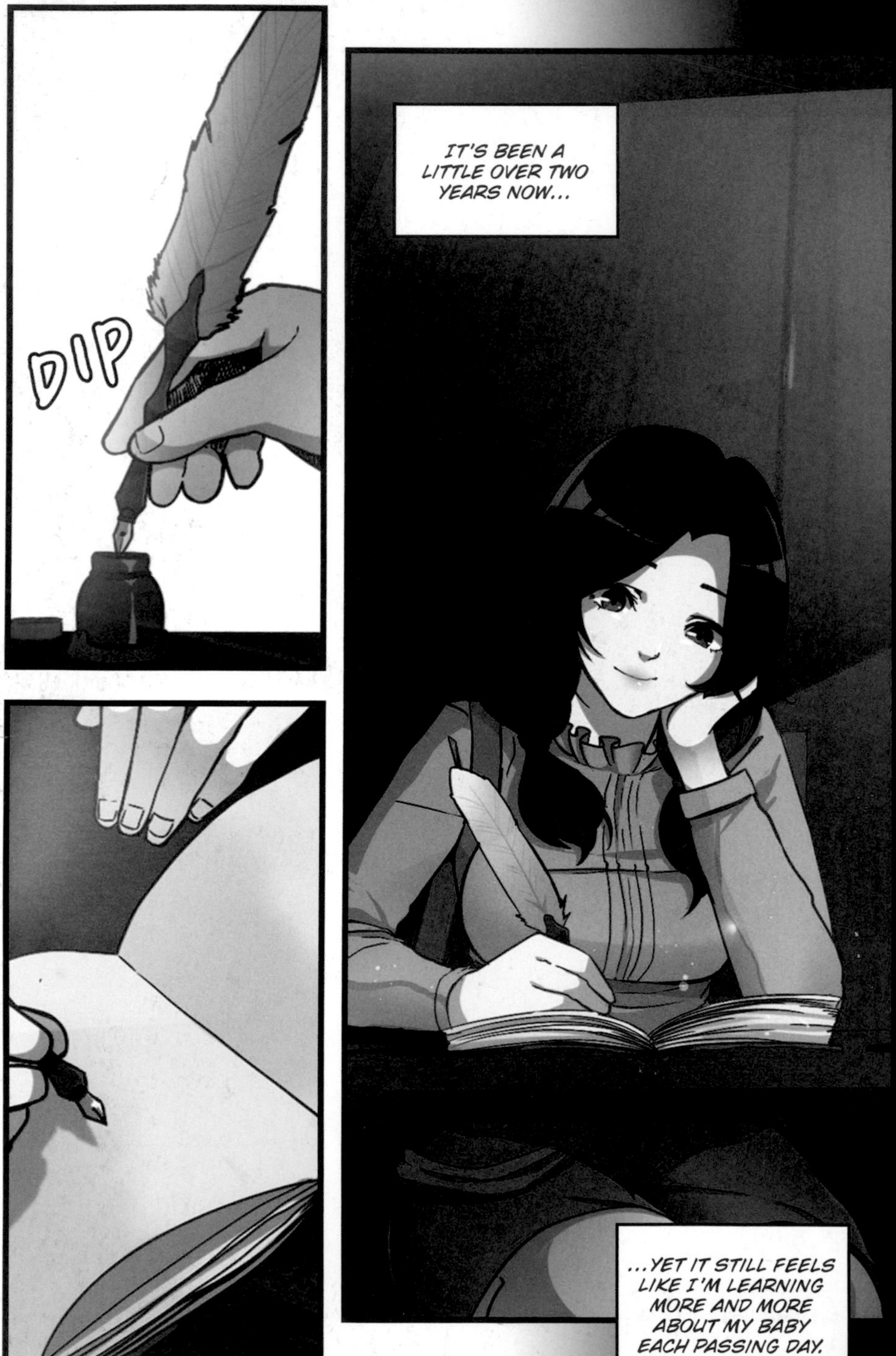
DIP
IT'S BEEN A LITTLE OVER TWO YEARS NOW...
...YET IT STILL FEELS LIKE I'M LEARNING MORE AND MORE ABOUT MY BABY EACH PASSING DAY.

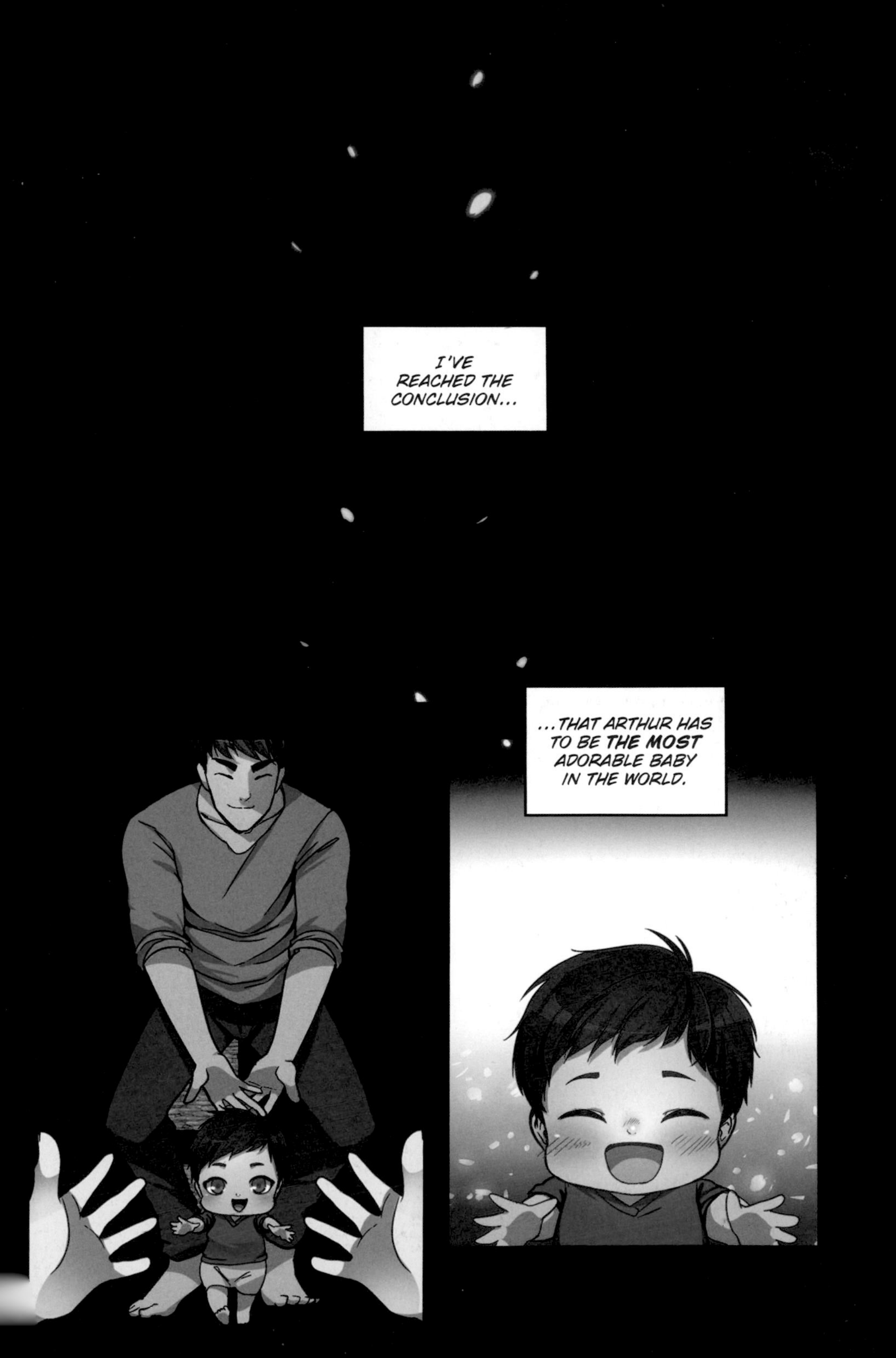
I'VE REACHED THE CONCLUSION...
...THAT ARTHUR HAS TO BE **THE MOST** ADORABLE BABY IN THE WORLD.

WITH HIS LITTLE PATCH OF AUBURN HAIR...

...AND AZURE EYES THAT LOOK AT ME ALMOST INTELLIGENTLY...

I KNOW HE WILL GET INTO TROUBLE IN THE FUTURE IF I DON'T BECOME A STRICT AND DEPENDABLE MOTHER.

IT'S NOT LIKE I CAN RELY ON REY.

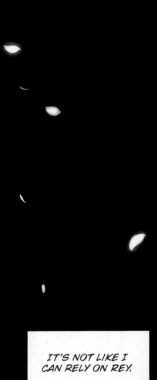

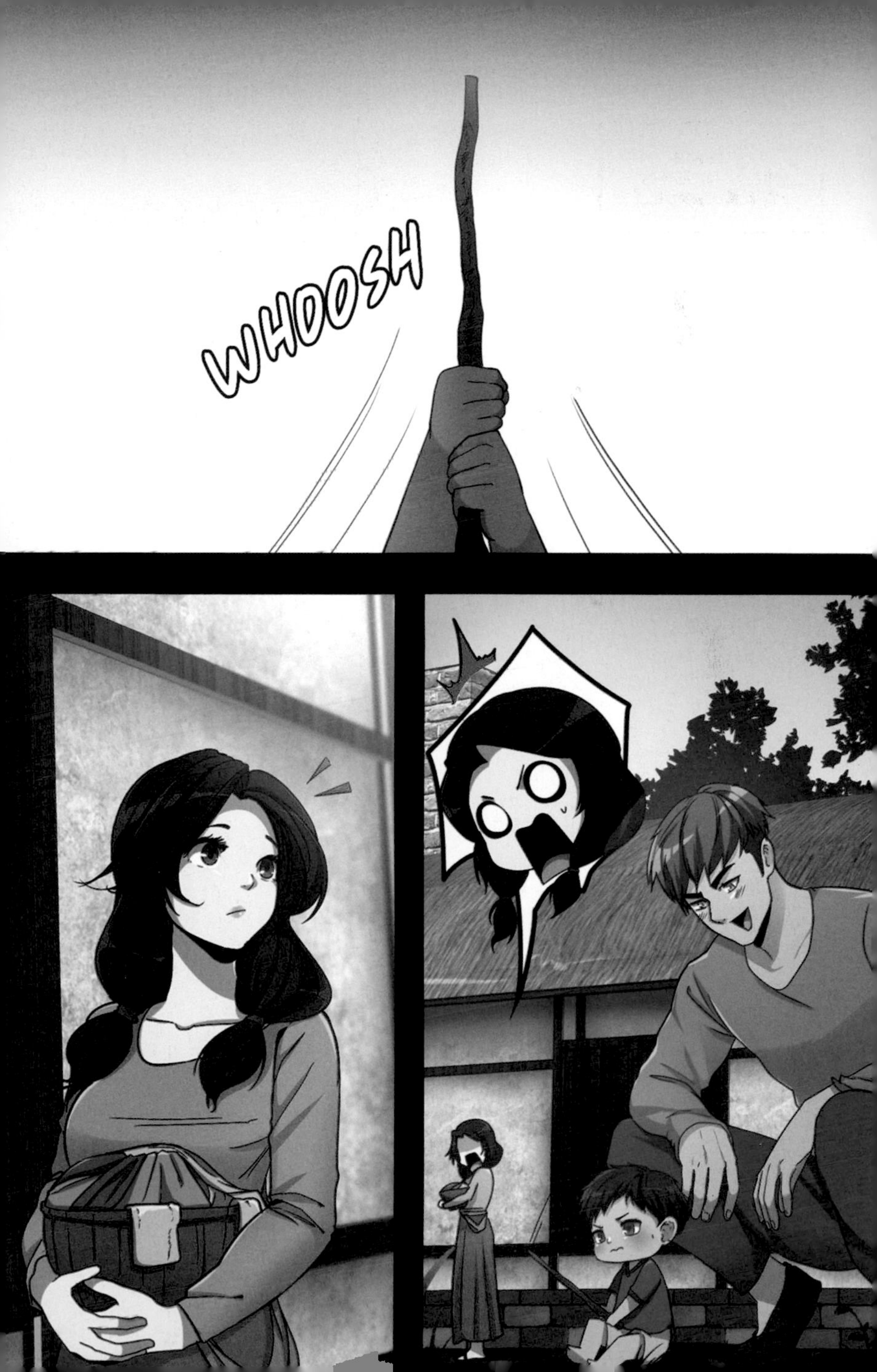
WHOOSH

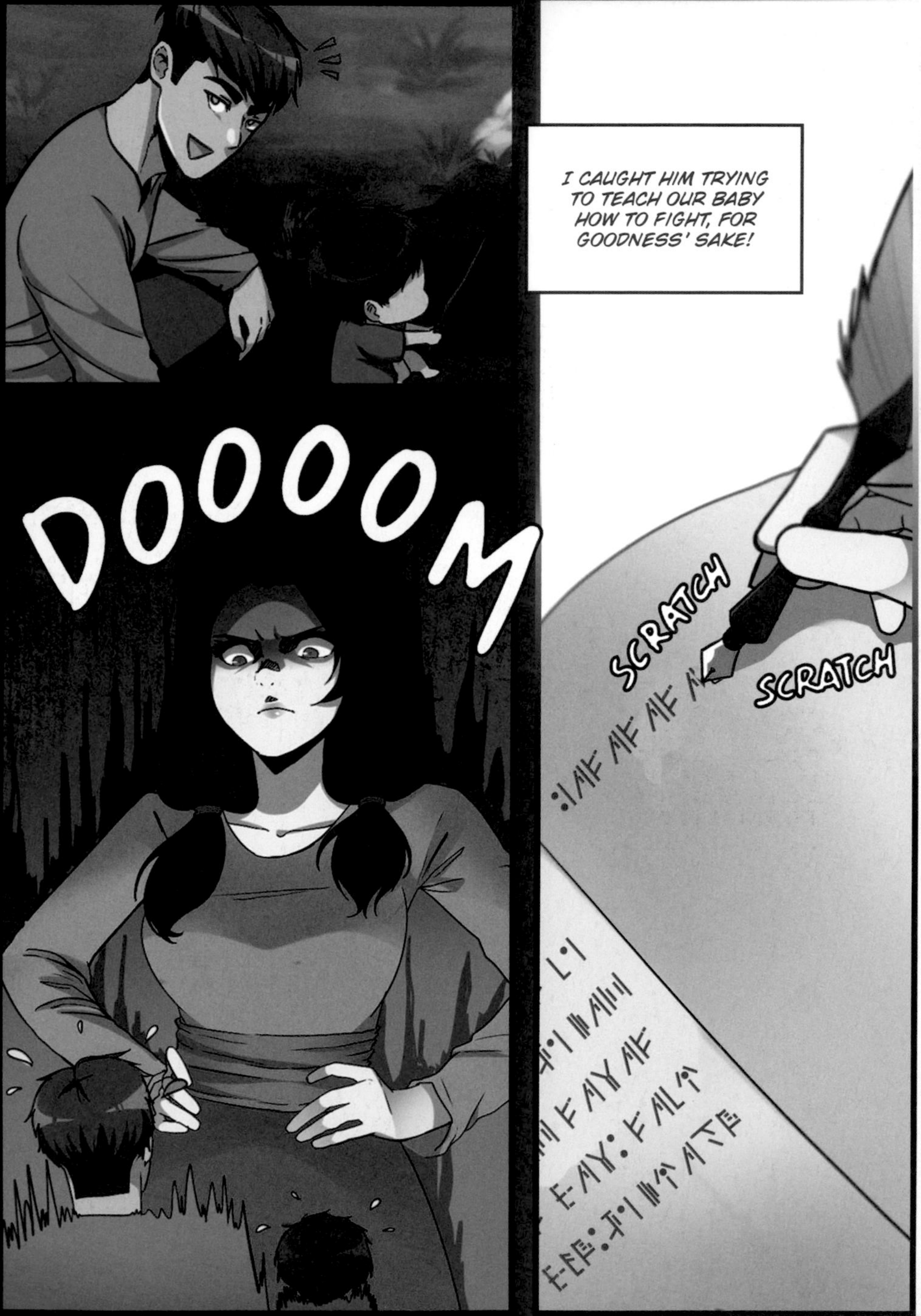
DOOOOM
I CAUGHT HIM TRYING TO TEACH OUR BABY HOW TO FIGHT, FOR GOODNESS' SAKE!
SCRATCH
SCRATCH

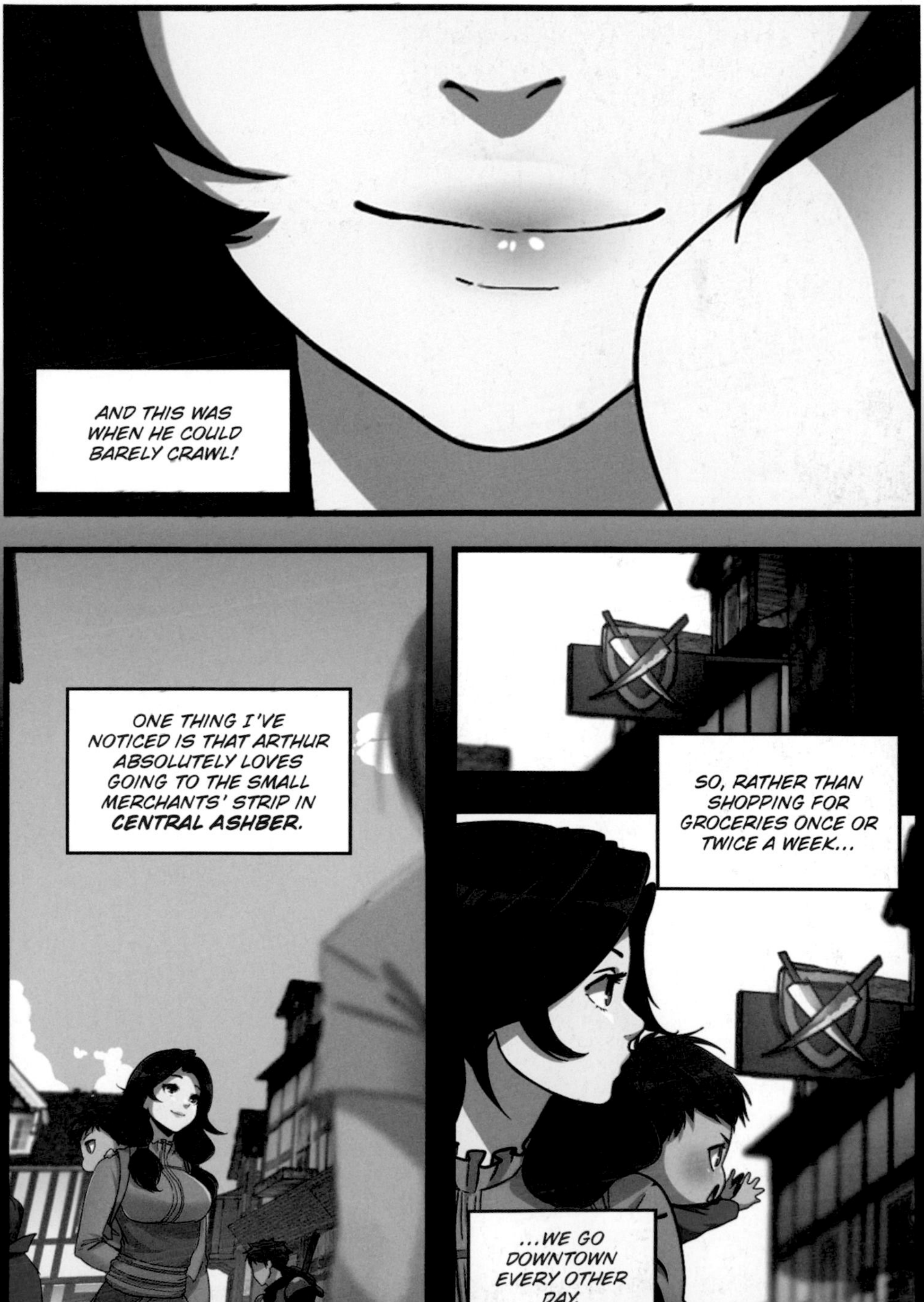

AND THIS WAS WHEN HE COULD BARELY CRAWL!
ONE THING I'VE NOTICED IS THAT ARTHUR ABSOLUTELY LOVES GOING TO THE SMALL MERCHANTS' STRIP IN **CENTRAL ASHBER.**
SO, RATHER THAN SHOPPING FOR GROCERIES ONCE OR TWICE A WEEK...
...WE GO DOWNTOWN EVERY OTHER DAY.

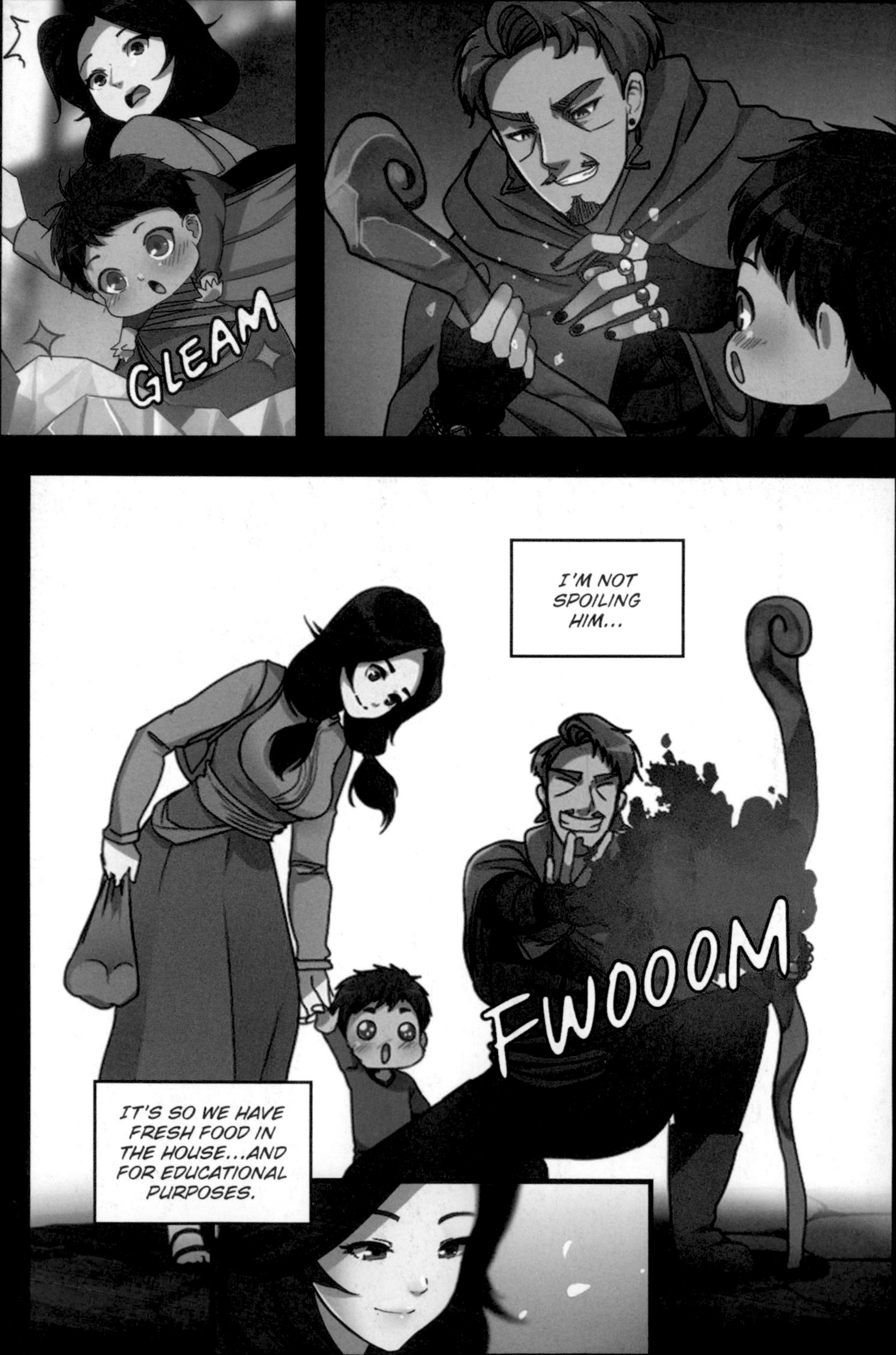
GLEAM
I'M NOT SPOILING HIM...
FWOOOM
IT'S SO WE HAVE FRESH FOOD IN THE HOUSE...AND FOR EDUCATIONAL PURPOSES.

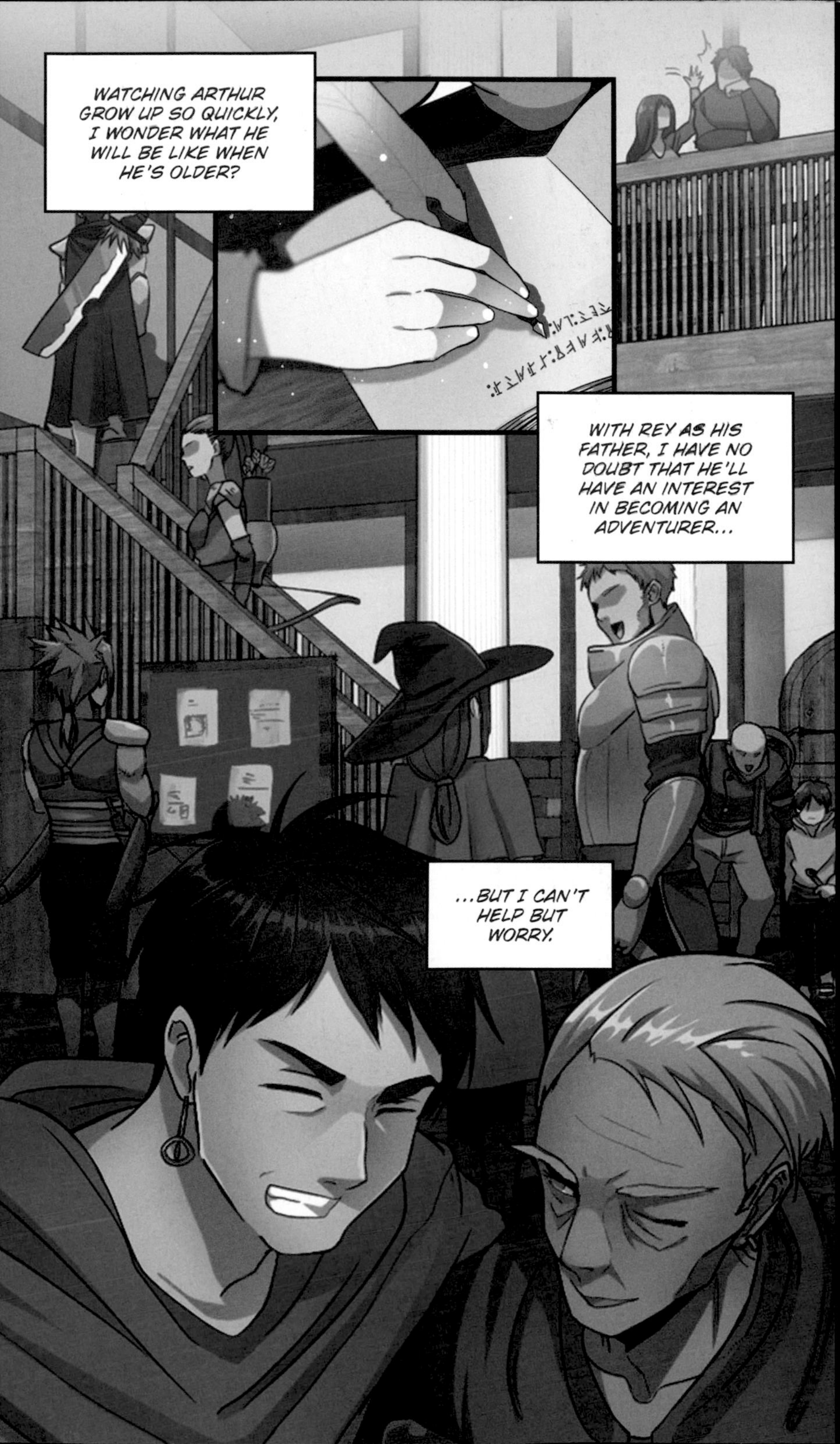
WATCHING ARTHUR GROW UP SO QUICKLY, I WONDER WHAT HE WILL BE LIKE WHEN HE'S OLDER?
WITH REY AS HIS FATHER, I HAVE NO DOUBT THAT HE'LL HAVE AN INTEREST IN BECOMING AN ADVENTURER...
...BUT I CAN'T HELP BUT WORRY.

I CAN ONLY HOPE HE FARES BETTER THAN THE NAIVE YOUNG TEENS HOPING TO MAKE IT BIG AS ADVENTURERS.

NOW, IF ONLY I COULD DO SOMETHING ABOUT HIS PERPETUAL HABIT OF SNEAKING INTO THE STUDY...

I'M TEMPTED TO MOVE HIS CRIB THERE...

...BUT THAT'S FOR ANOTHER DAY.

THUMP

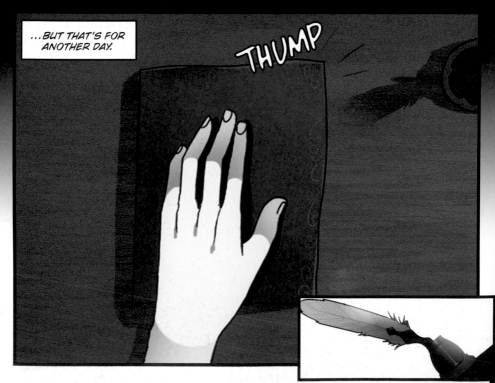

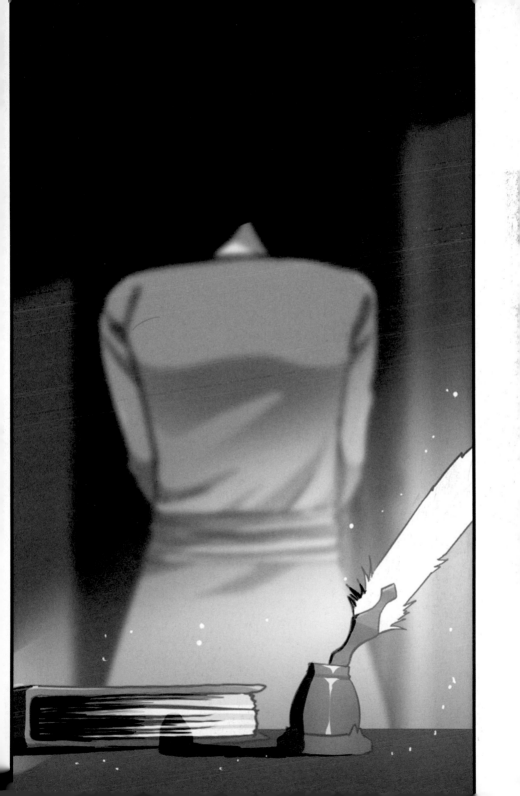

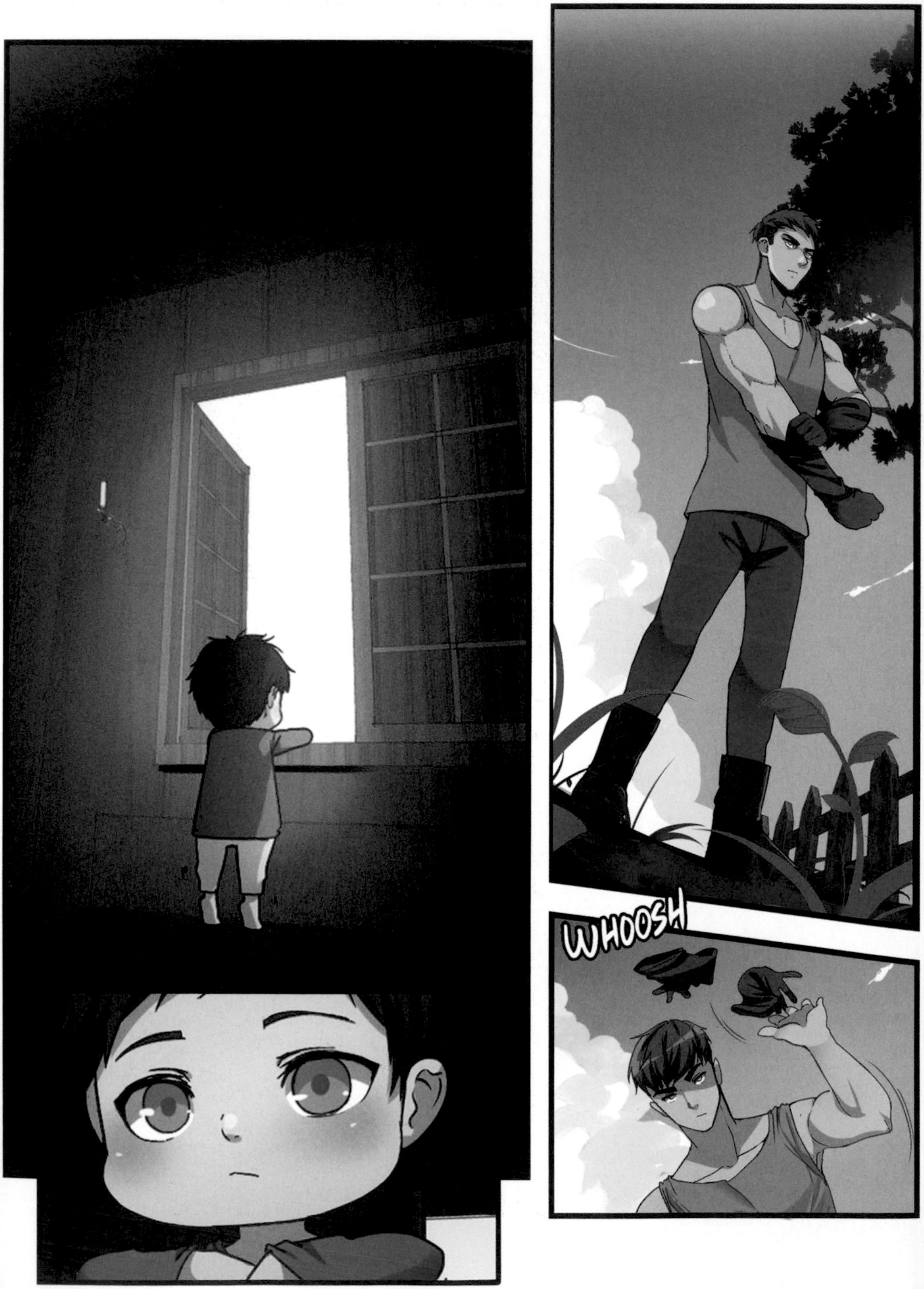
WHOOSH

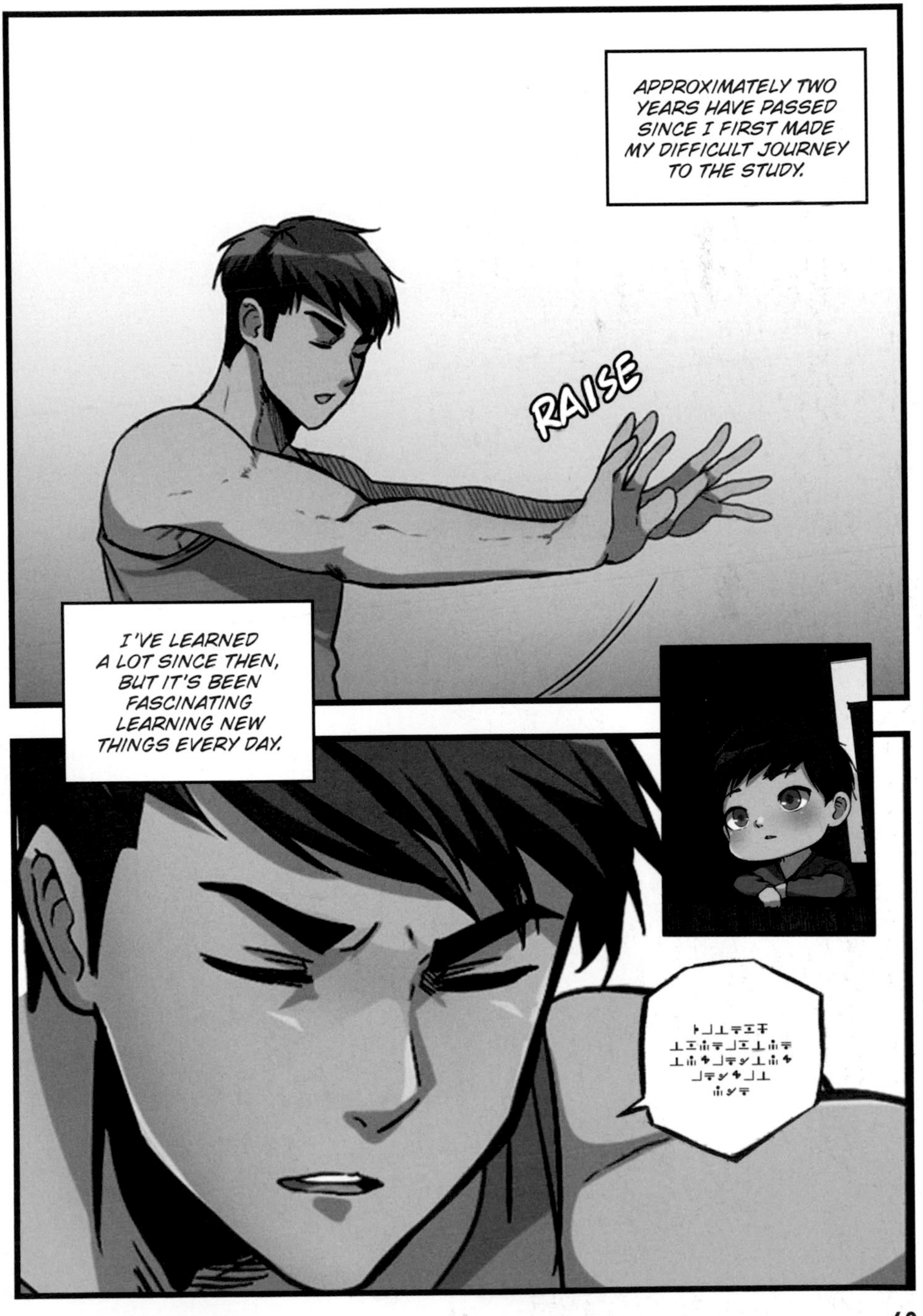
APPROXIMATELY TWO YEARS HAVE PASSED SINCE I FIRST MADE MY DIFFICULT JOURNEY TO THE STUDY.
RAISE
I'VE LEARNED A LOT SINCE THEN, BUT IT'S BEEN FASCINATING LEARNING NEW THINGS EVERY DAY.

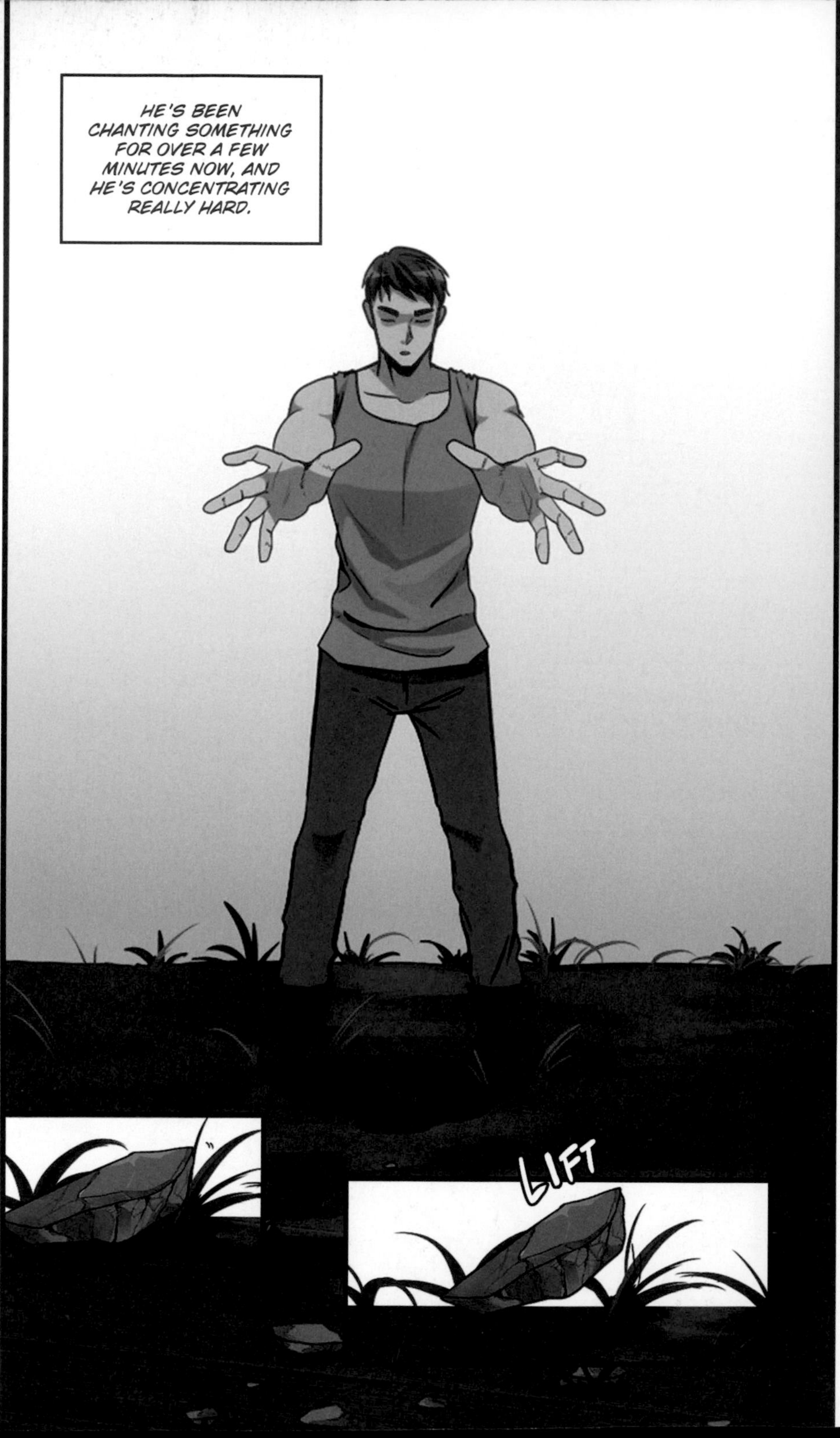
HE'S BEEN CHANTING SOMETHING FOR OVER A FEW MINUTES NOW, AND HE'S CONCENTRATING REALLY HARD.
LIFT

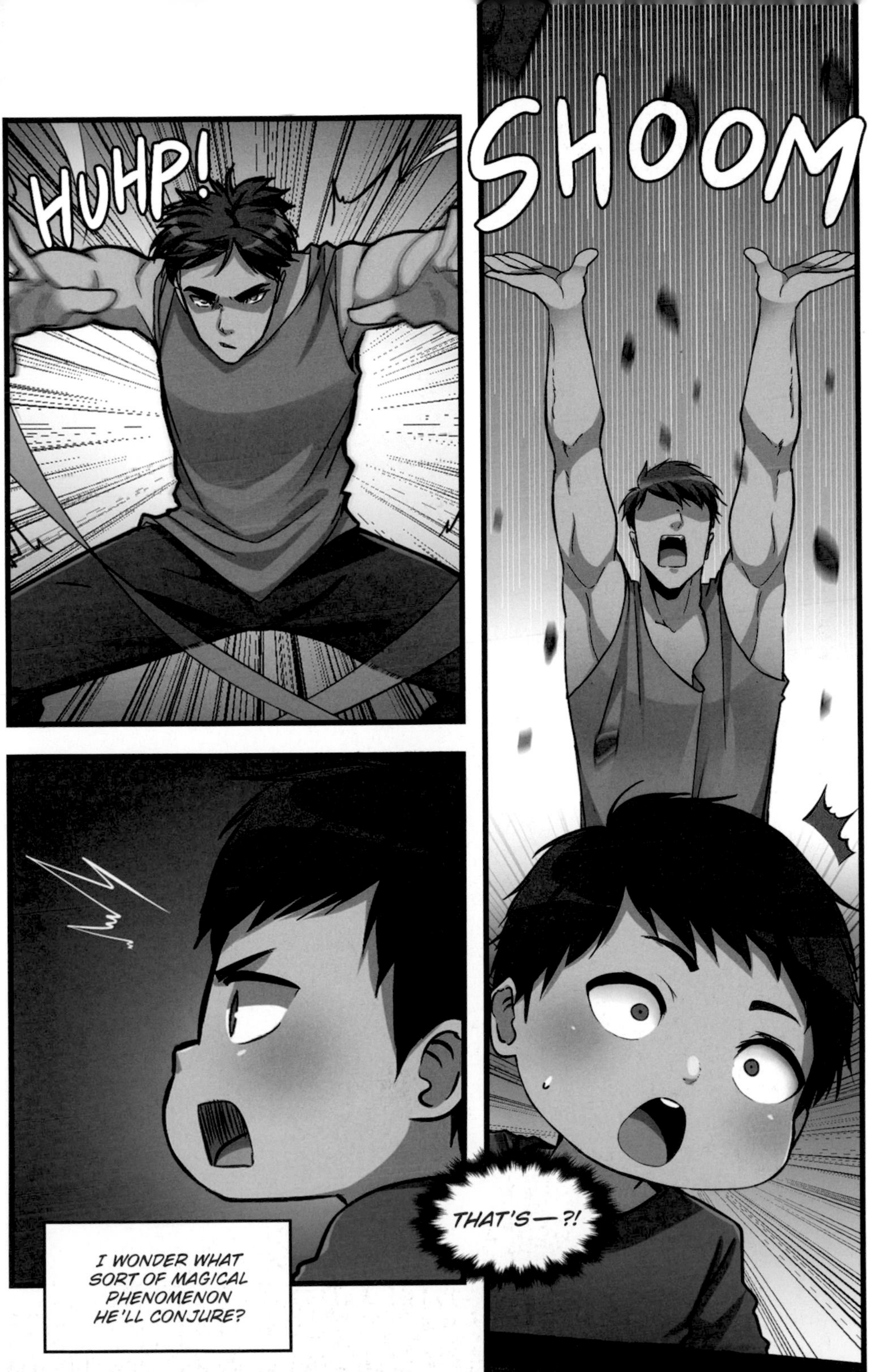
HUHP!
SHOOM
I WONDER WHAT SORT OF MAGICAL PHENOMENON HE'LL CONJURE?
THAT'S—?!

THE
BEGINNING
AFTER
THE
END

CHAPTER 4—Almost There

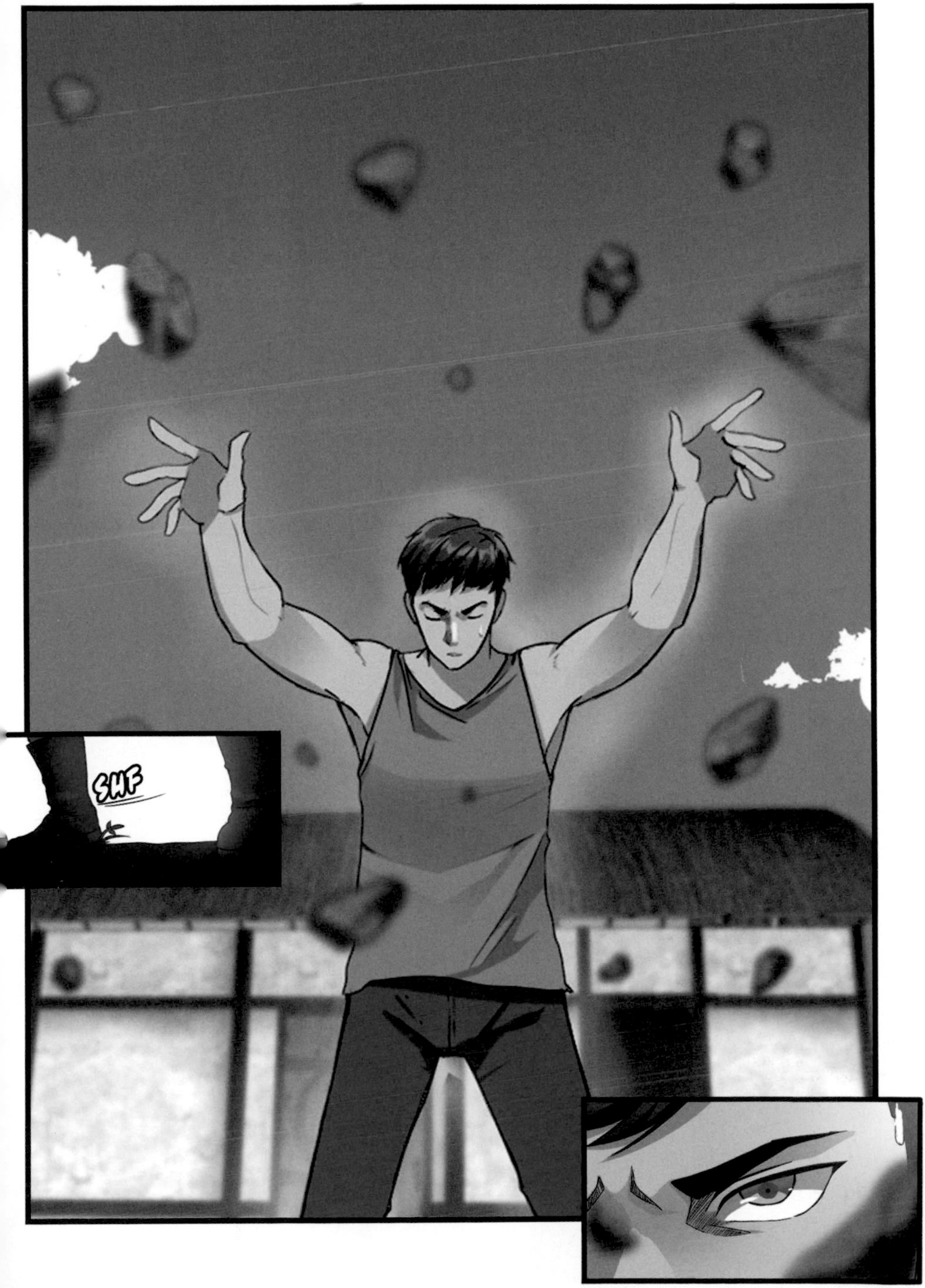
SHF

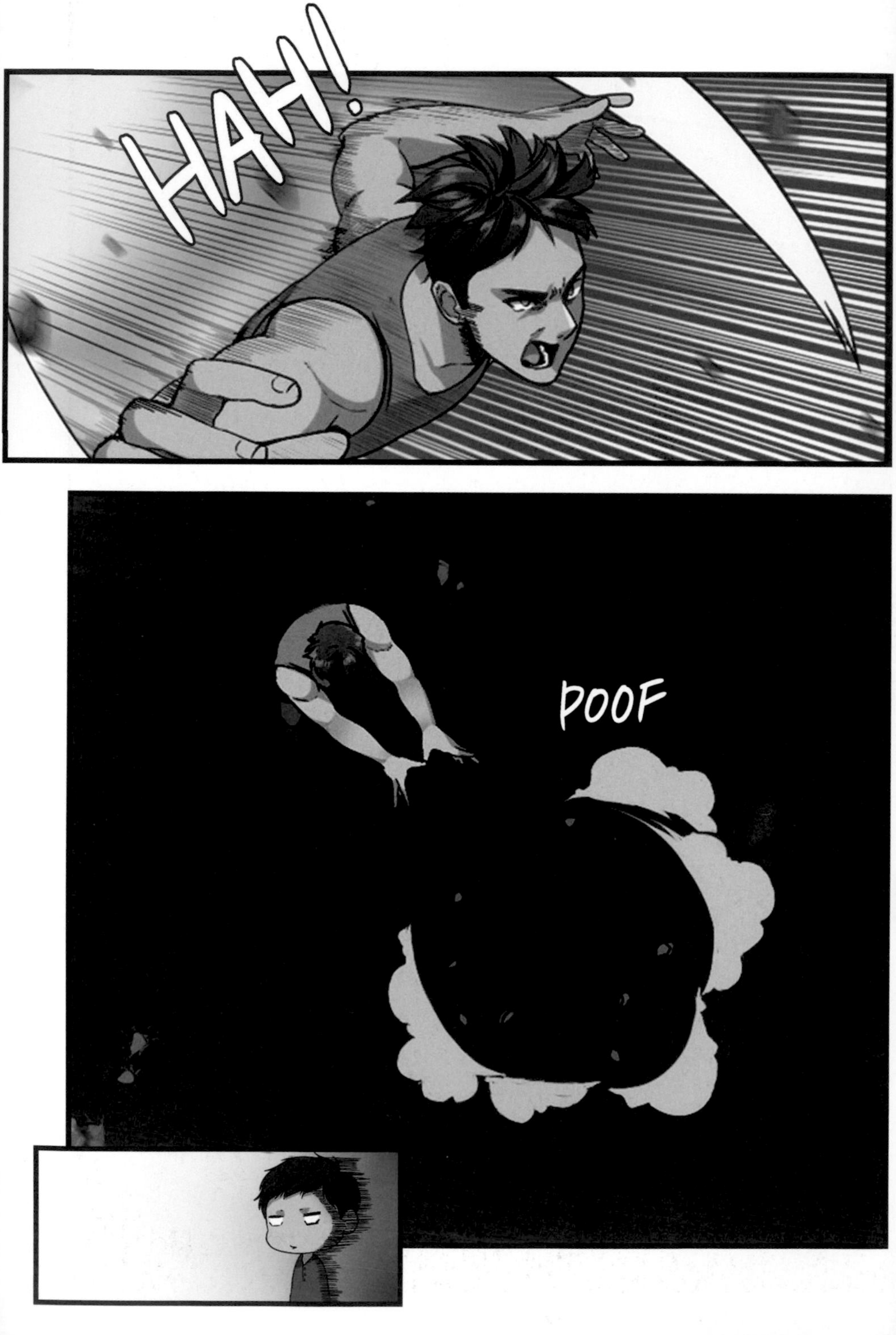
HAH!
POOF

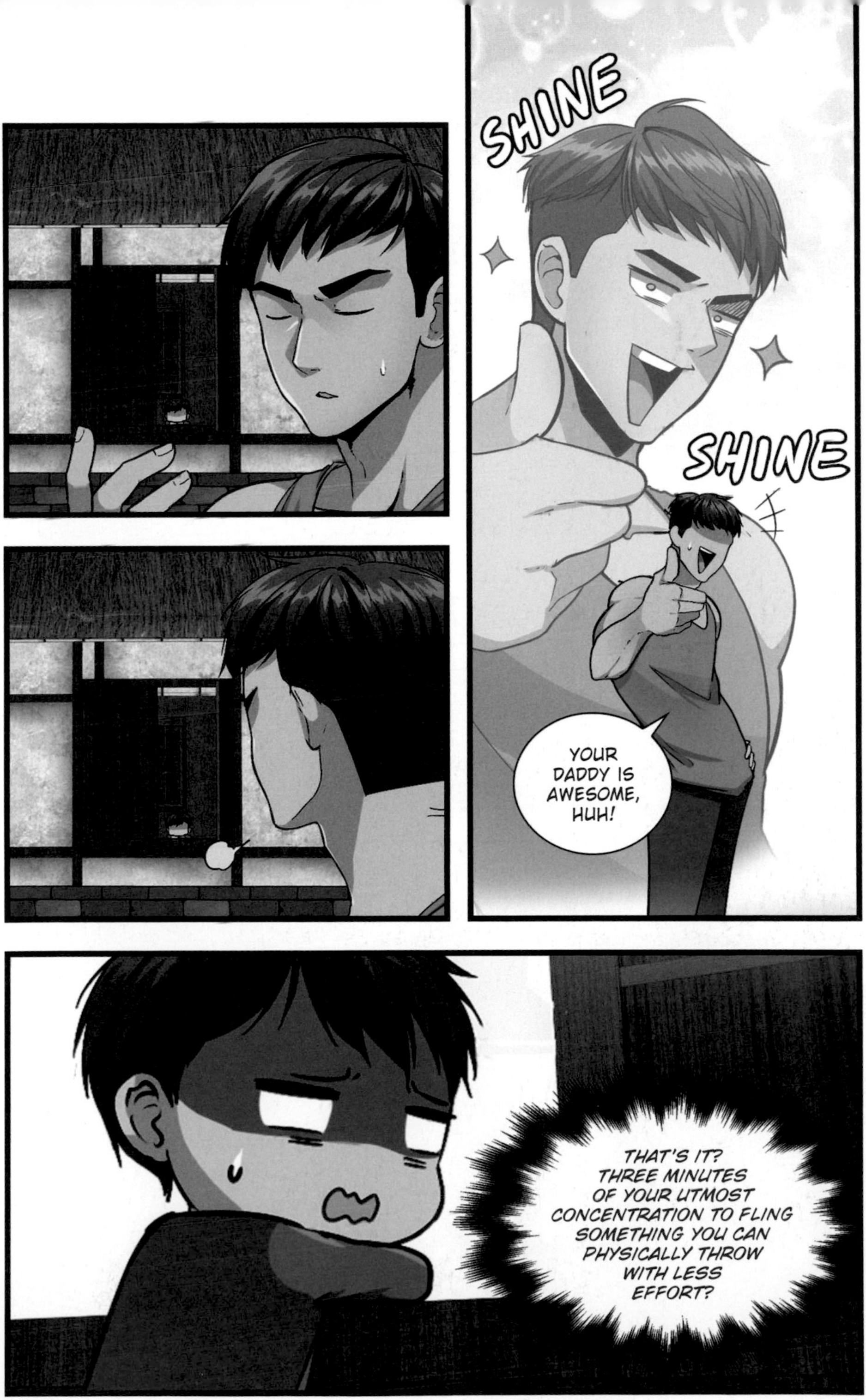
SHINE
SHINE
YOUR DADDY IS AWESOME, HUH!
THAT'S IT? THREE MINUTES OF YOUR UTMOST CONCENTRATION TO FLING SOMETHING YOU CAN PHYSICALLY THROW WITH LESS EFFORT?

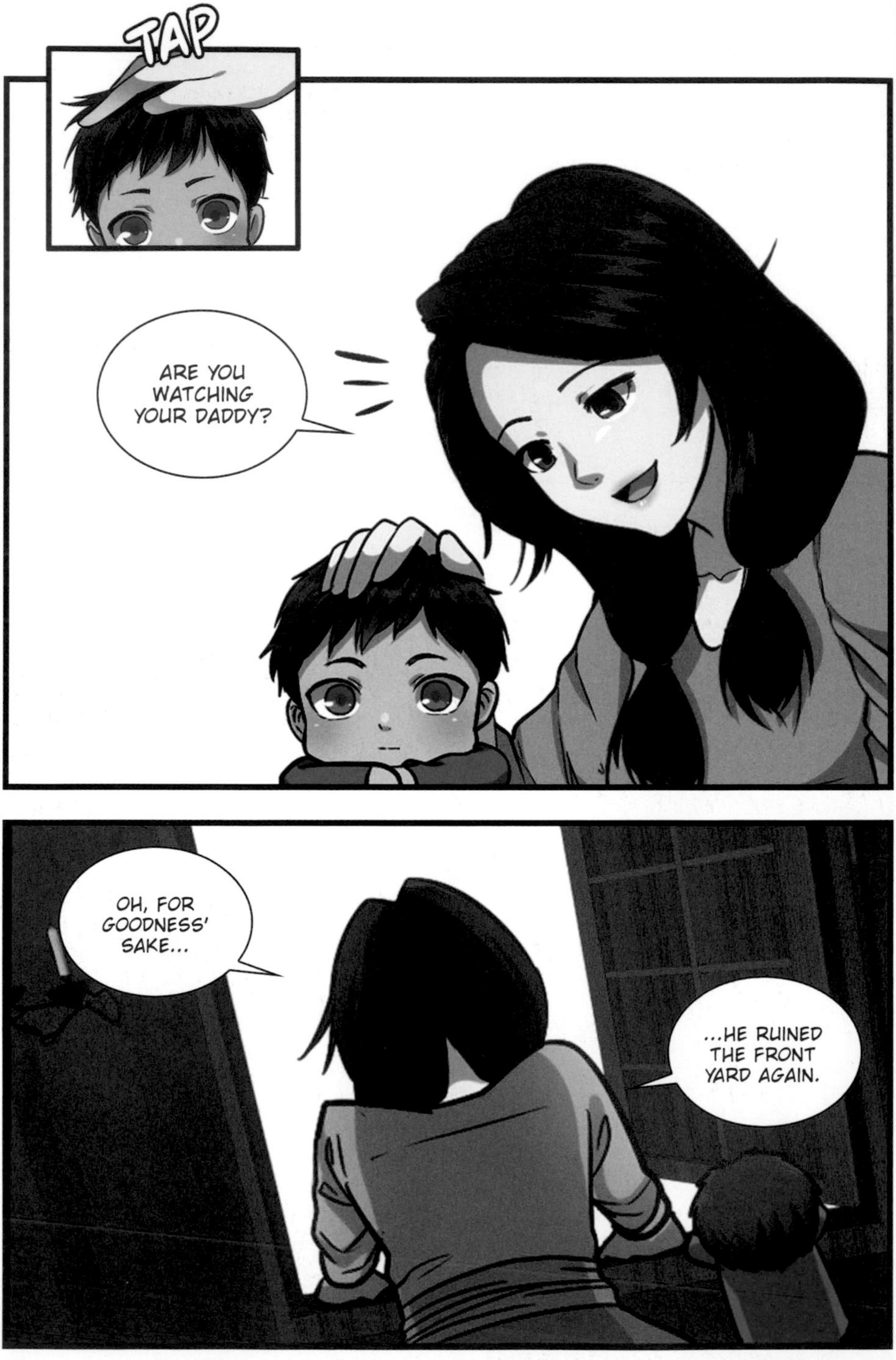
TAP
ARE YOU WATCHING YOUR DADDY?
OH, FOR GOODNESS' SAKE...
...HE RUINED THE FRONT YARD AGAIN.

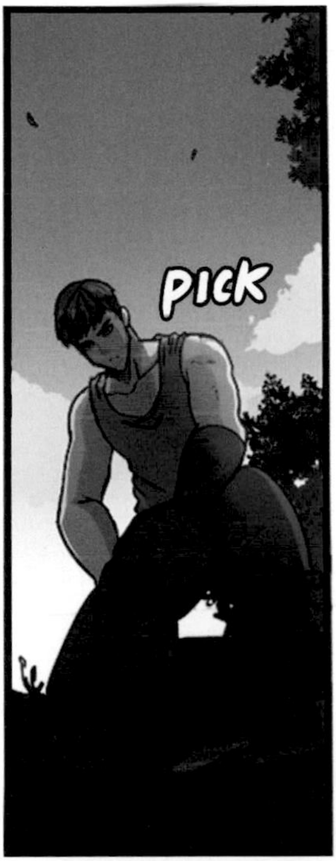
PICK

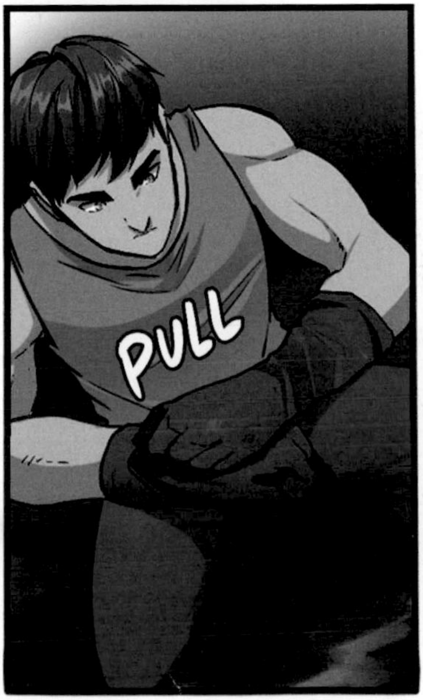
PULL

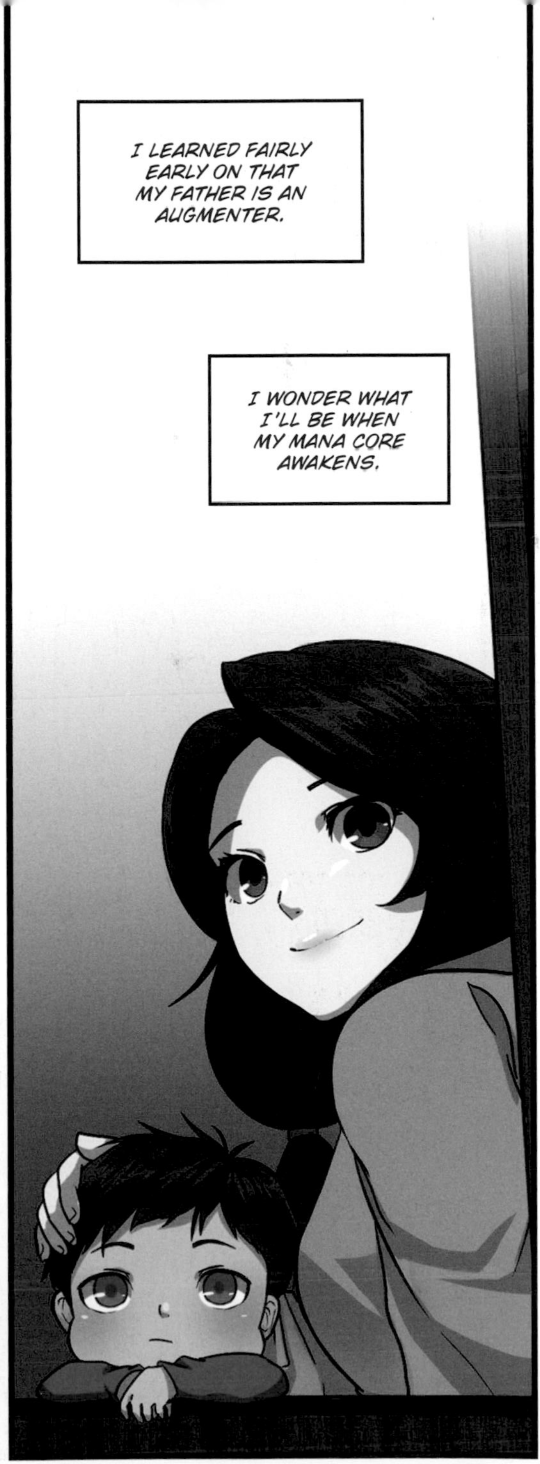
I LEARNED FAIRLY EARLY ON THAT MY FATHER IS AN AUGMENTER.
I WONDER WHAT I'LL BE WHEN MY MANA CORE AWAKENS.

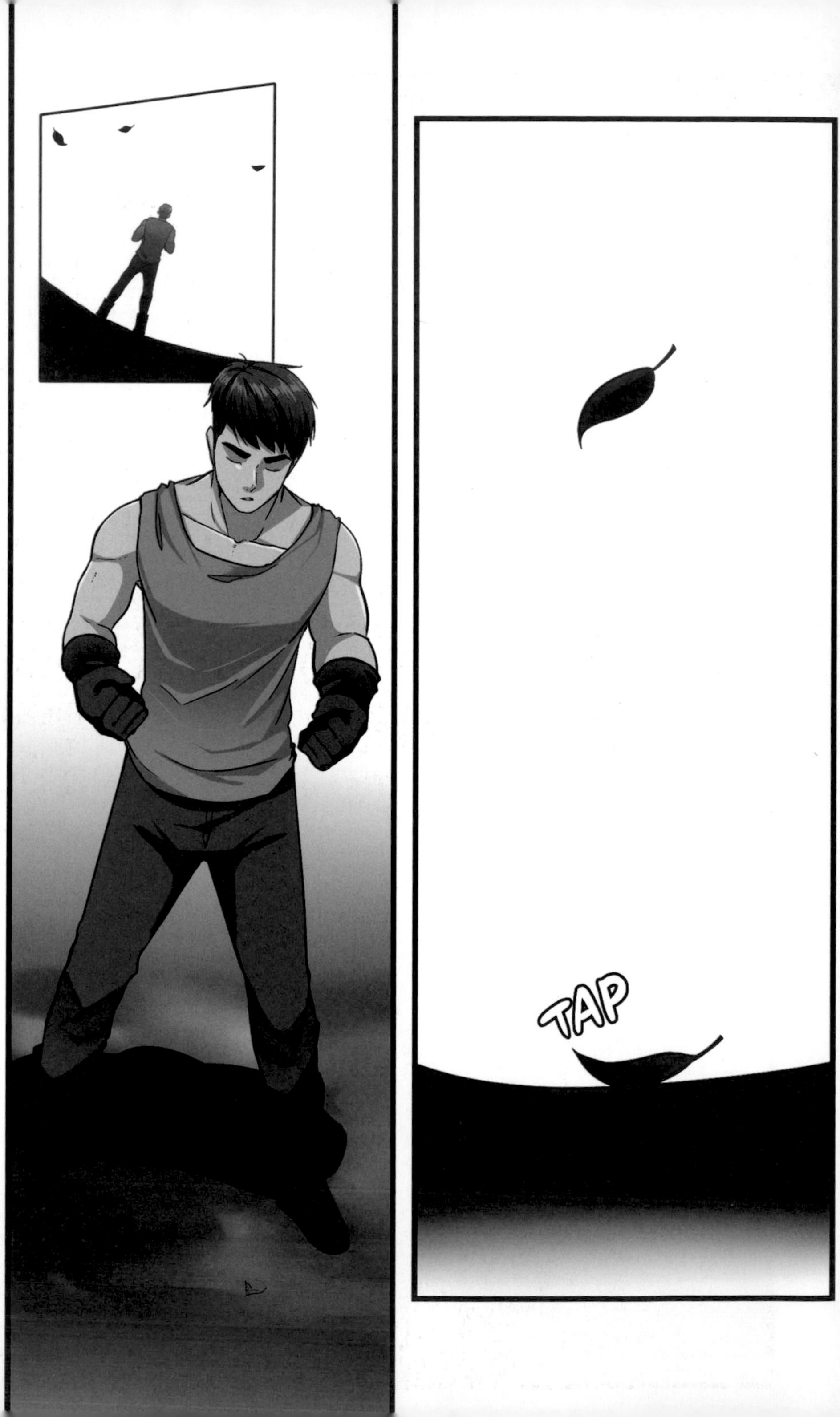
TAP

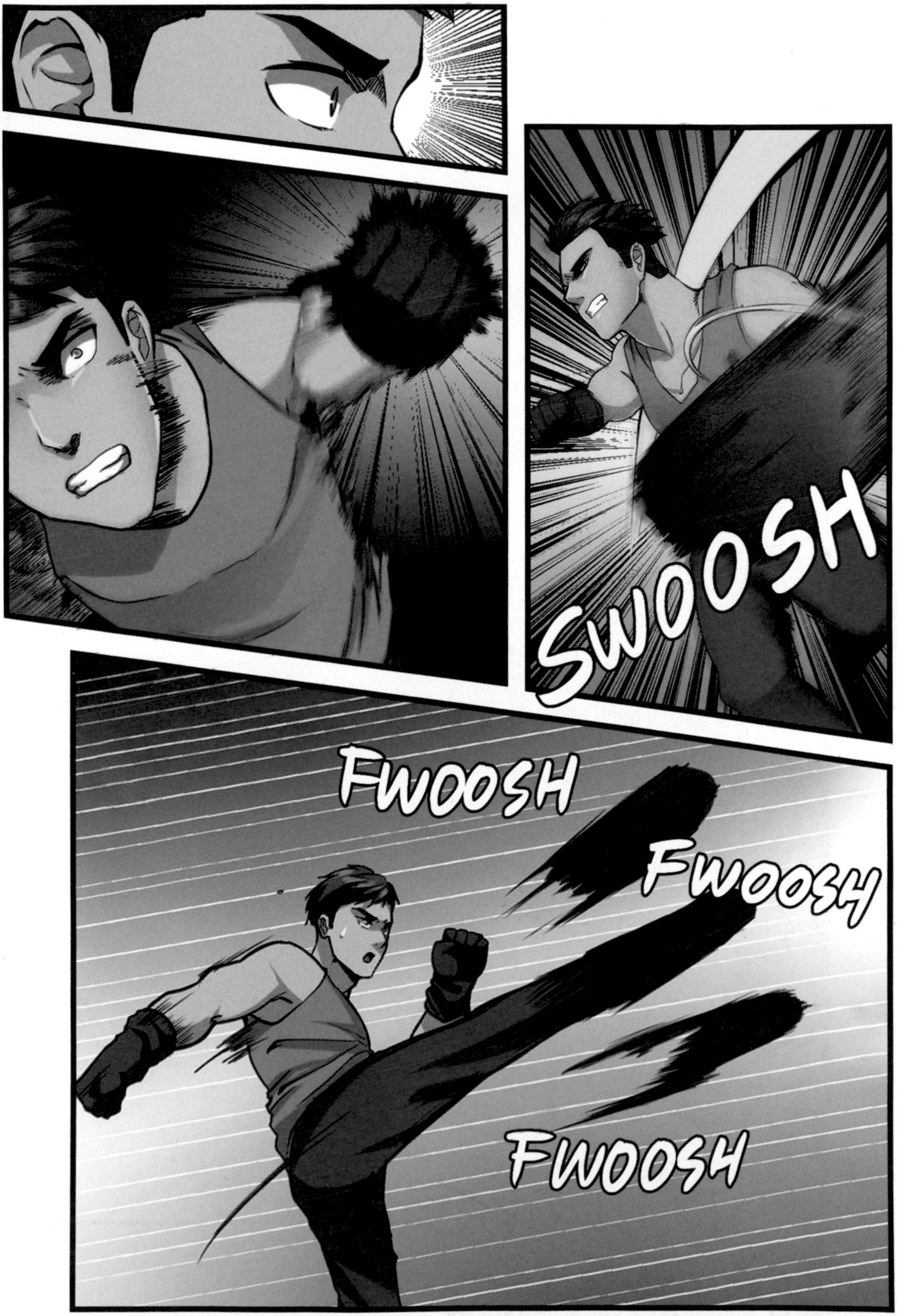
SWOOSH
FWOOSH
FWOOSH
FWOOSH

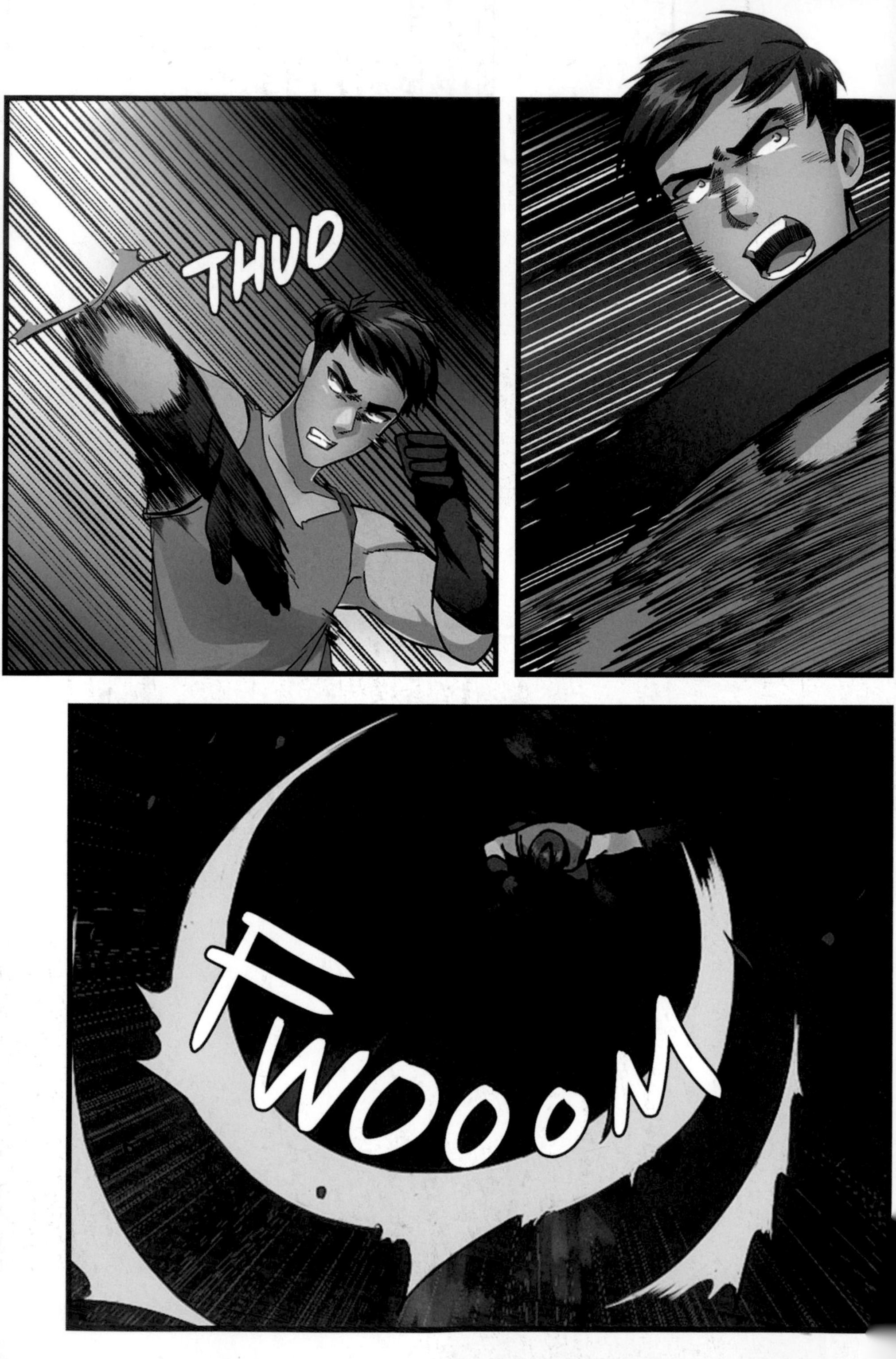
THUD
FWOOOM

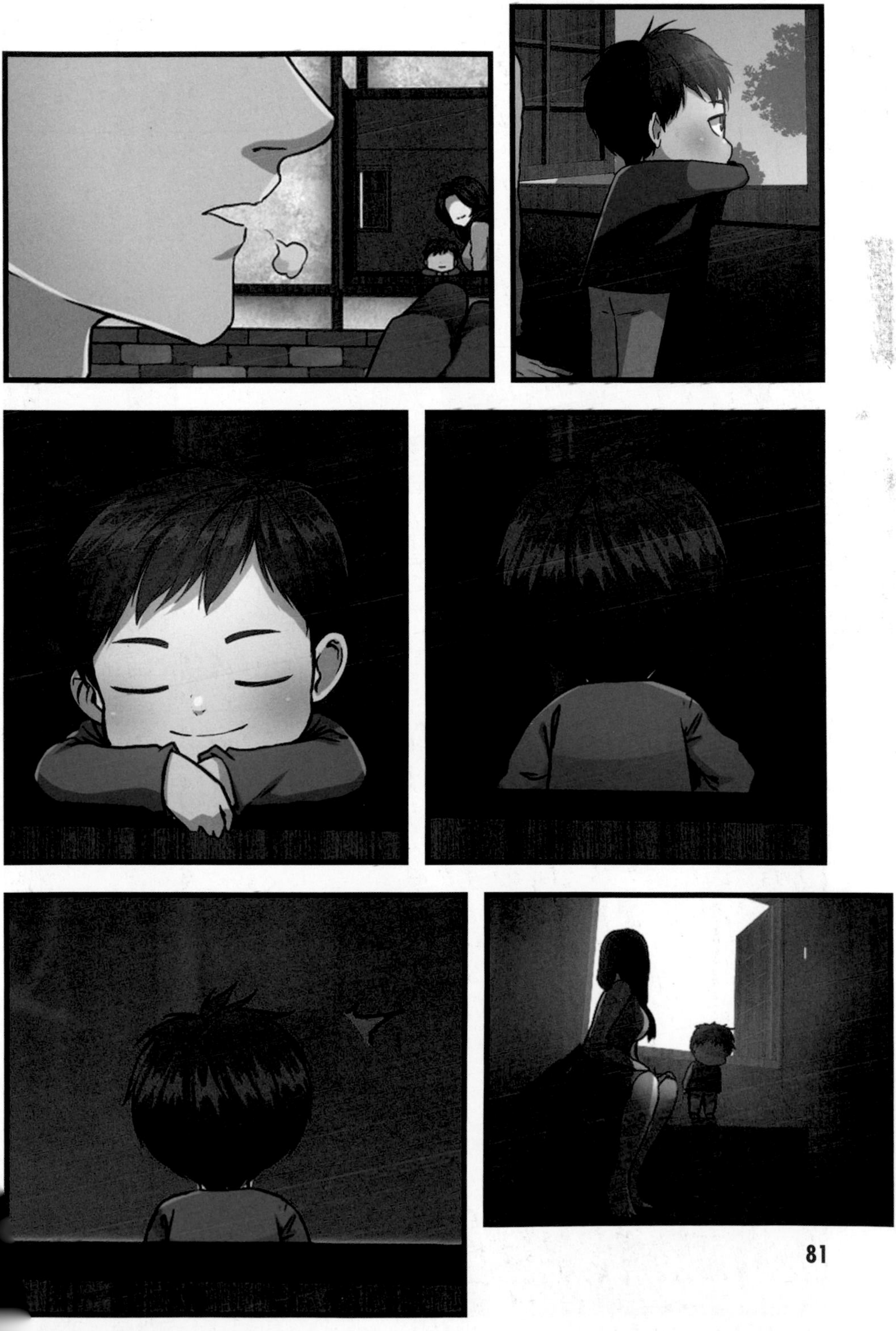

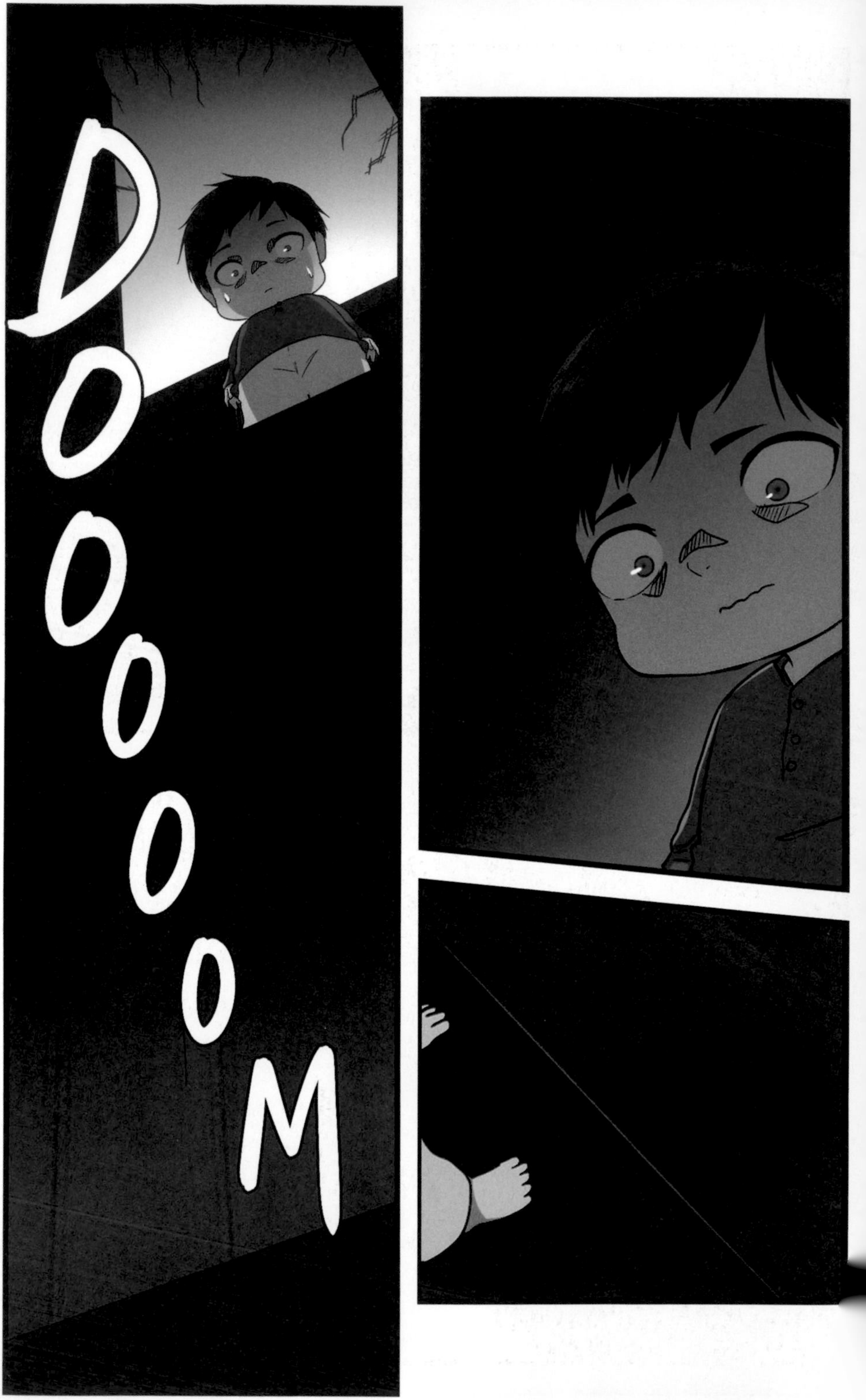
DOOOOOM

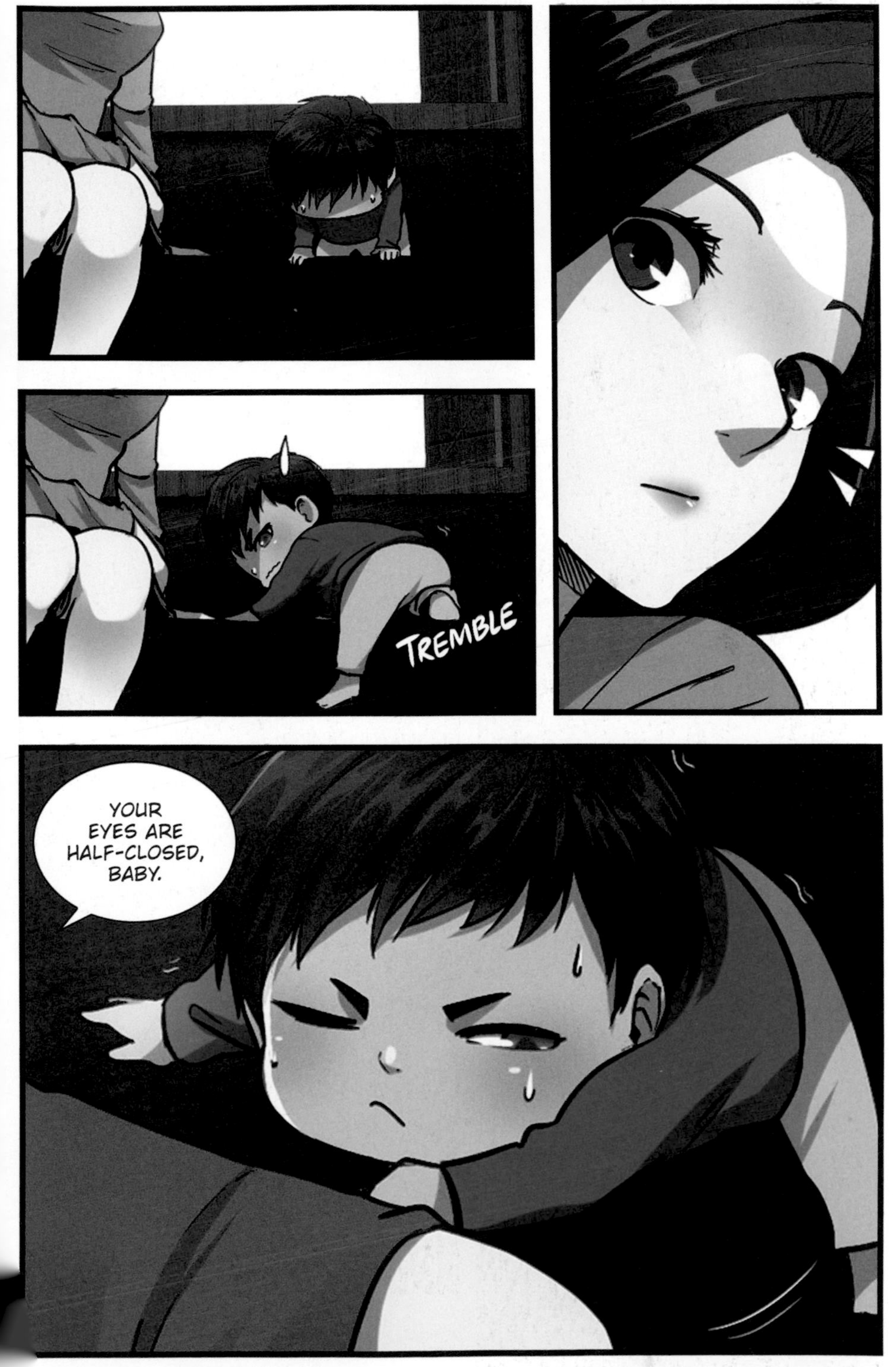
TREMBLE
YOUR EYES ARE HALF-CLOSED, BABY.

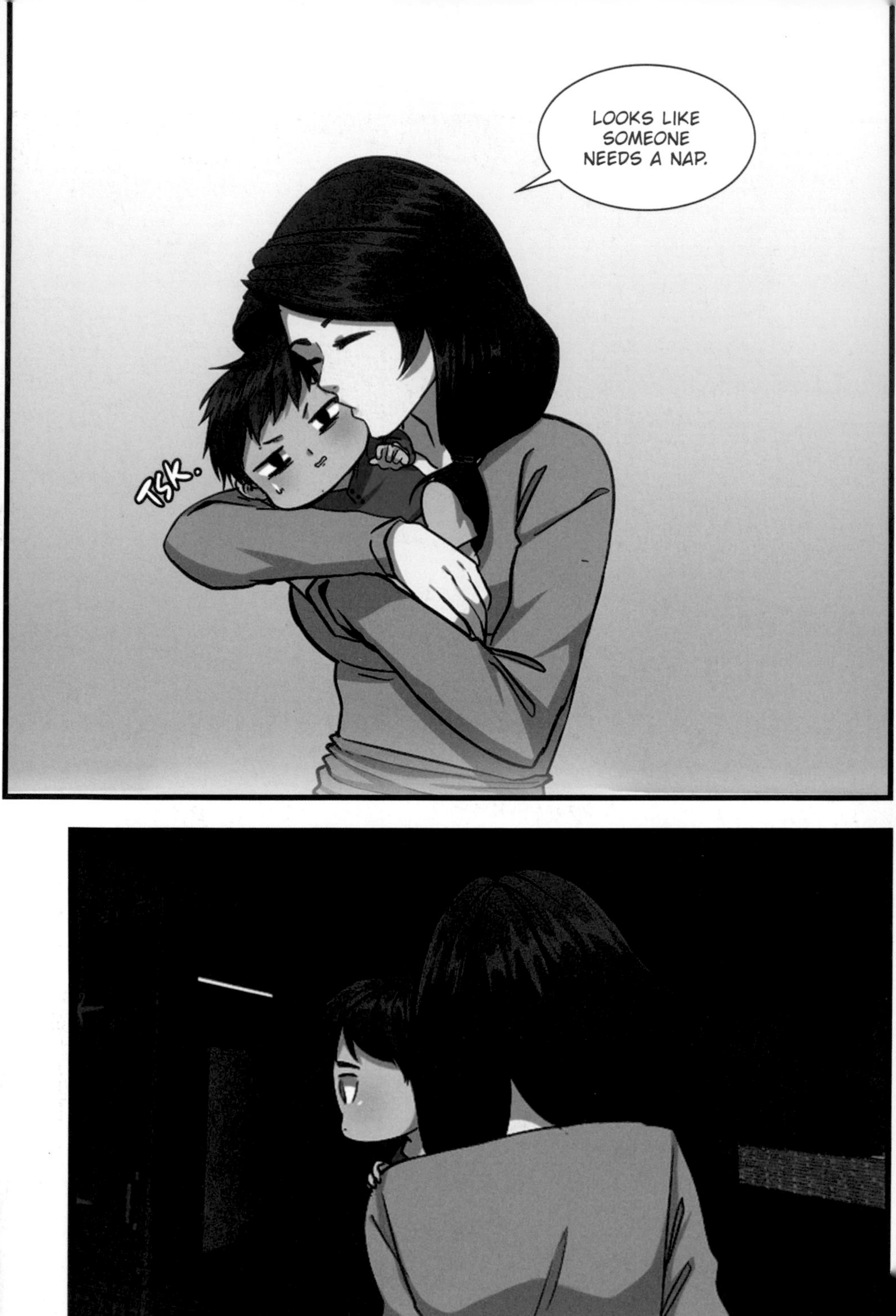
LOOKS LIKE SOMEONE NEEDS A NAP.
TSK.

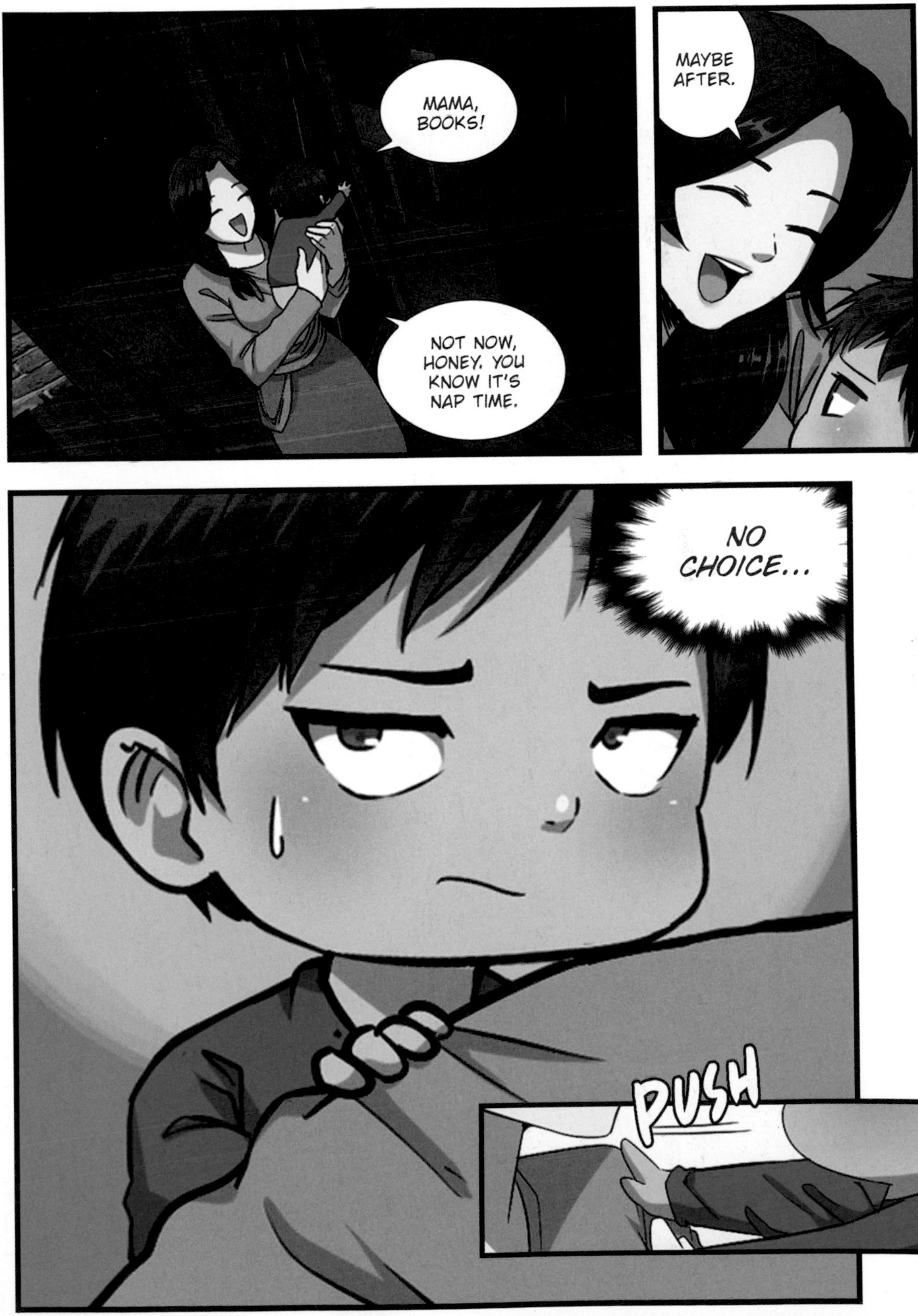
MAMA, BOOKS!
NOT NOW, HONEY. YOU KNOW IT'S NAP TIME.
MAYBE AFTER.
NO CHOICE...
PUSH

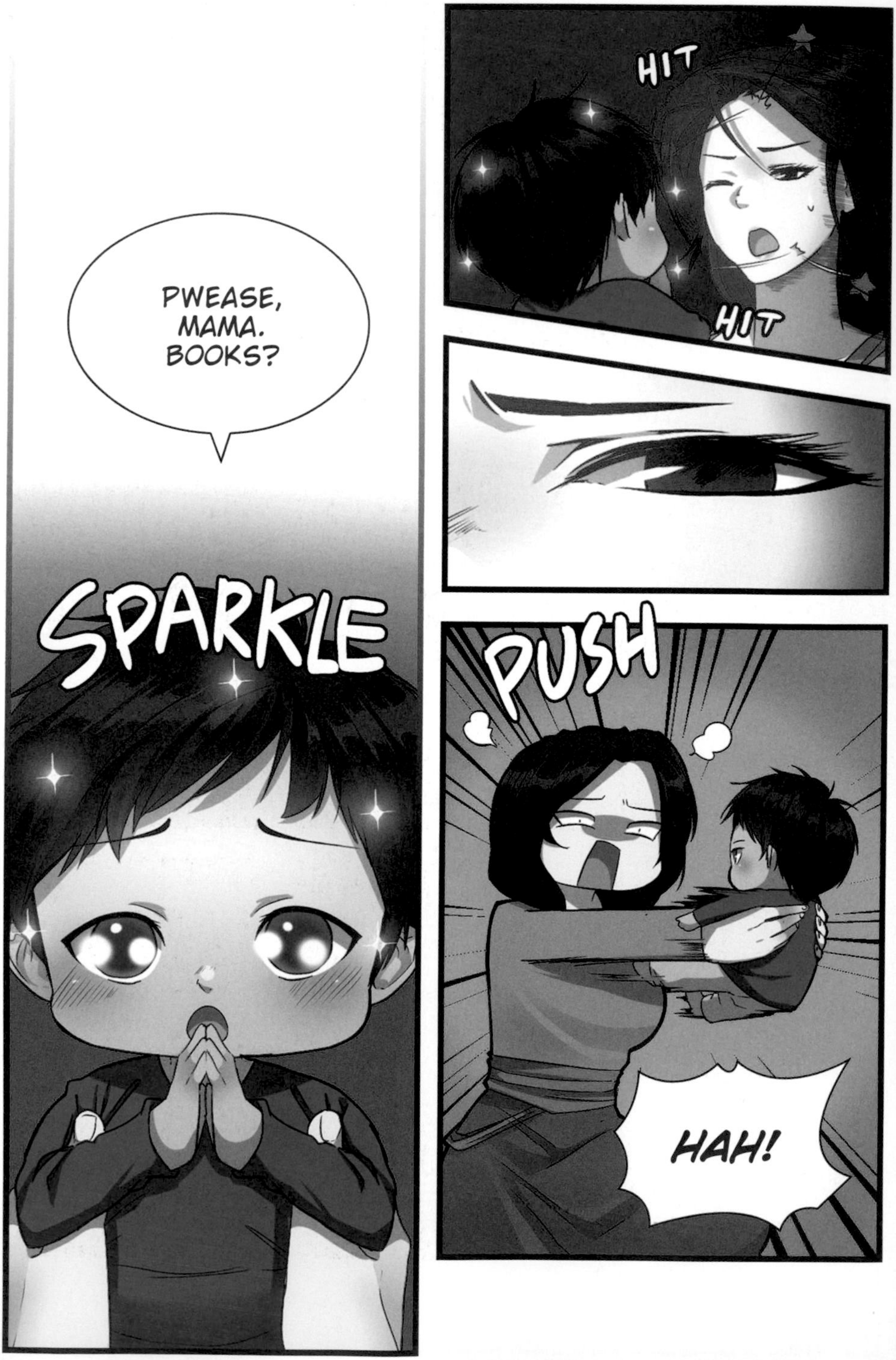
PWEASE, MAMA. BOOKS?
SPARKLE
HIT
HIT
PUSH
HAH!

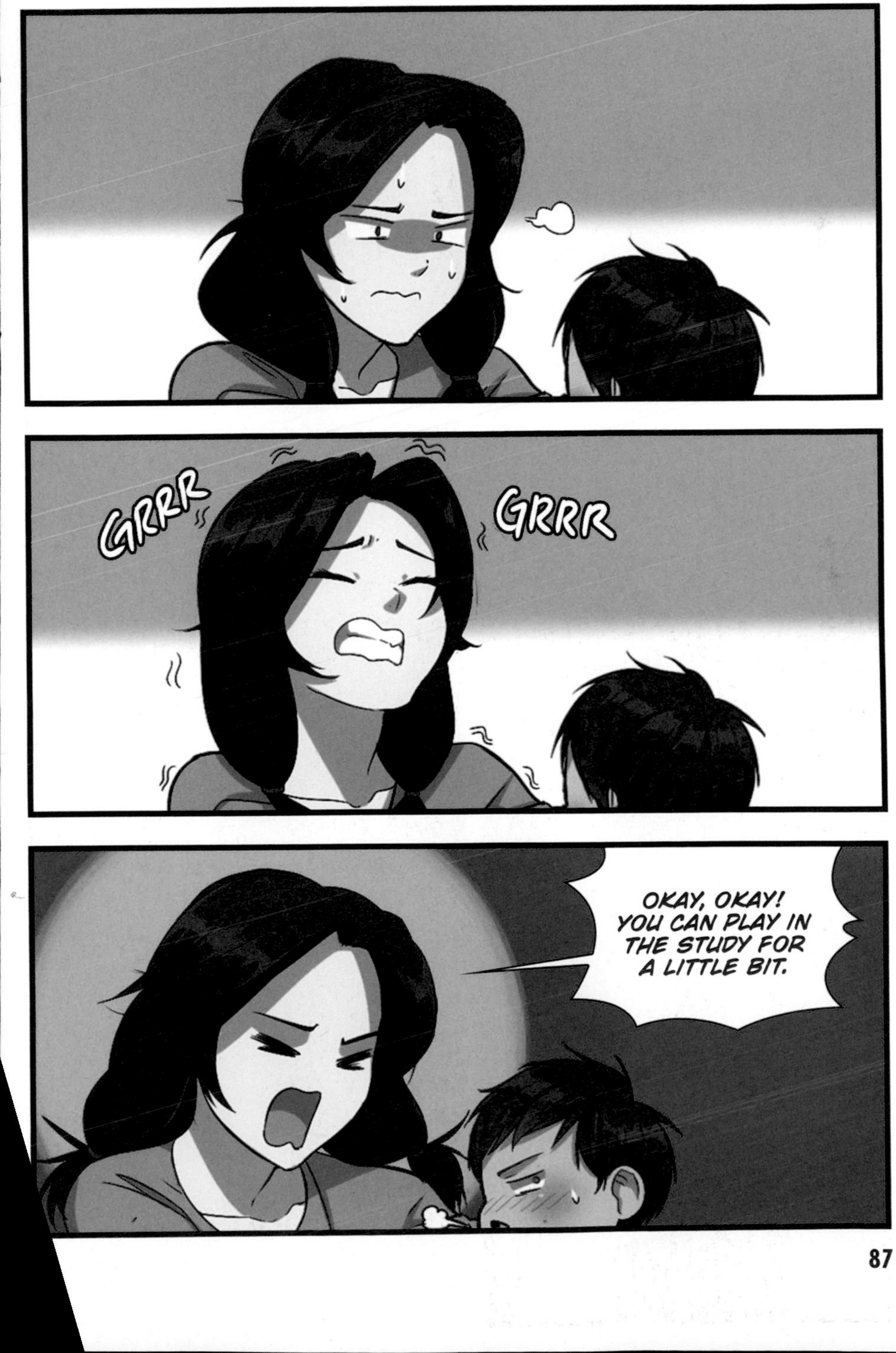
GRRR
GRRR
OKAY, OKAY! YOU CAN PLAY IN THE STUDY FOR A LITTLE BIT.

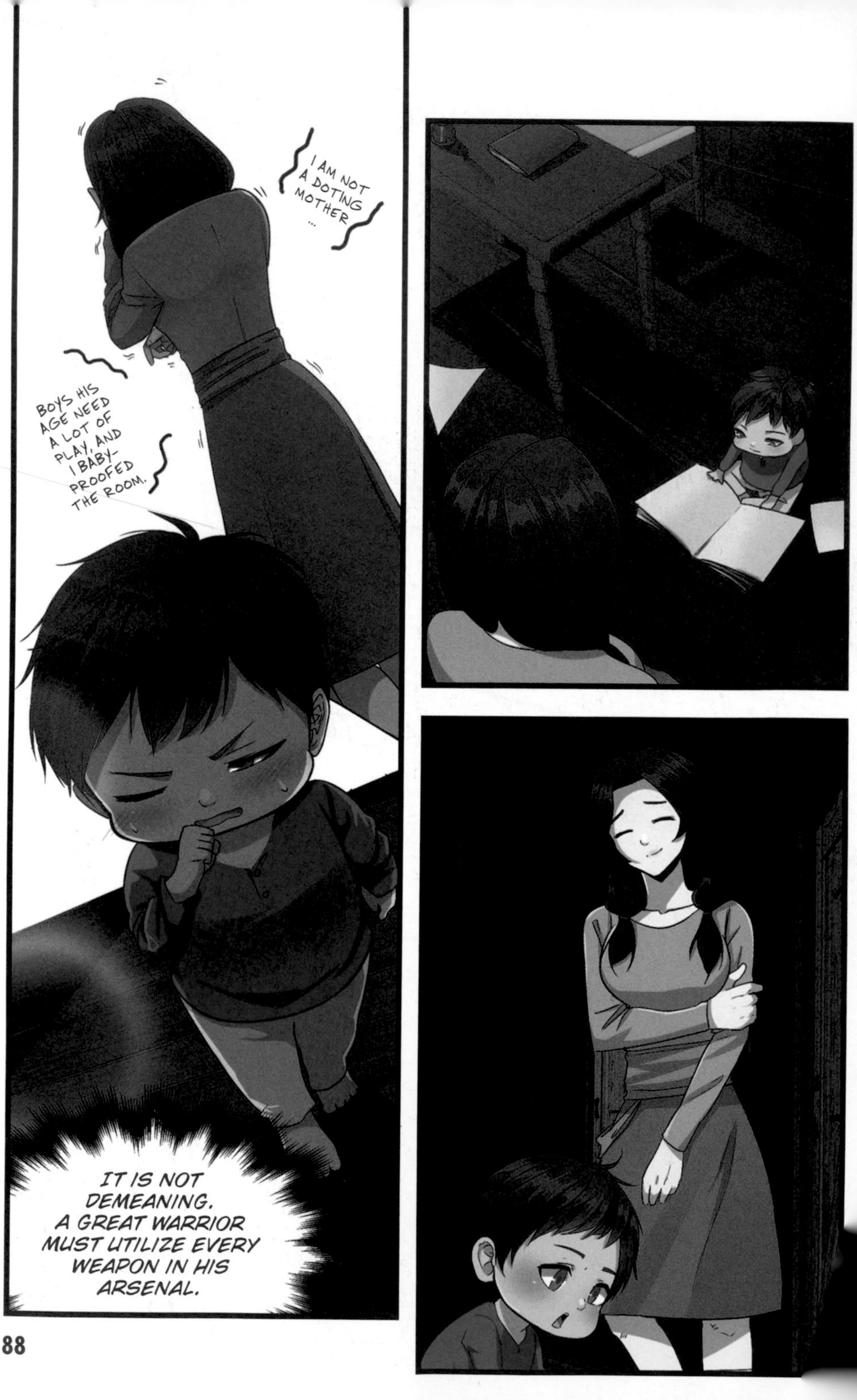
I AM NOT A DOTING MOTHER ...
BOYS HIS AGE NEED A LOT OF PLAY, AND I BABY-PROOFED THE ROOM.
IT IS NOT DEMEANING. A GREAT WARRIOR MUST UTILIZE EVERY WEAPON IN HIS ARSENAL.

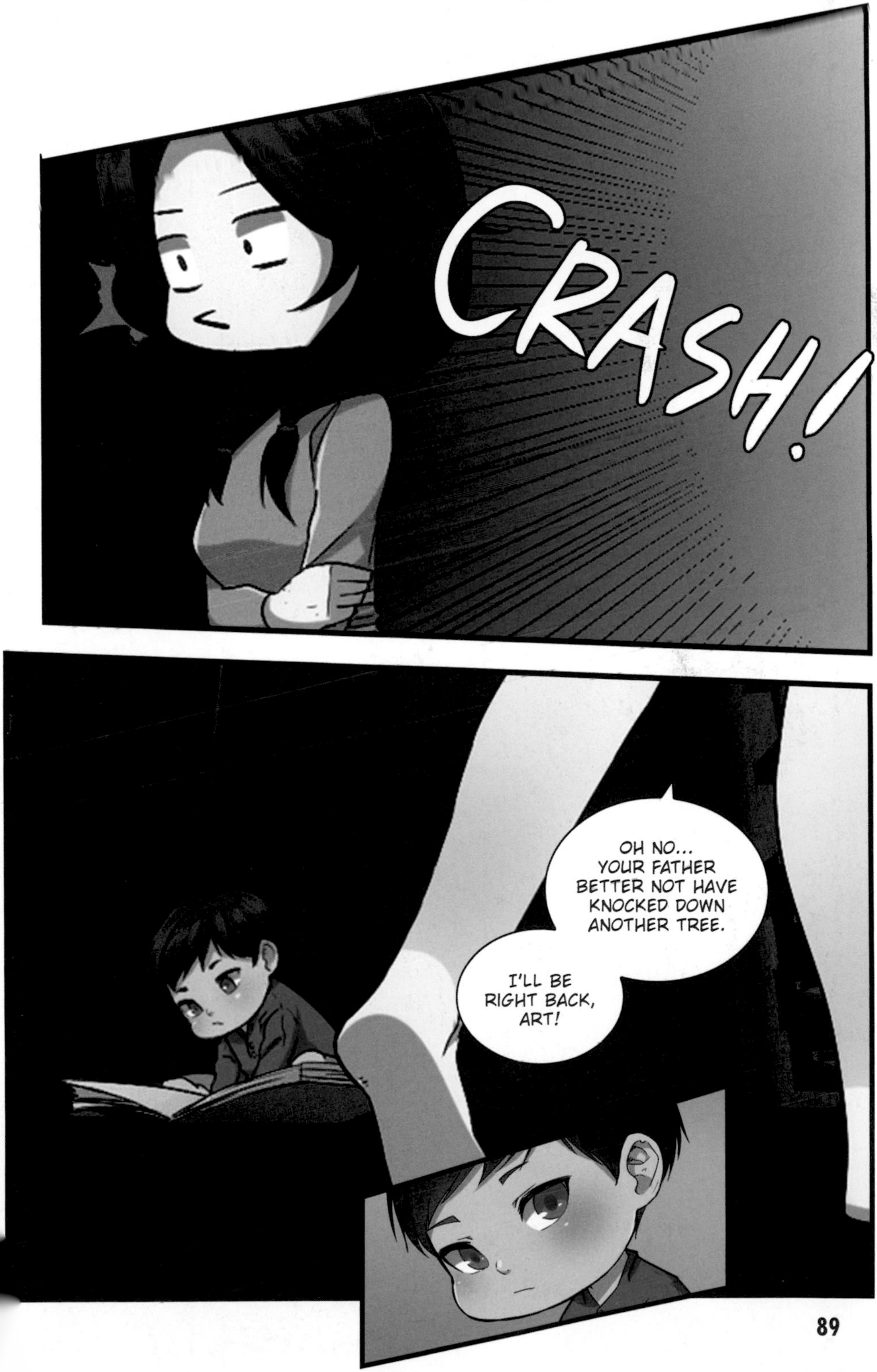
CRASH!
OH NO... YOUR FATHER BETTER NOT HAVE KNOCKED DOWN ANOTHER TREE.
I'LL BE RIGHT BACK, ART!

MY BIGGEST ACCOMPLISHMENT, ASIDE FROM THE ACCUMULATED KNOWLEDGE OF THIS WORLD...

...IS MY PROGRESS IN FORMING MY MANA CORE.

I SPENT THESE LAST TWO YEARS MOVING THE TENS OF THOUSANDS OF TINY FRAGMENTS OF MANA INSIDE MY BODY...

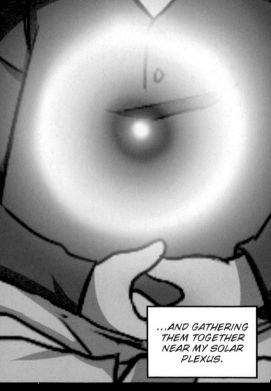

...AND GATHERING THEM TOGETHER NEAR MY SOLAR PLEXUS.

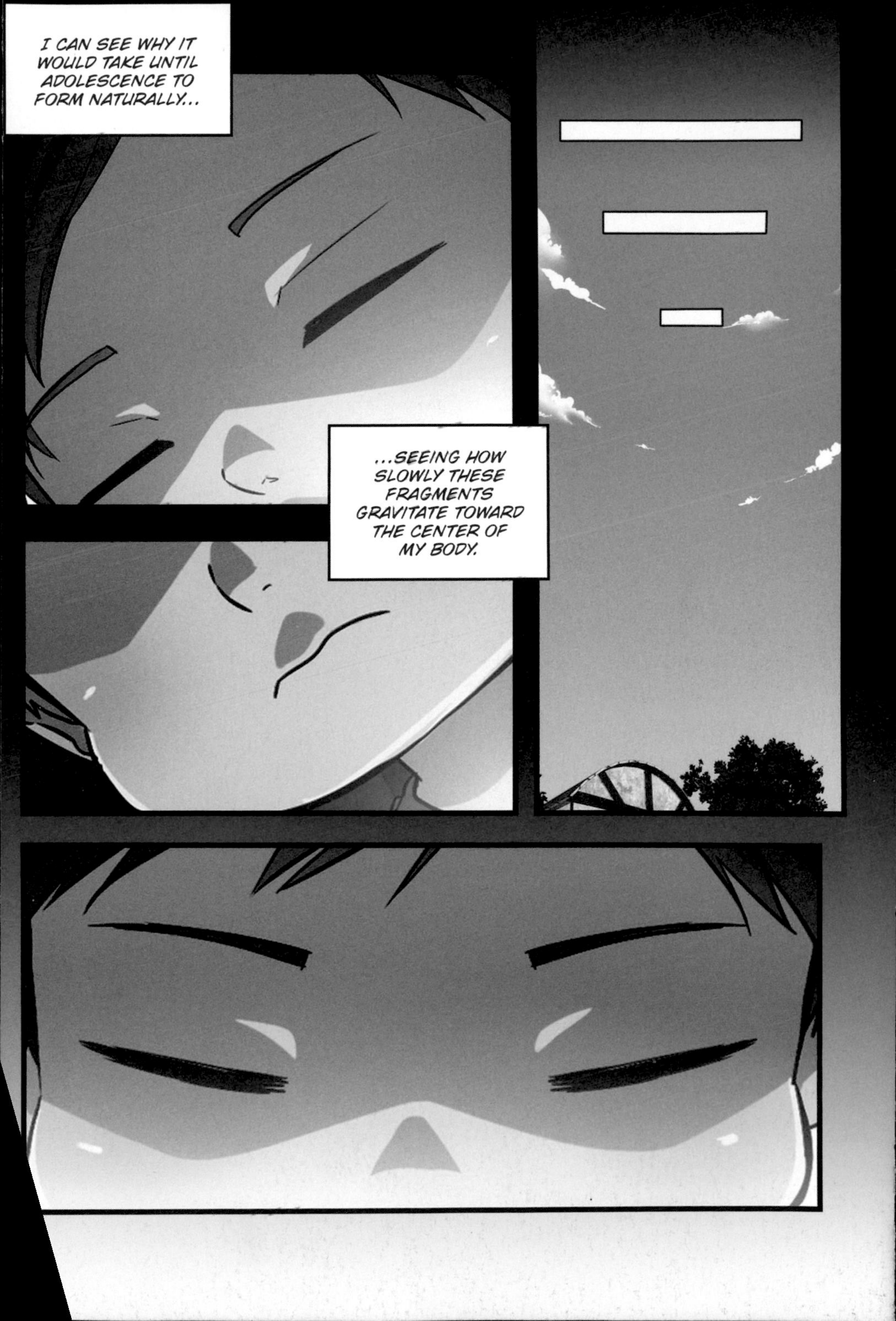
I CAN SEE WHY IT WOULD TAKE UNTIL ADOLESCENCE TO FORM NATURALLY...
...SEEING HOW SLOWLY THESE FRAGMENTS GRAVITATE TOWARD THE CENTER OF MY BODY.

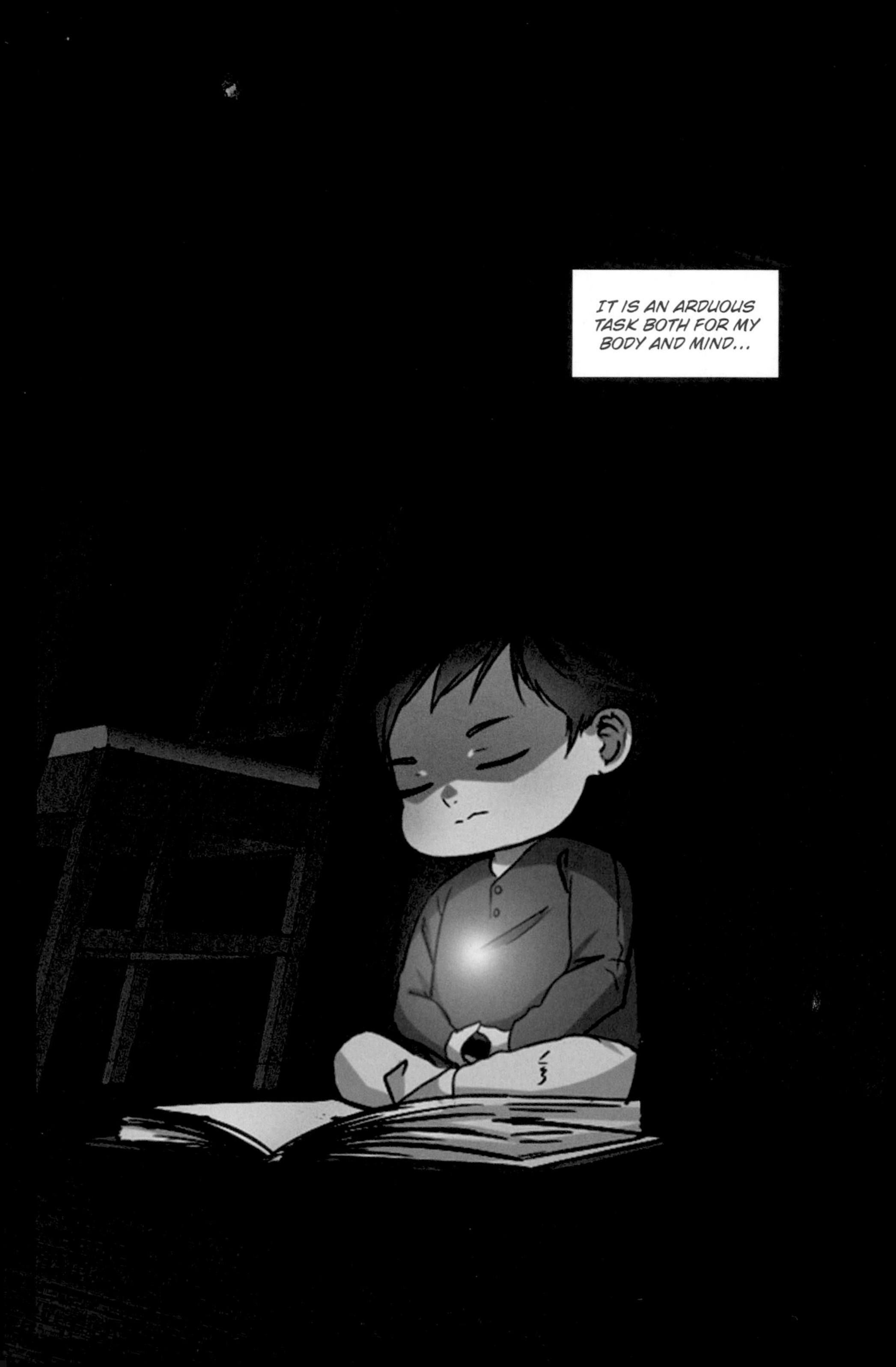
IT IS AN ARDUOUS TASK BOTH FOR MY BODY AND MIND...

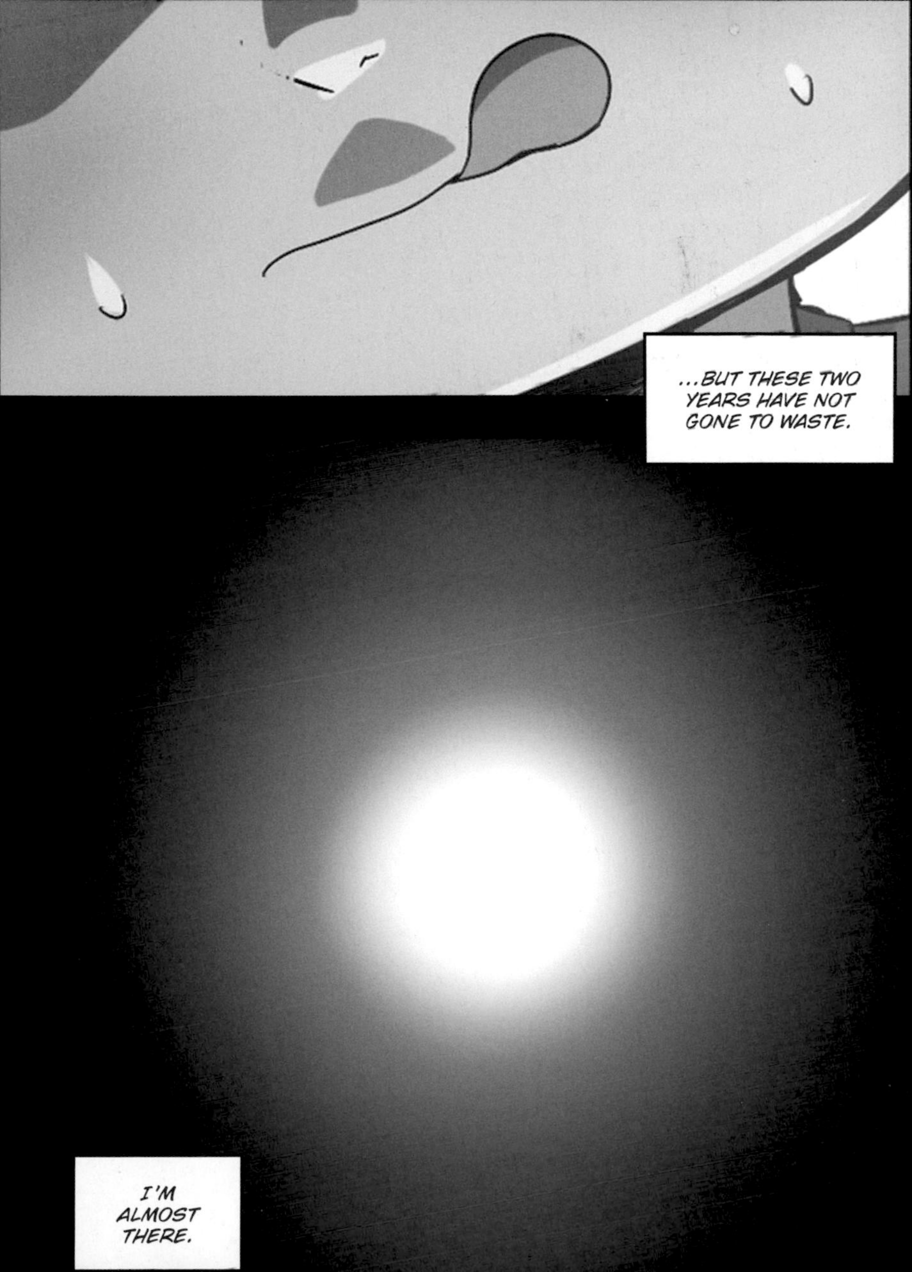
...BUT THESE TWO YEARS HAVE NOT GONE TO WASTE.
I'M ALMOST THERE.

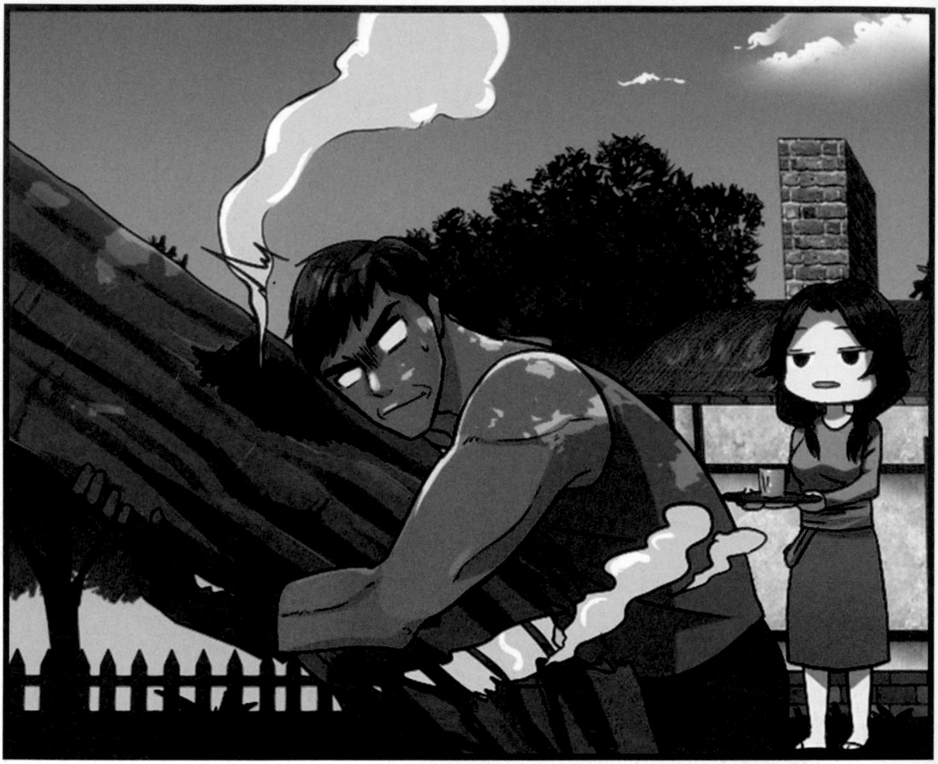
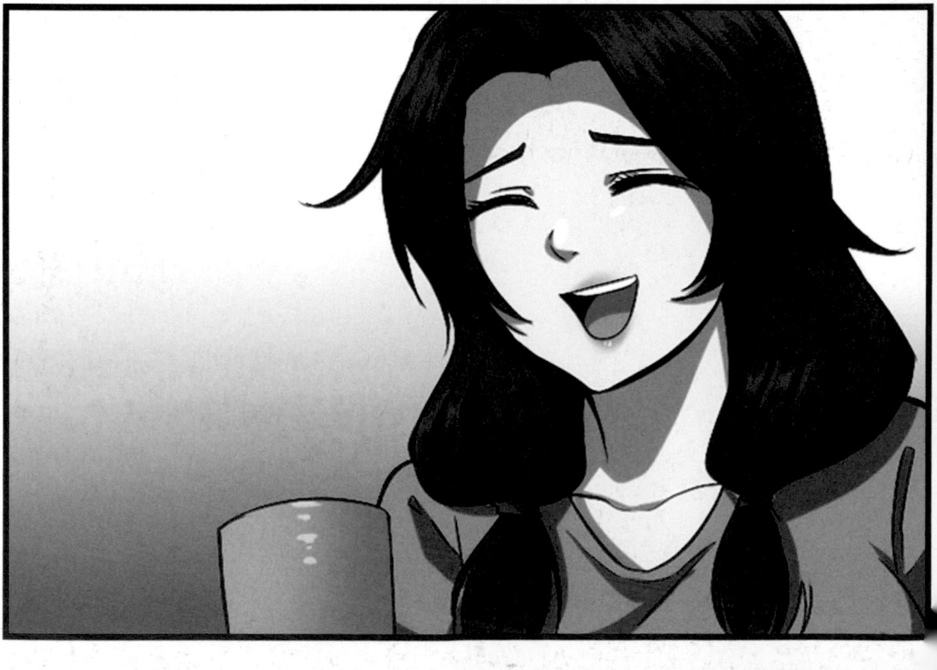

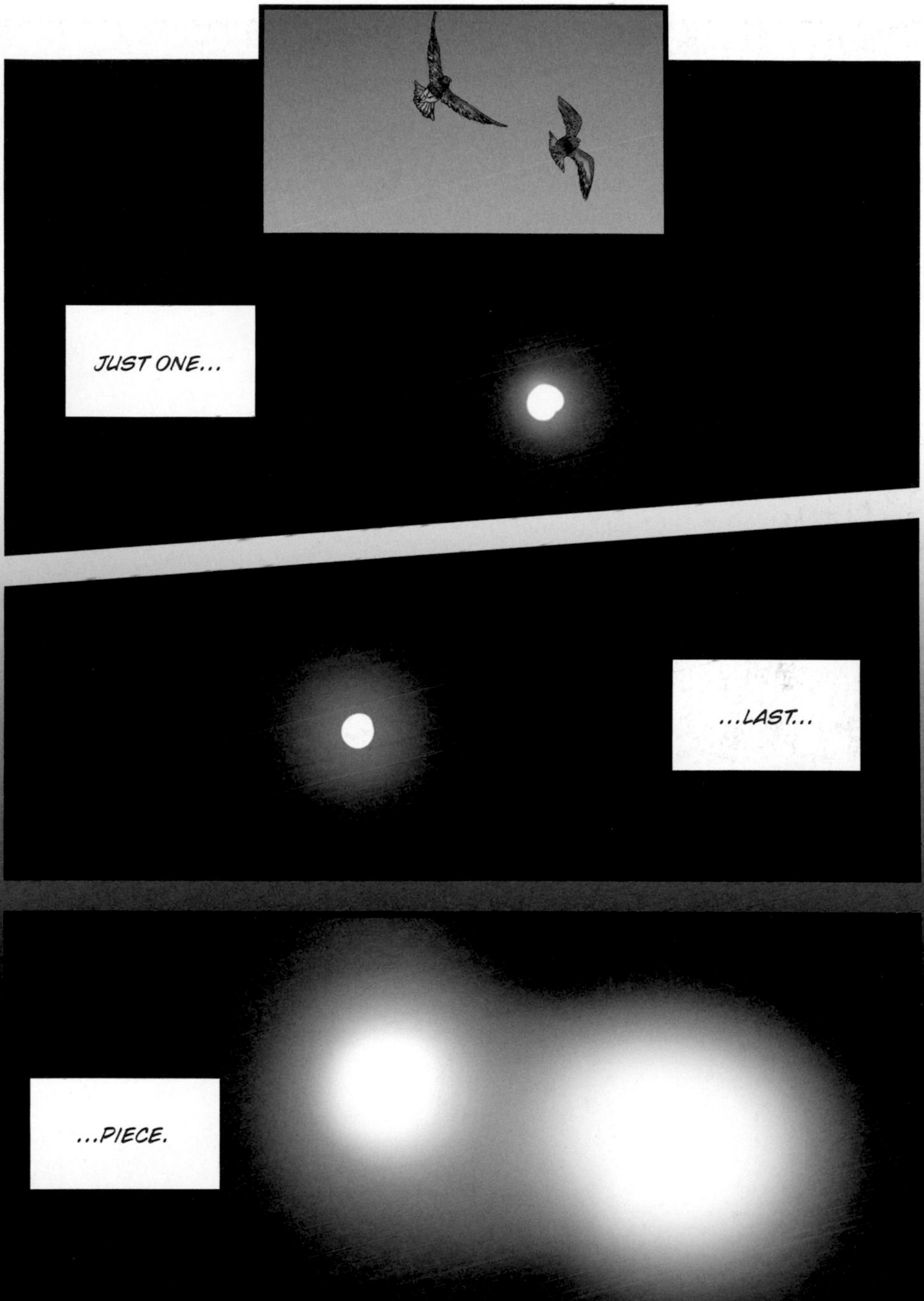
JUST ONE...
...LAST...
...PIECE.

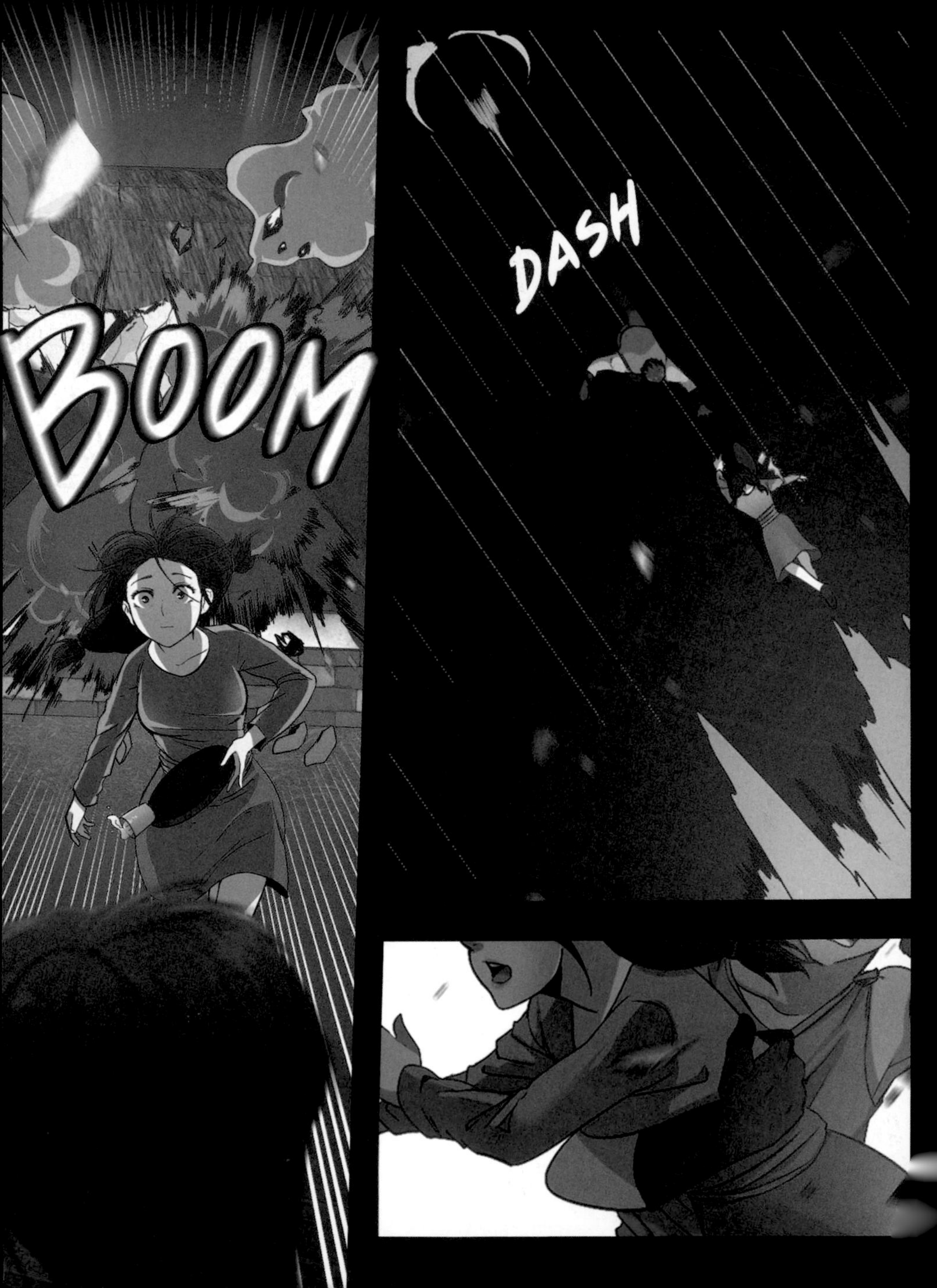
BOOM
DASH

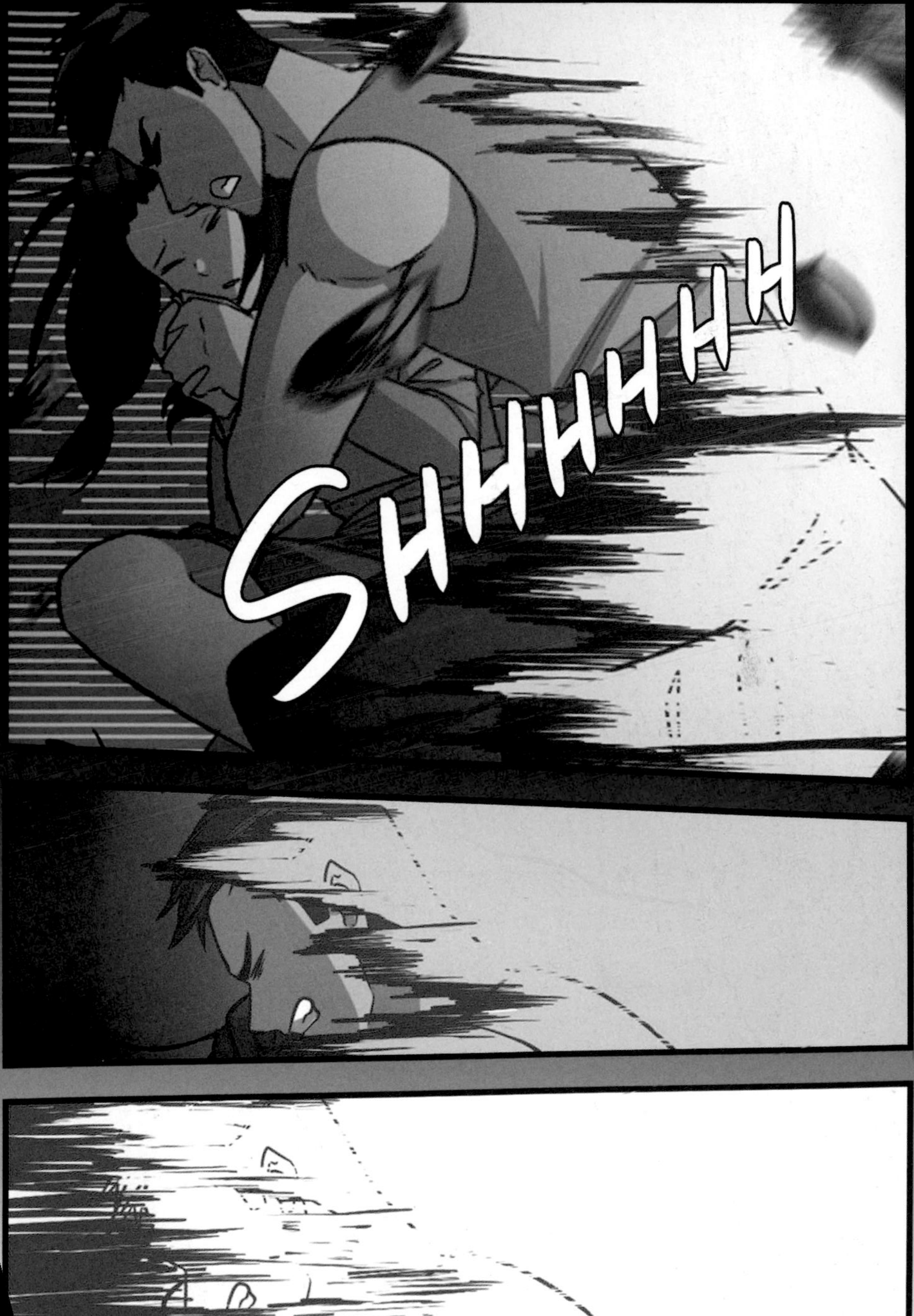
SHHHHHH

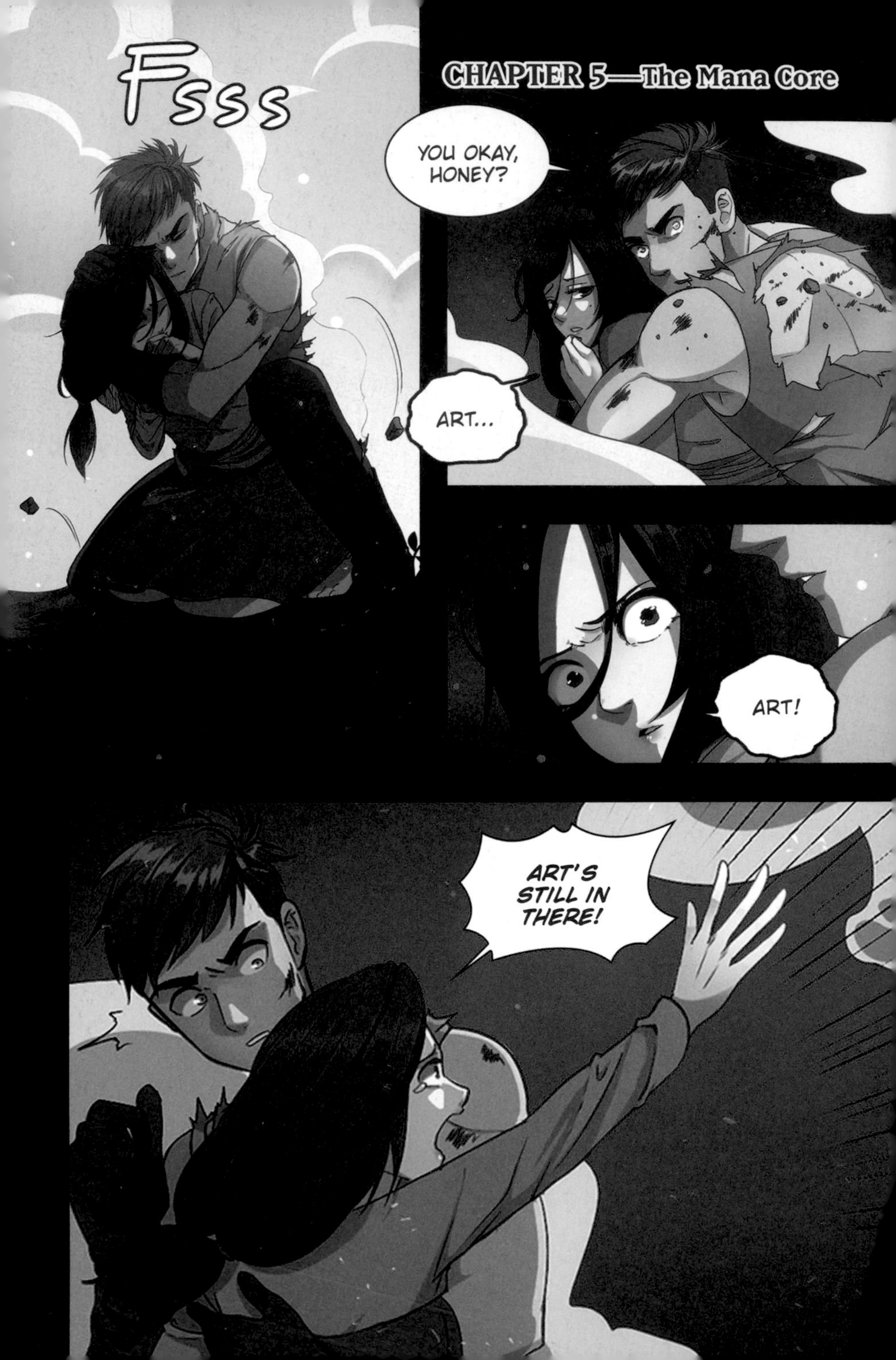
Fsss
CHAPTER 5—The Mana Core
YOU OKAY, HONEY?
ART...
ART!
ART'S STILL IN THERE!

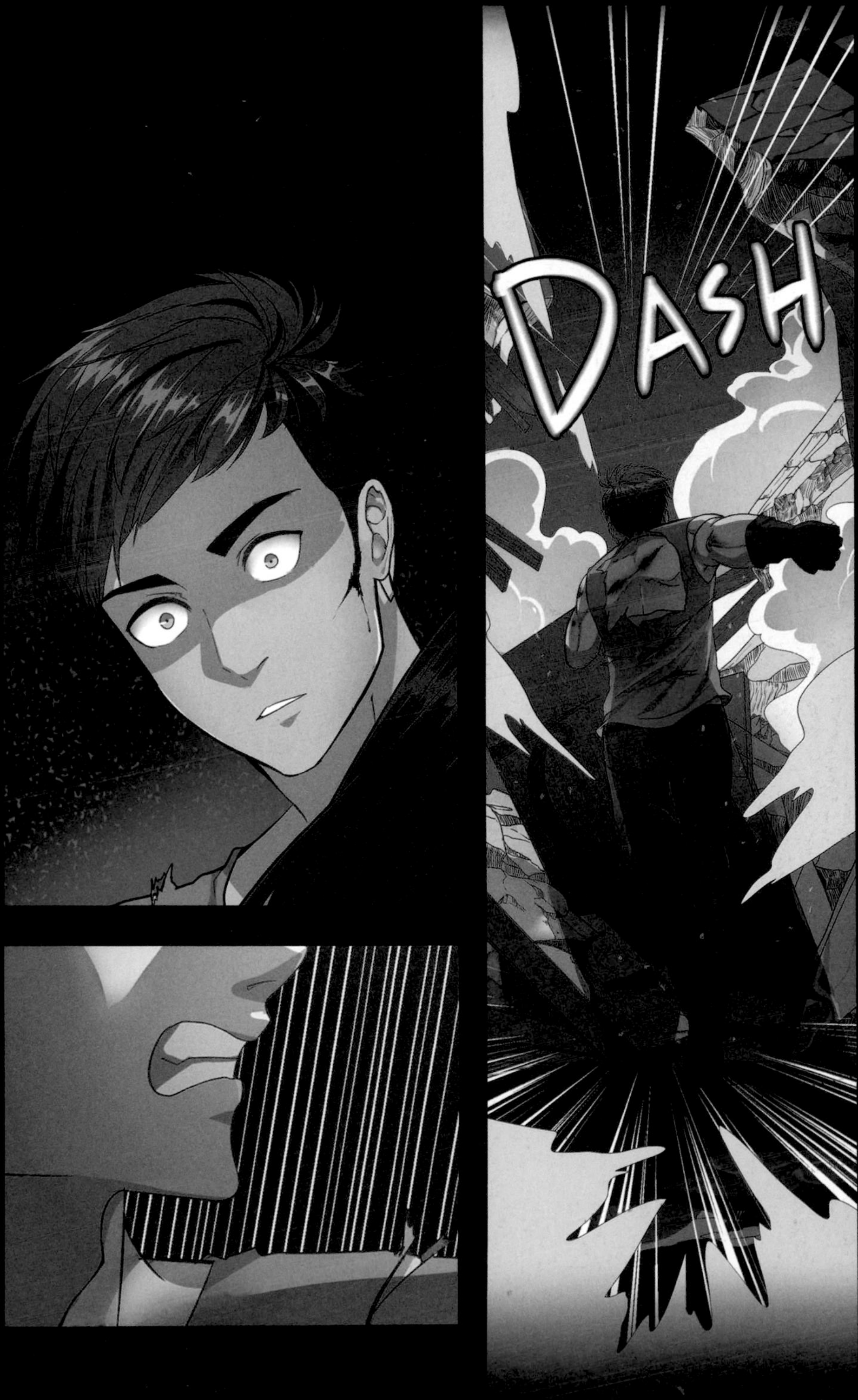
DASH

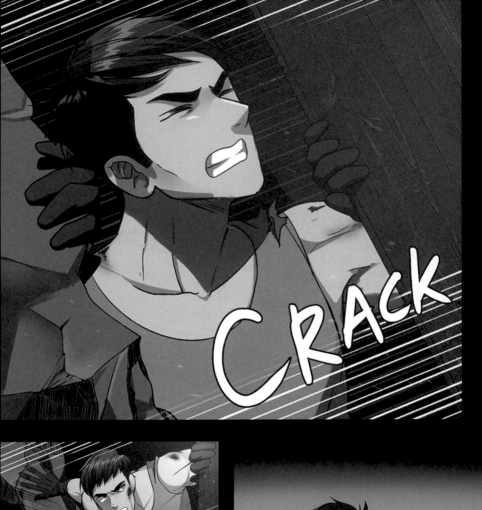

CRACK

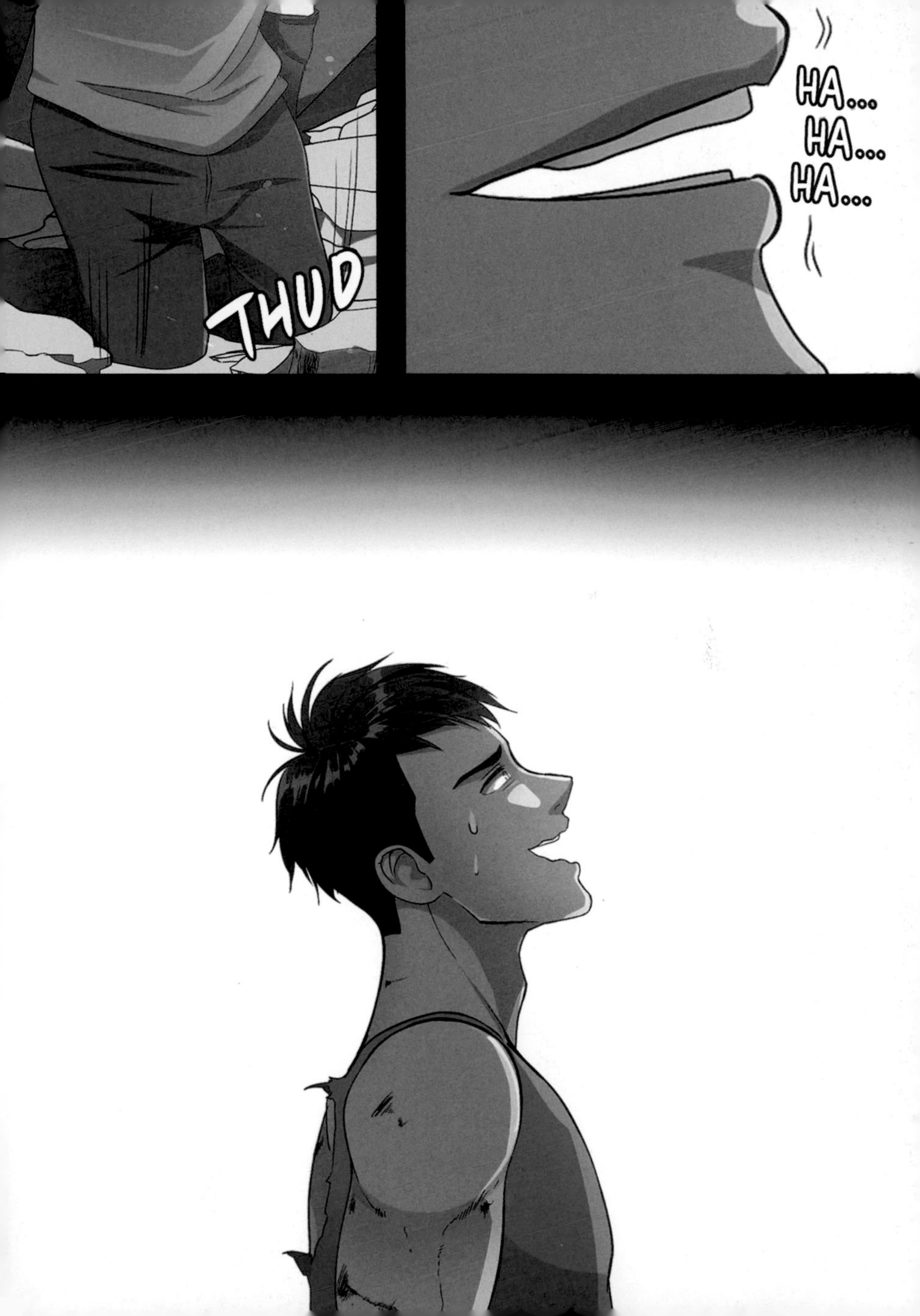
THUD
HA...
HA...
HA...

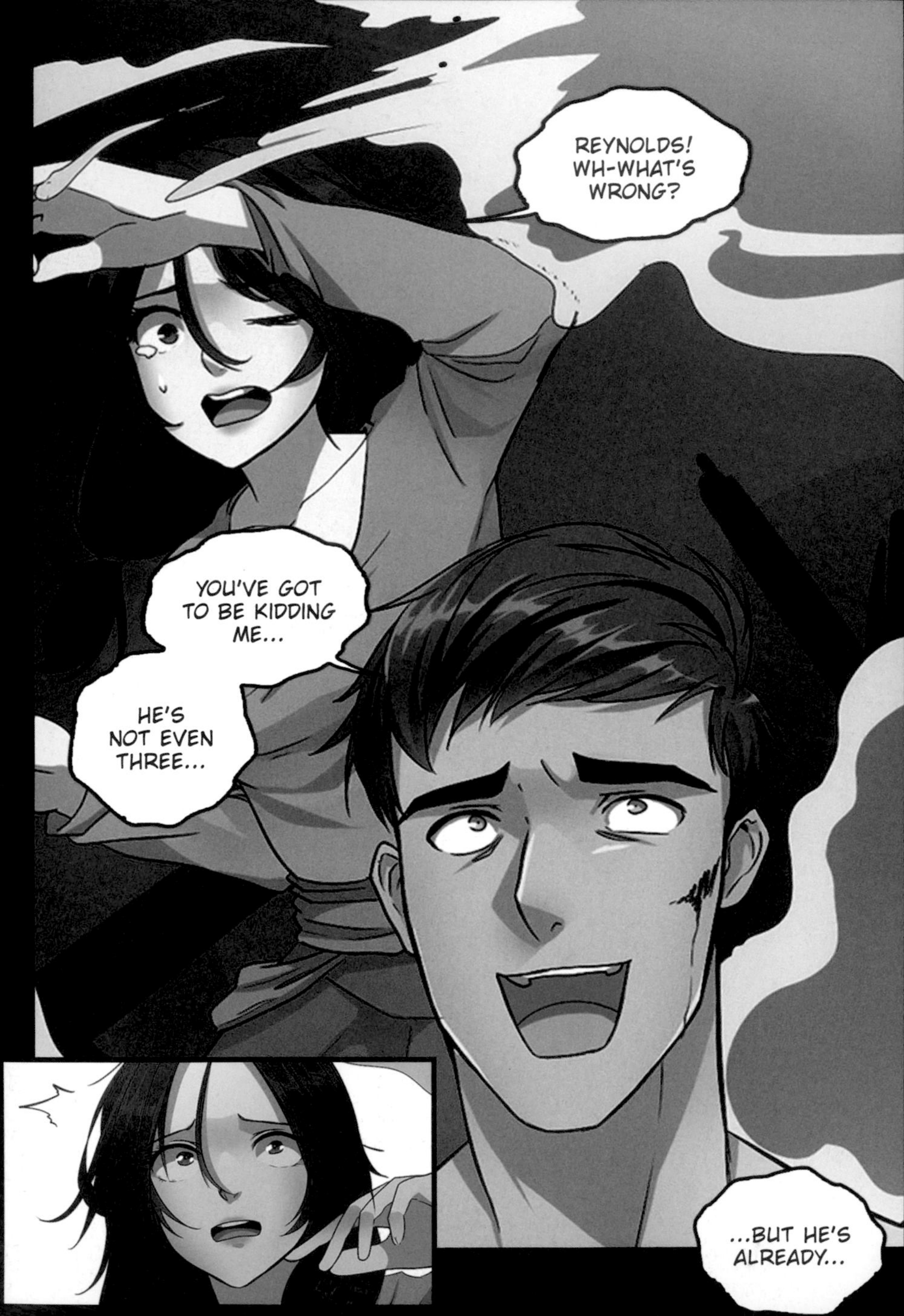
REYNOLDS! WH-WHAT'S WRONG?
YOU'VE GOT TO BE KIDDING ME...
HE'S NOT EVEN THREE...
...BUT HE'S ALREADY...

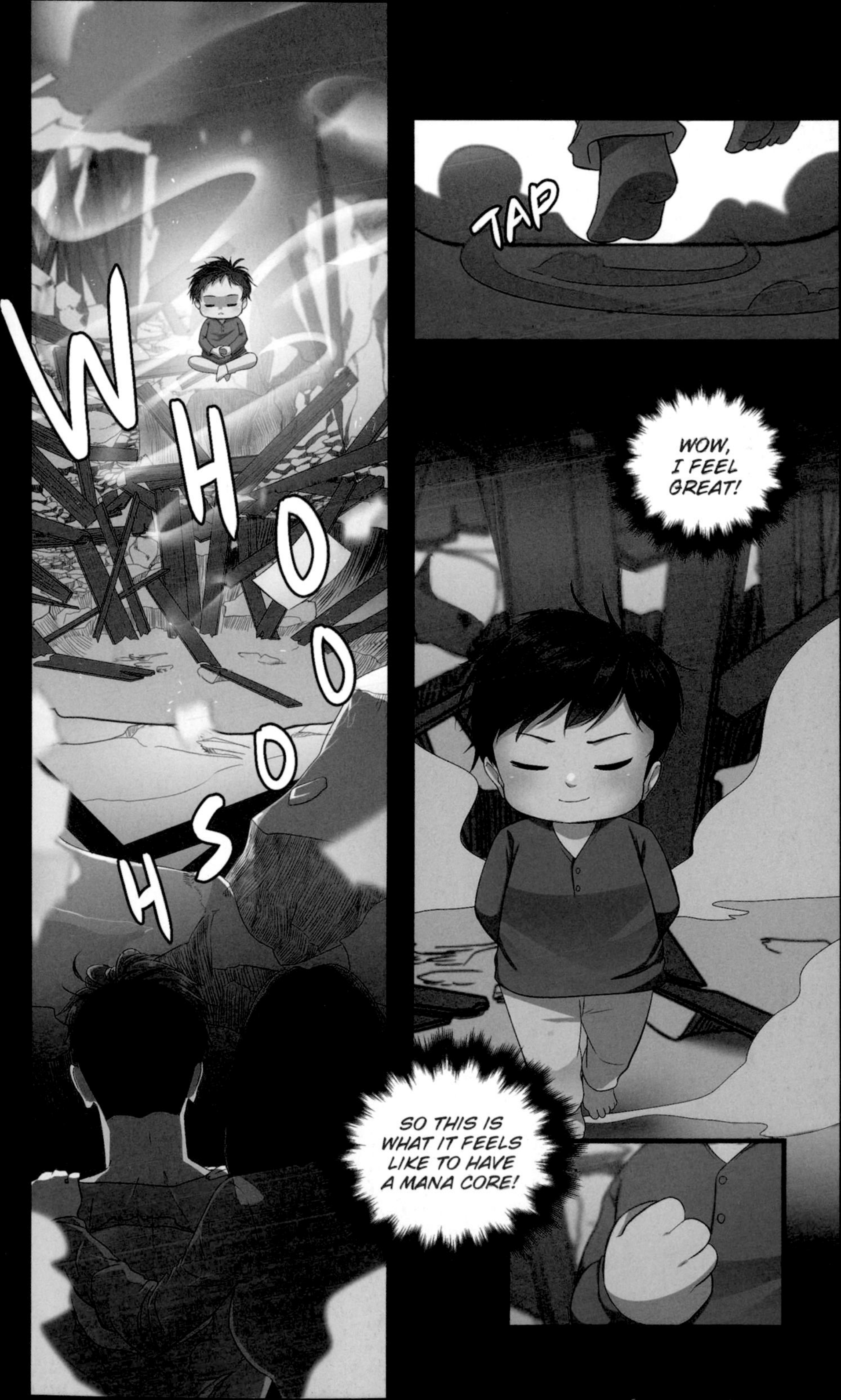
WHOOOSH
TAP
WOW, I FEEL GREAT!
SO THIS IS WHAT IT FEELS LIKE TO HAVE A MANA CORE!

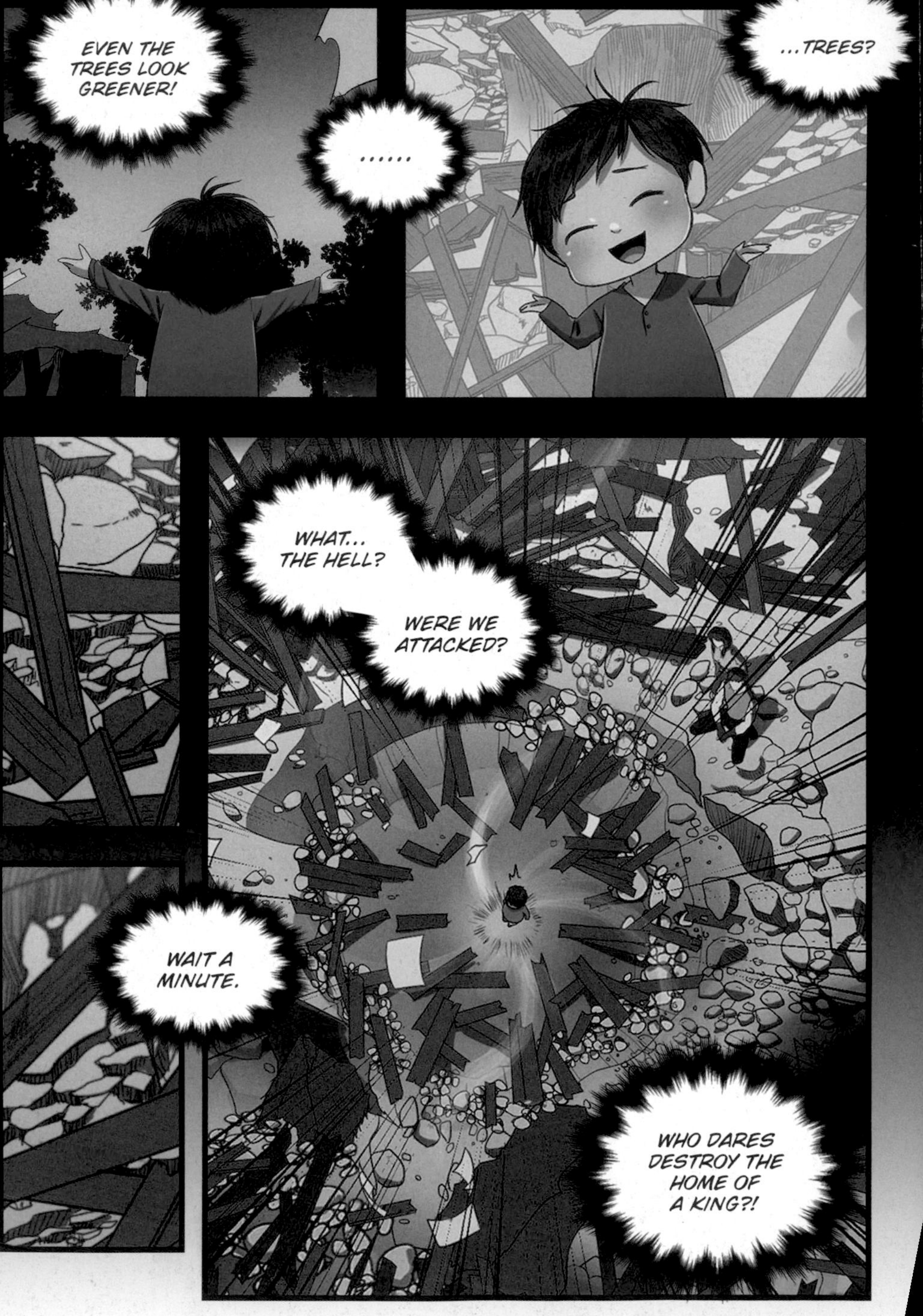
EVEN THE TREES LOOK GREENER!
......
...TREES?
WHAT... THE HELL?
WERE WE ATTACKED?
WAIT A MINUTE.
WHO DARES DESTROY THE HOME OF A KING?!

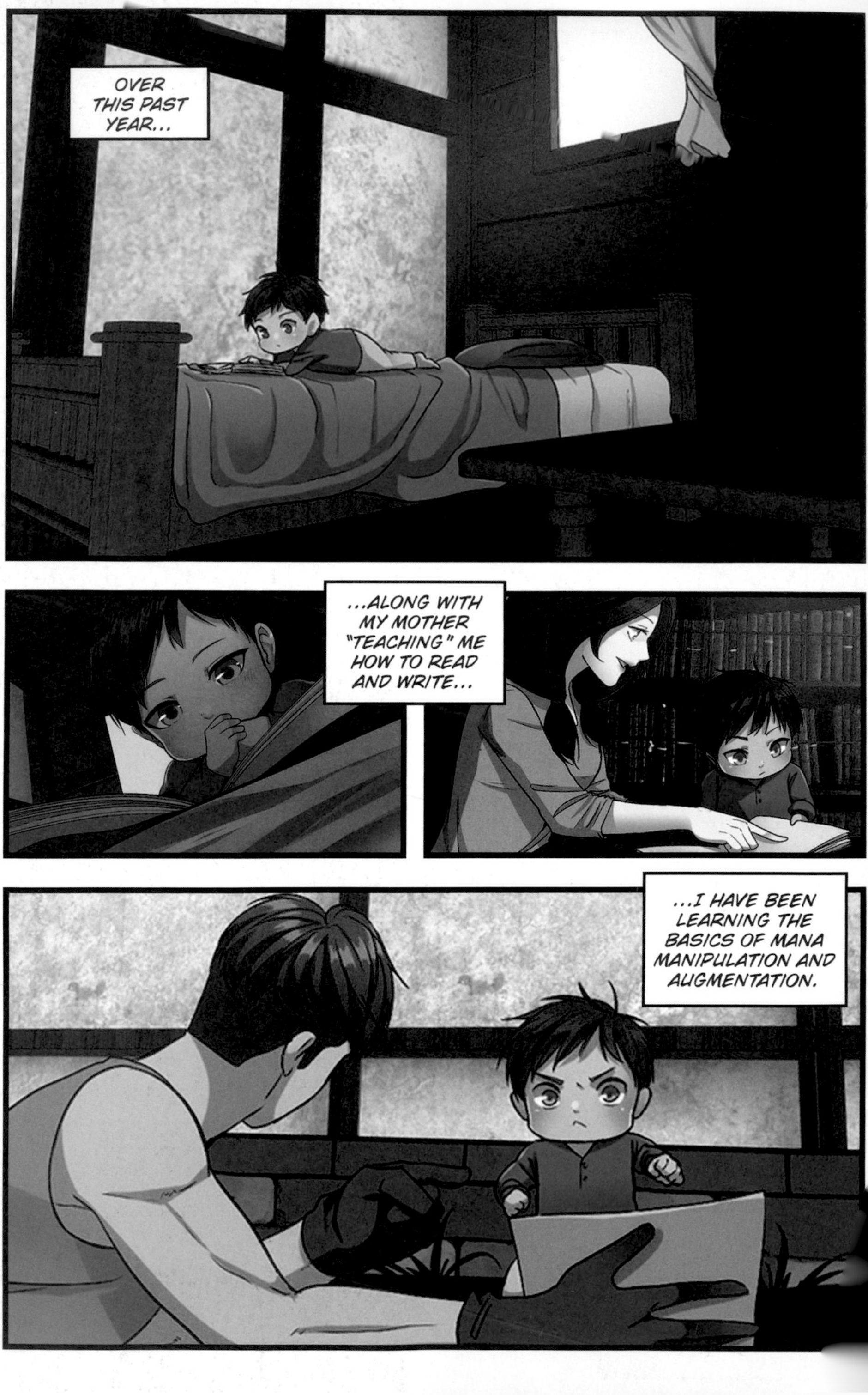

OVER THIS PAST YEAR...
...ALONG WITH MY MOTHER "TEACHING" ME HOW TO READ AND WRITE...
...I HAVE BEEN LEARNING THE BASICS OF MANA MANIPULATION AND AUGMENTATION.

AT FIRST, SINCE MY BODY WAS TOO SMALL TO BE SPARRING, WE DID BASIC BODY WORKOUTS.

IT WASN'T TOO LONG AGO THAT MY FATHER FINALLY DECIDED I WOULD BE OKAY TO PRACTICE...

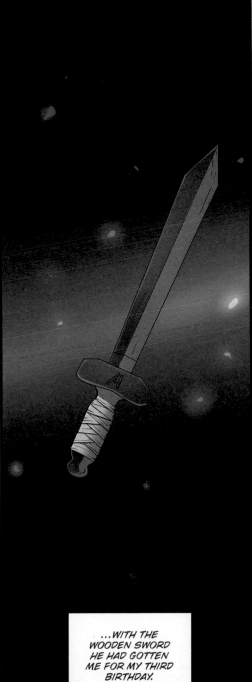

...WITH THE WOODEN SWORD HE HAD GOTTEN ME FOR MY THIRD BIRTHDAY.

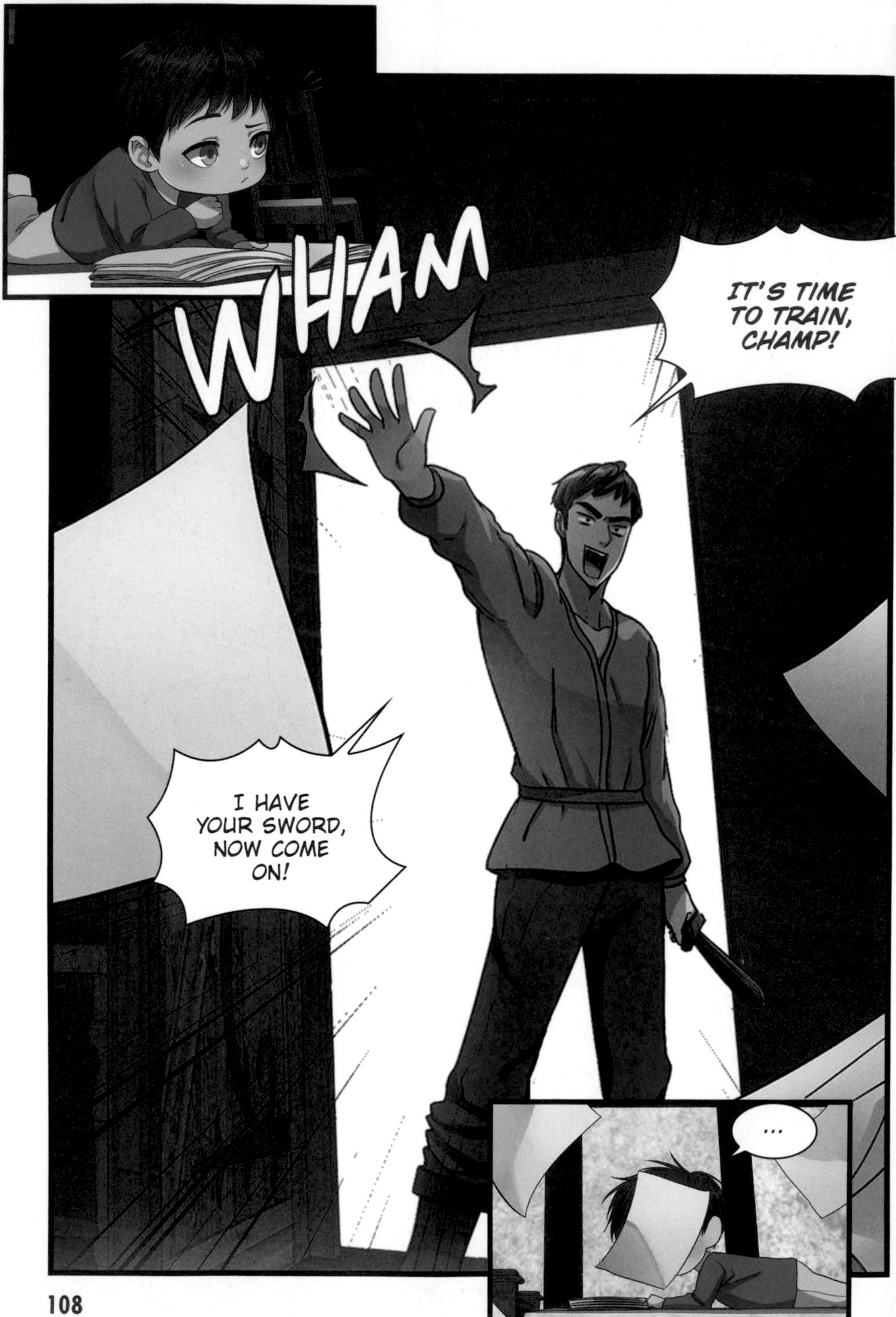
WHAM
IT'S TIME TO TRAIN, CHAMP!
I HAVE YOUR SWORD, NOW COME ON!
...

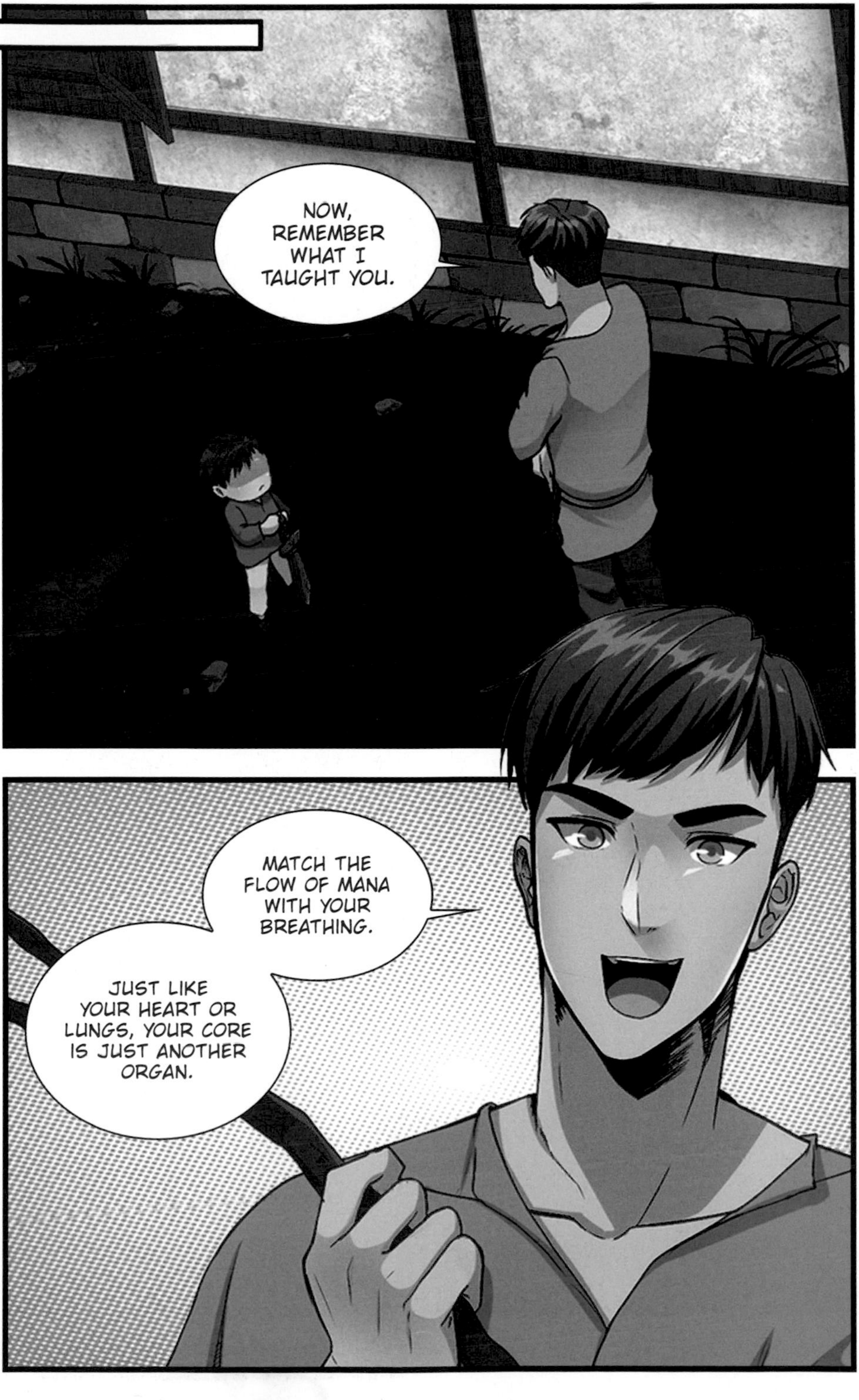
NOW, REMEMBER WHAT I TAUGHT YOU.
MATCH THE FLOW OF MANA WITH YOUR BREATHING.
JUST LIKE YOUR HEART OR LUNGS, YOUR CORE IS JUST ANOTHER ORGAN.

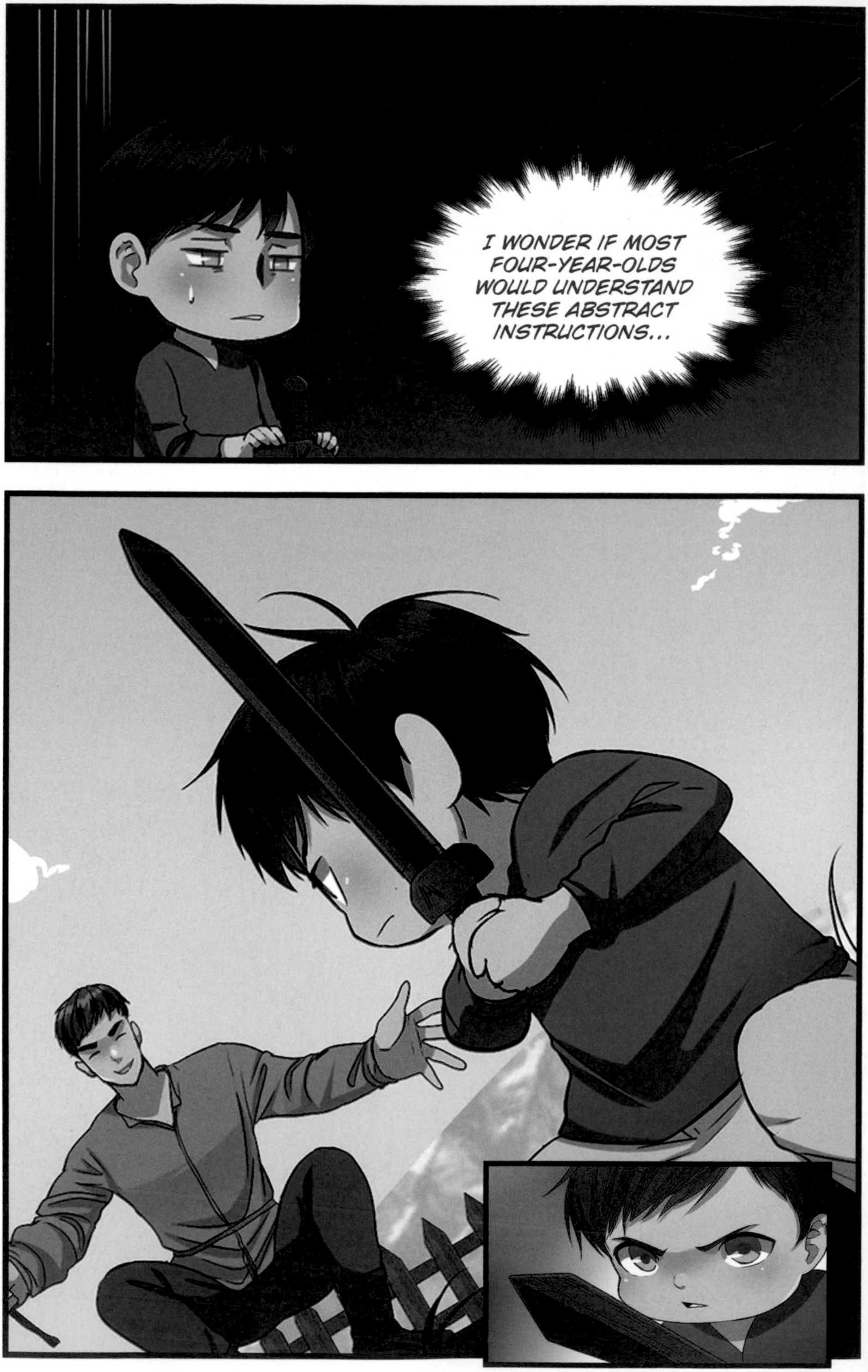
I WONDER IF MOST FOUR-YEAR-OLDS WOULD UNDERSTAND THESE ABSTRACT INSTRUCTIONS...

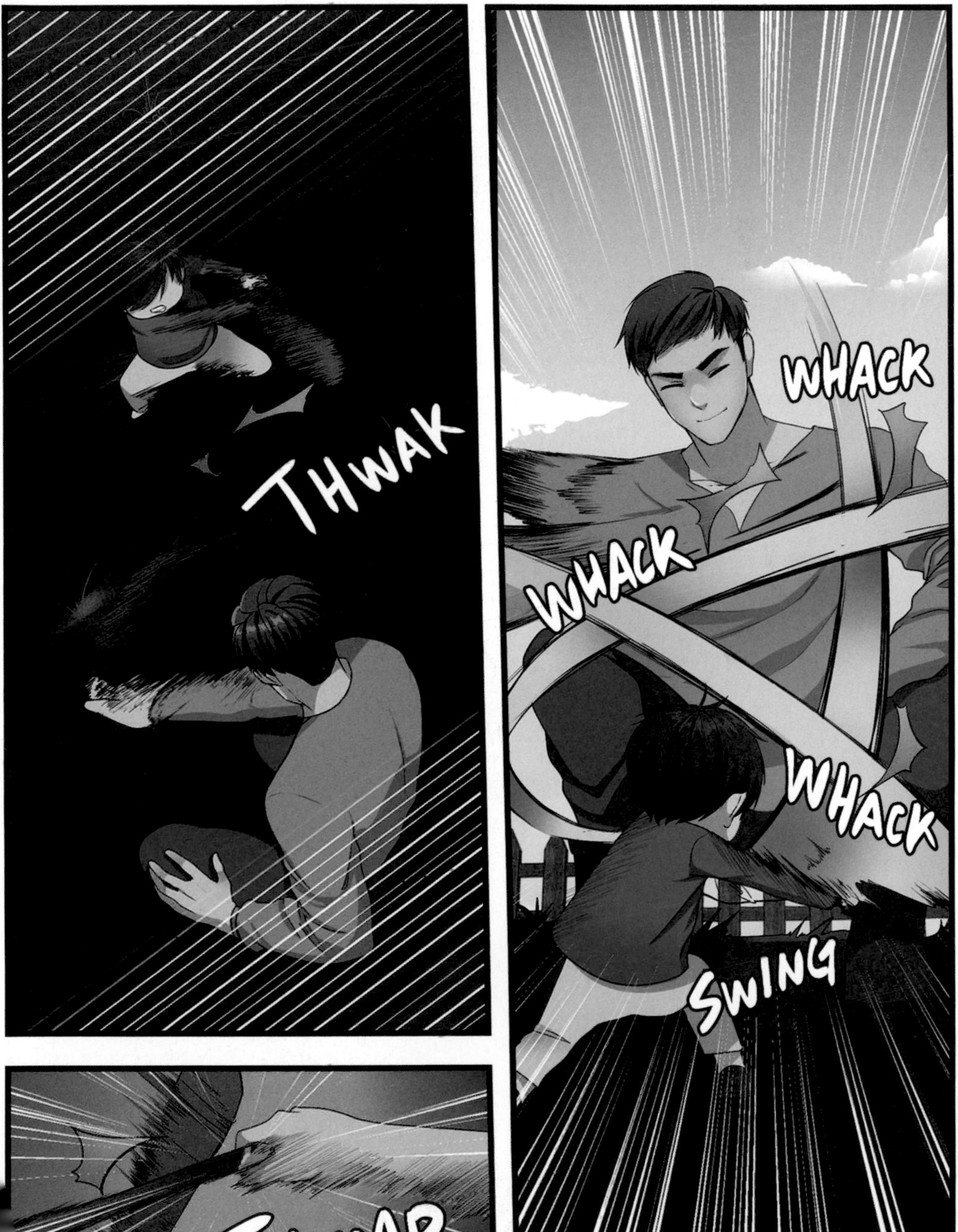
THWAK
THUMP
WHACK
WHACK
WHACK
SWING

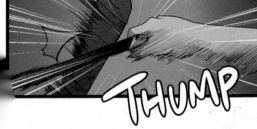

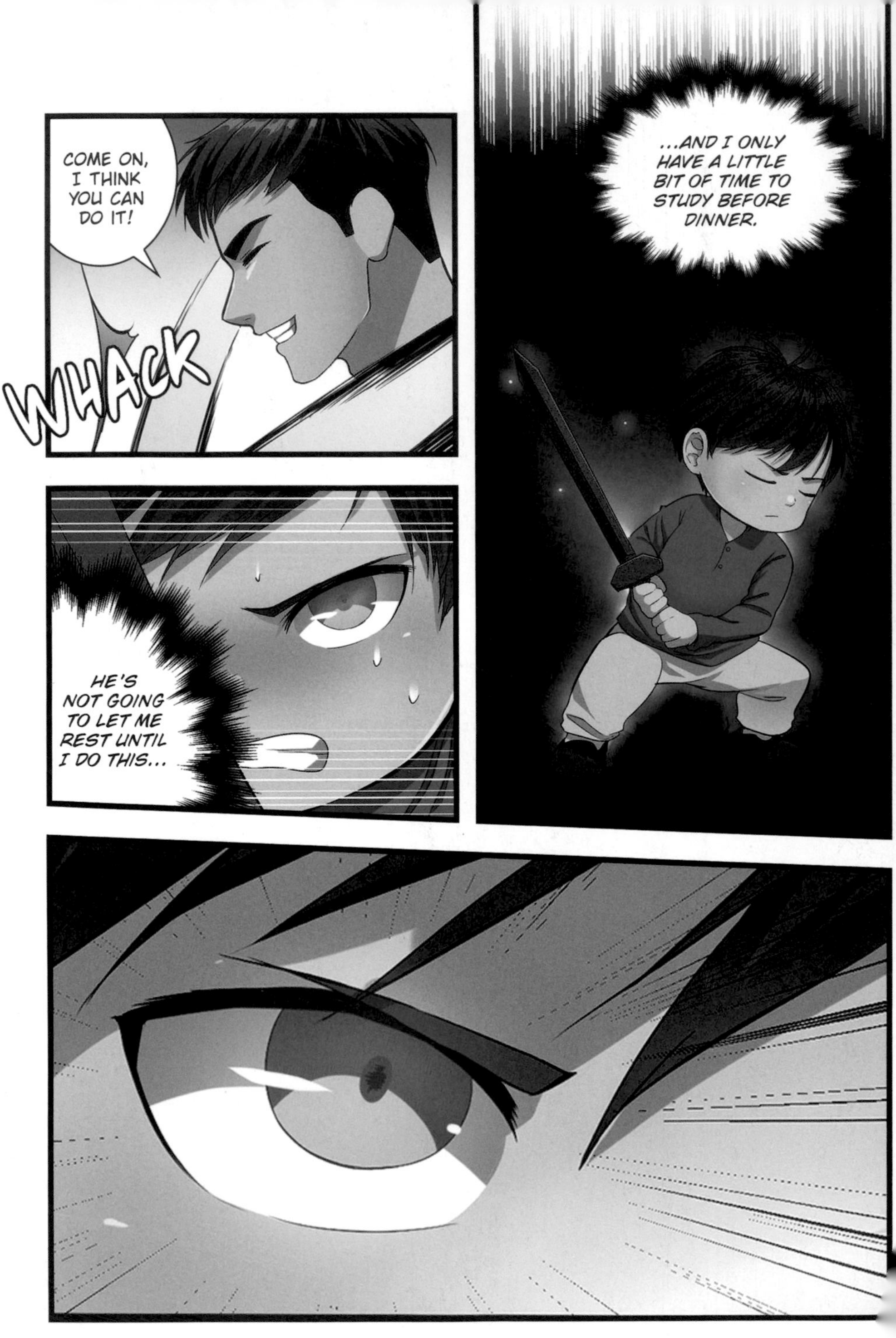

COME ON, I THINK YOU CAN DO IT!
WHACK
HE'S NOT GOING TO LET ME REST UNTIL I DO THIS...
...AND I ONLY HAVE A LITTLE BIT OF TIME TO STUDY BEFORE DINNER.

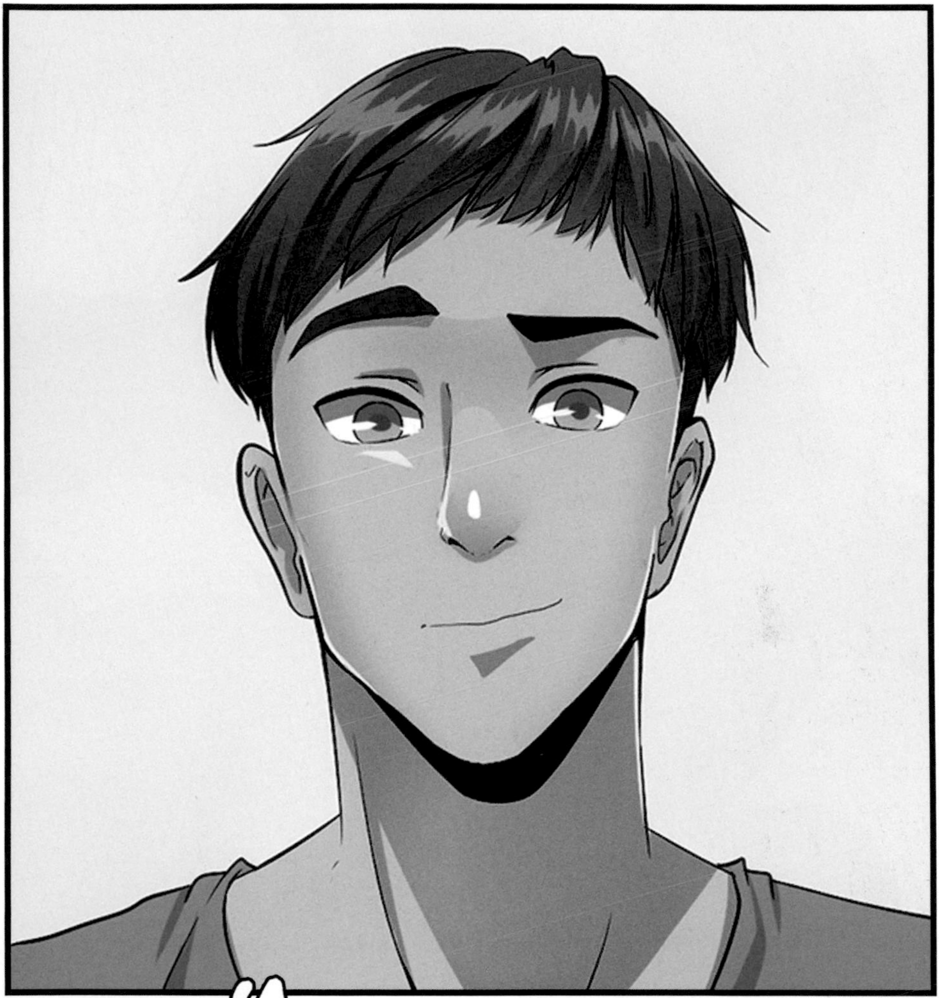

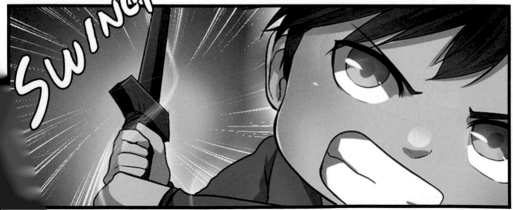

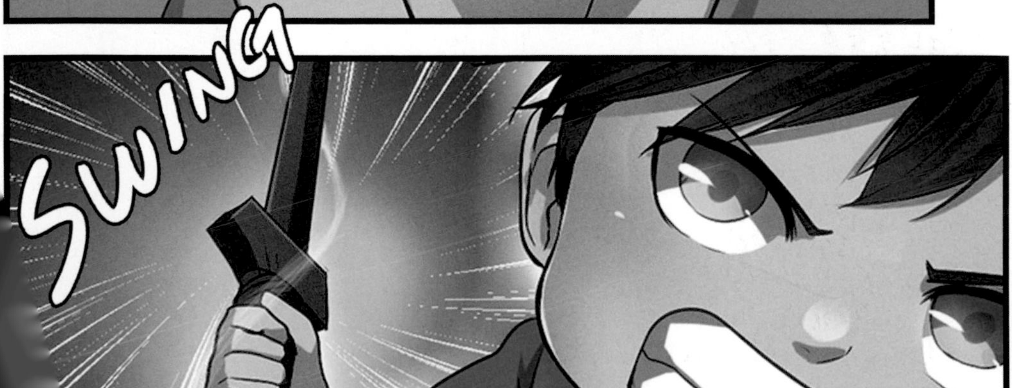
SWING

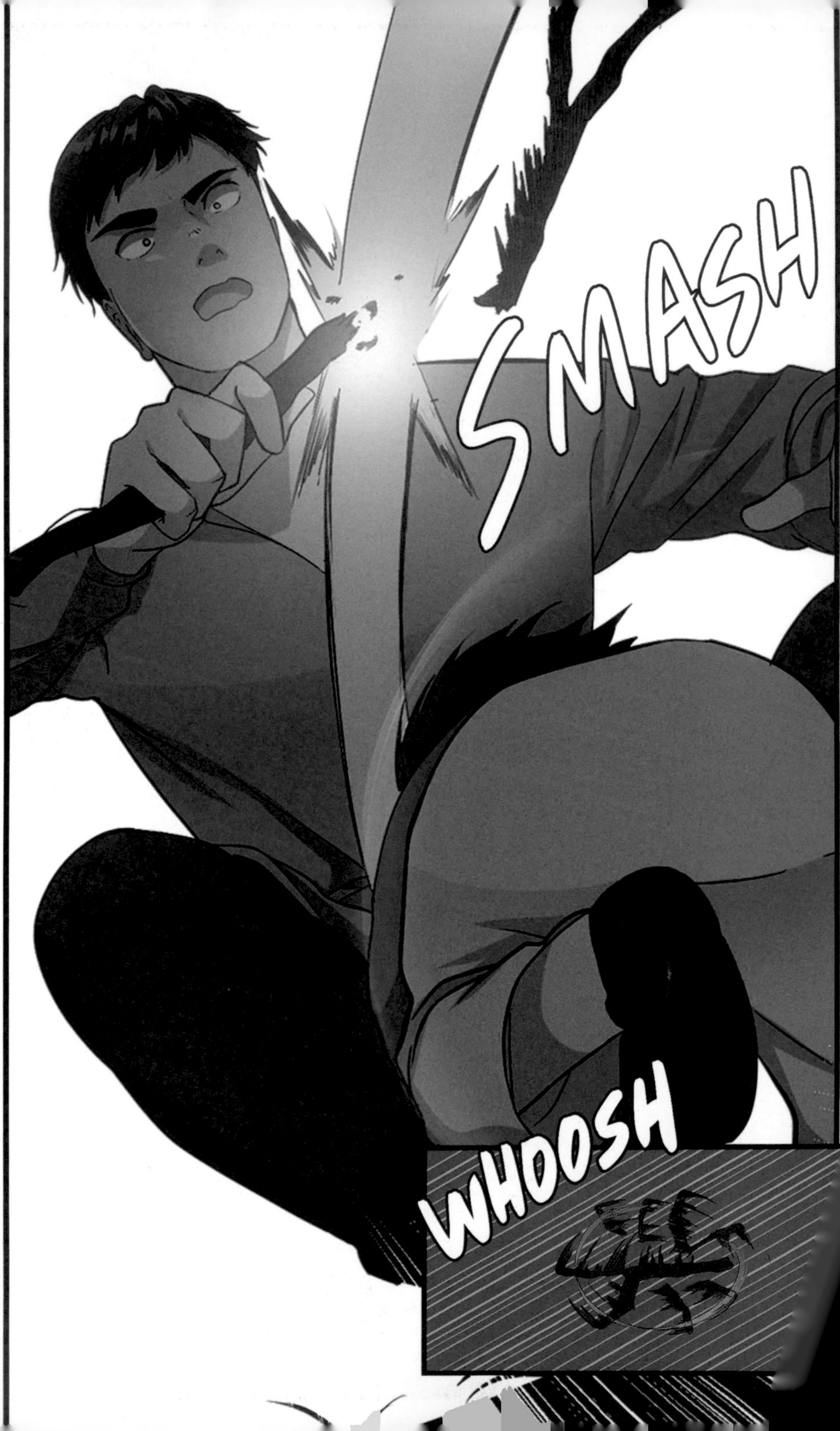
SMASH
WHOOSH

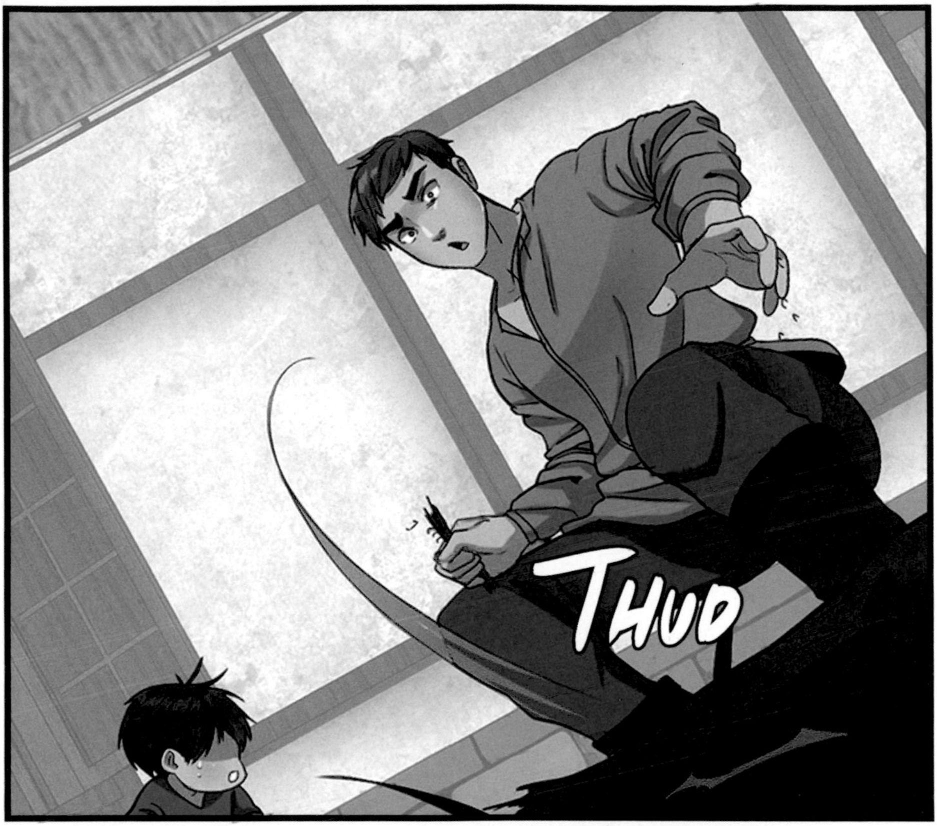
THUD

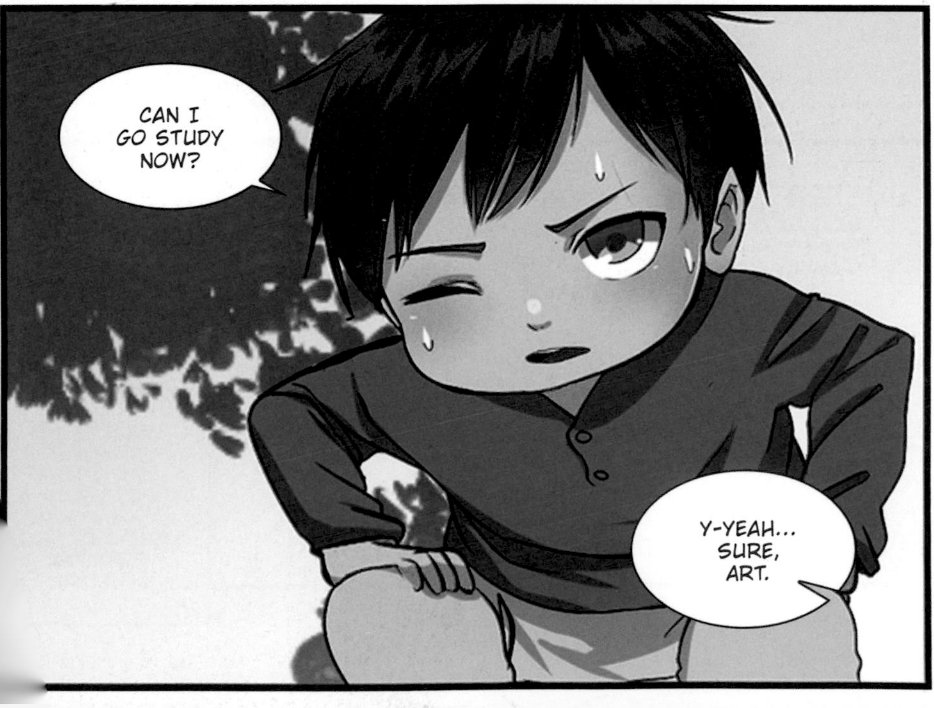
CAN I GO STUDY NOW?
Y-YEAH... SURE, ART.

IN THIS WORLD, STRENGTH IS MEASURED BY THE COLOR OF YOUR MANA CORE.

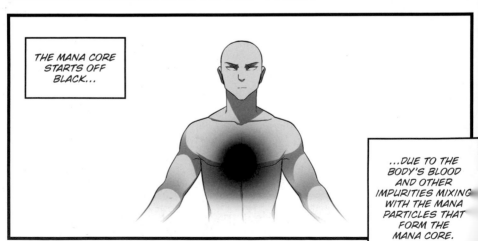

THE MANA CORE STARTS OFF BLACK...

...DUE TO THE BODY'S BLOOD AND OTHER IMPURITIES MIXING WITH THE MANA PARTICLES THAT FORM THE MANA CORE.

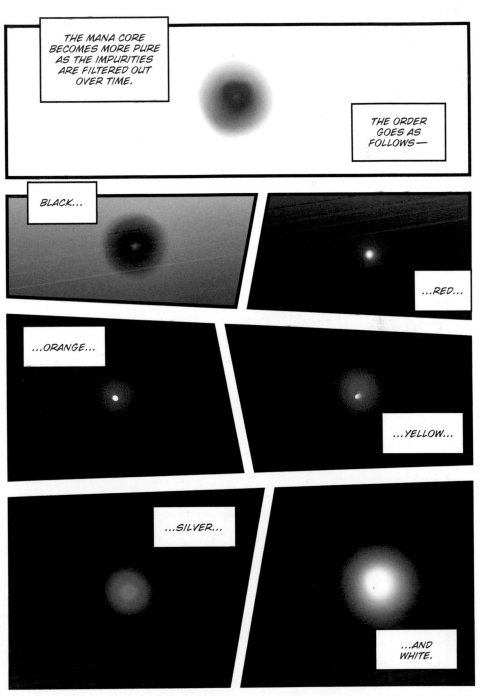

THE MANA CORE BECOMES MORE PURE AS THE IMPURITIES ARE FILTERED OUT OVER TIME.

THE ORDER GOES AS FOLLOWS—

BLACK...

...RED...

...ORANGE...

...YELLOW...

...SILVER...

...AND WHITE.

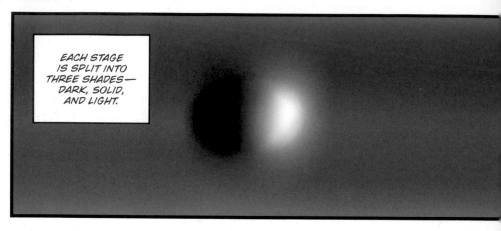

EACH STAGE IS SPLIT INTO THREE SHADES— DARK, SOLID, AND LIGHT.

THE LIGHTER THE MANA CORE, THE PURER IT IS, AND THE MORE POWER IT HAS.

AAAAR-THUR!

TIME FOR DINNER!

CURSES...

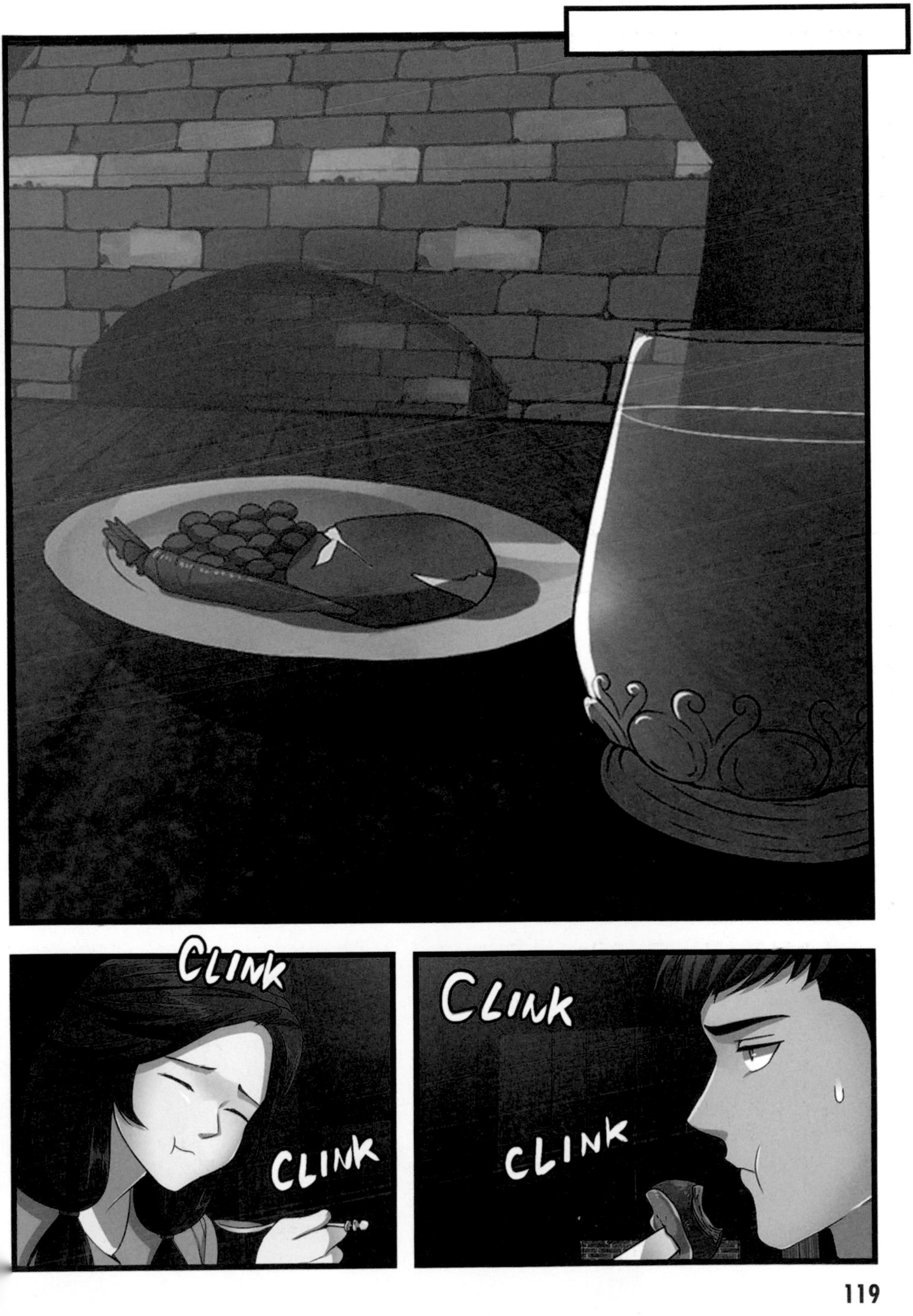
CLINK
CLINK
CLINK
CLINK

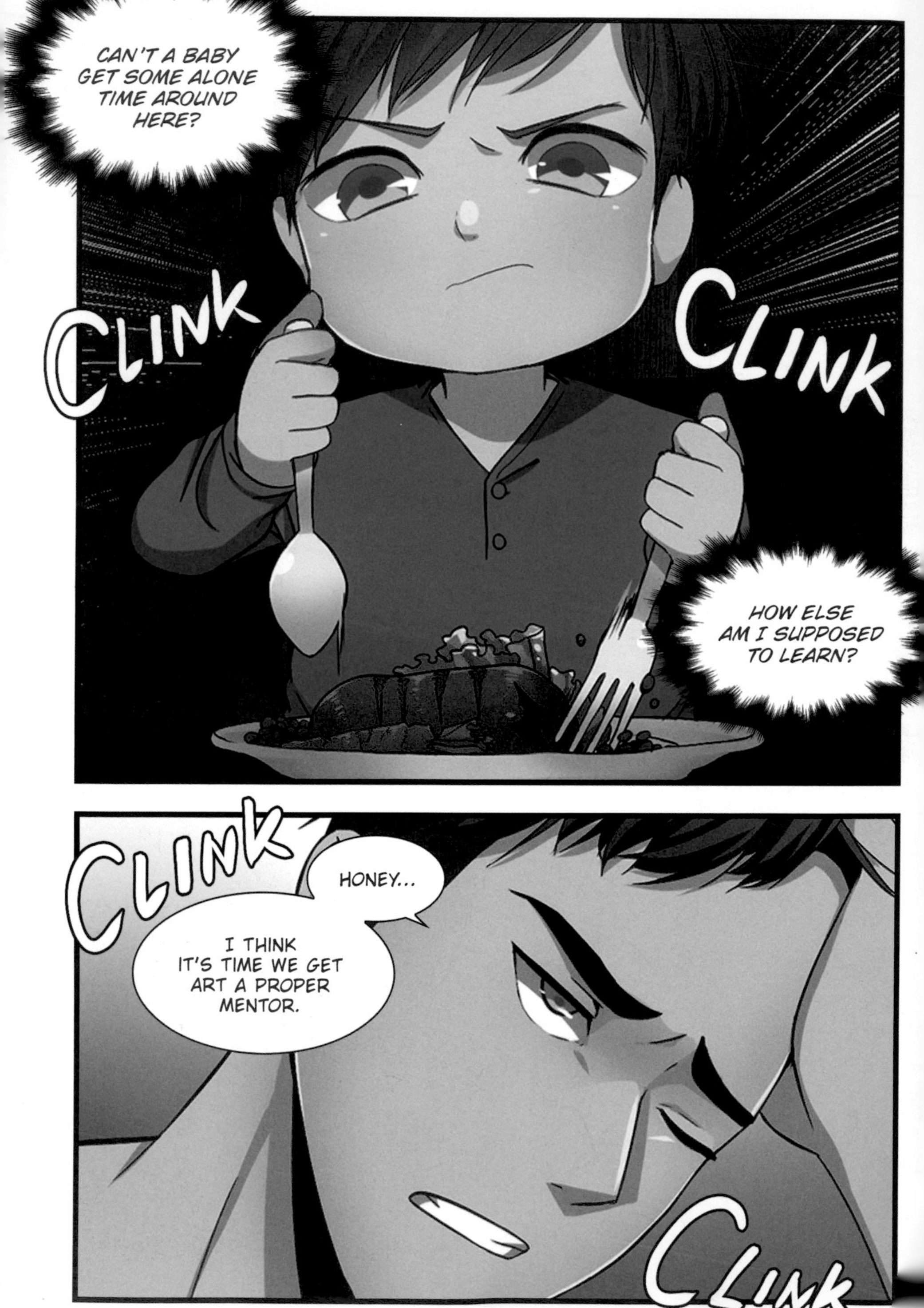
CAN'T A BABY GET SOME ALONE TIME AROUND HERE?
CLINK
CLINK
HOW ELSE AM I SUPPOSED TO LEARN?
CLINK
HONEY...
I THINK IT'S TIME WE GET ART A PROPER MENTOR.
CLINK

THE BEGINNING AFTER THE END

CHAPTER 6
Let the Journey Begin

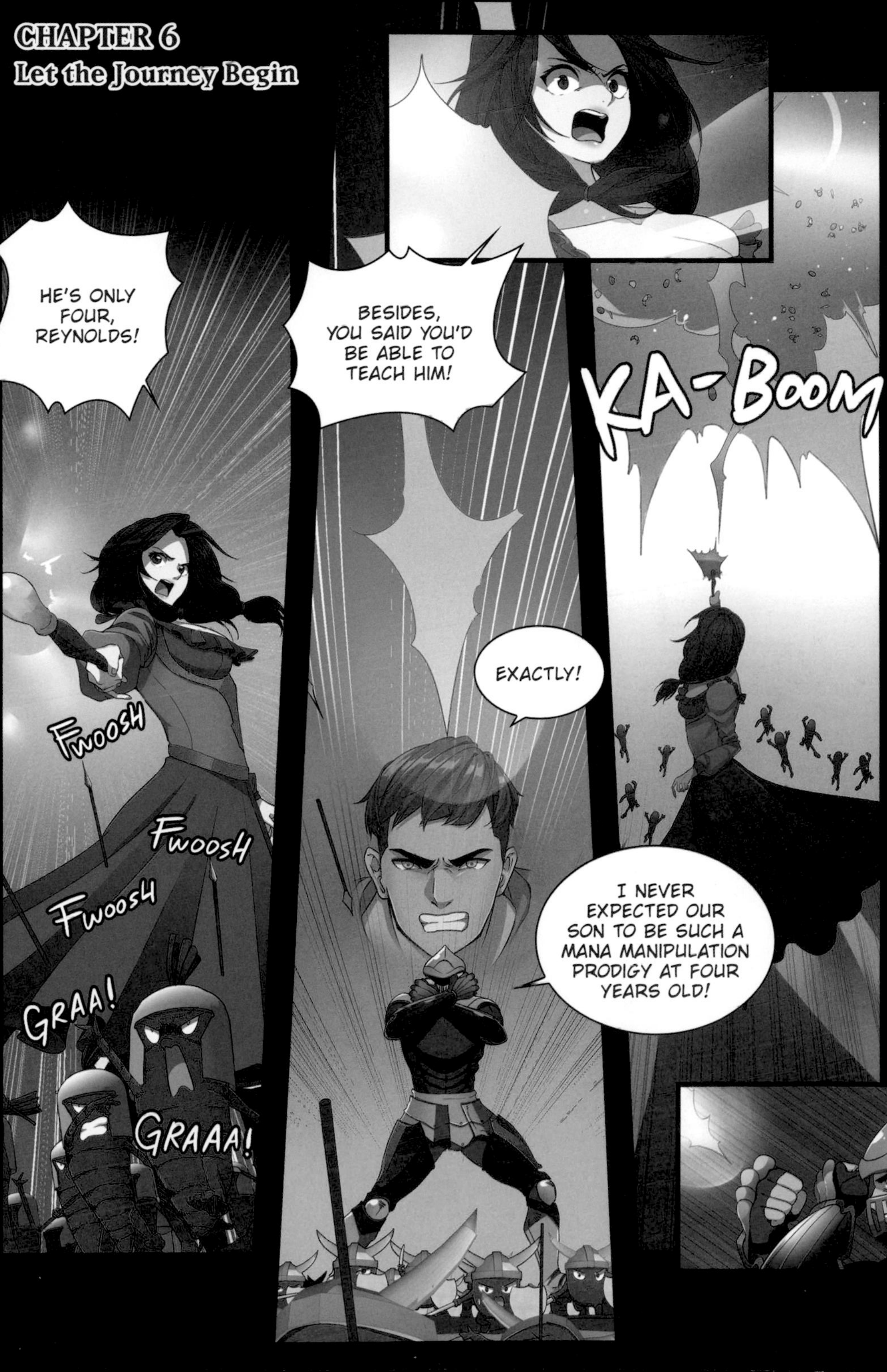

HE'S ONLY FOUR, REYNOLDS!
BESIDES, YOU SAID YOU'D BE ABLE TO TEACH HIM!
KA-BOOM
FWOOSH
FWOOSH
FWOOSH
GRAA!
GRAAA!
EXACTLY!
I NEVER EXPECTED OUR SON TO BE SUCH A MANA MANIPULATION PRODIGY AT FOUR YEARS OLD!

I'M HOLDING HIM BACK!
HE'S GOT SO MUCH POTENTIAL!
I'M NOT HAVING MY CHILD LEAVE HOME TO SOME CITY HUNDREDS OF MILES AWAY!
XYRUS ISN'T JUST SOME CITY! AND I'LL MAKE SURE MY FRIEND TAKES CARE OF HIM!
SIGH

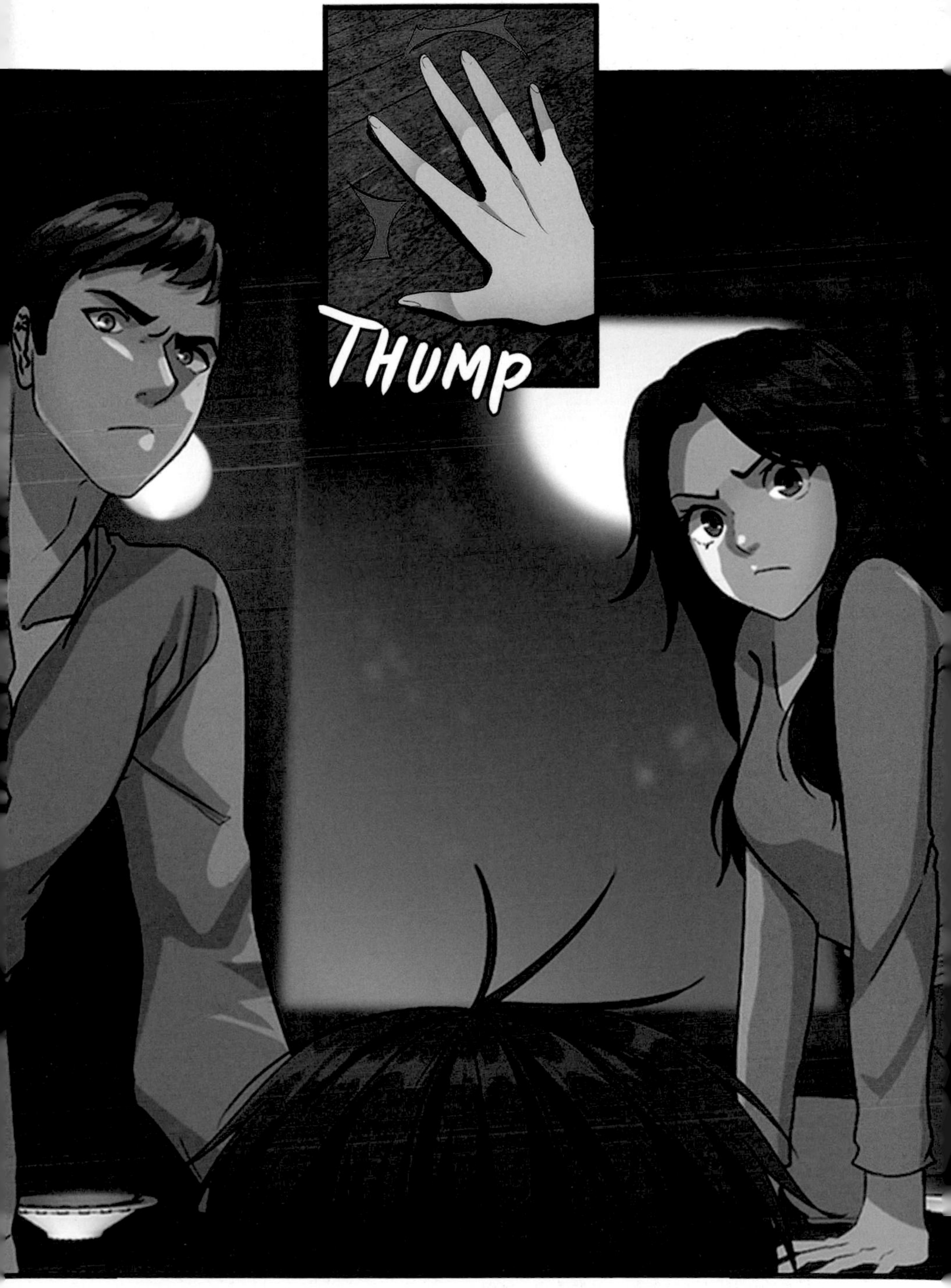
THUMP

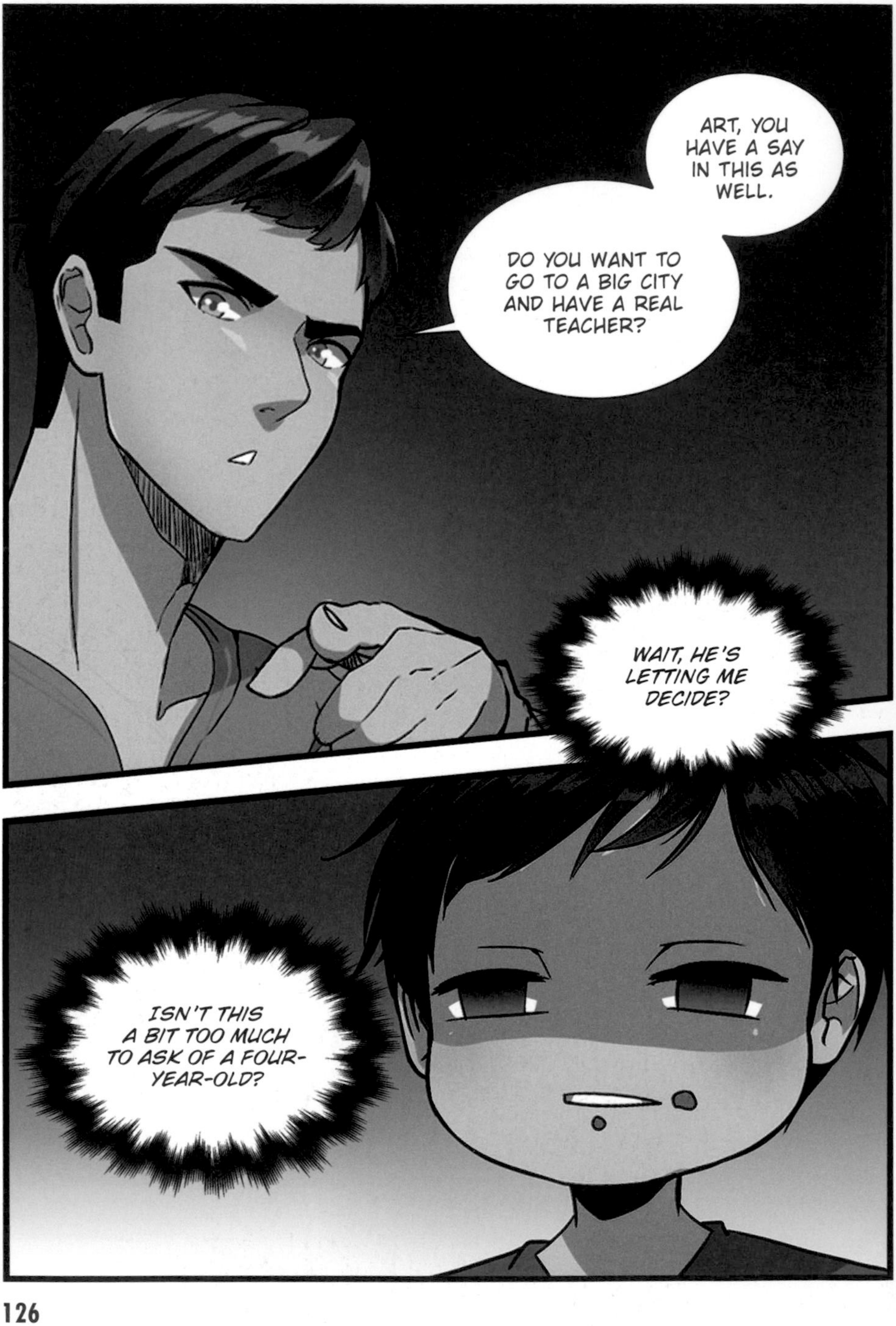
ART, YOU HAVE A SAY IN THIS AS WELL.
DO YOU WANT TO GO TO A BIG CITY AND HAVE A REAL TEACHER?
WAIT, HE'S LETTING ME DECIDE?
ISN'T THIS A BIT TOO MUCH TO ASK OF A FOUR-YEAR-OLD?

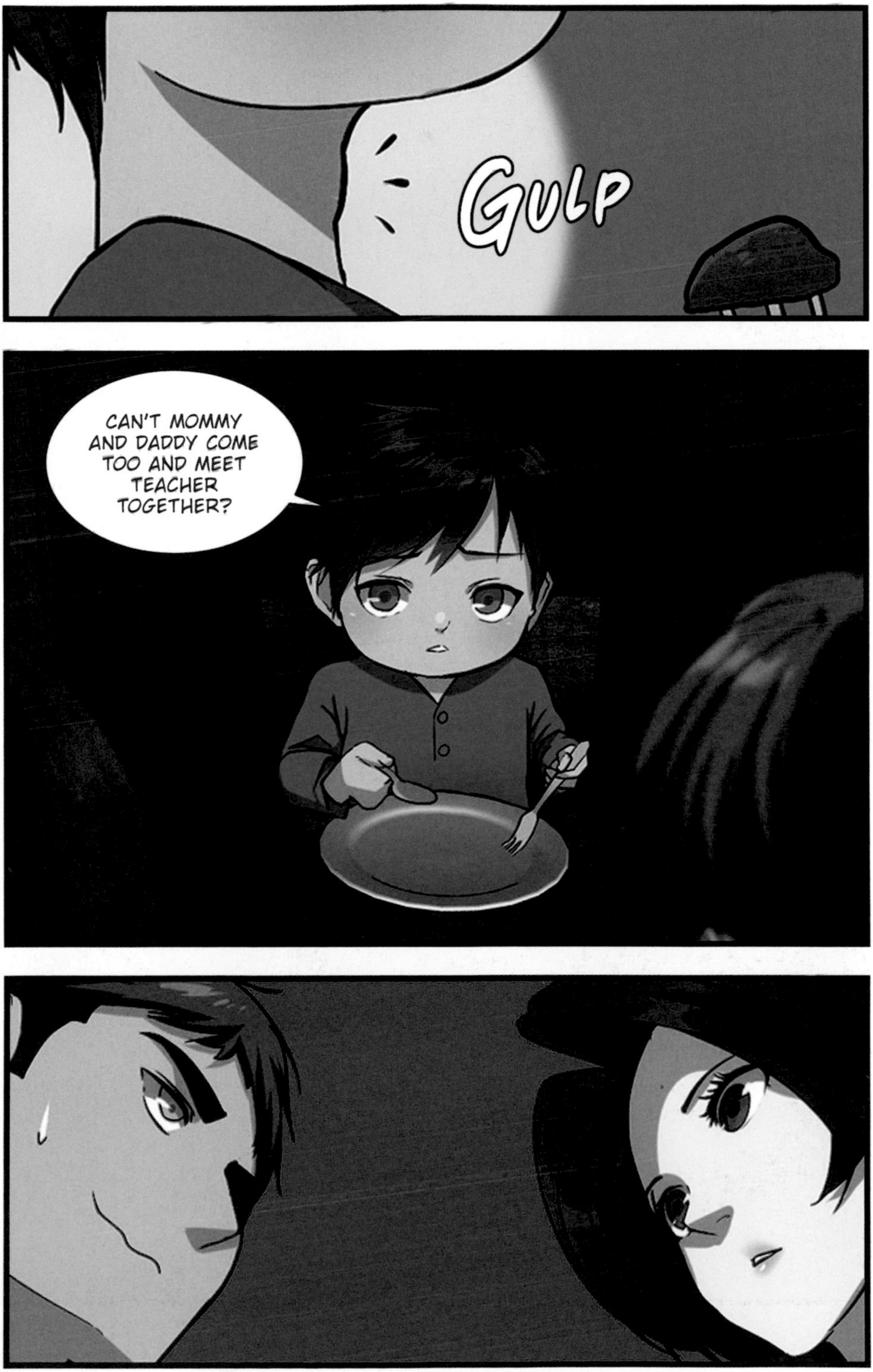
GULP
CAN'T MOMMY AND DADDY COME TOO AND MEET TEACHER TOGETHER?

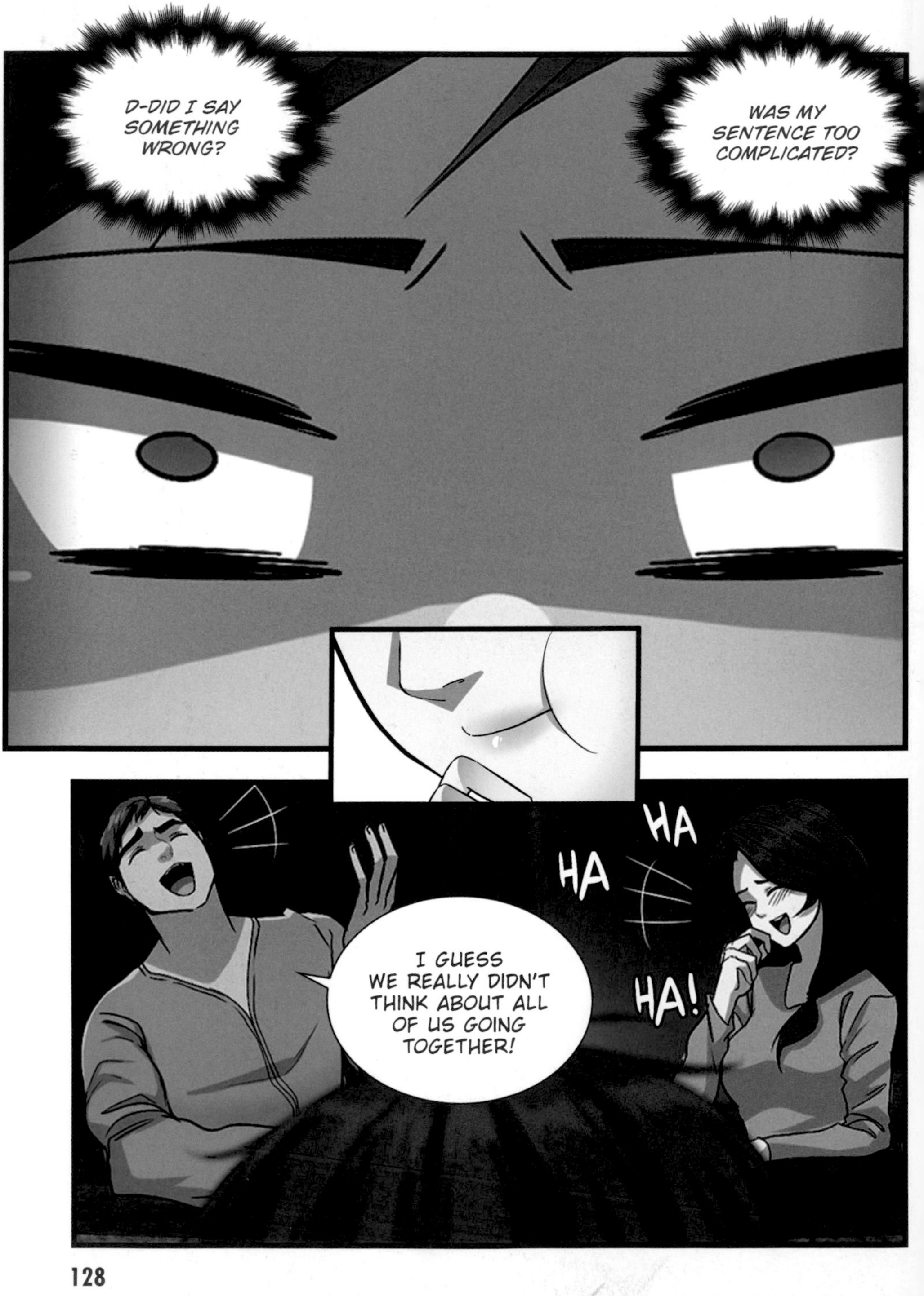
D-DID I SAY SOMETHING WRONG?
WAS MY SENTENCE TOO COMPLICATED?
I GUESS WE REALLY DIDN'T THINK ABOUT ALL OF US GOING TOGETHER!
HA
HA
HA!

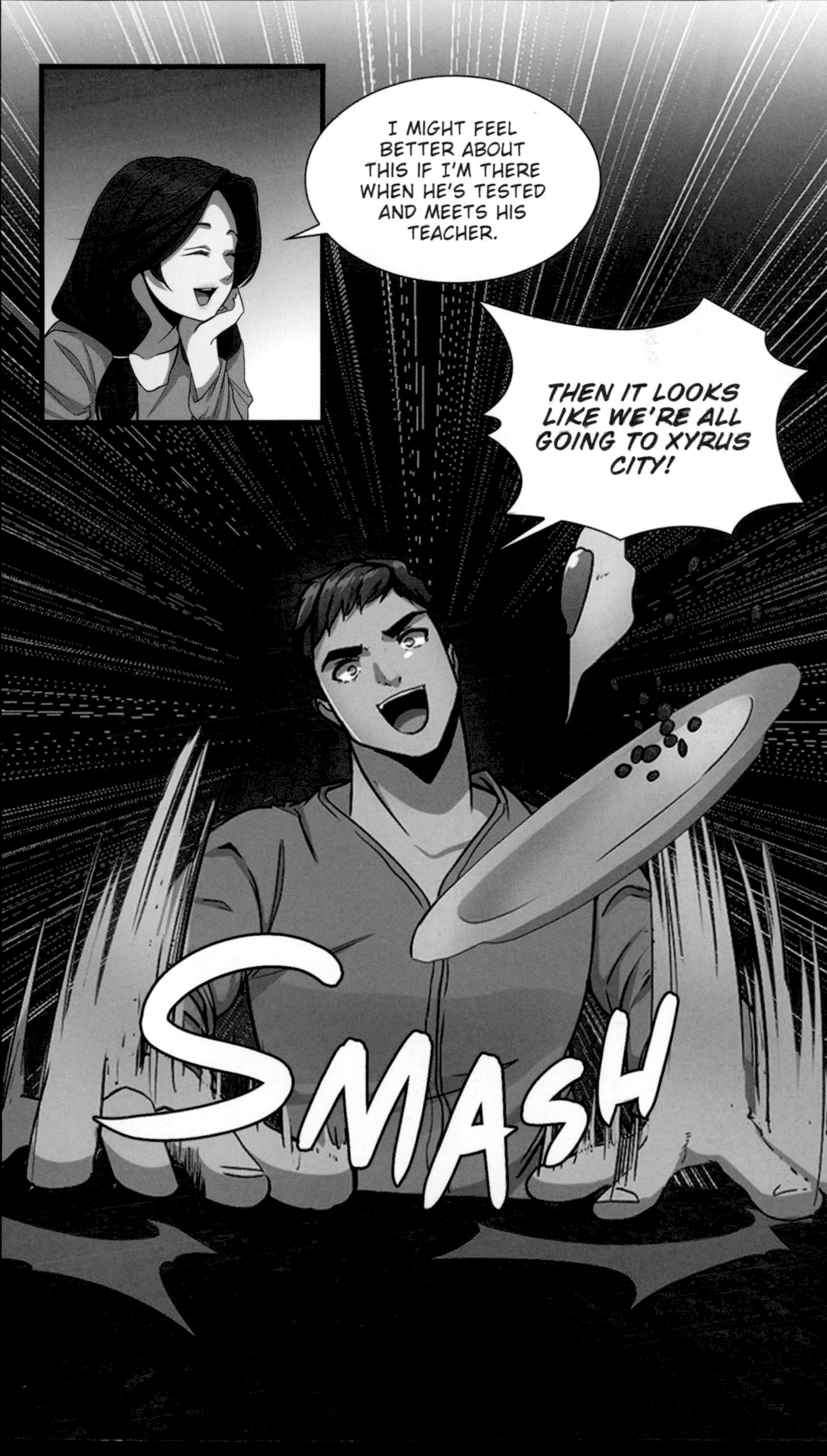

I MIGHT FEEL BETTER ABOUT THIS IF I'M THERE WHEN HE'S TESTED AND MEETS HIS TEACHER.
THEN IT LOOKS LIKE WE'RE ALL GOING TO XYRUS CITY!
SMASH

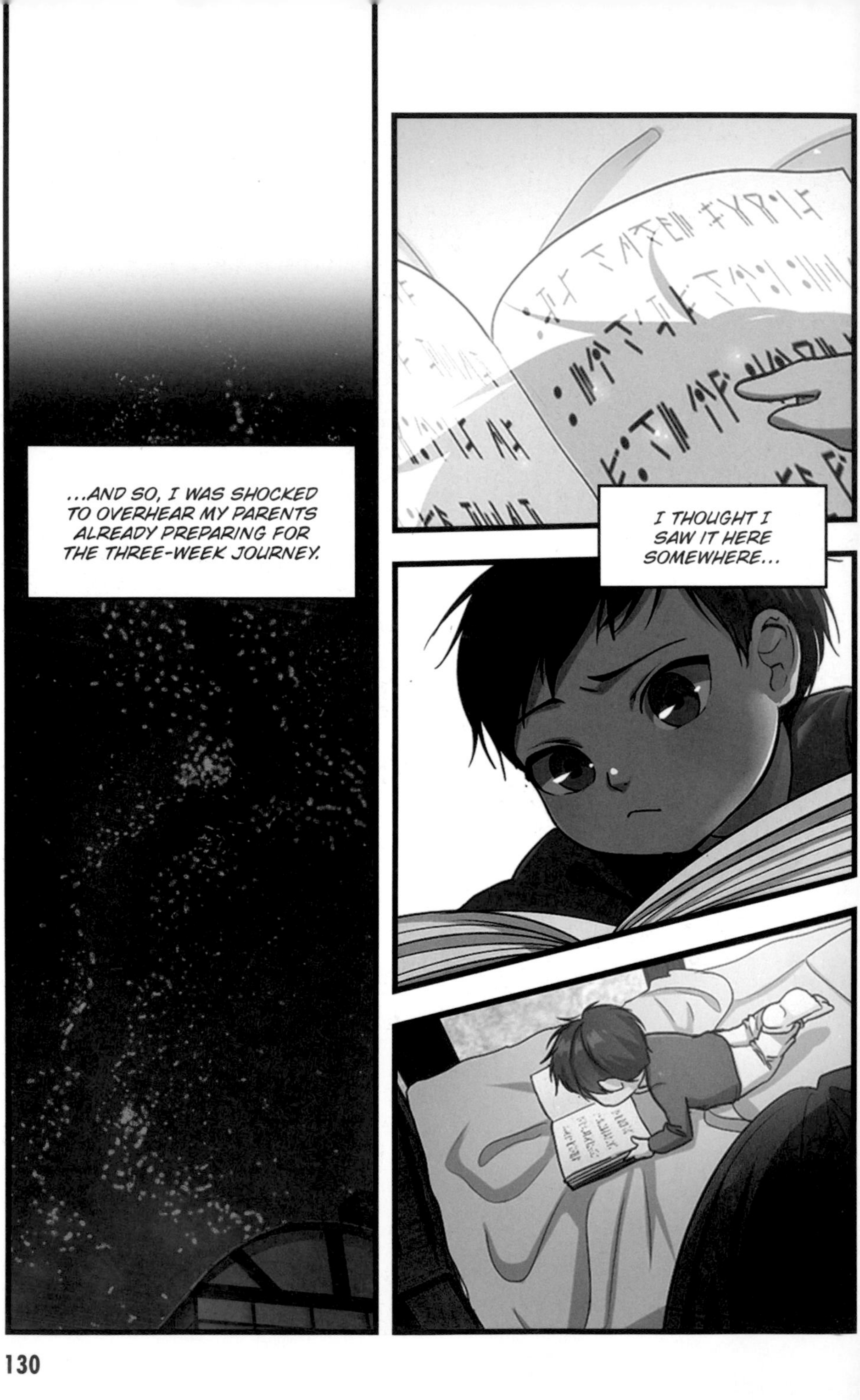
...AND SO, I WAS SHOCKED TO OVERHEAR MY PARENTS ALREADY PREPARING FOR THE THREE-WEEK JOURNEY.
I THOUGHT I SAW IT HERE SOMEWHERE...

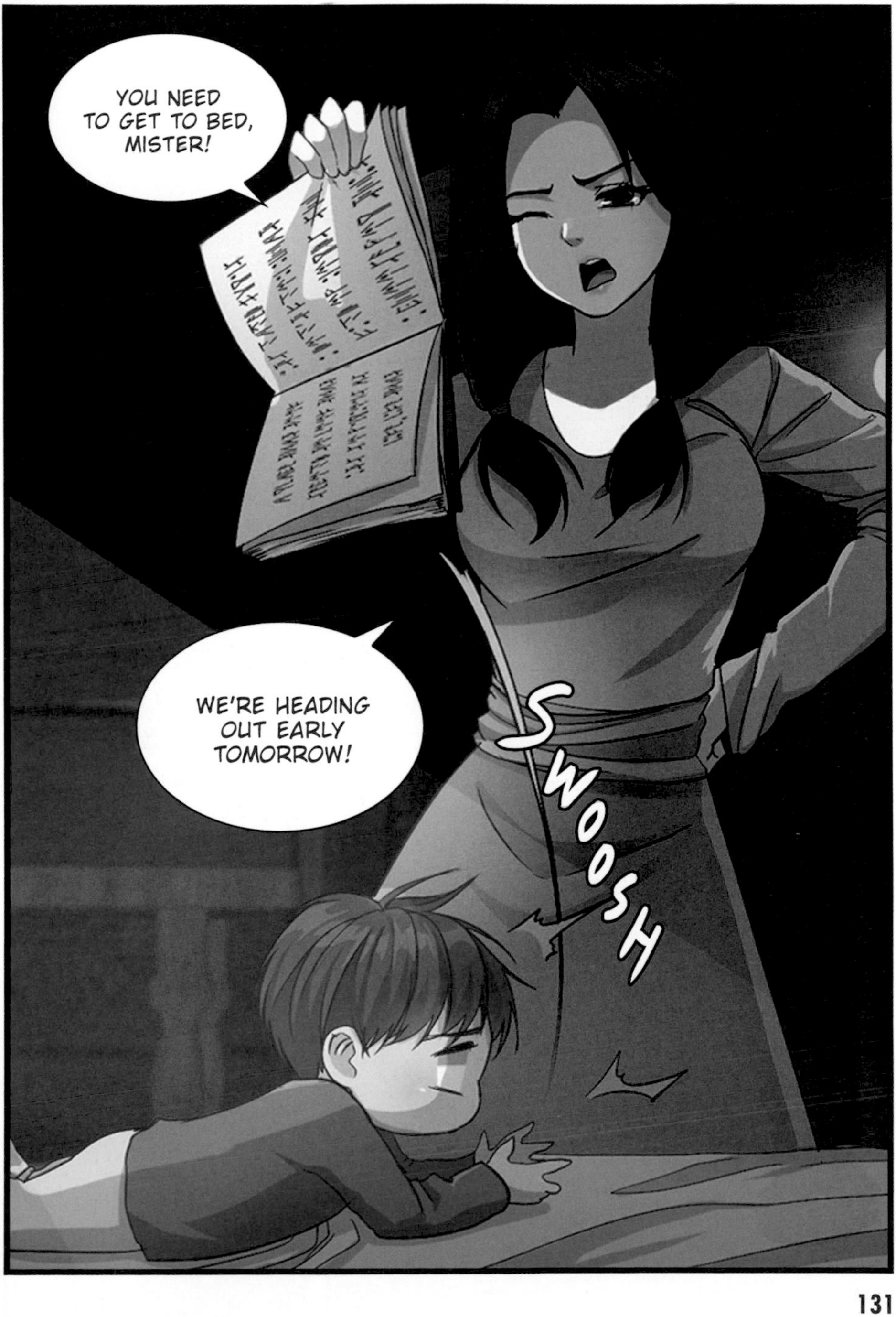
YOU NEED TO GET TO BED, MISTER!
WE'RE HEADING OUT EARLY TOMORROW!
SWOOSH

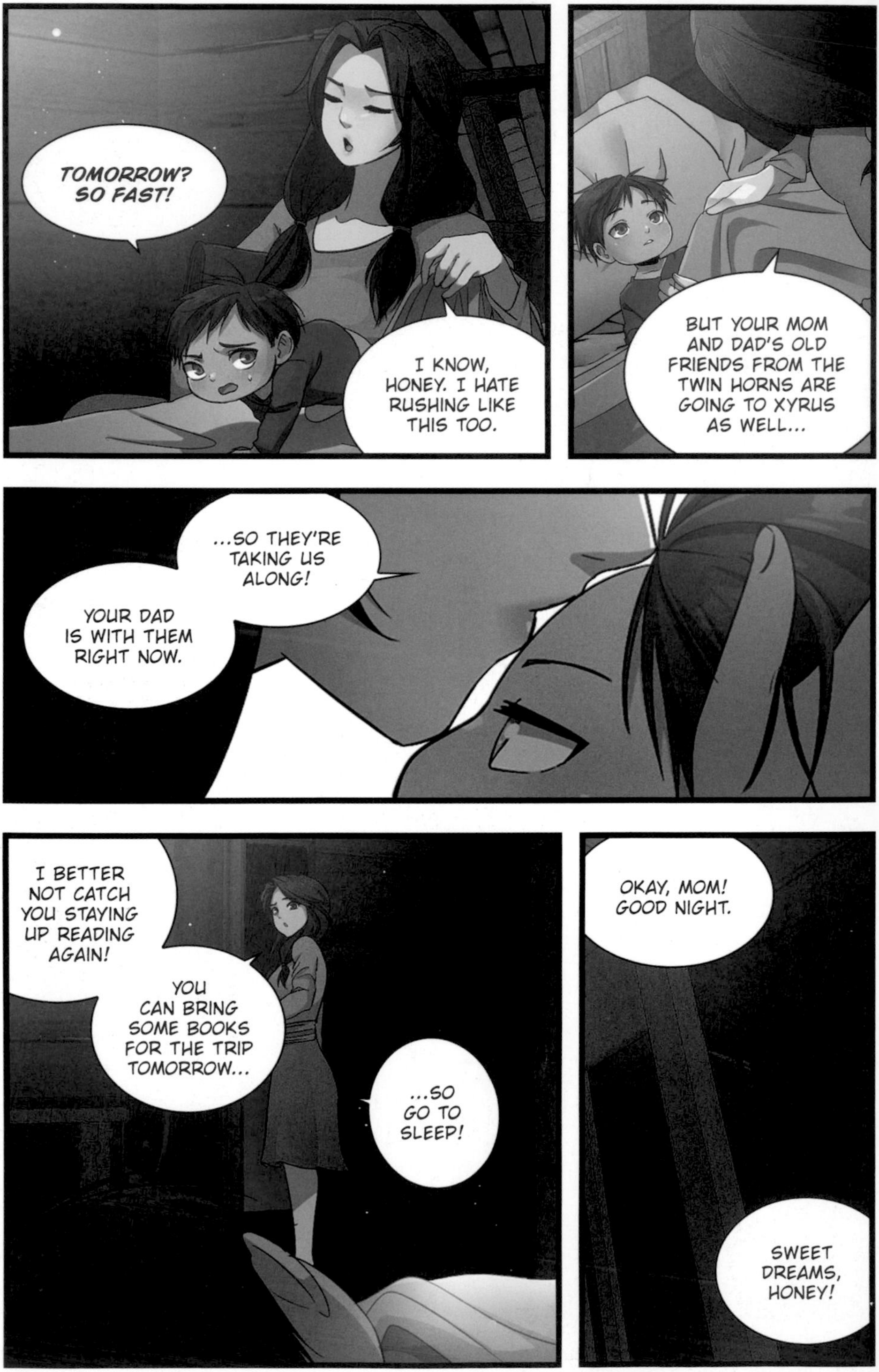
TOMORROW? SO FAST!
I KNOW, HONEY. I HATE RUSHING LIKE THIS TOO.
BUT YOUR MOM AND DAD'S OLD FRIENDS FROM THE TWIN HORNS ARE GOING TO XYRUS AS WELL...
...SO THEY'RE TAKING US ALONG!
YOUR DAD IS WITH THEM RIGHT NOW.
I BETTER NOT CATCH YOU STAYING UP READING AGAIN!
YOU CAN BRING SOME BOOKS FOR THE TRIP TOMORROW...
...SO GO TO SLEEP!
OKAY, MOM! GOOD NIGHT.
SWEET DREAMS, HONEY!

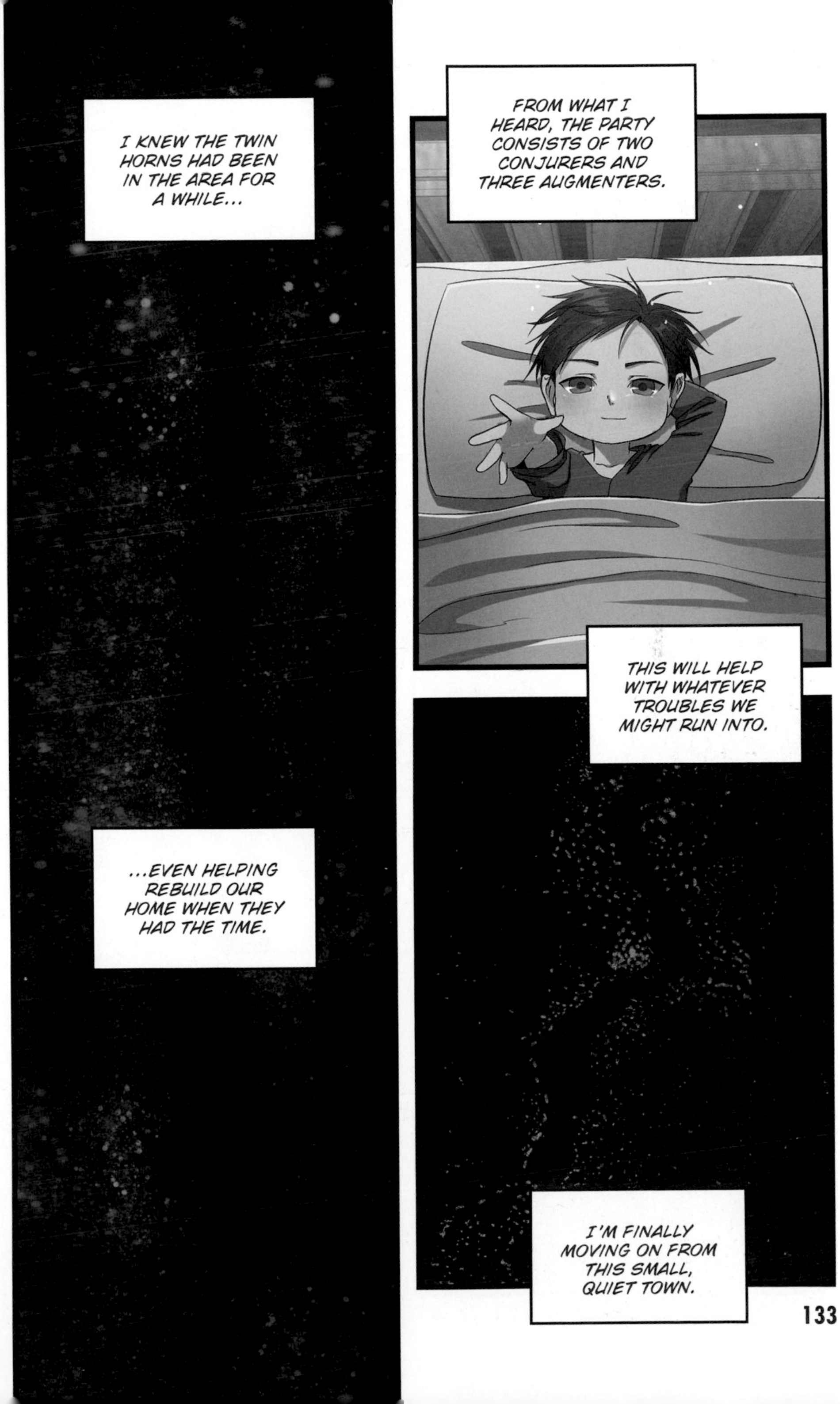
I KNEW THE TWIN HORNS HAD BEEN IN THE AREA FOR A WHILE...
...EVEN HELPING REBUILD OUR HOME WHEN THEY HAD THE TIME.
FROM WHAT I HEARD, THE PARTY CONSISTS OF TWO CONJURERS AND THREE AUGMENTERS.
THIS WILL HELP WITH WHATEVER TROUBLES WE MIGHT RUN INTO.
I'M FINALLY MOVING ON FROM THIS SMALL, QUIET TOWN.

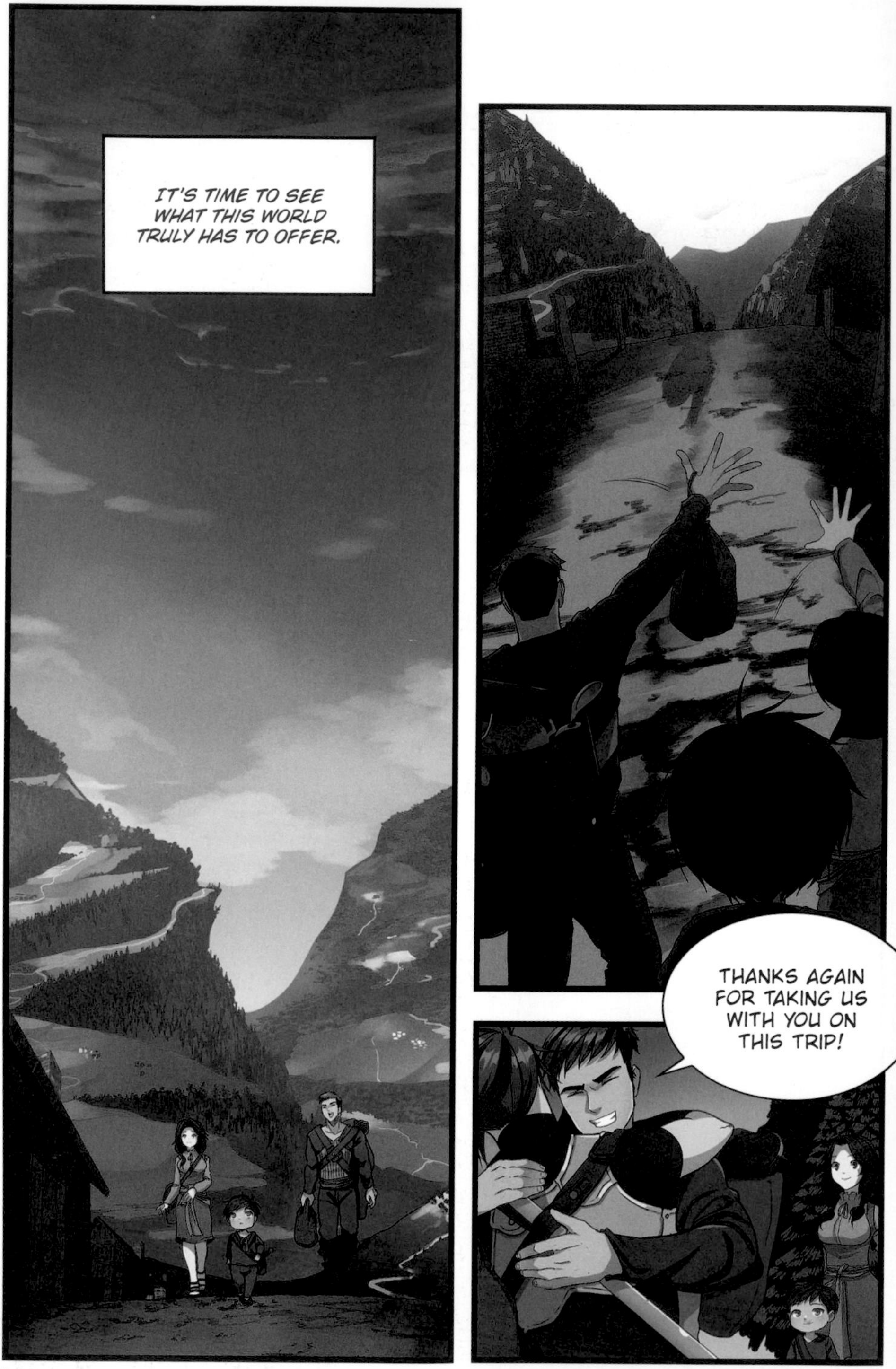
IT'S TIME TO SEE WHAT THIS WORLD TRULY HAS TO OFFER.
THANKS AGAIN FOR TAKING US WITH YOU ON THIS TRIP!

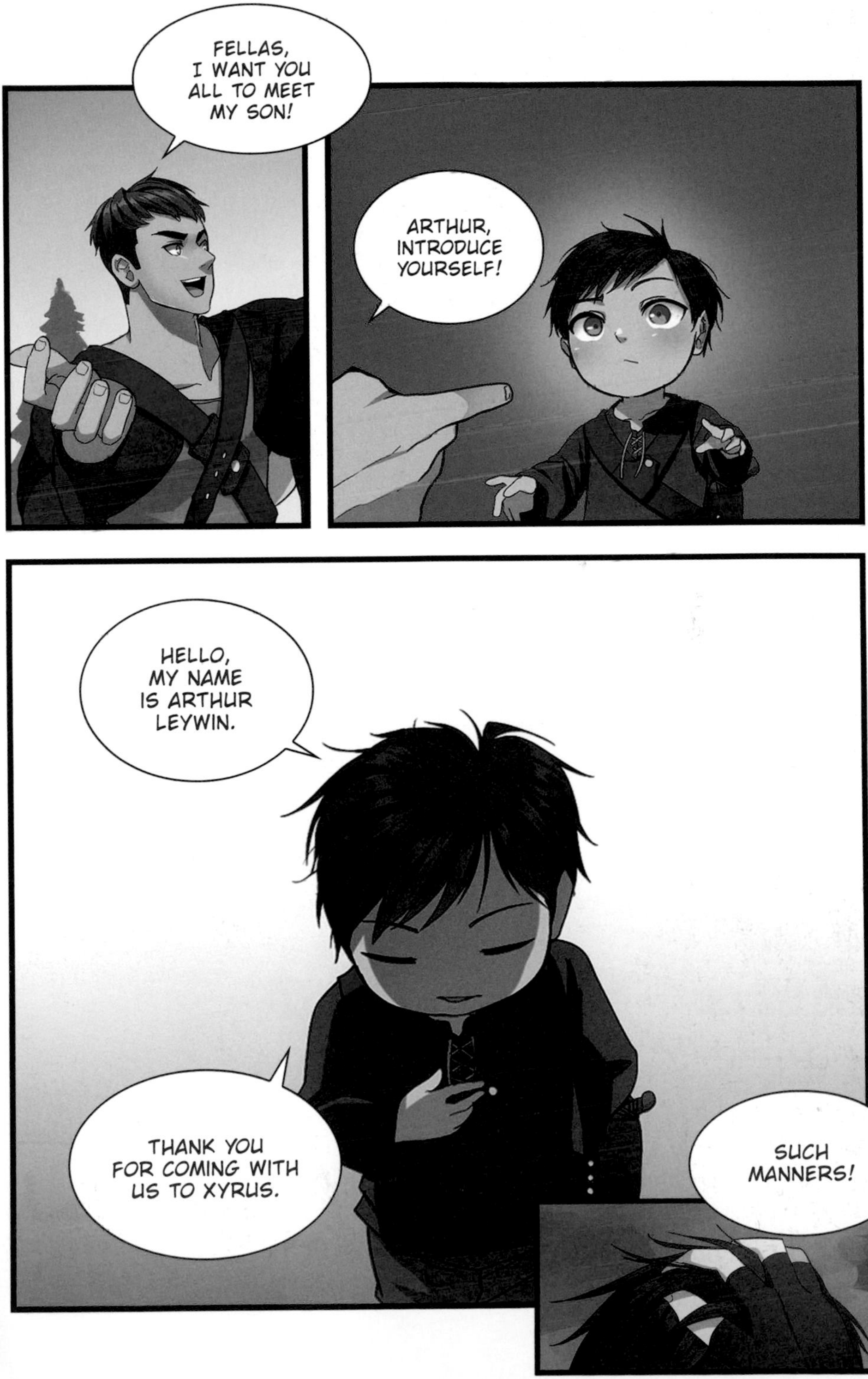
FELLAS, I WANT YOU ALL TO MEET MY SON!
ARTHUR, INTRODUCE YOURSELF!
HELLO, MY NAME IS ARTHUR LEYWIN.
THANK YOU FOR COMING WITH US TO XYRUS.
SUCH MANNERS!

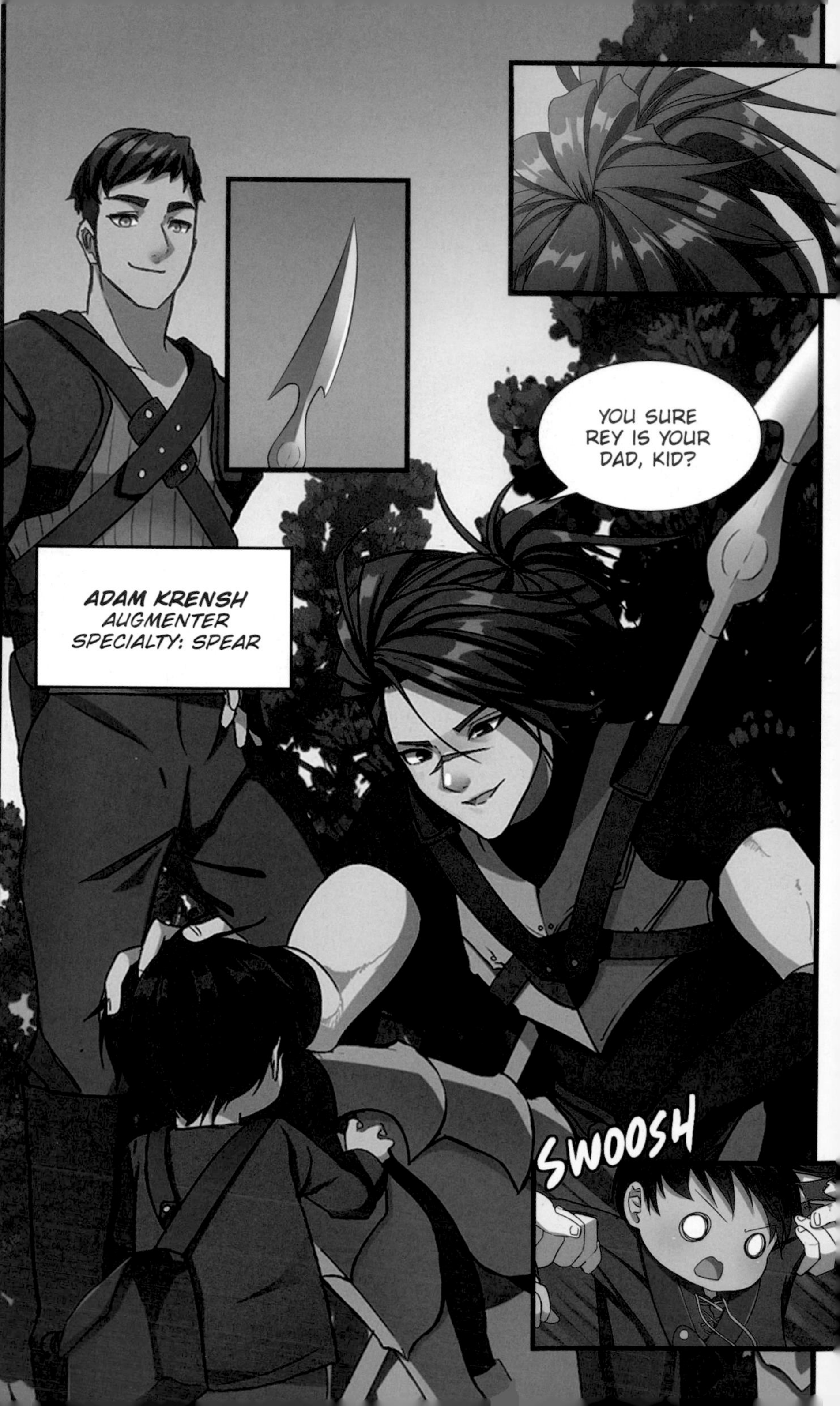
ADAM KRENSH
AUGMENTER
SPECIALTY: SPEAR
YOU SURE REY IS YOUR DAD, KID?
SWOOSH

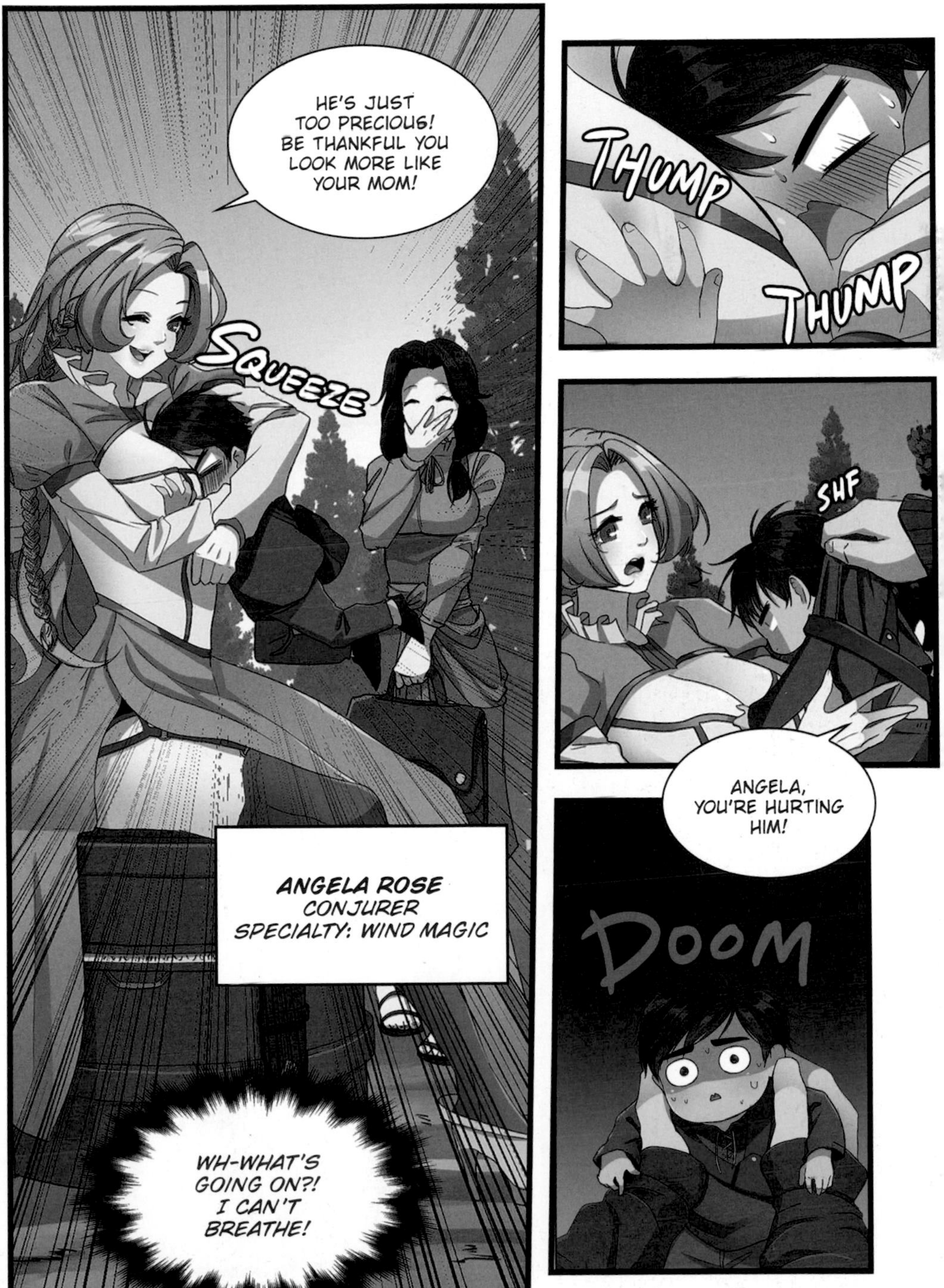
HE'S JUST TOO PRECIOUS! BE THANKFUL YOU LOOK MORE LIKE YOUR MOM!
SQUEEZE
ANGELA ROSE
CONJURER
SPECIALTY: WIND MAGIC
WH-WHAT'S GOING ON?! I CAN'T BREATHE!
THUMP
THUMP
SHF
ANGELA, YOU'RE HURTING HIM!
DOOM

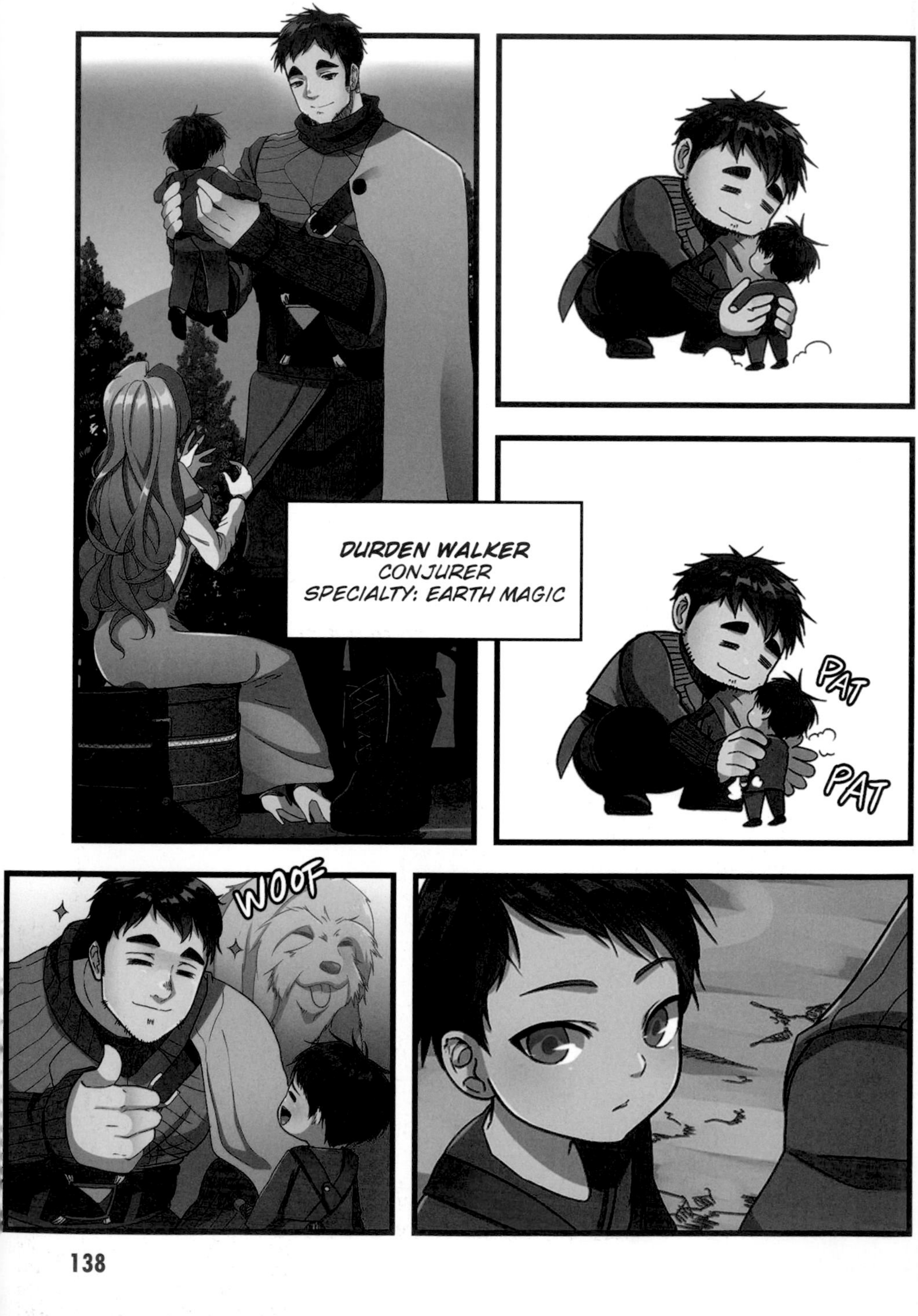
DURDEN WALKER
CONJURER
SPECIALTY: EARTH MAGIC
PAT
PAT
WOOF

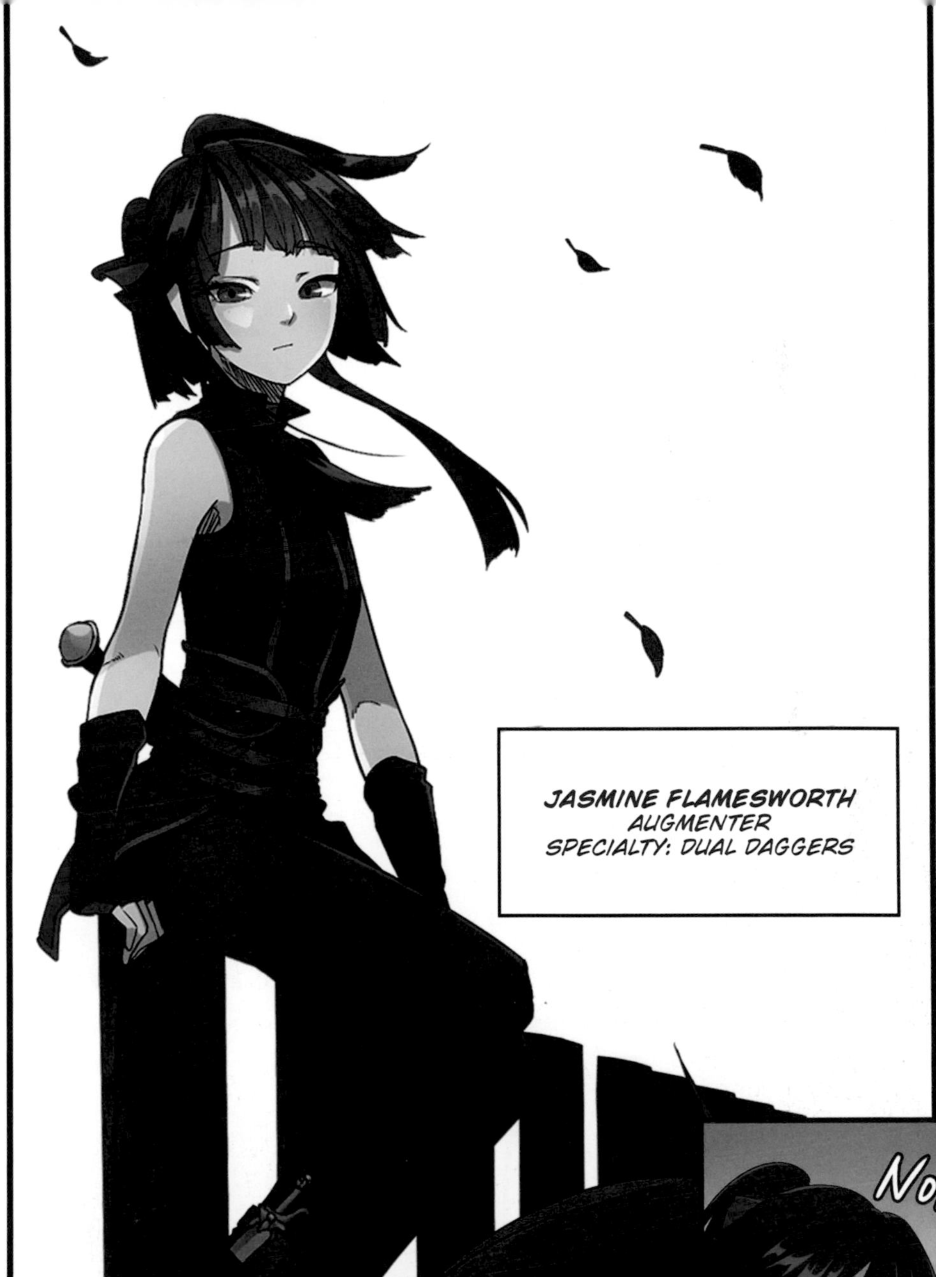
JASMINE FLAMESWORTH
AUGMENTER
SPECIALTY: DUAL DAGGERS

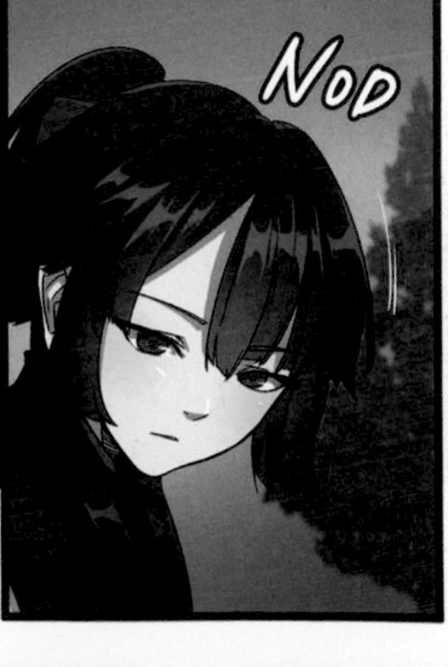
NOD

DON'T MIND HER, SHE JUST NEEDS TO GET USED TO YOU.

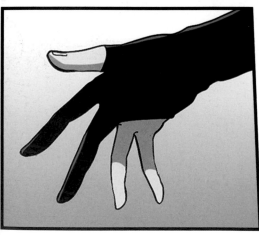

NICE TO MEET YOU, ARTHUR.

MY NAME IS *HELEN SHARD.*

HELEN SHARD
AUGMENTER
SPECIALTY: MAGIC ARCHERY

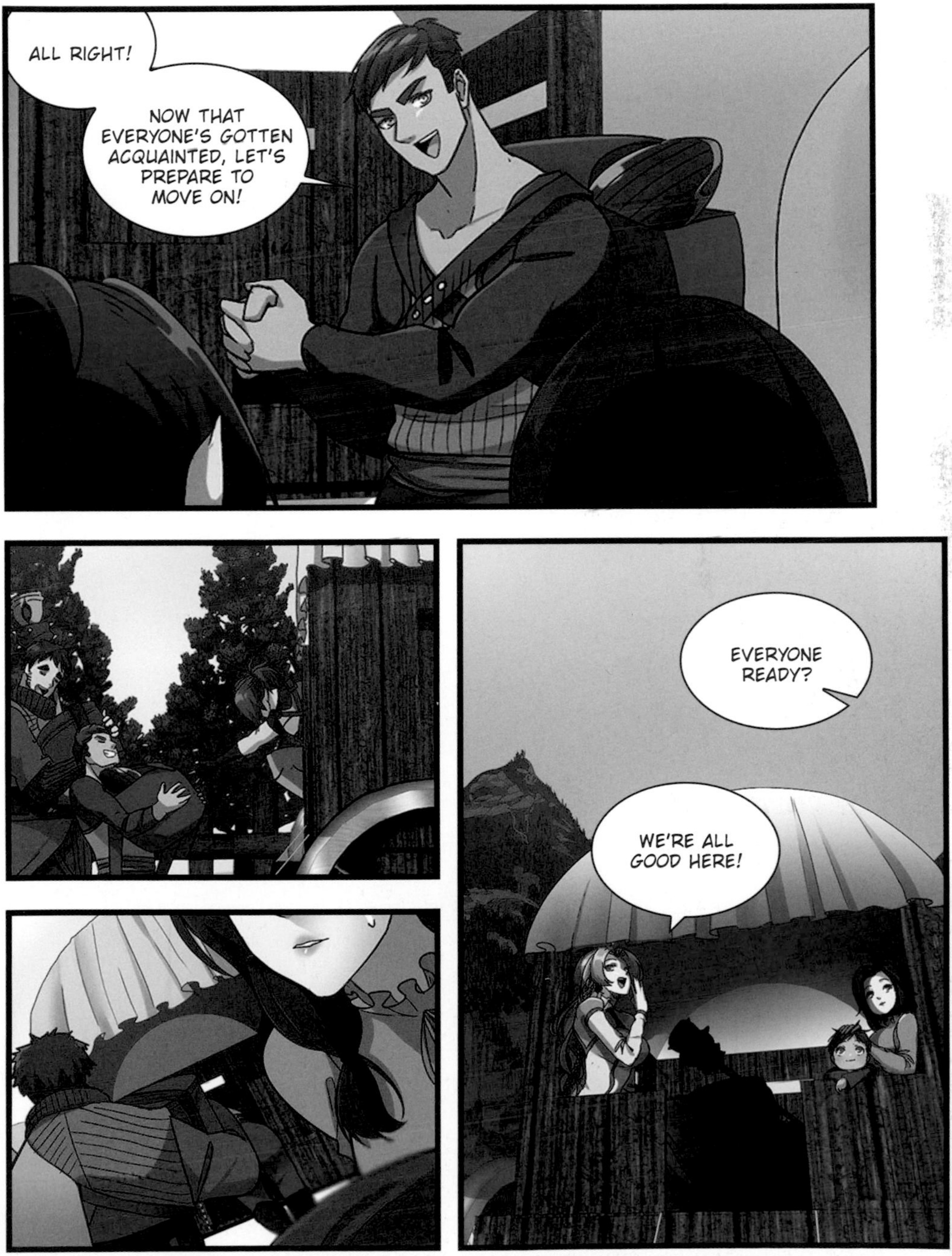
ALL RIGHT!
NOW THAT EVERYONE'S GOTTEN ACQUAINTED, LET'S PREPARE TO MOVE ON!
EVERYONE READY?
WE'RE ALL GOOD HERE!

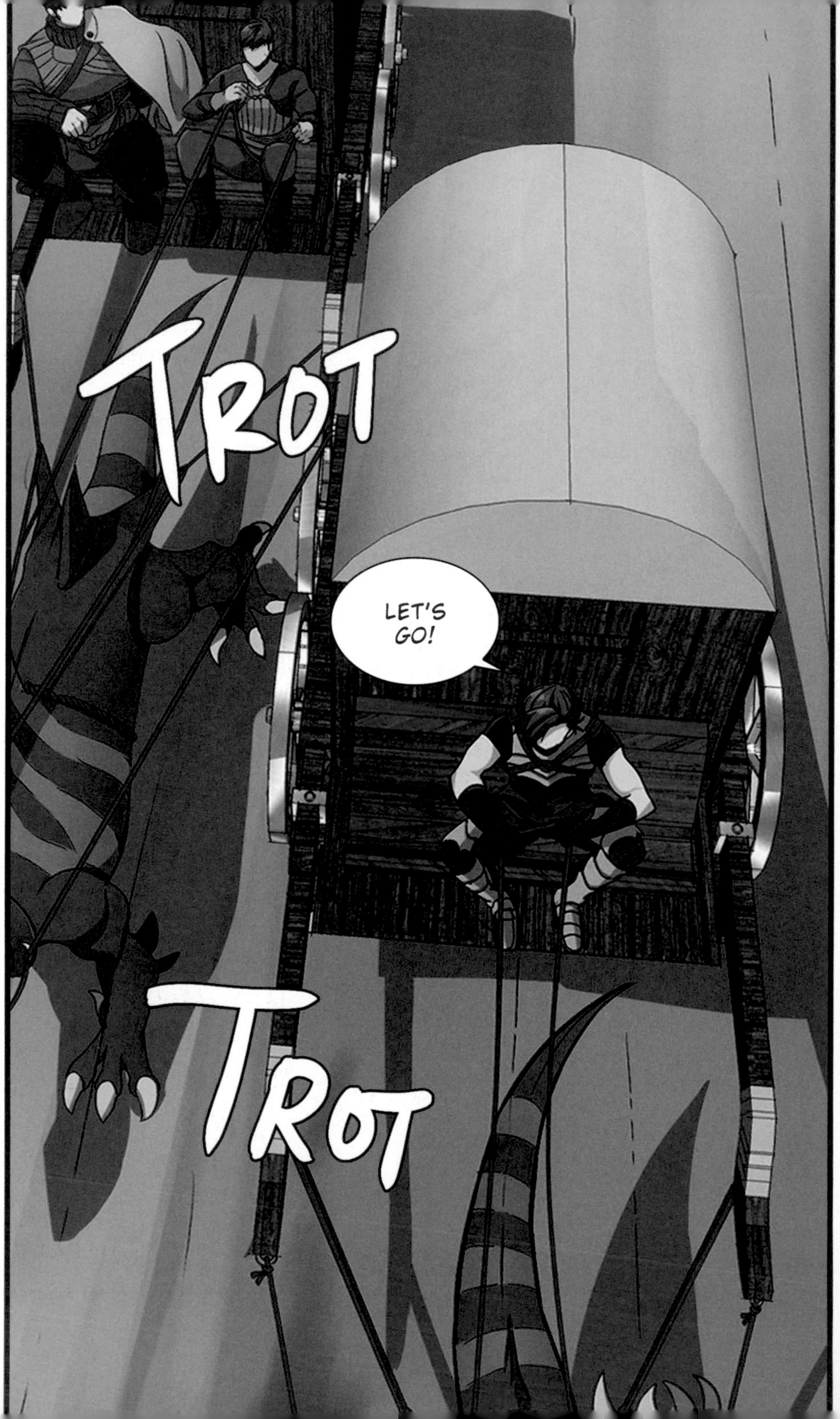
TROT
LET'S GO!
TROT

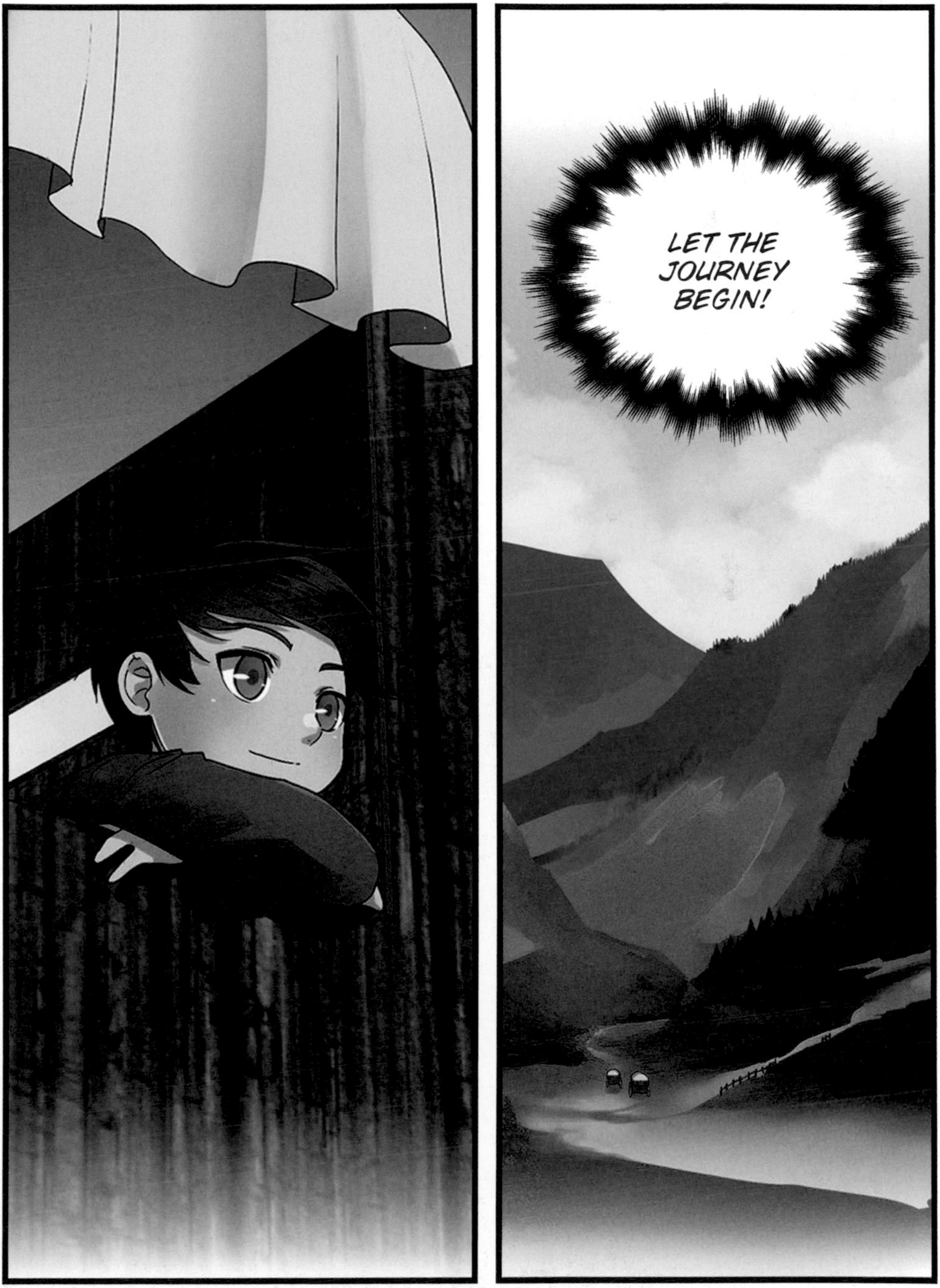
LET THE JOURNEY BEGIN!

THE BEGINNING AFTER THE END

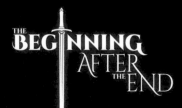

CHAPTER 7—The Sparring Match

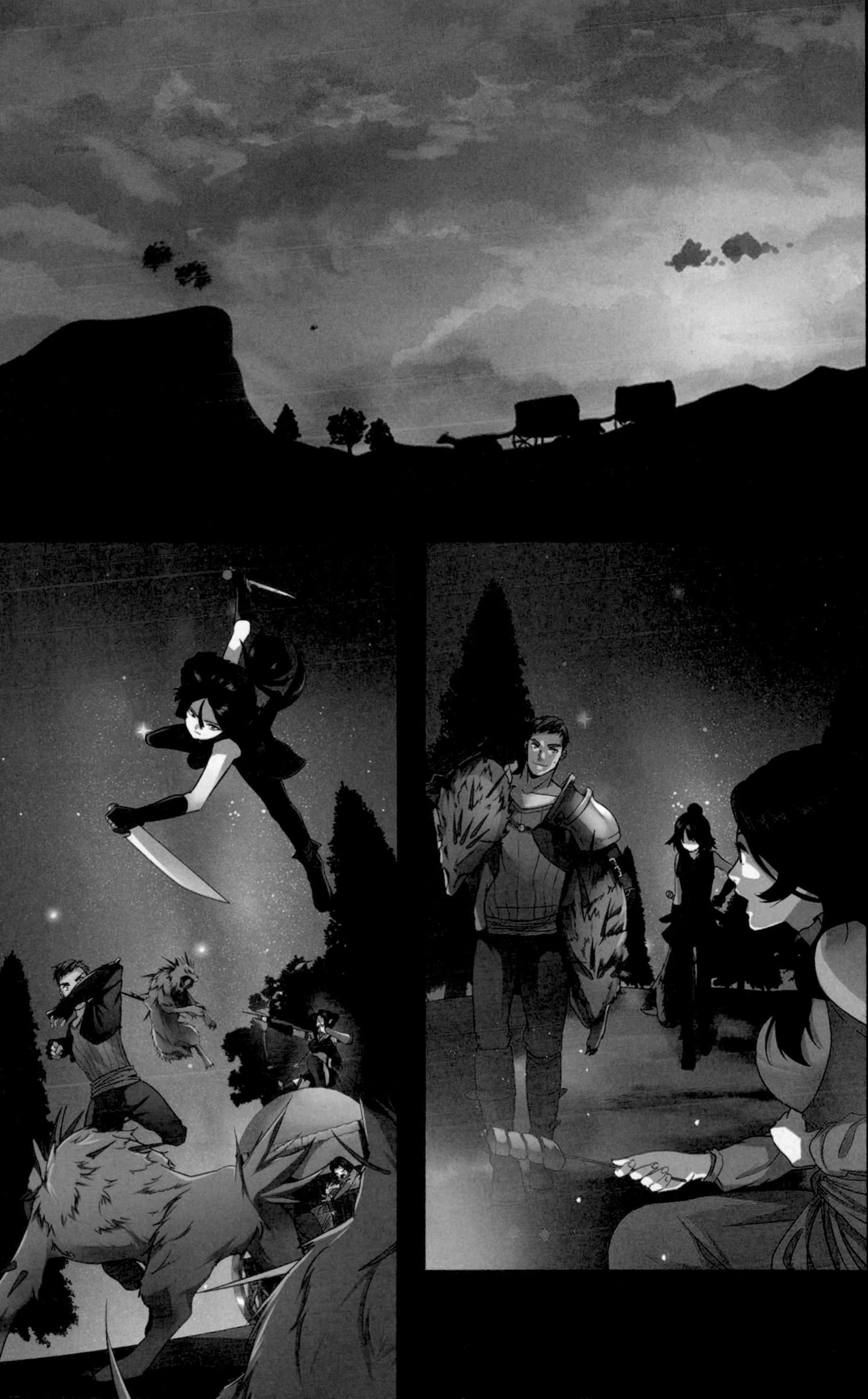

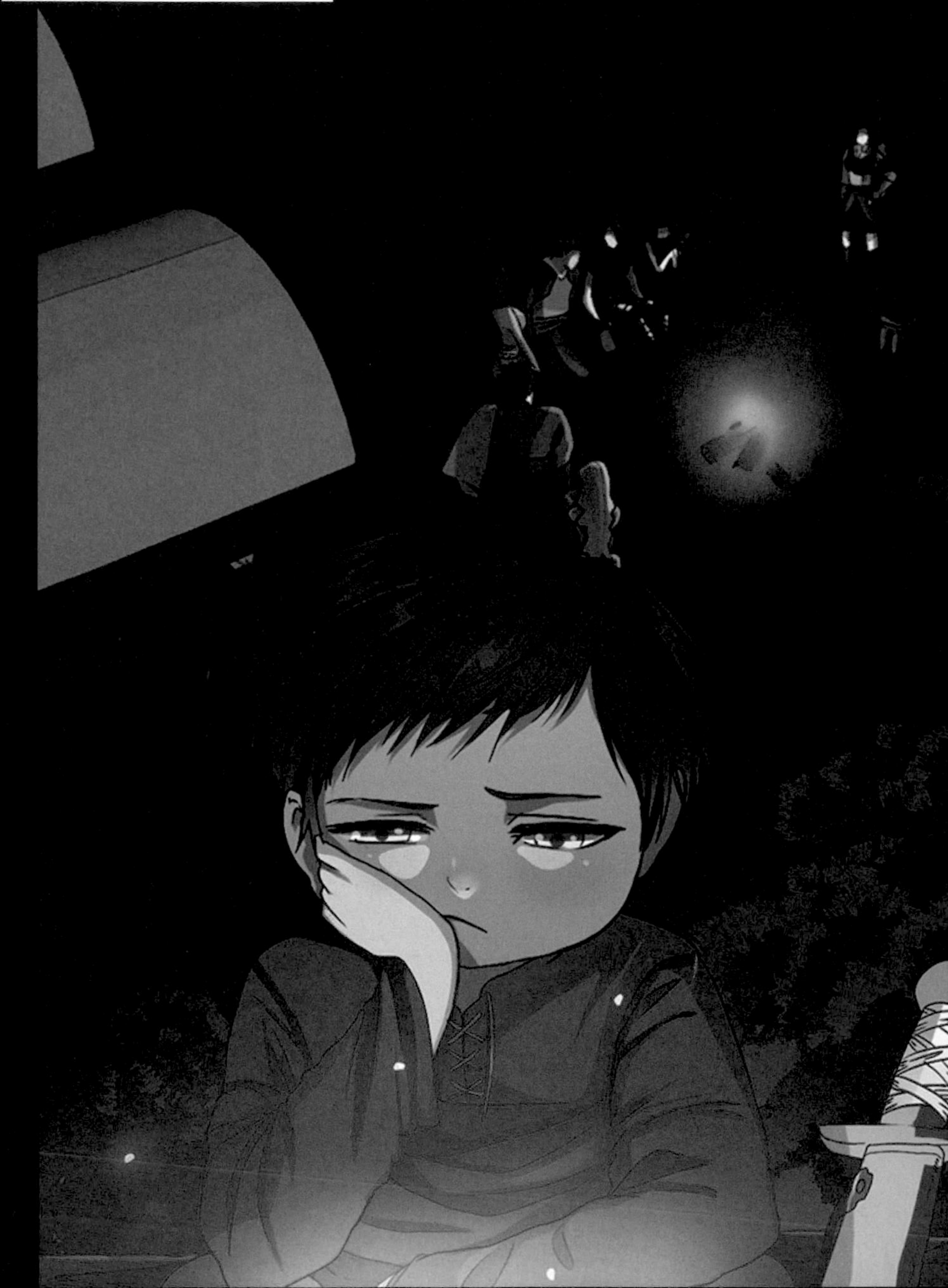

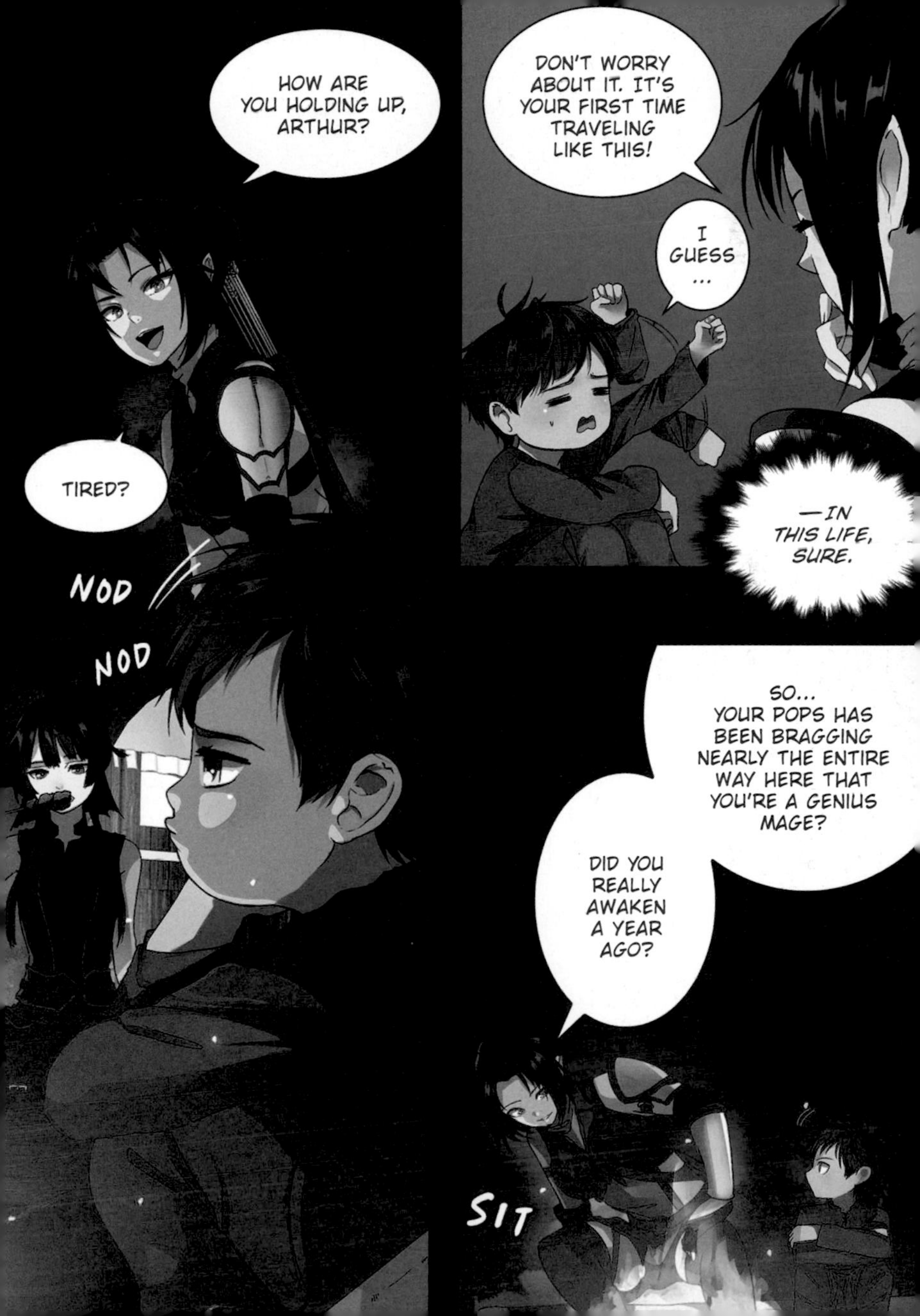
DON'T WORRY ABOUT IT. IT'S YOUR FIRST TIME TRAVELING LIKE THIS!
I GUESS ...
—IN THIS LIFE, SURE.
HOW ARE YOU HOLDING UP, ARTHUR?
TIRED?
NOD
NOD
SO... YOUR POPS HAS BEEN BRAGGING NEARLY THE ENTIRE WAY HERE THAT YOU'RE A GENIUS MAGE?
DID YOU REALLY AWAKEN A YEAR AGO?
SIT

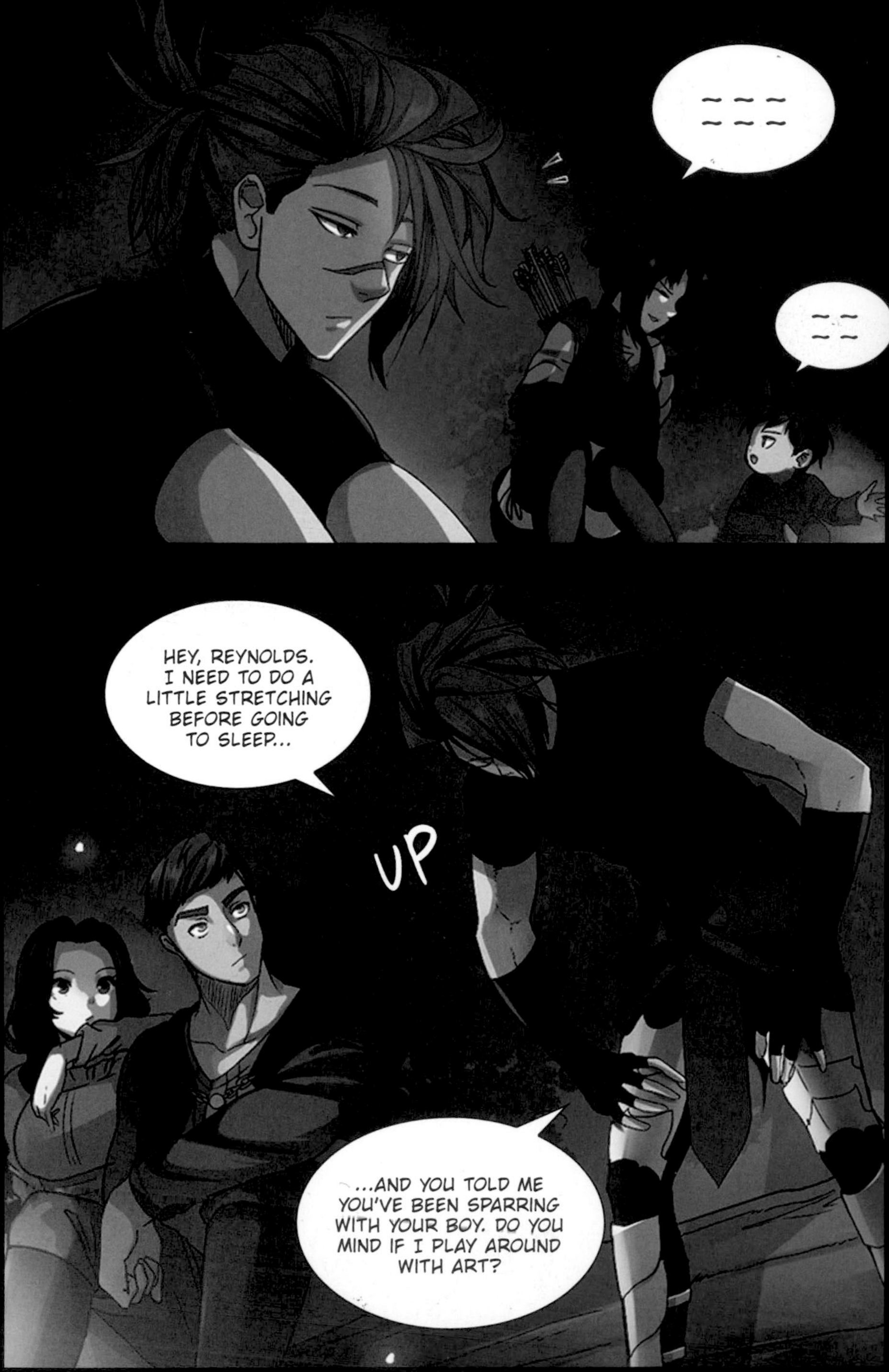
HEY, REYNOLDS. I NEED TO DO A LITTLE STRETCHING BEFORE GOING TO SLEEP...
UP
...AND YOU TOLD ME YOU'VE BEEN SPARRING WITH YOUR BOY. DO YOU MIND IF I PLAY AROUND WITH ART?

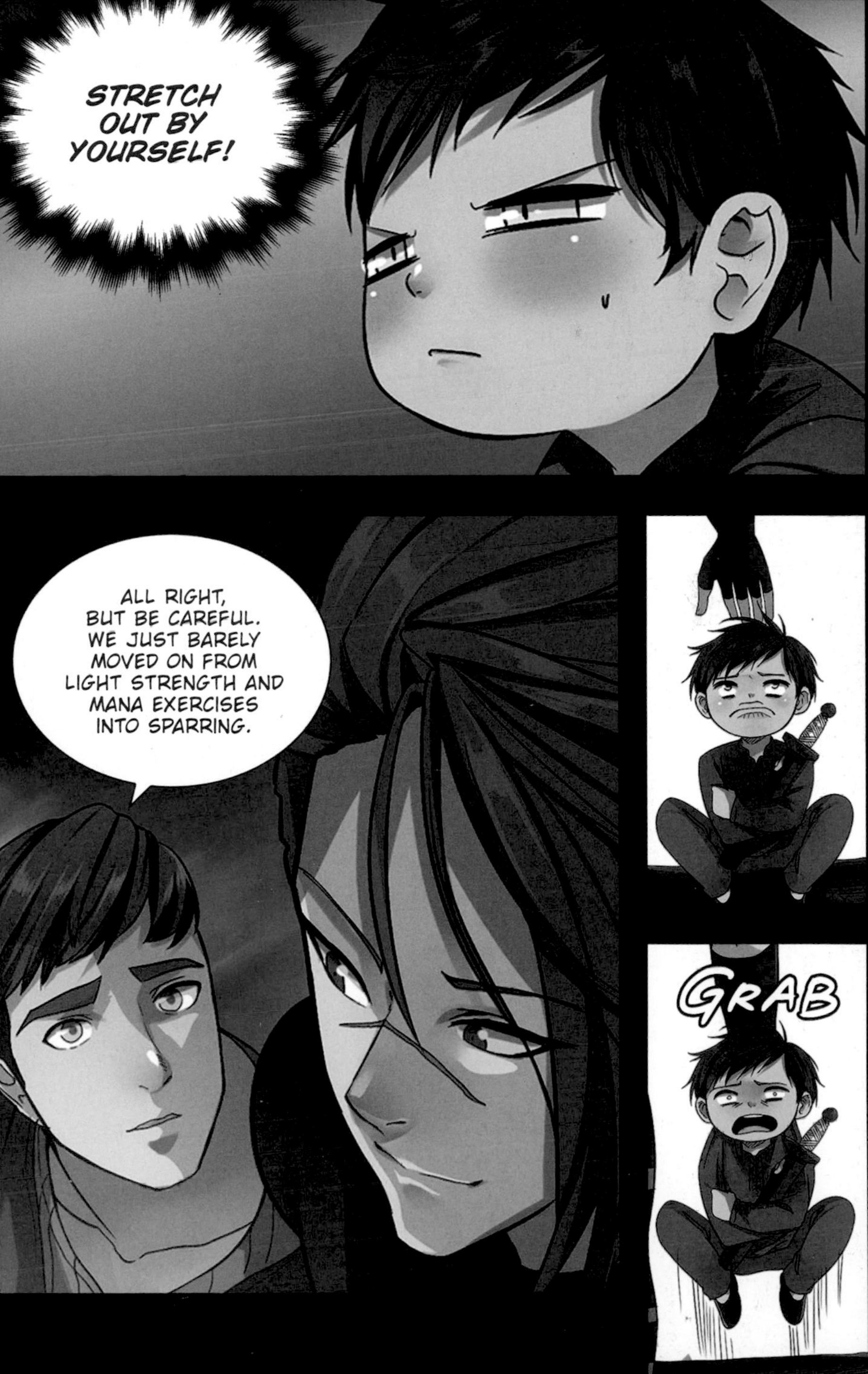
STRETCH OUT BY YOURSELF!
ALL RIGHT, BUT BE CAREFUL. WE JUST BARELY MOVED ON FROM LIGHT STRENGTH AND MANA EXERCISES INTO SPARRING.
GRAB

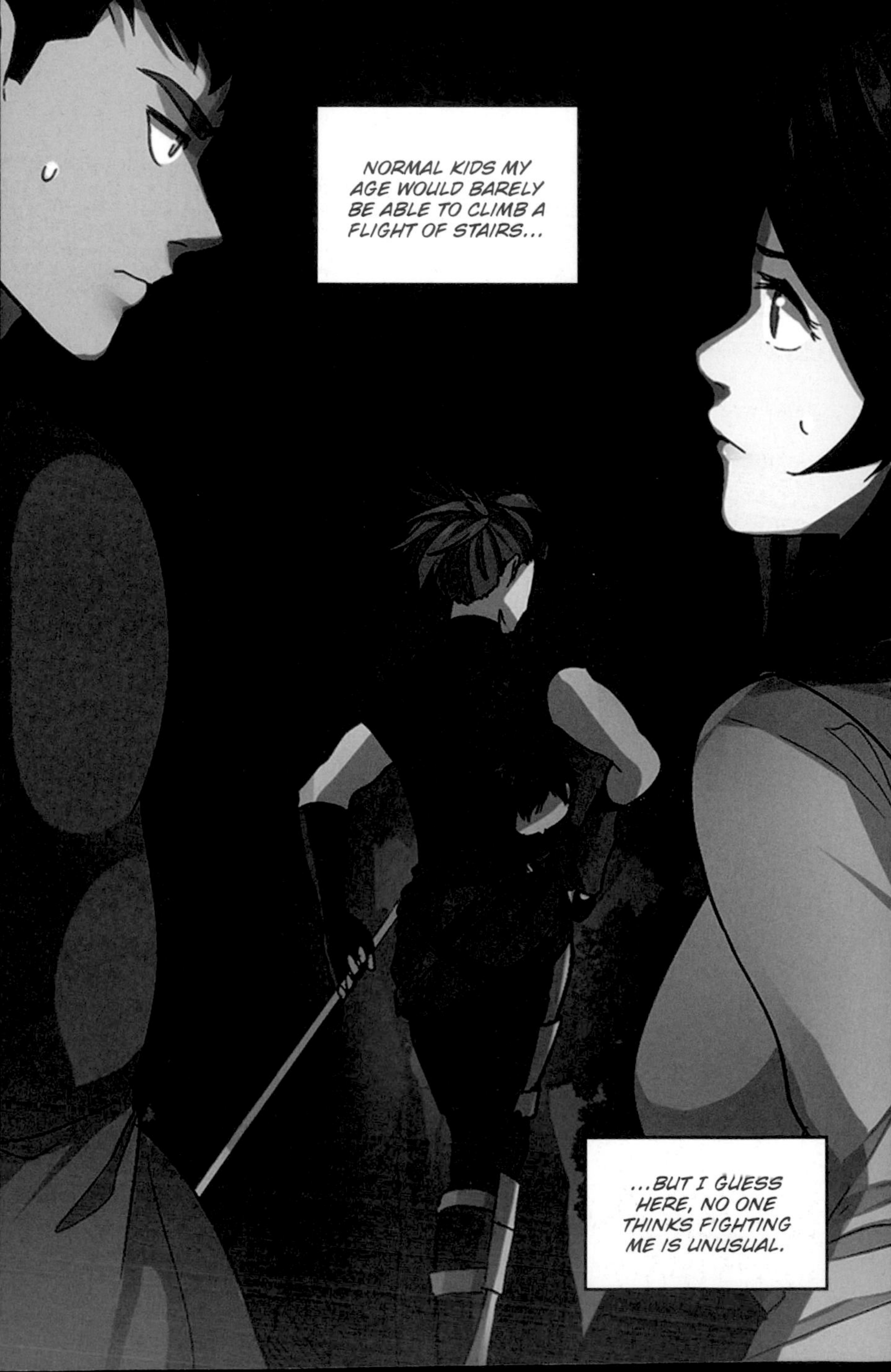
NORMAL KIDS MY AGE WOULD BARELY BE ABLE TO CLIMB A FLIGHT OF STAIRS...
...BUT I GUESS HERE, NO ONE THINKS FIGHTING ME IS UNUSUAL.

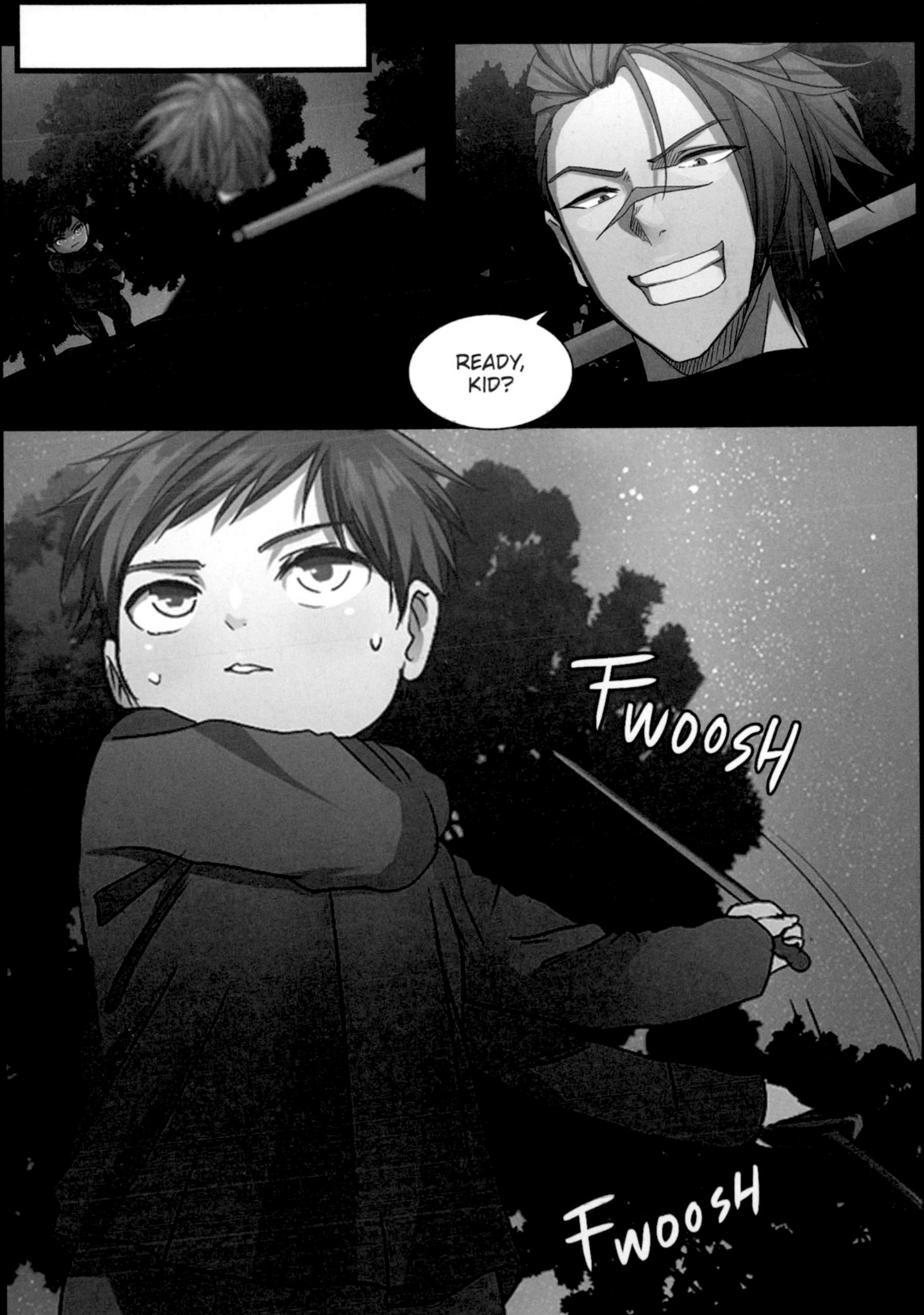
READY, KID?
FWOOSH
FWOOSH

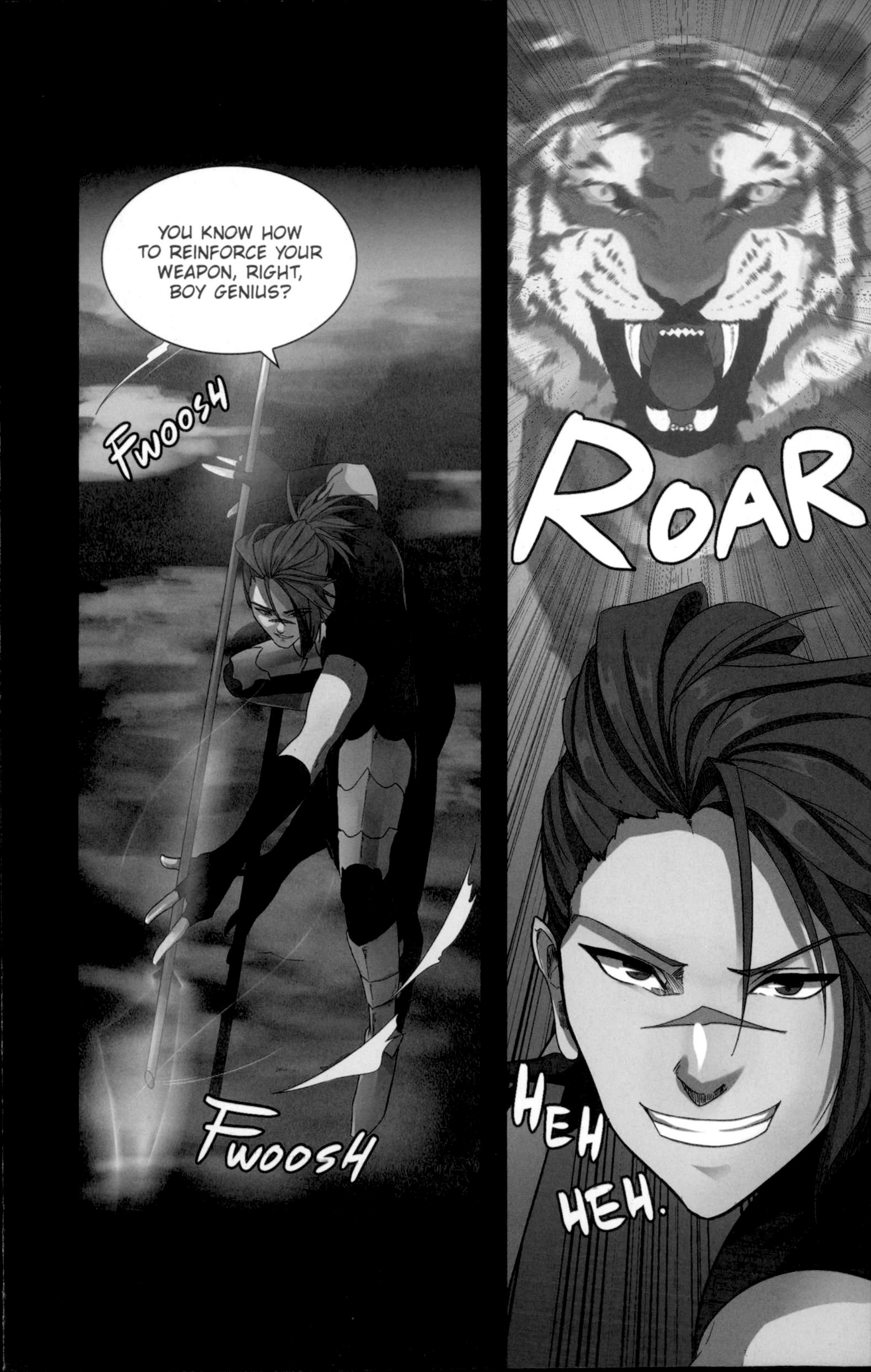

YOU KNOW HOW TO REINFORCE YOUR WEAPON, RIGHT, BOY GENIUS?
FWOOSH
FWOOSH
ROAR
HEH HEH.

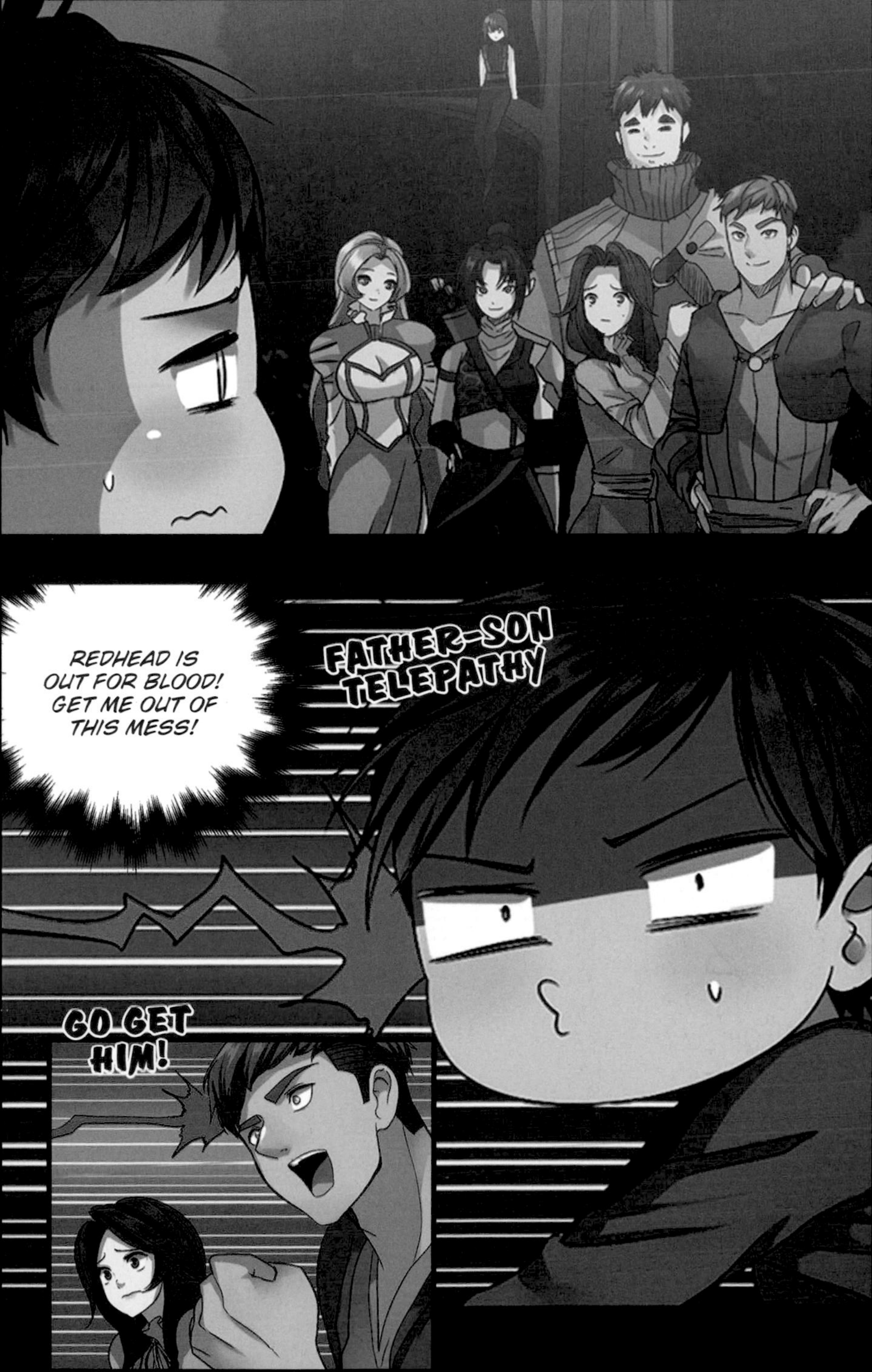
REDHEAD IS OUT FOR BLOOD! GET ME OUT OF THIS MESS!
FATHER-SON TELEPATHY
GO GET HIM!

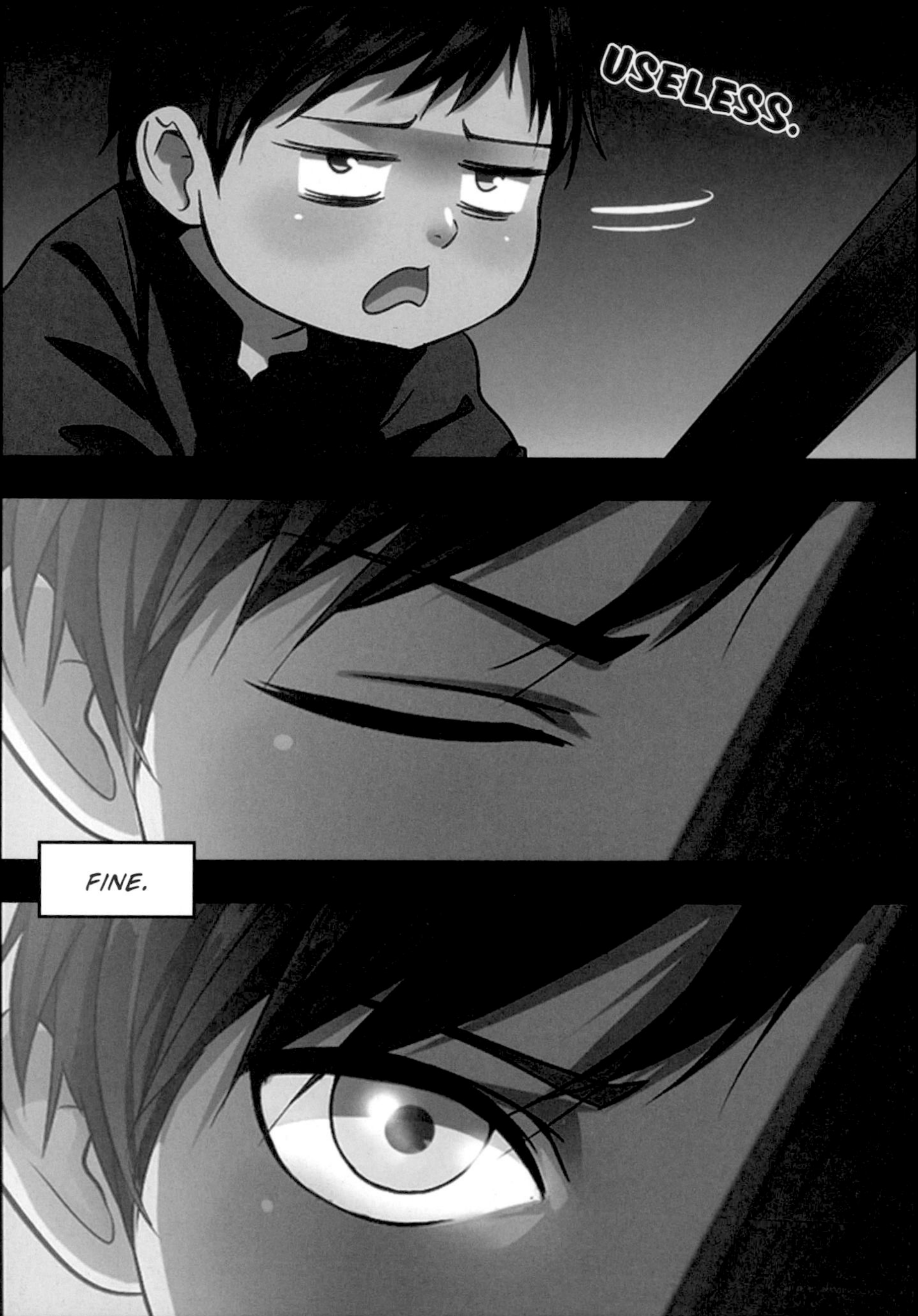
USELESS.
FINE.

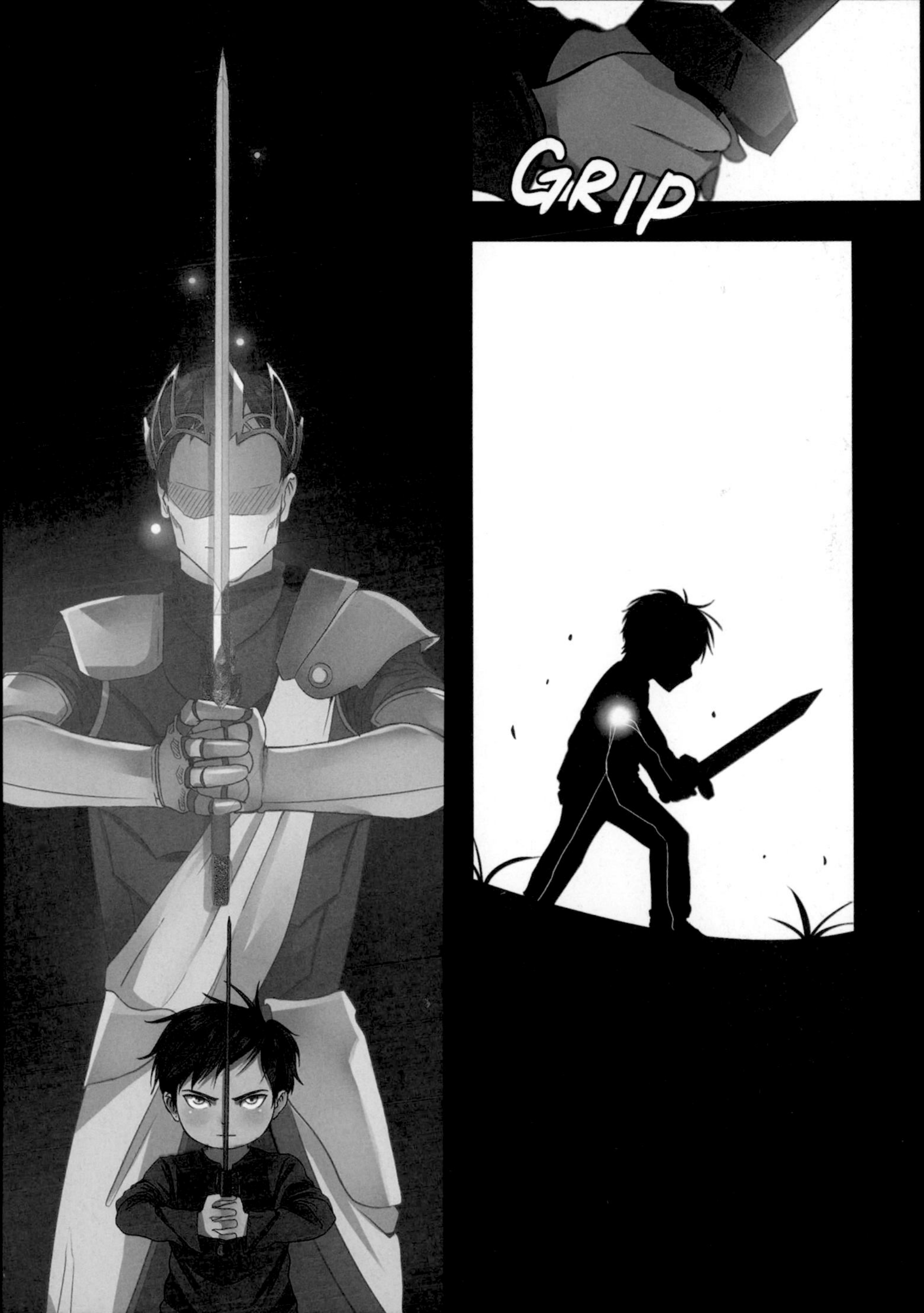
GRIP

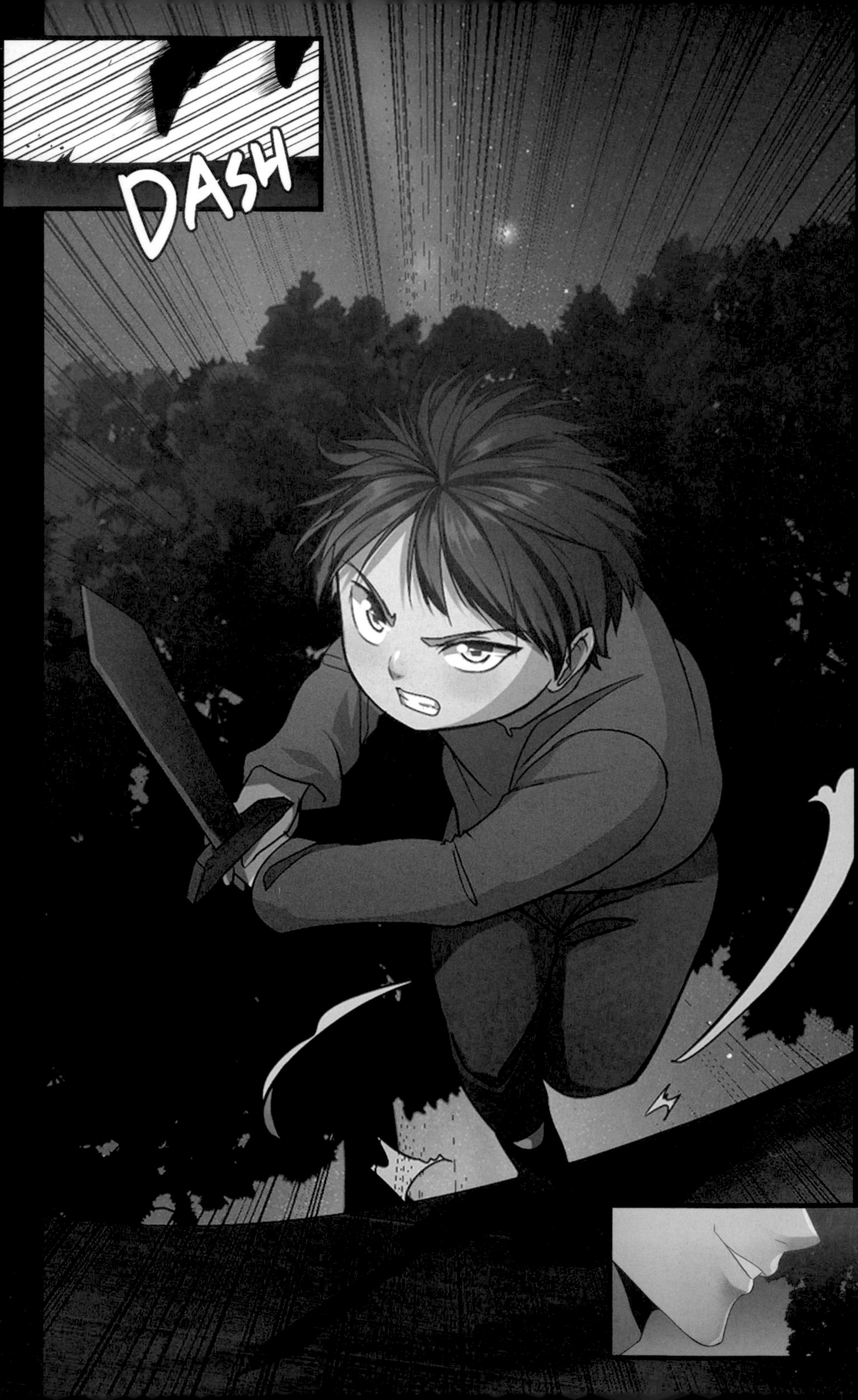
DASH

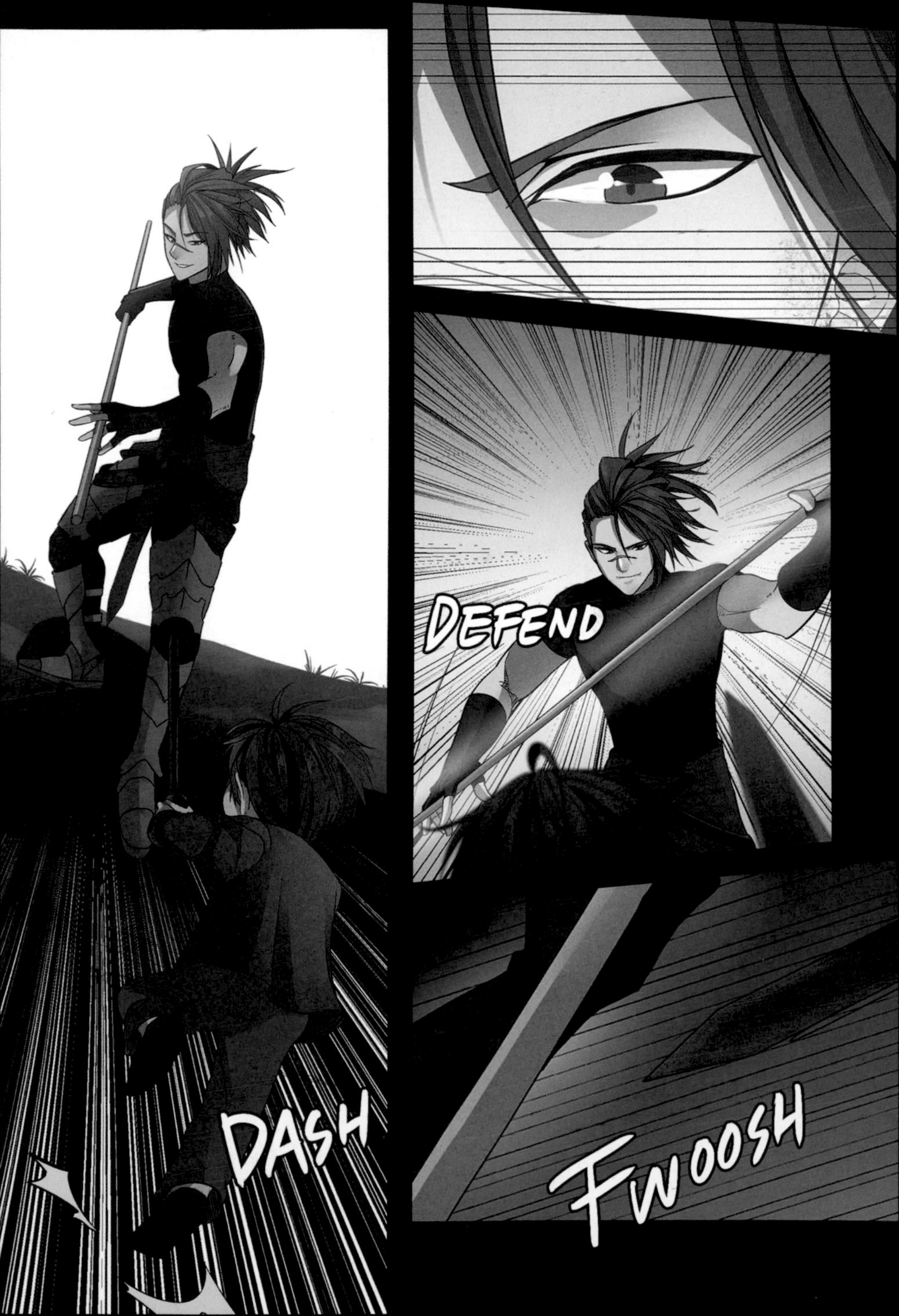
DASH
DEFEND
FWOOSH

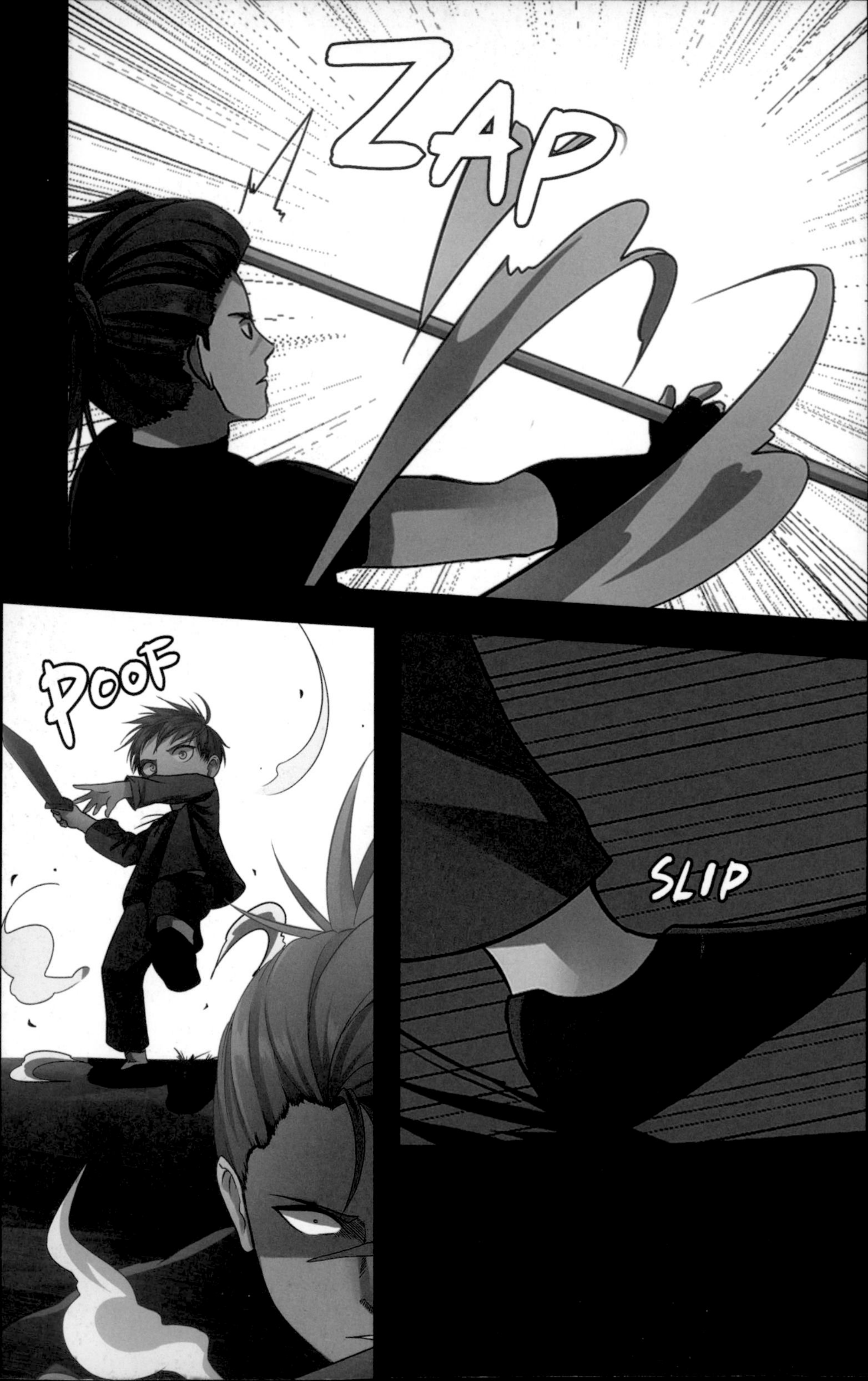
ZAP
POOF
SLIP

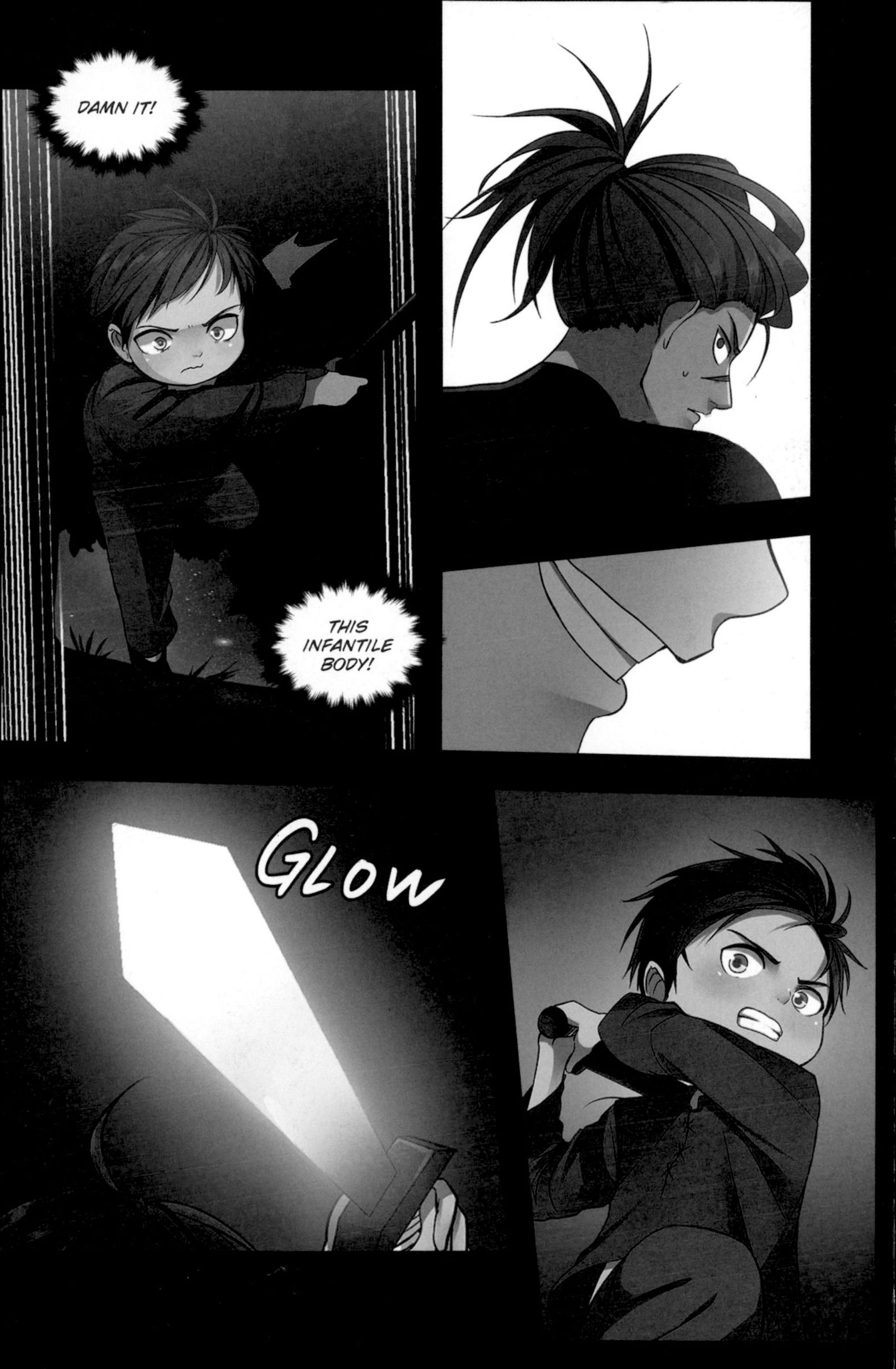
DAMN IT!
THIS INFANTILE BODY!
GLOW

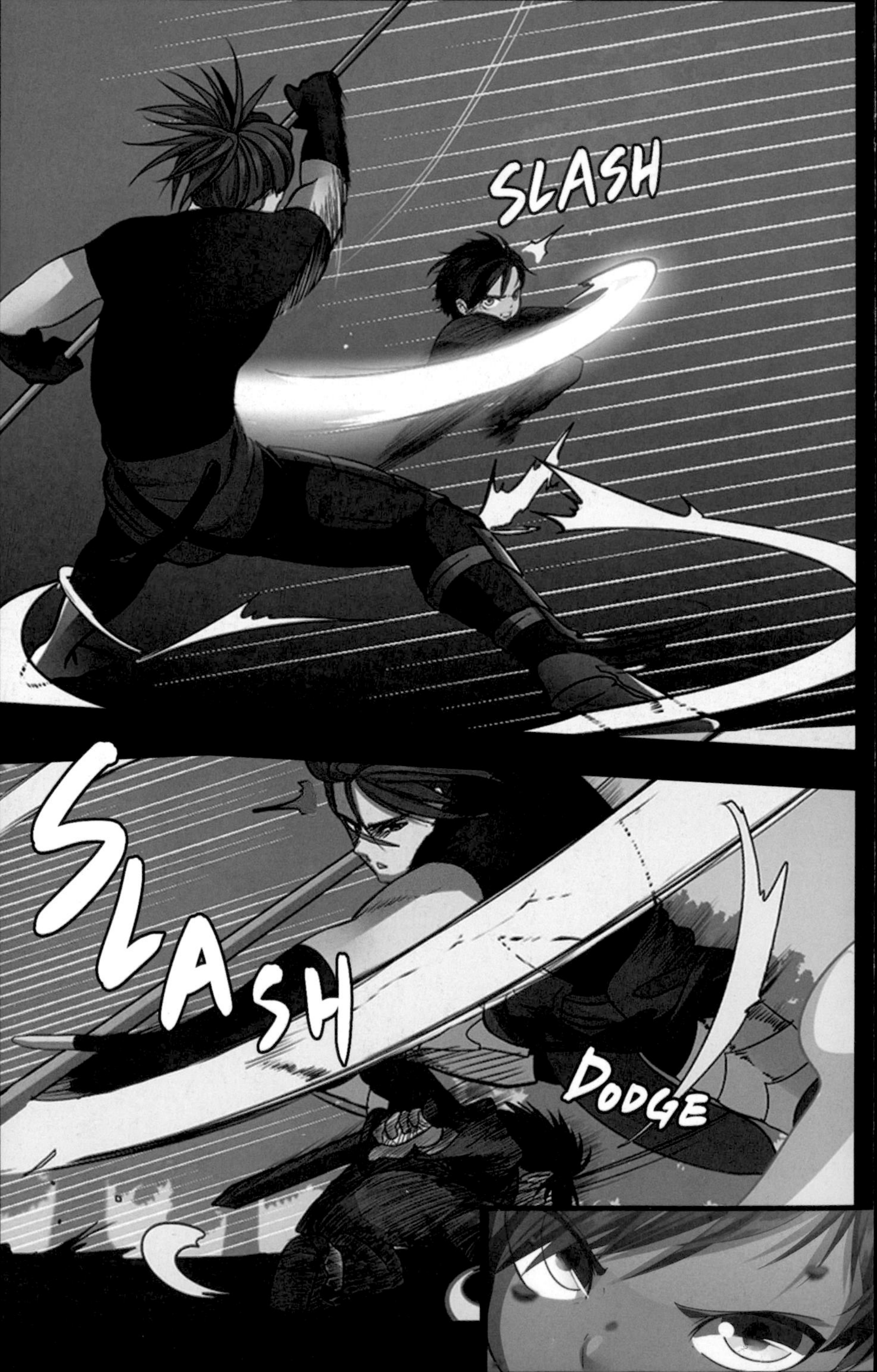
SLASH
SLASH
DODGE

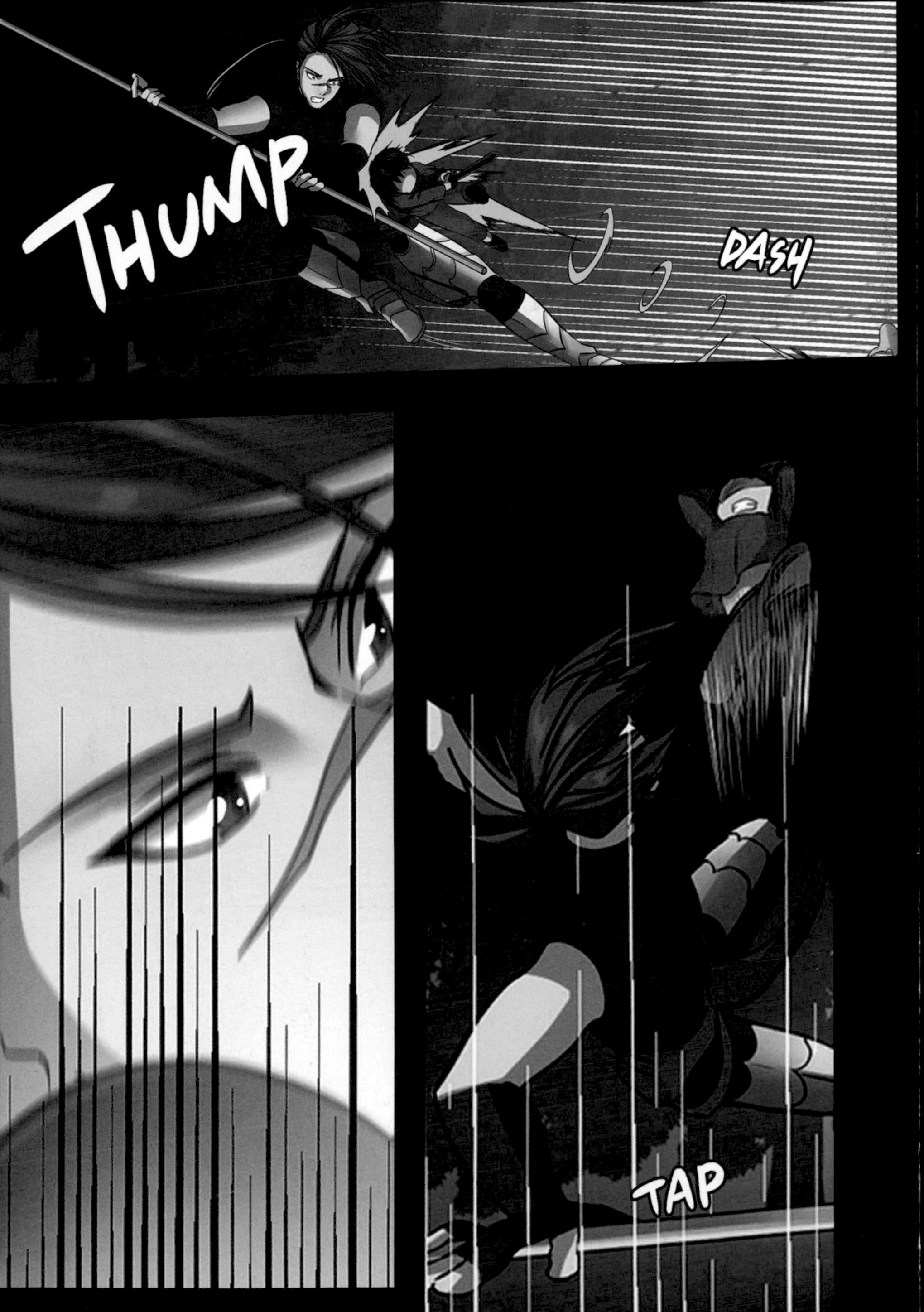
THUMP
DASH
TAP

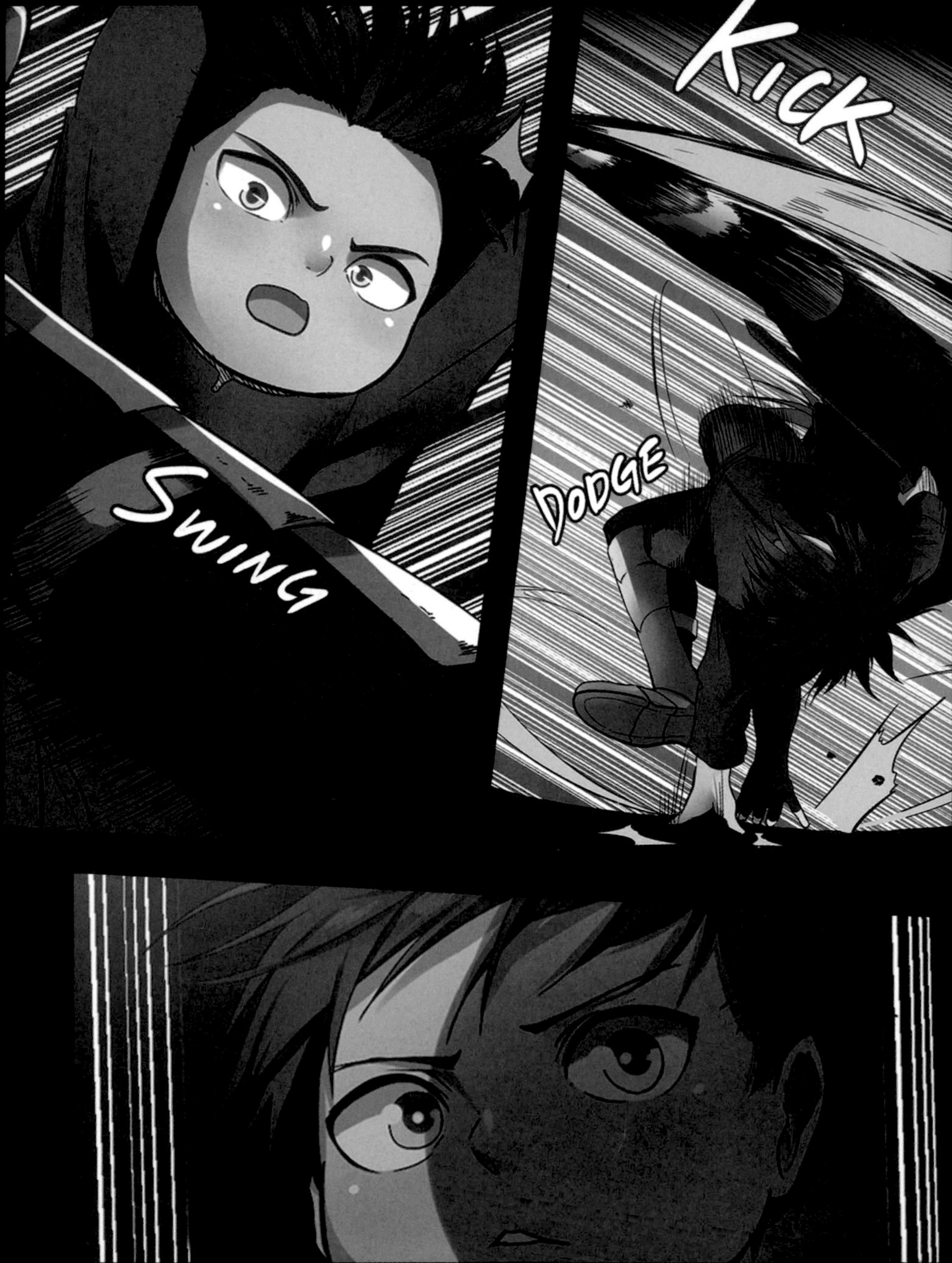
KICK
DODGE
SWING

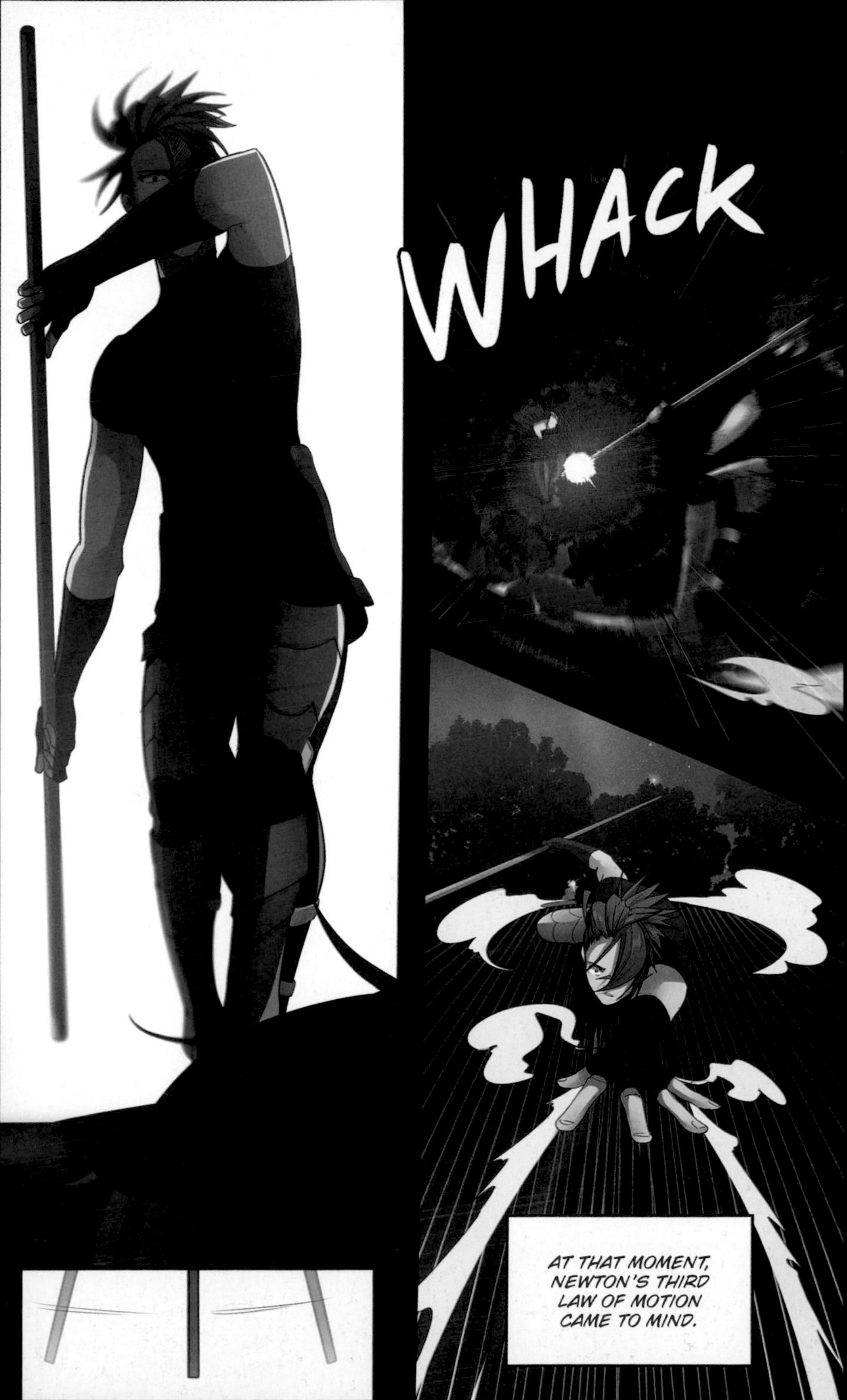
WHACK
AT THAT MOMENT, NEWTON'S THIRD LAW OF MOTION CAME TO MIND.

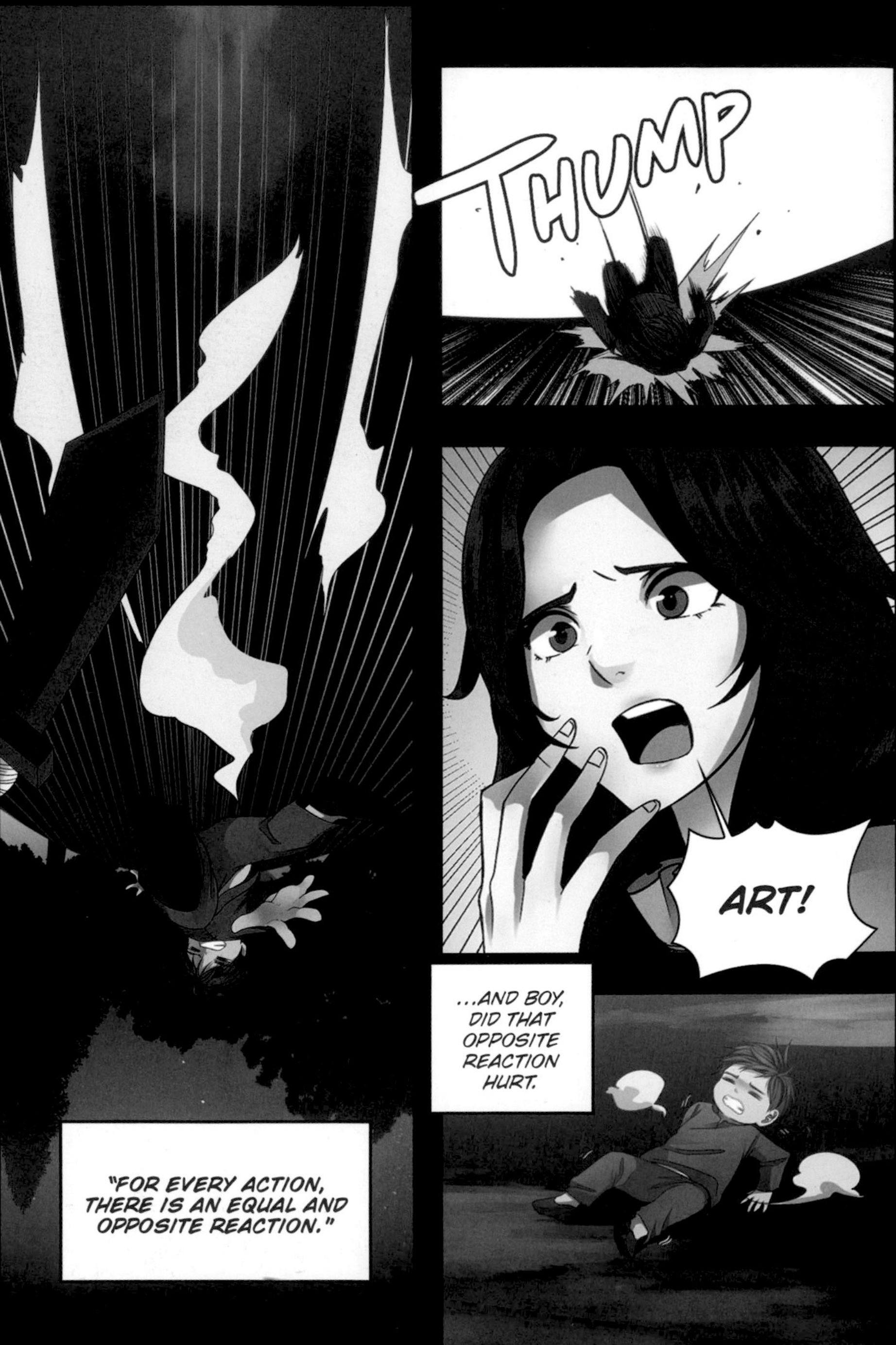

THUMP
ART!
...AND BOY, DID THAT OPPOSITE REACTION HURT.
"FOR EVERY ACTION, THERE IS AN EQUAL AND OPPOSITE REACTION."

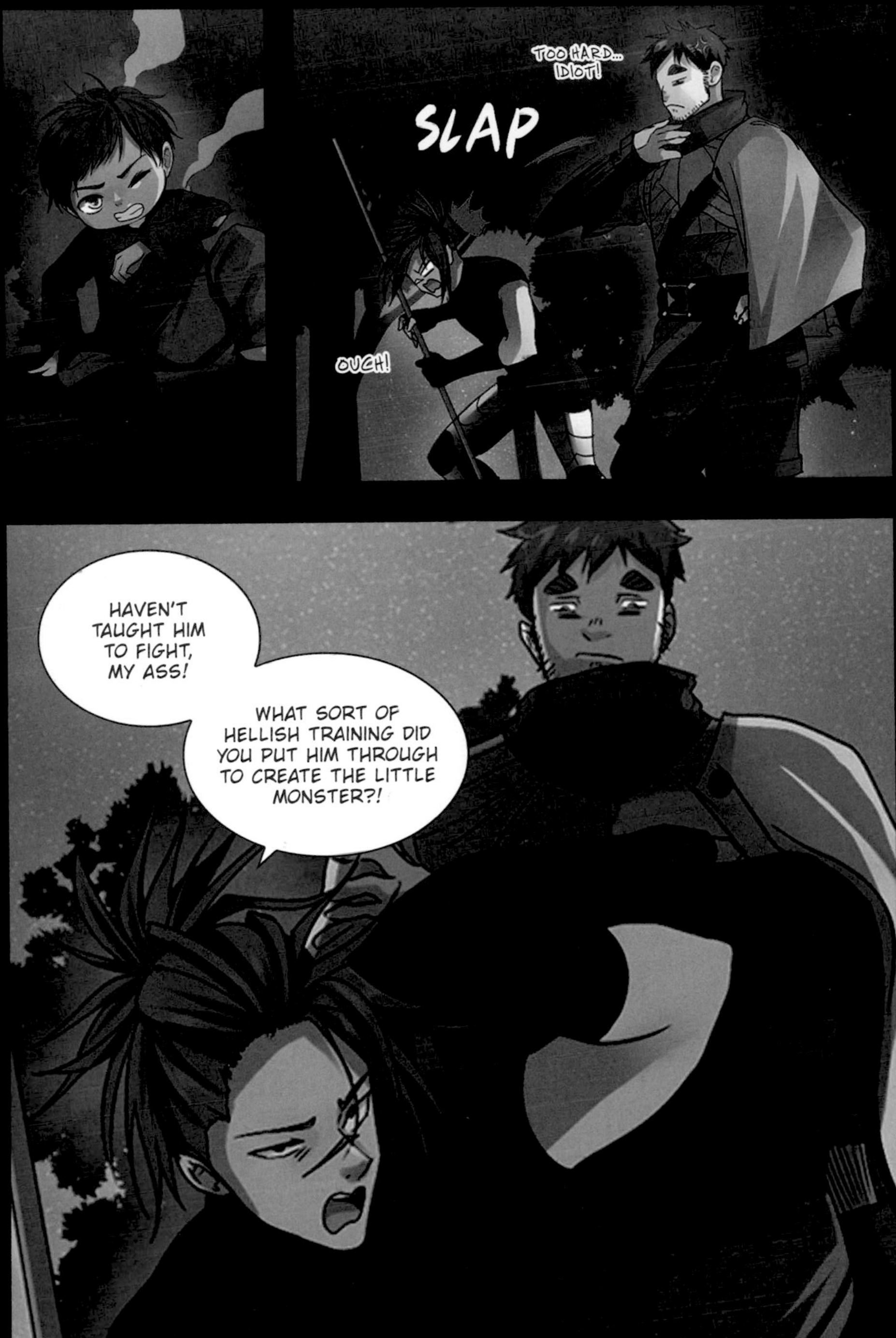
TOO HARD... IDIOT!
SLAP
OUCH!
HAVEN'T TAUGHT HIM TO FIGHT, MY ASS!
WHAT SORT OF HELLISH TRAINING DID YOU PUT HIM THROUGH TO CREATE THE LITTLE MONSTER?!

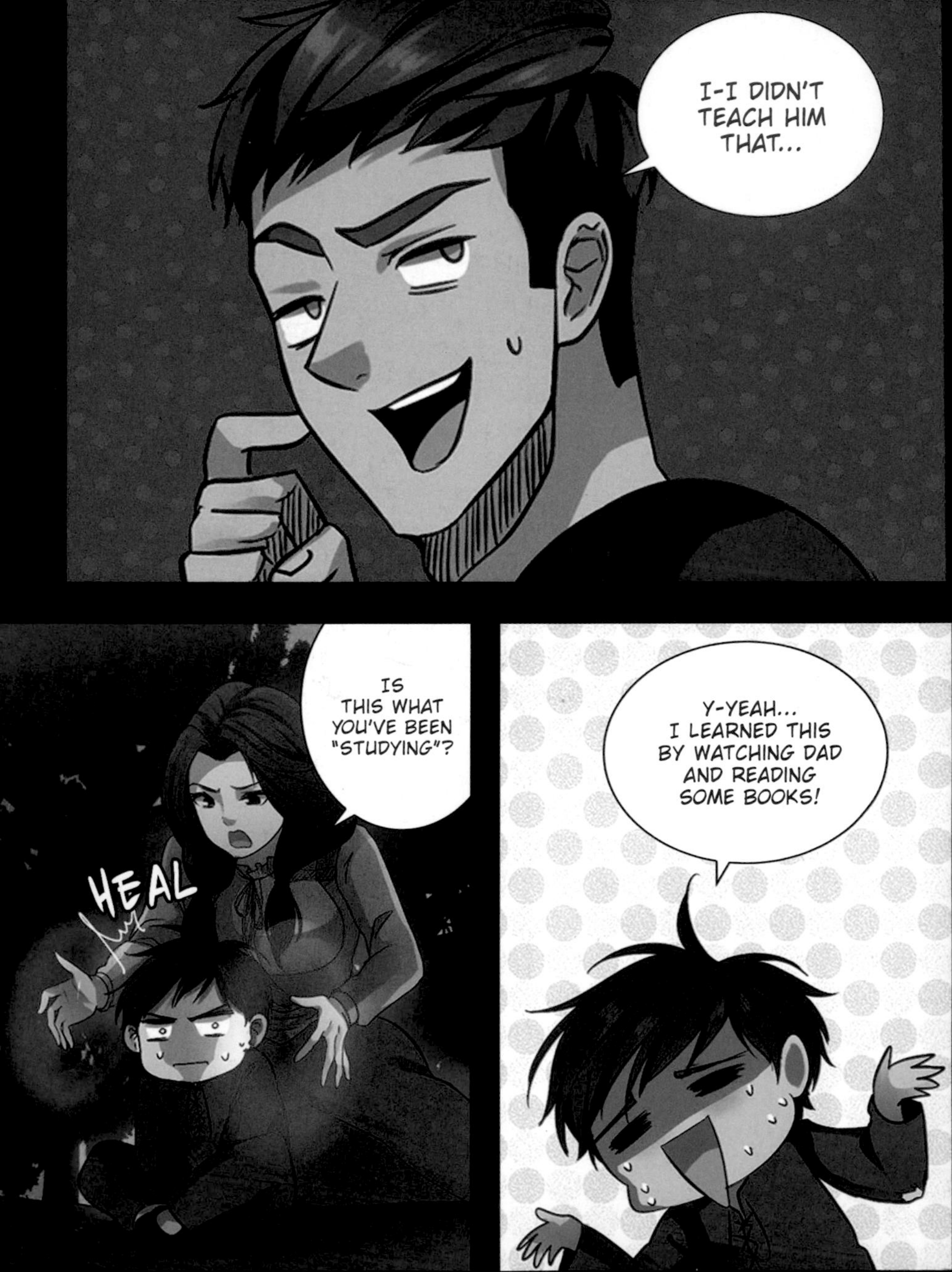
I-I DIDN'T TEACH HIM THAT...
IS THIS WHAT YOU'VE BEEN "STUDYING"?
HEAL
Y-YEAH... I LEARNED THIS BY WATCHING DAD AND READING SOME BOOKS!

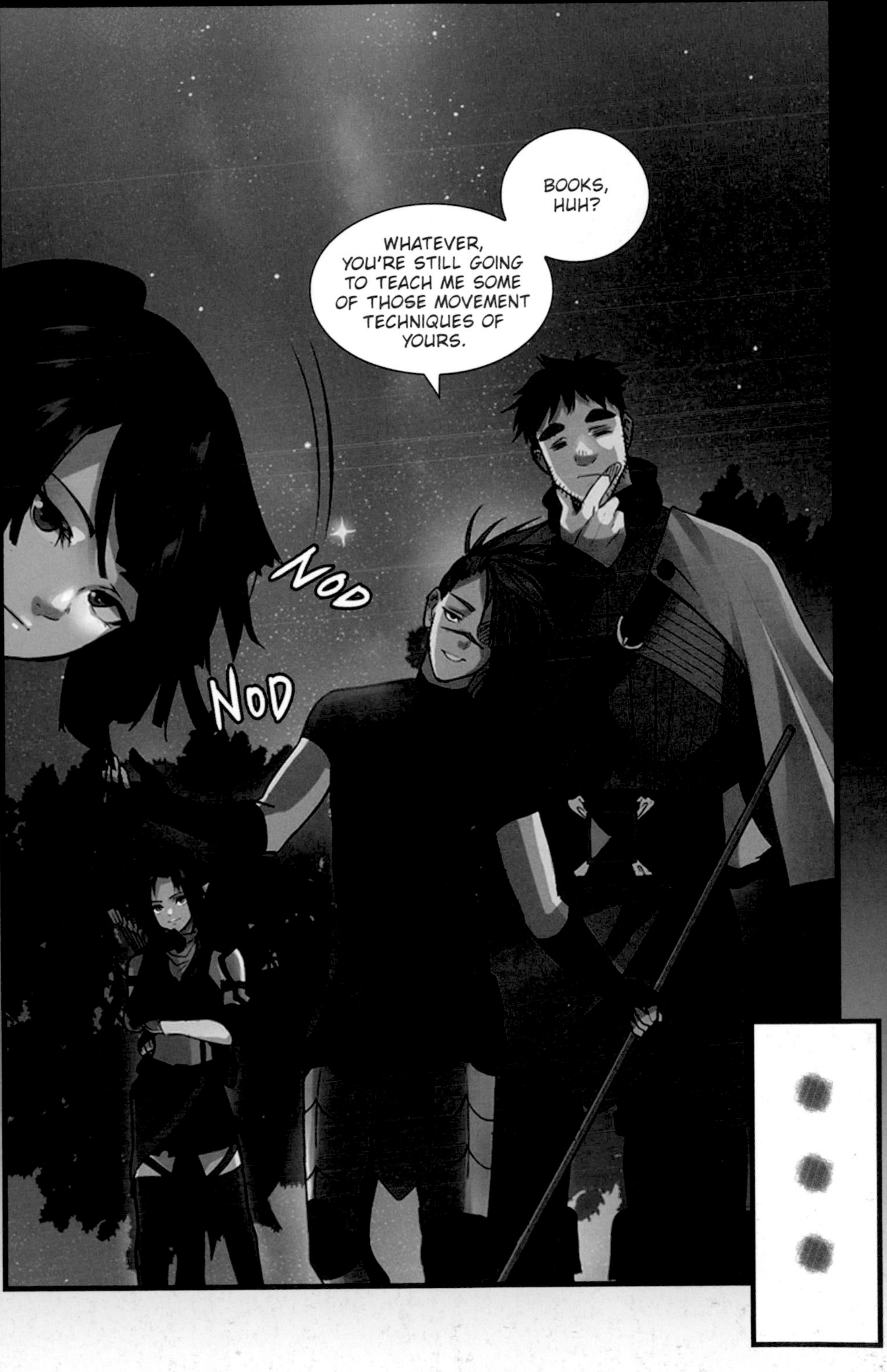
BOOKS, HUH?
WHATEVER, YOU'RE STILL GOING TO TEACH ME SOME OF THOSE MOVEMENT TECHNIQUES OF YOURS.
NOD
NOD

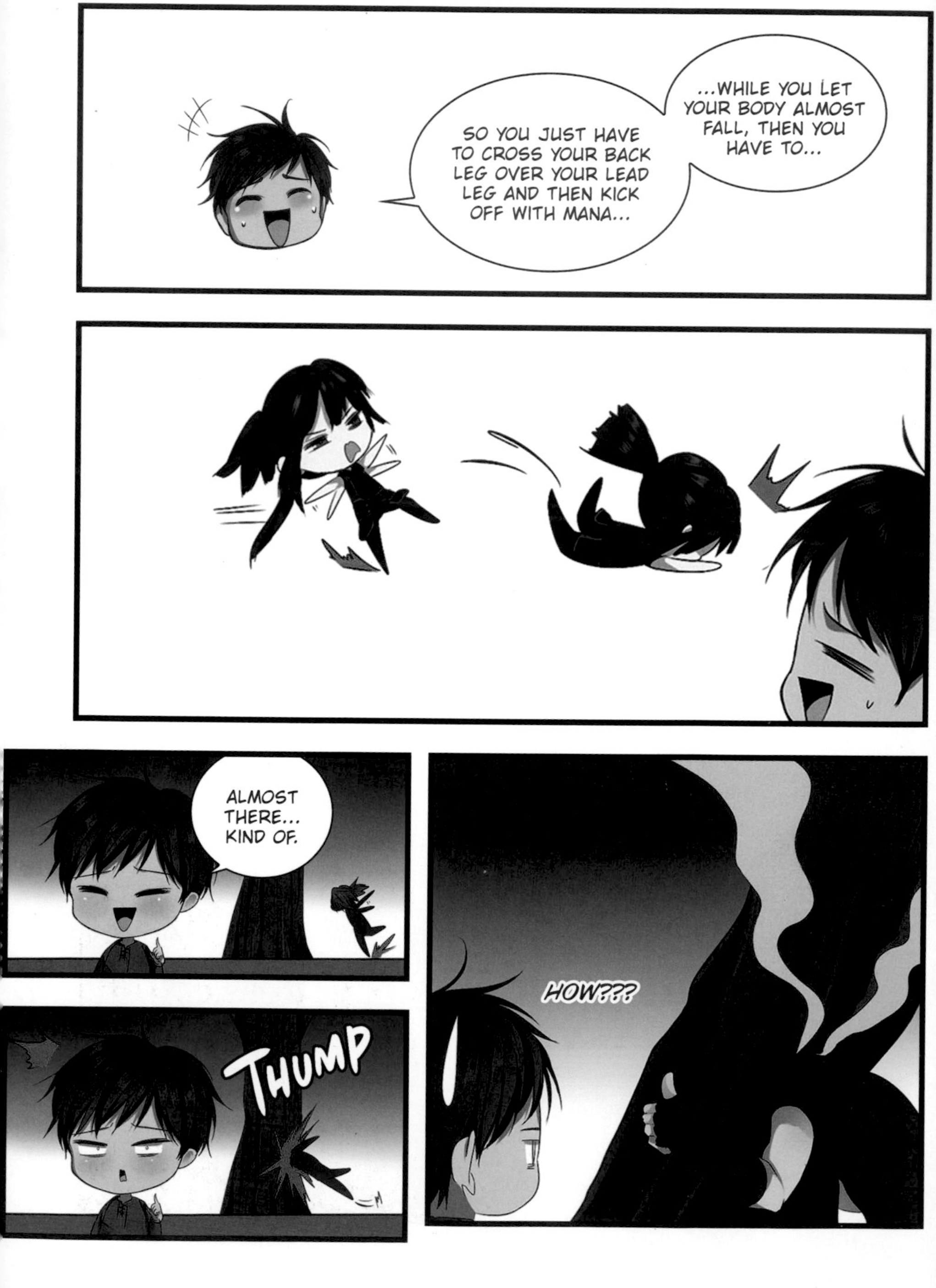

SO YOU JUST HAVE TO CROSS YOUR BACK LEG OVER YOUR LEAD LEG AND THEN KICK OFF WITH MANA...
...WHILE YOU LET YOUR BODY ALMOST FALL, THEN YOU HAVE TO...
ALMOST THERE... KIND OF.
THUMP
HOW???

THE
BEGINNING
AFTER
THE
END

CHAPTER 8—Ambush

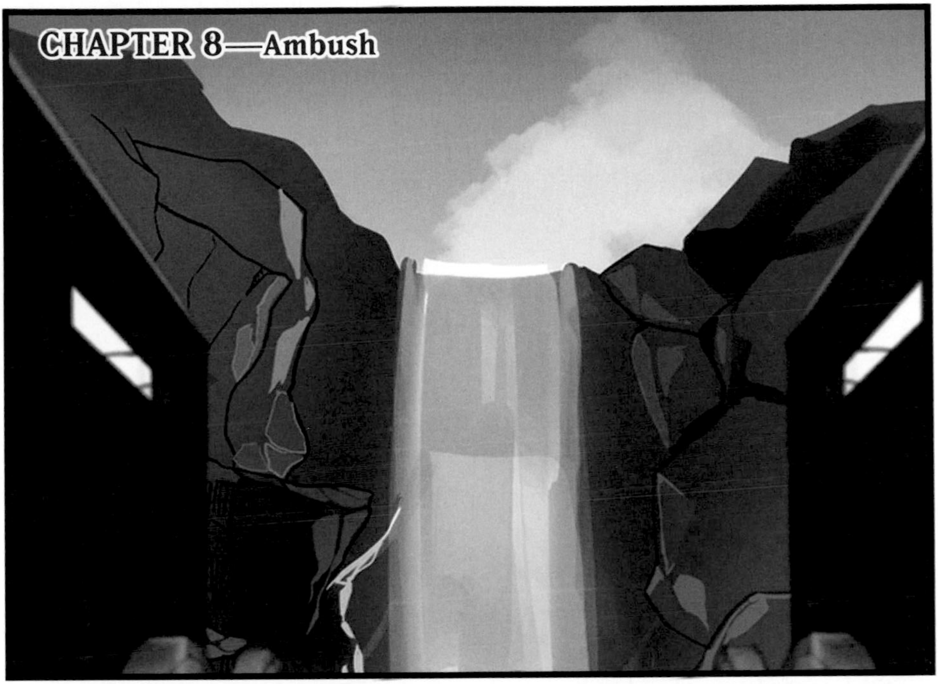

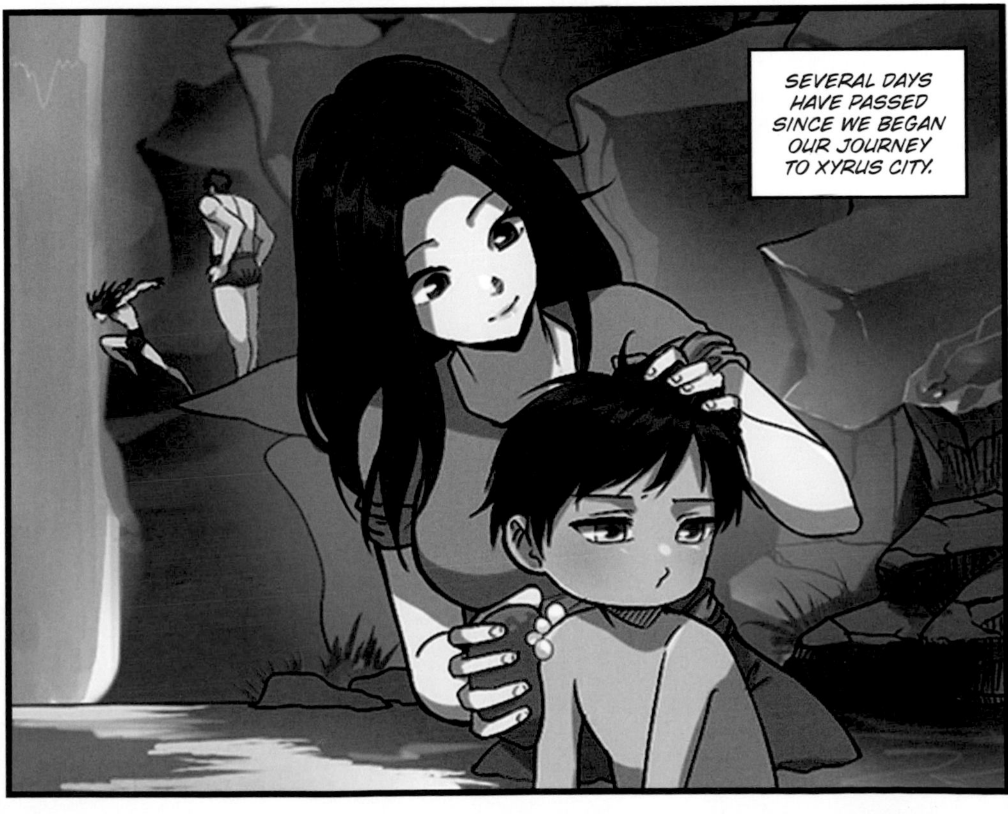
SEVERAL DAYS HAVE PASSED SINCE WE BEGAN OUR JOURNEY TO XYRUS CITY.

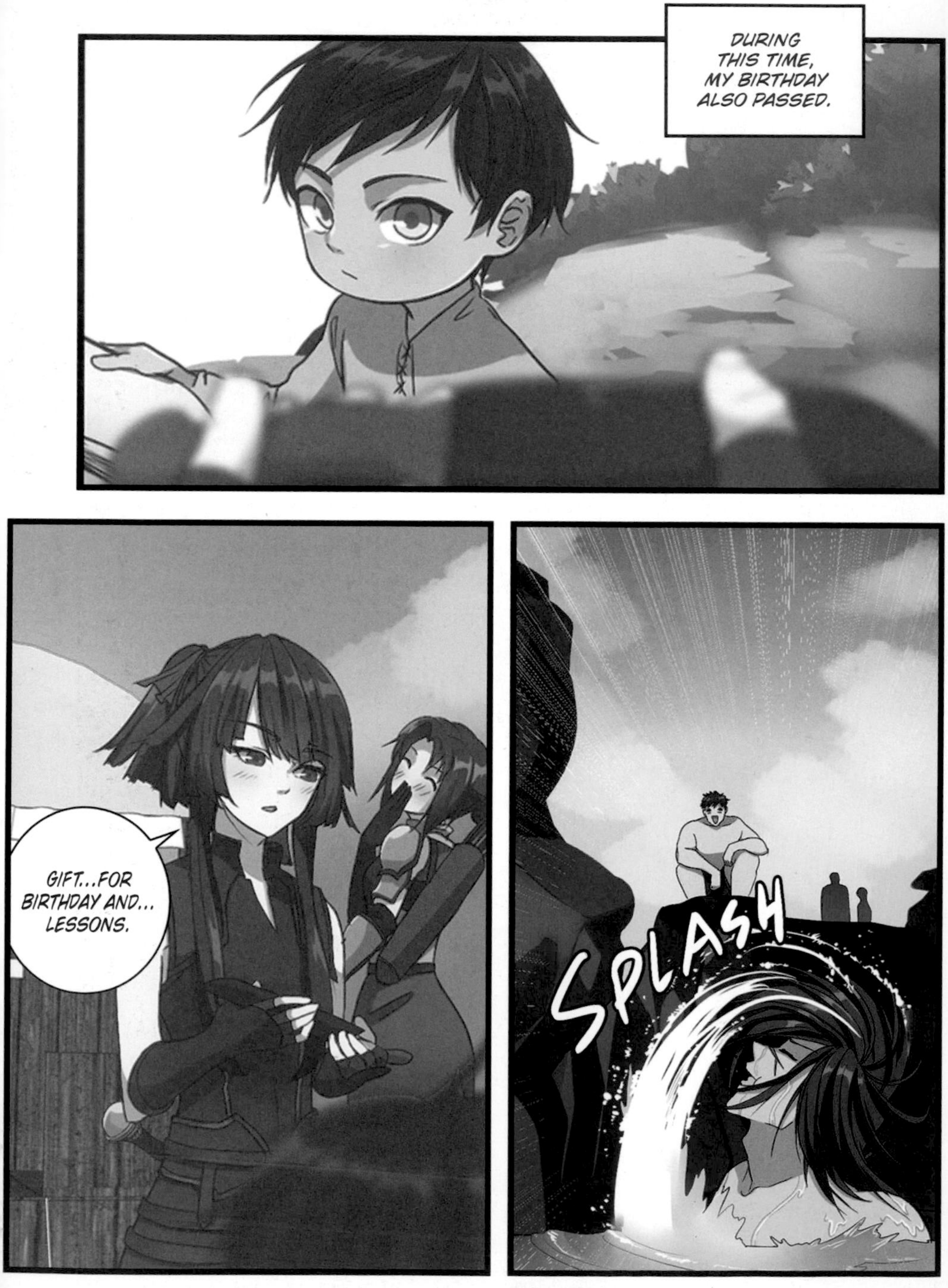
DURING THIS TIME, MY BIRTHDAY ALSO PASSED.
GIFT...FOR BIRTHDAY AND... LESSONS.
SPLASH

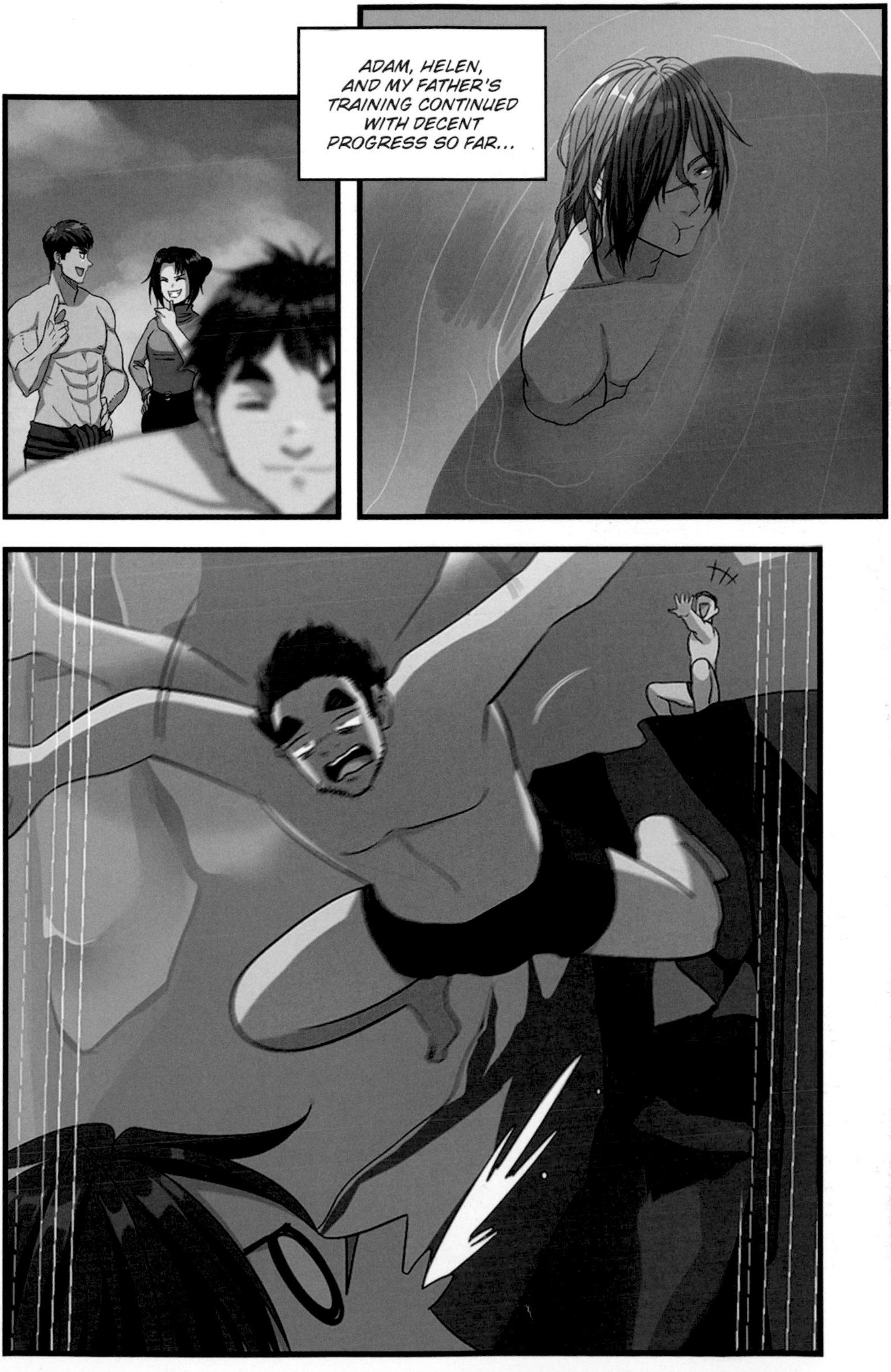
ADAM, HELEN, AND MY FATHER'S TRAINING CONTINUED WITH DECENT PROGRESS SO FAR...

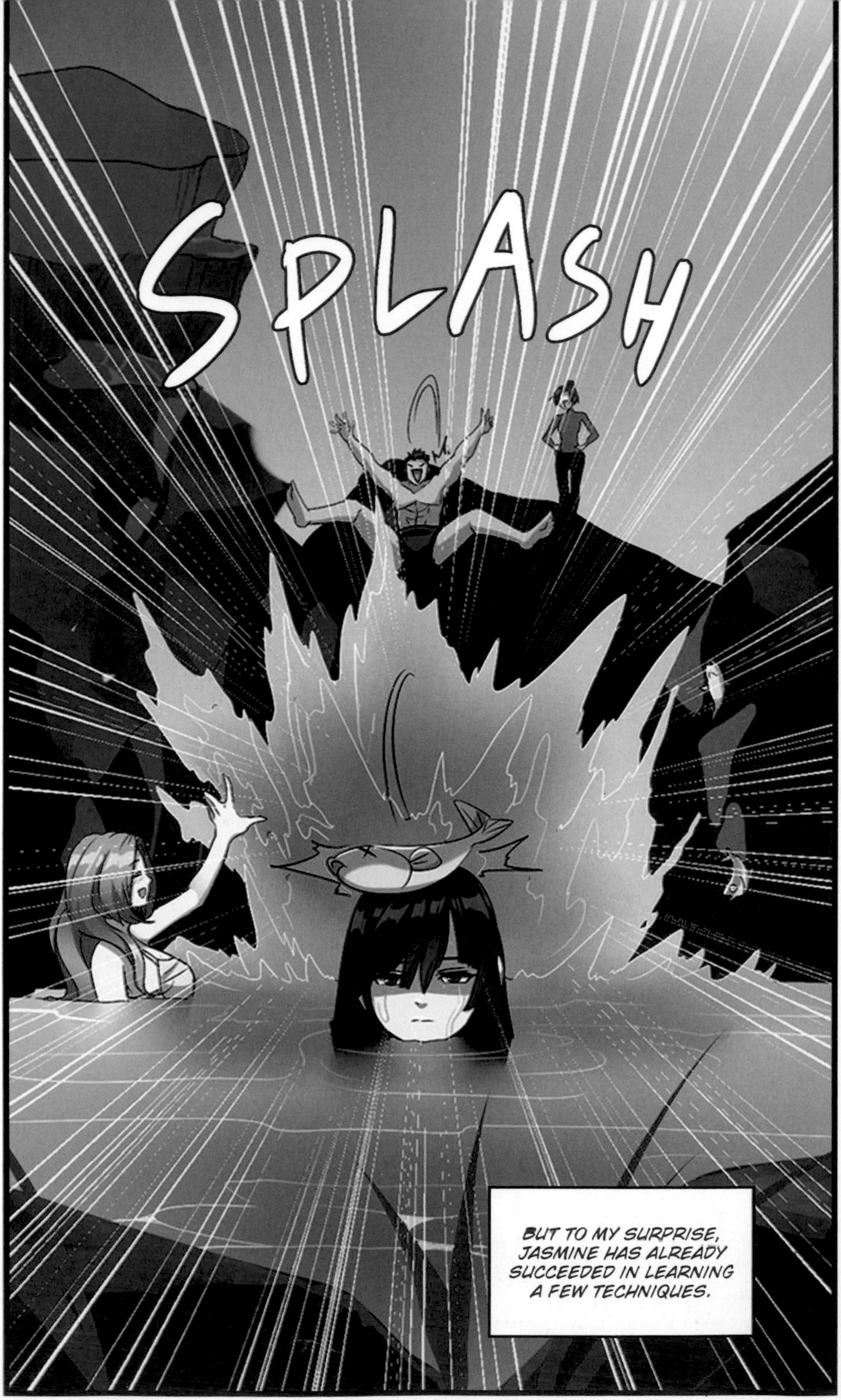
SPLASH
BUT TO MY SURPRISE, JASMINE HAS ALREADY SUCCEEDED IN LEARNING A FEW TECHNIQUES.

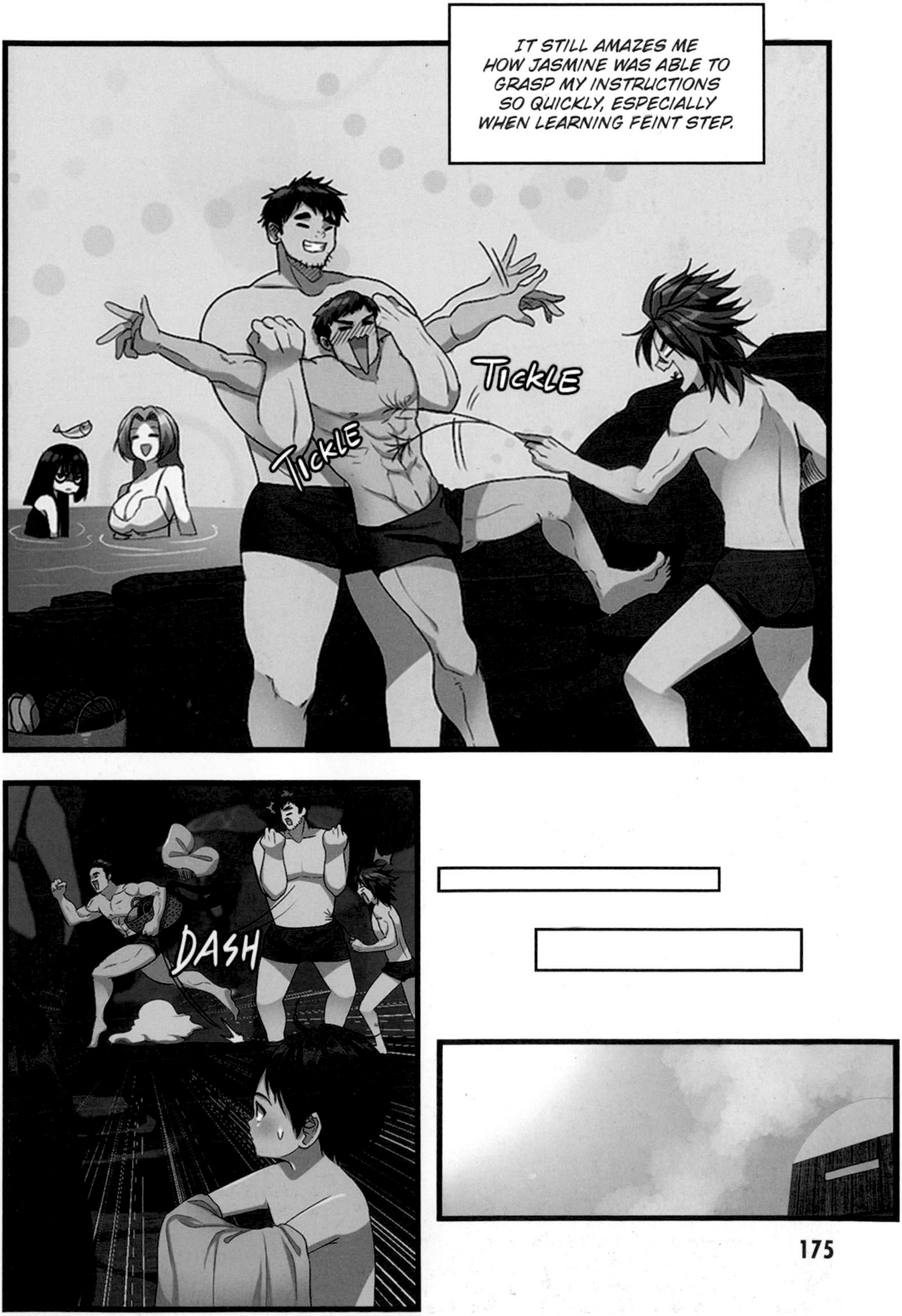
IT STILL AMAZES ME HOW JASMINE WAS ABLE TO GRASP MY INSTRUCTIONS SO QUICKLY, ESPECIALLY WHEN LEARNING FEINT STEP.
TICKLE
TICKLE
DASH

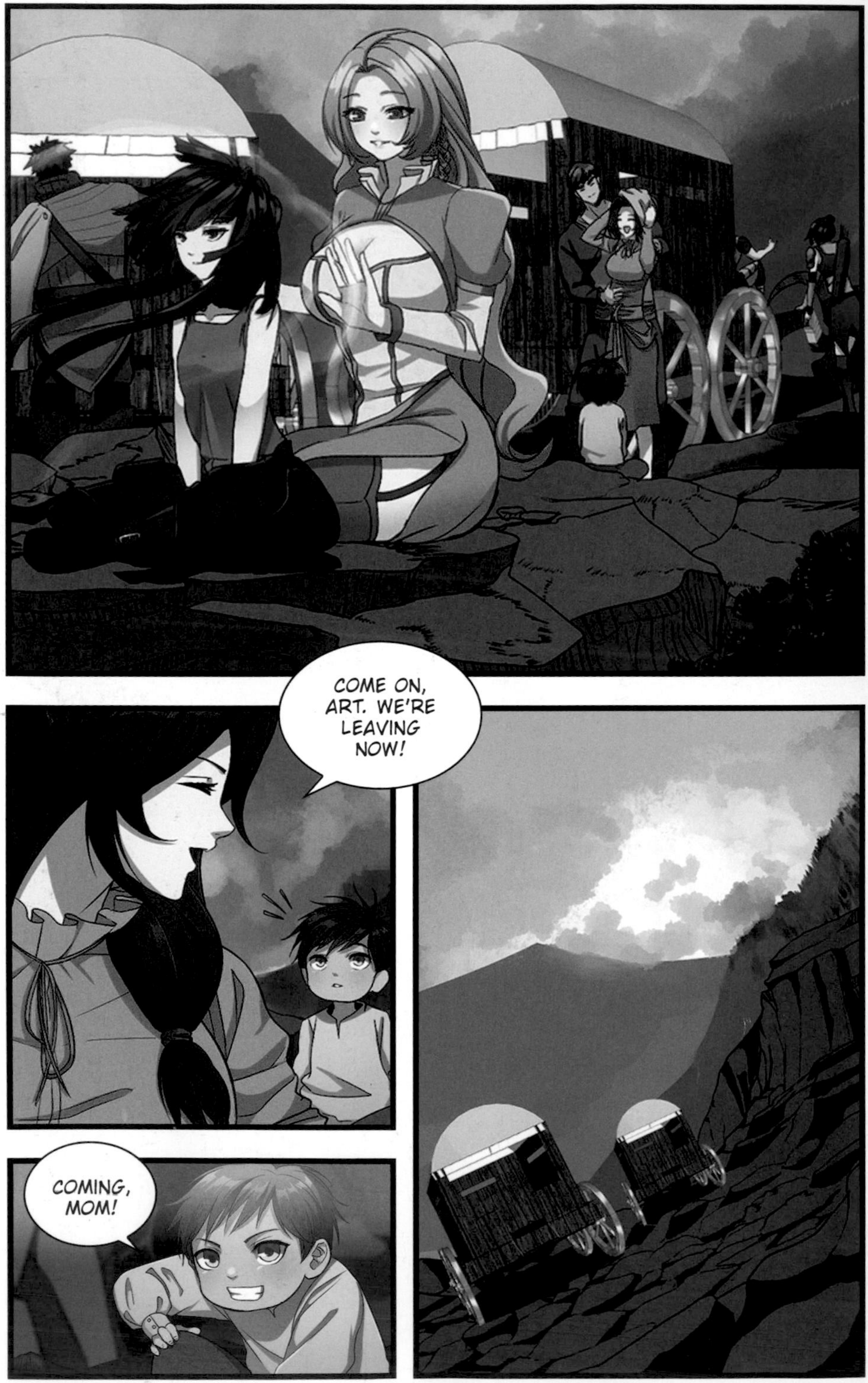
COME ON, ART. WE'RE LEAVING NOW!
COMING, MOM!

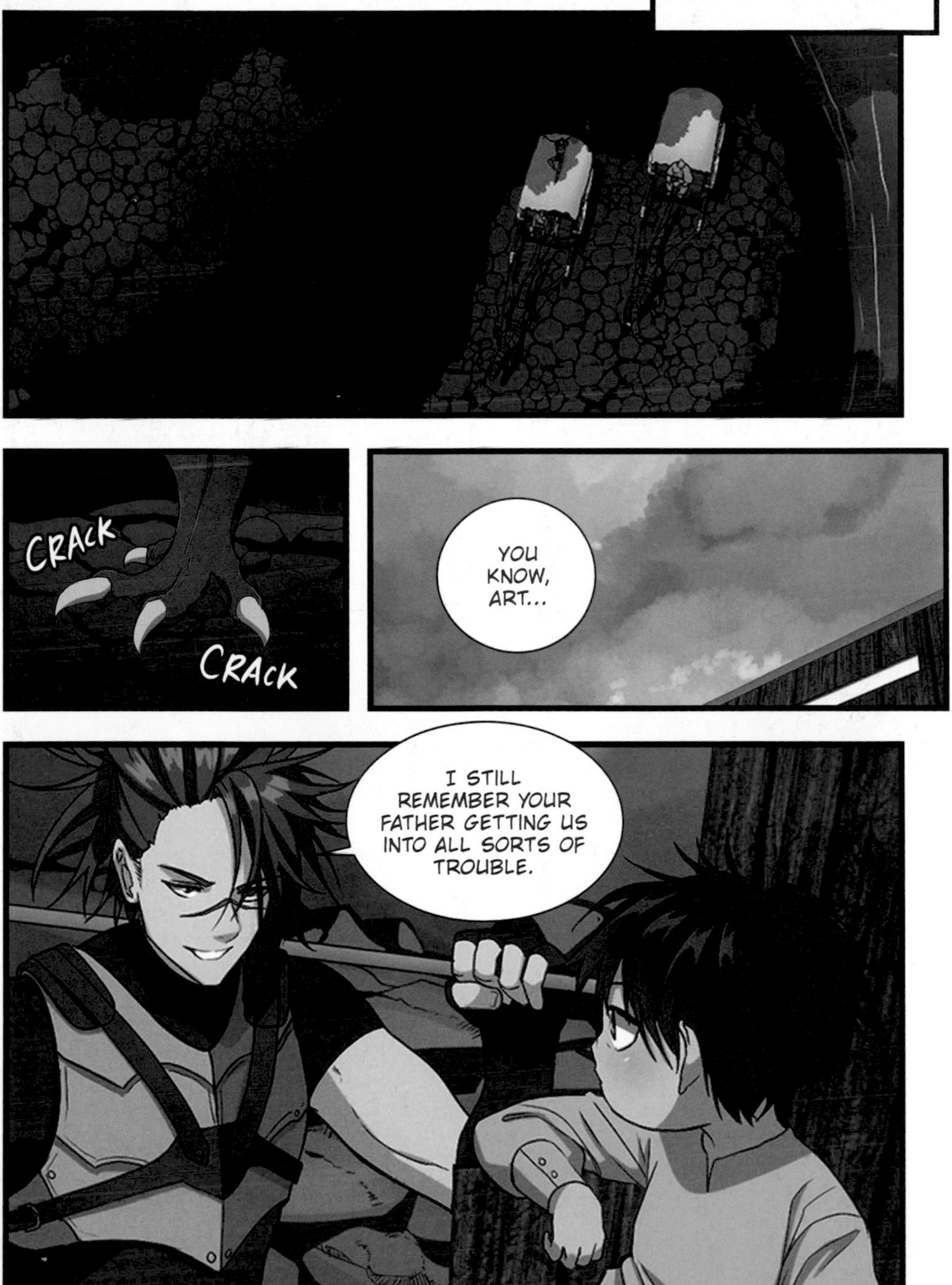
CRACK
CRACK
YOU KNOW, ART...
I STILL REMEMBER YOUR FATHER GETTING US INTO ALL SORTS OF TROUBLE.

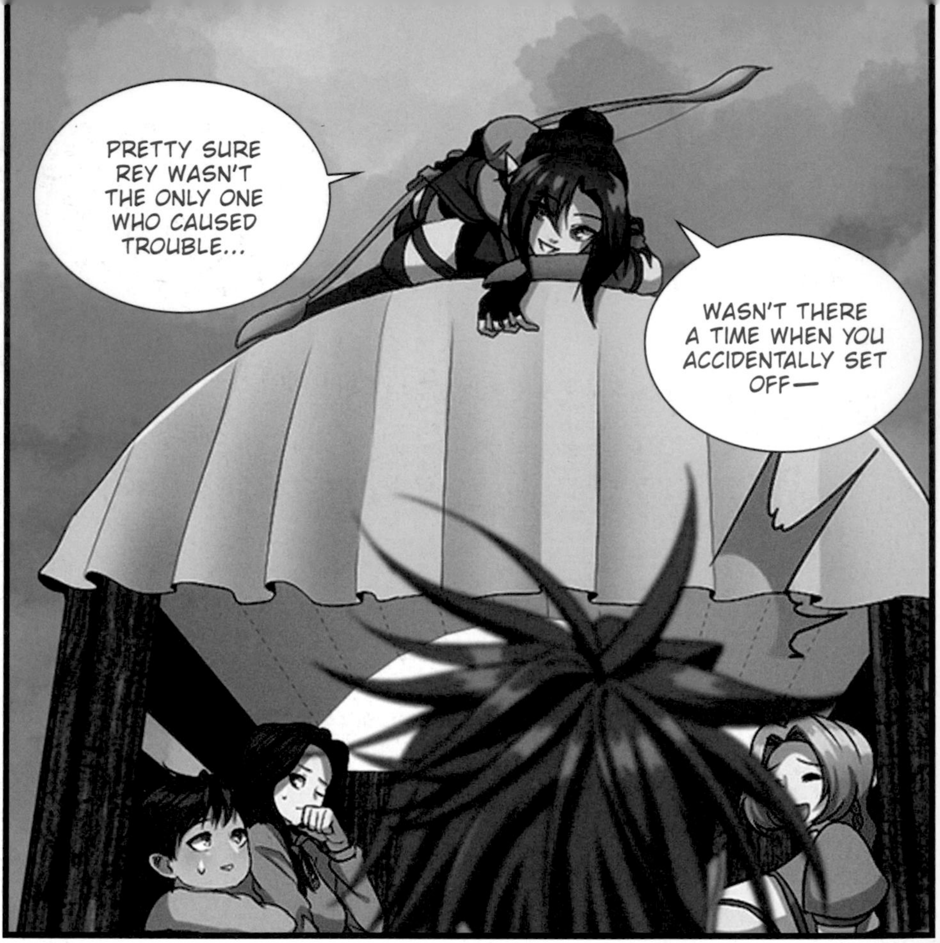
PRETTY SURE REY WASN'T THE ONLY ONE WHO CAUSED TROUBLE...
WASN'T THERE A TIME WHEN YOU ACCIDENTALLY SET OFF—

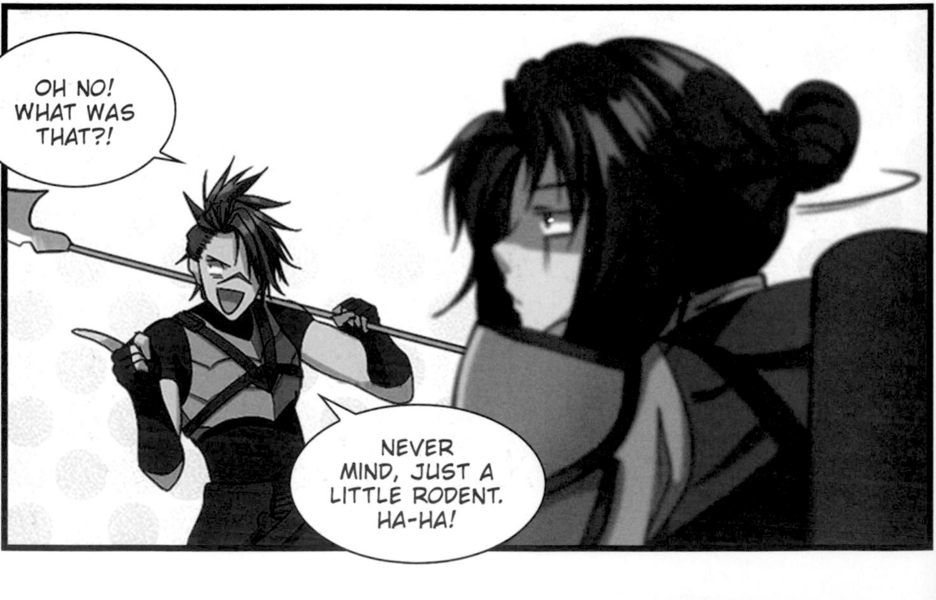
OH NO! WHAT WAS THAT?!
NEVER MIND, JUST A LITTLE RODENT. HA-HA!

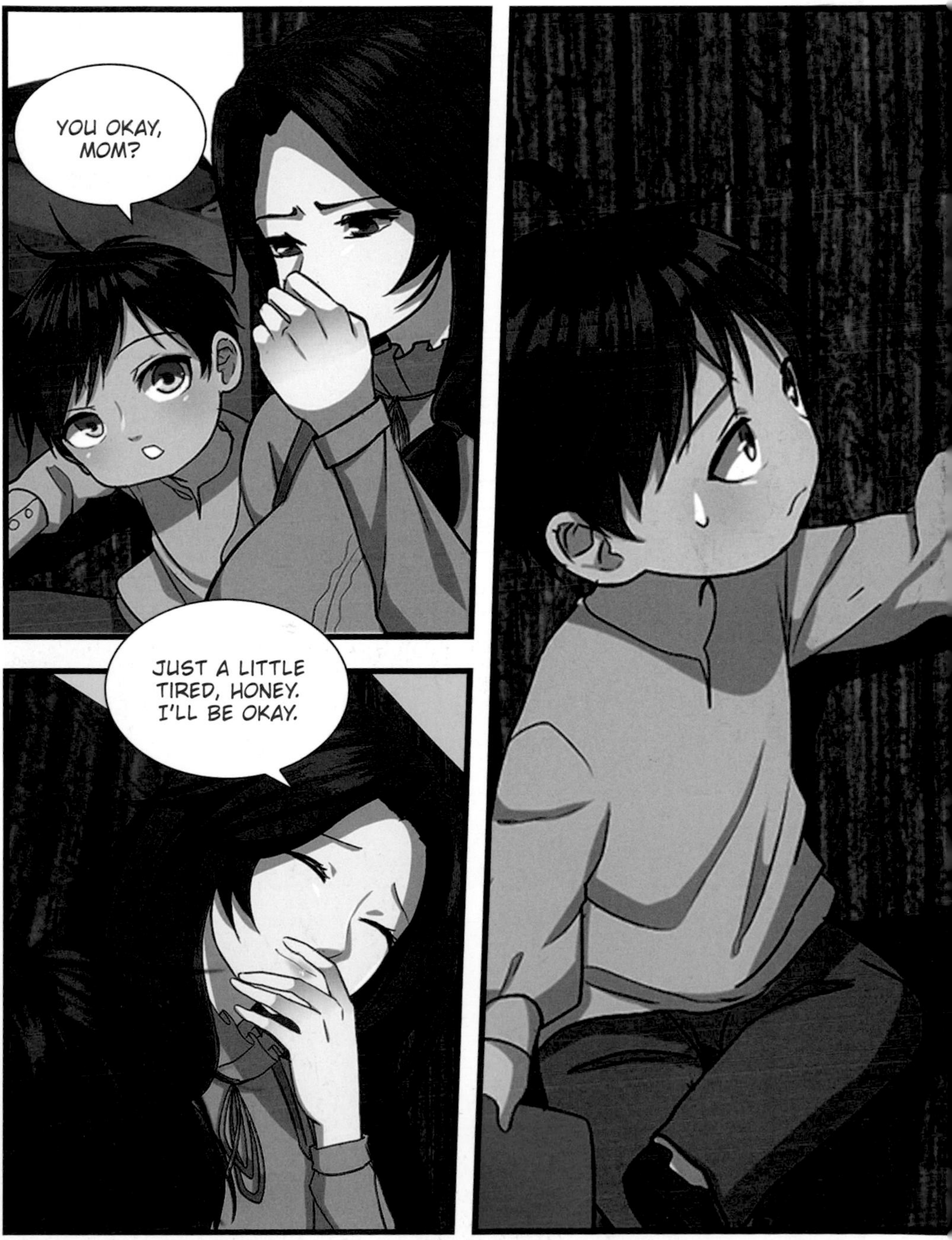
YOU OKAY, MOM?
JUST A LITTLE TIRED, HONEY. I'LL BE OKAY.

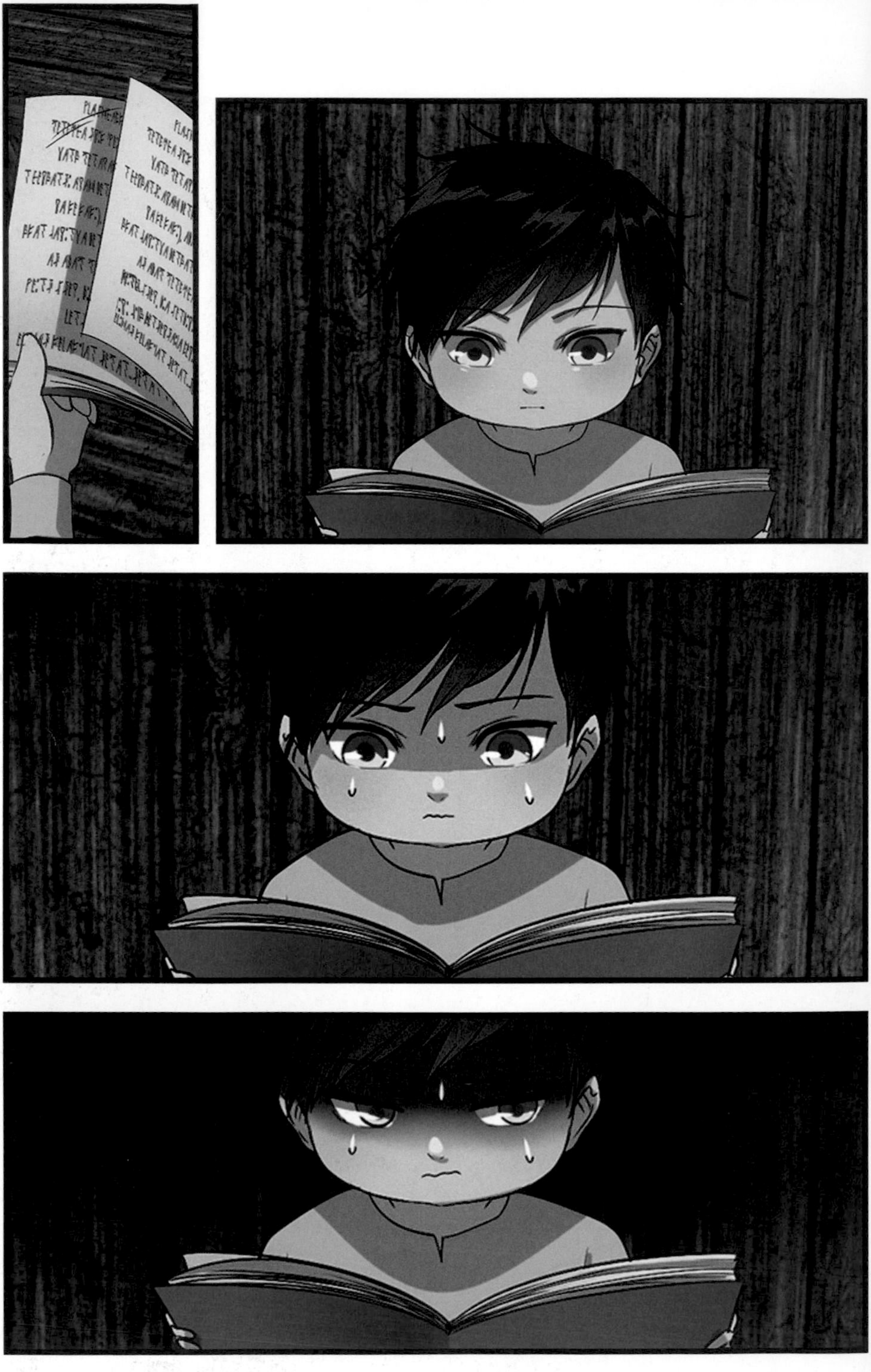

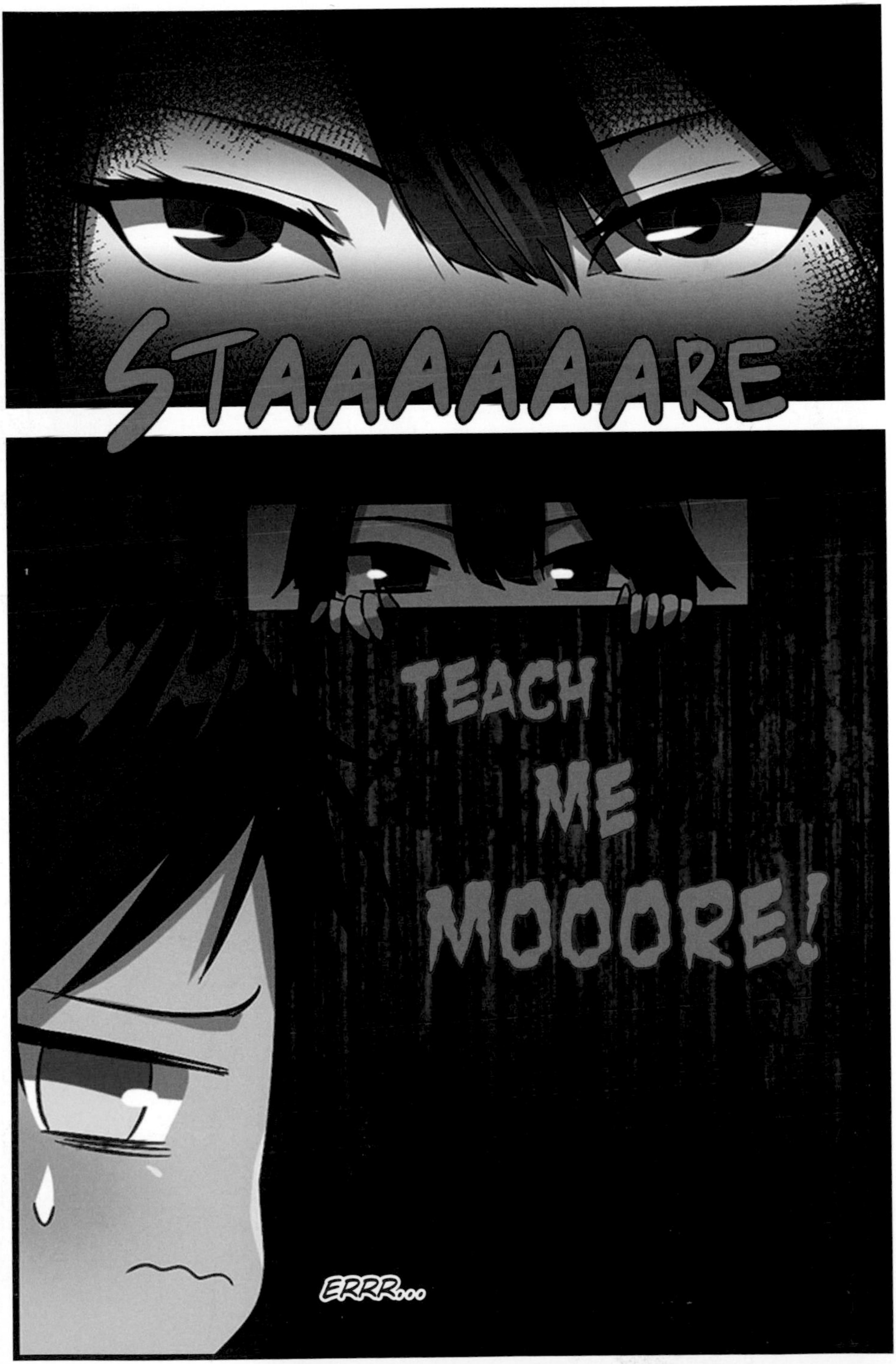
STAAAAAARE
TEACH ME MOOORE!
ERRR...

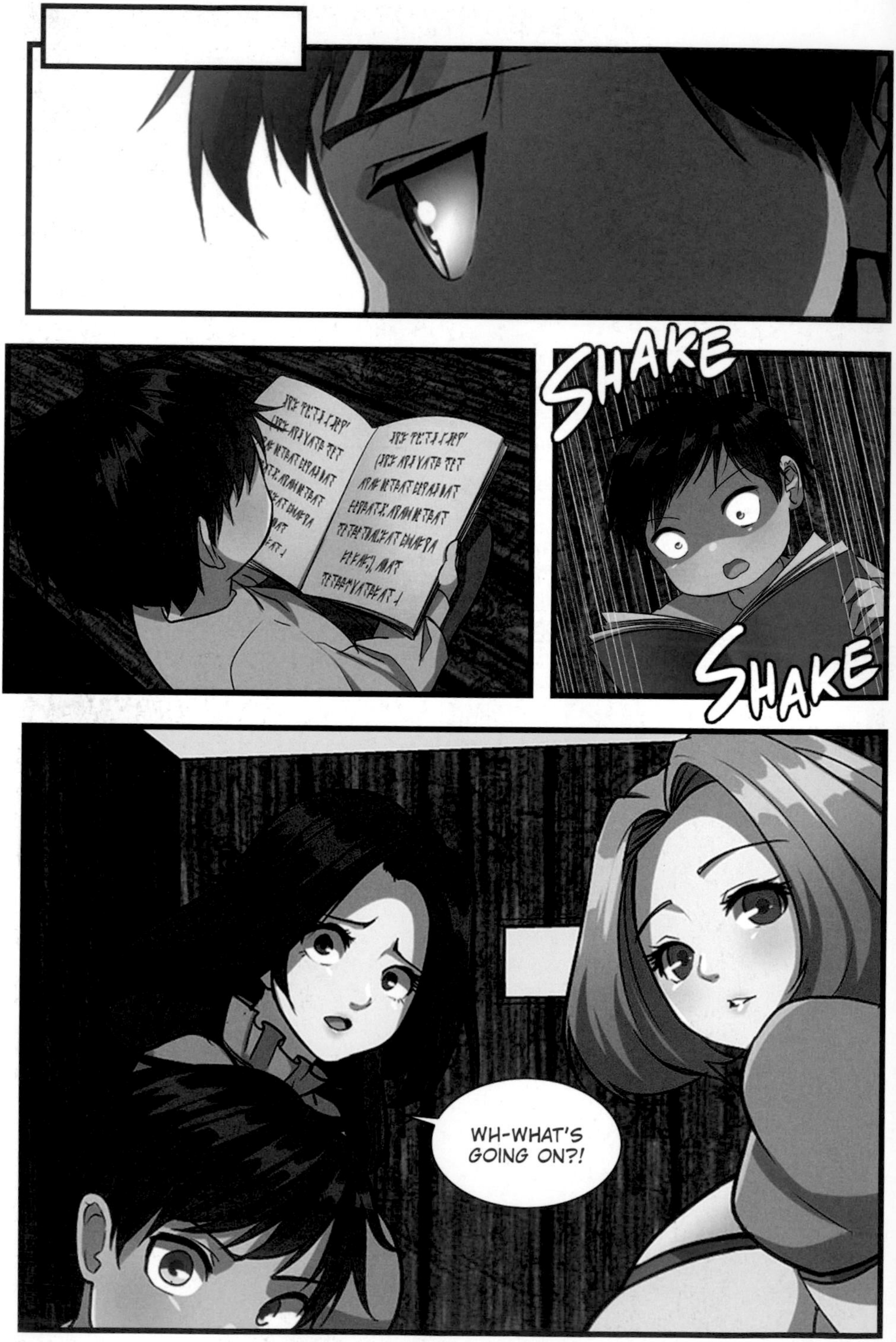
SHAKE
SHAKE
WH-WHAT'S GOING ON?!

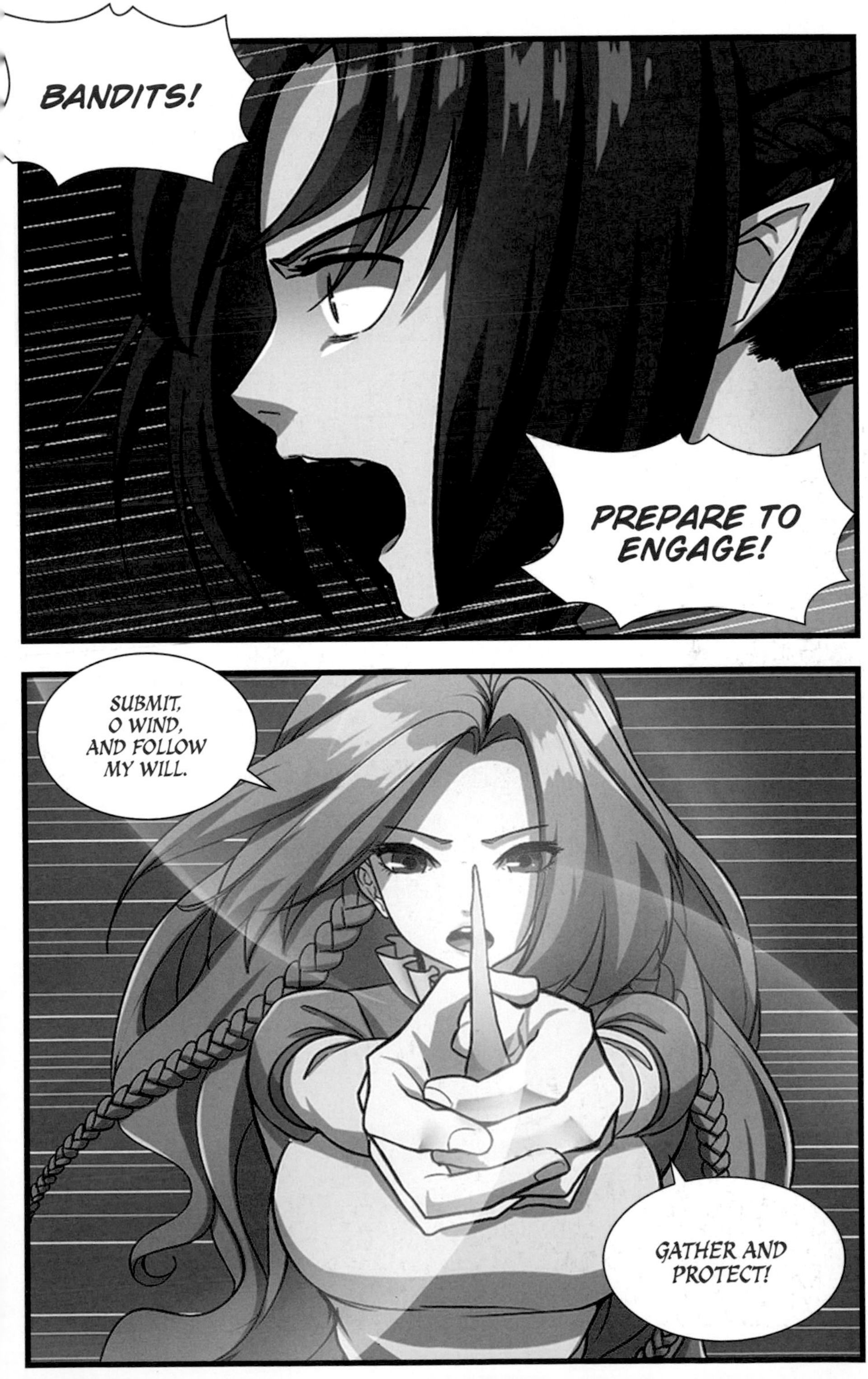
BANDITS!
PREPARE TO ENGAGE!
SUBMIT, O WIND, AND FOLLOW MY WILL.
GATHER AND PROTECT!

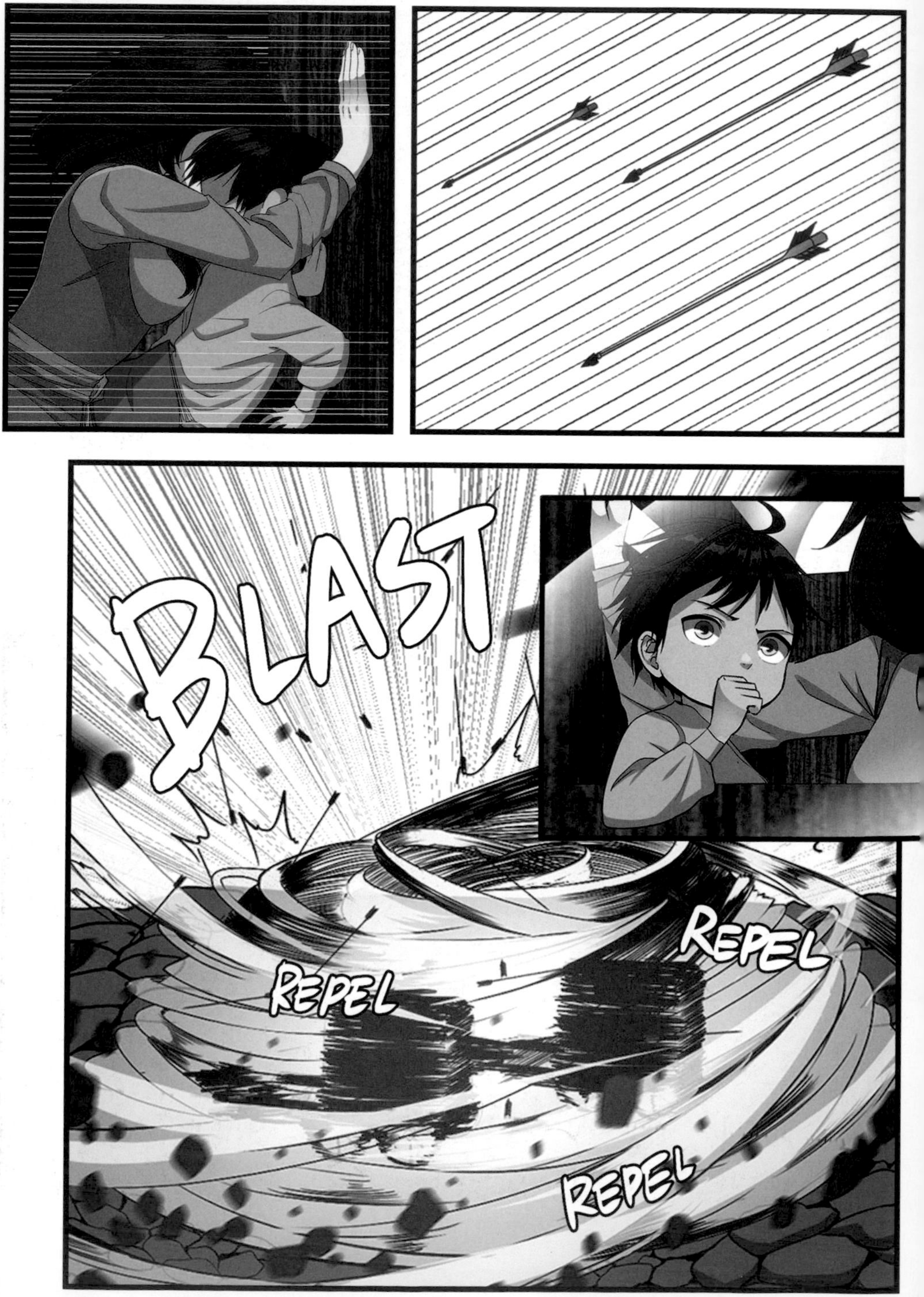
BLAST
REPEL
REPEL
REPEL

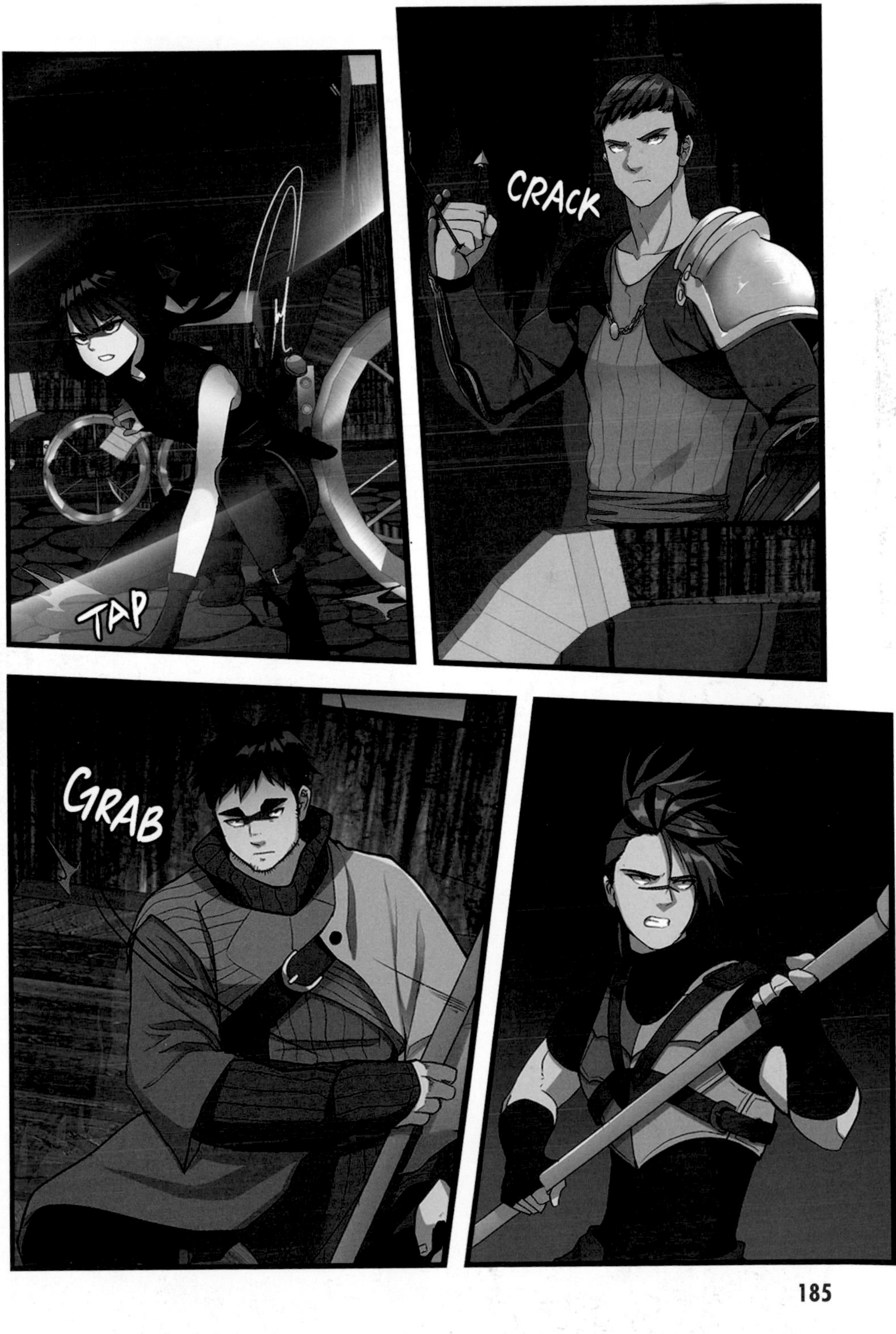
TAP
CRACK
GRAB

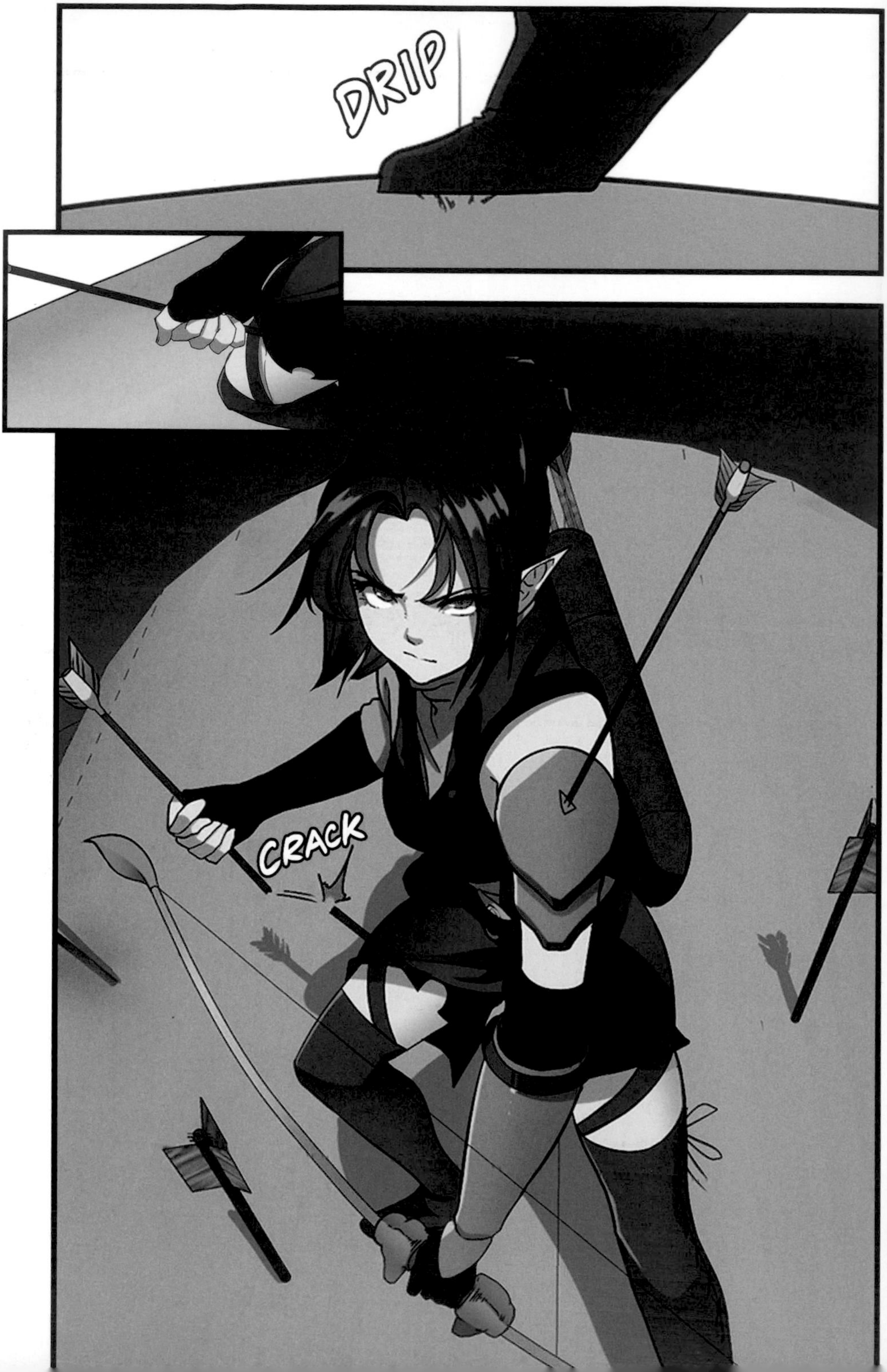
DRIP
CRACK

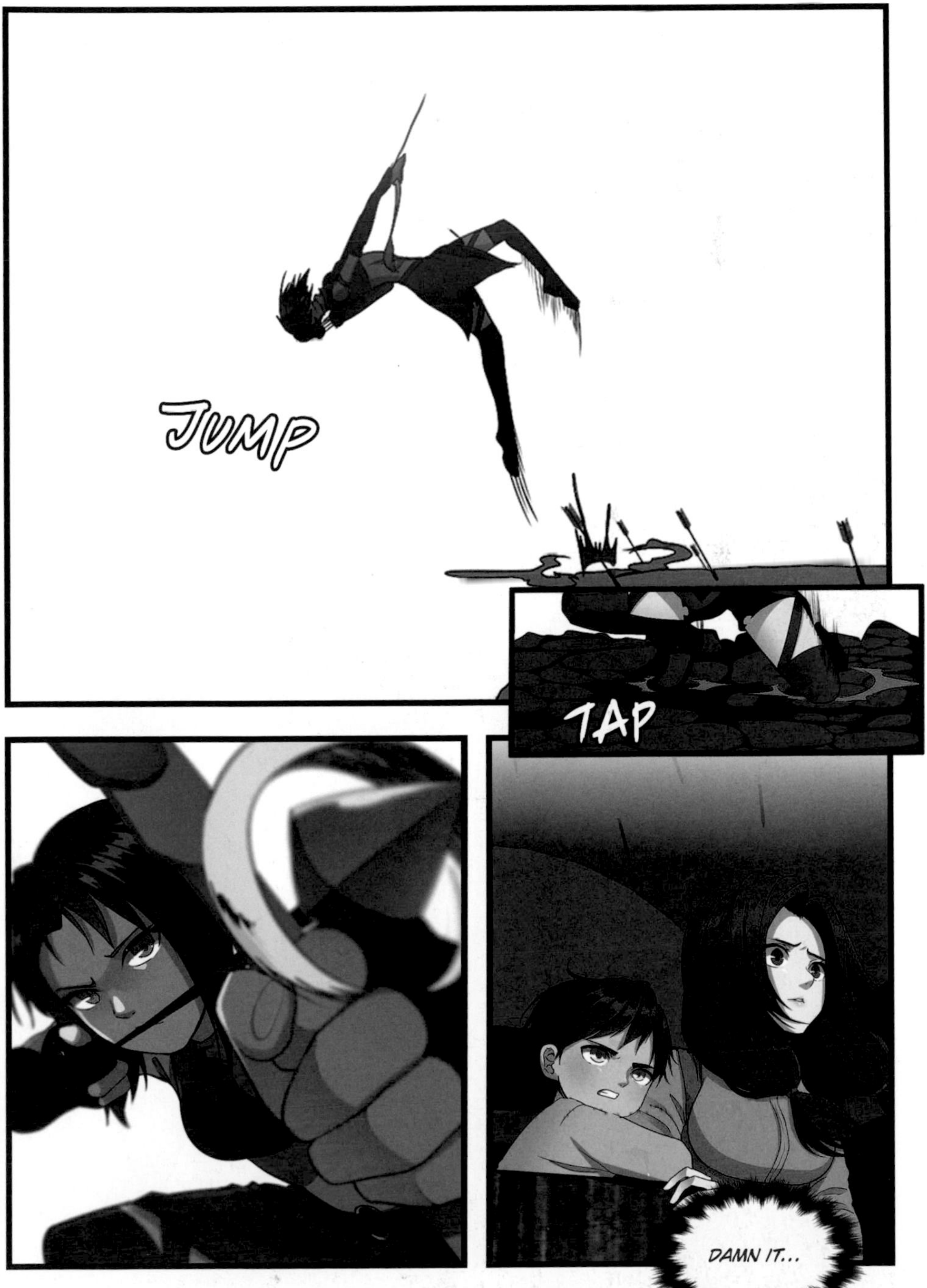
JUMP
TAP
DAMN IT...

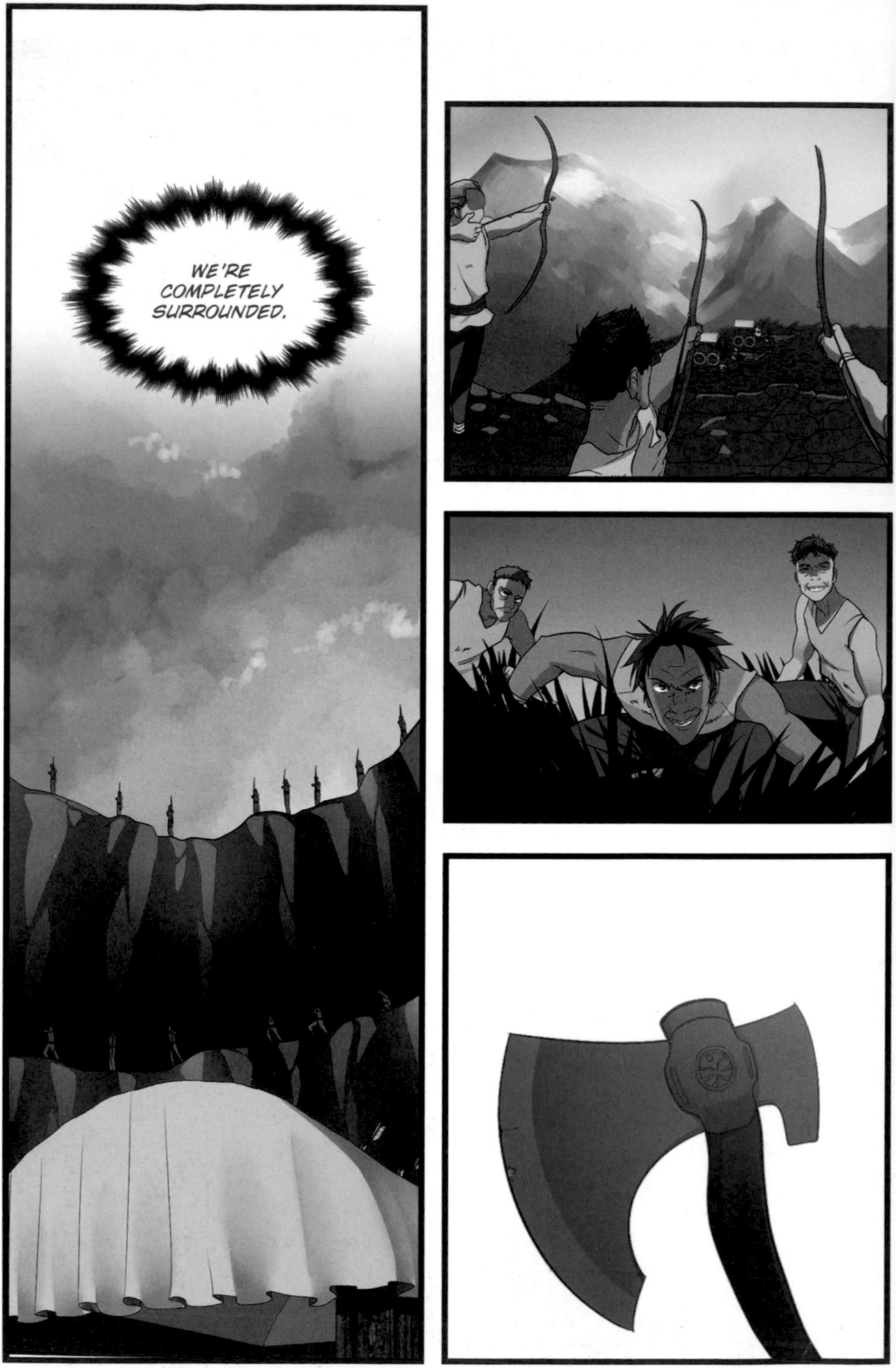
WE'RE COMPLETELY SURROUNDED.

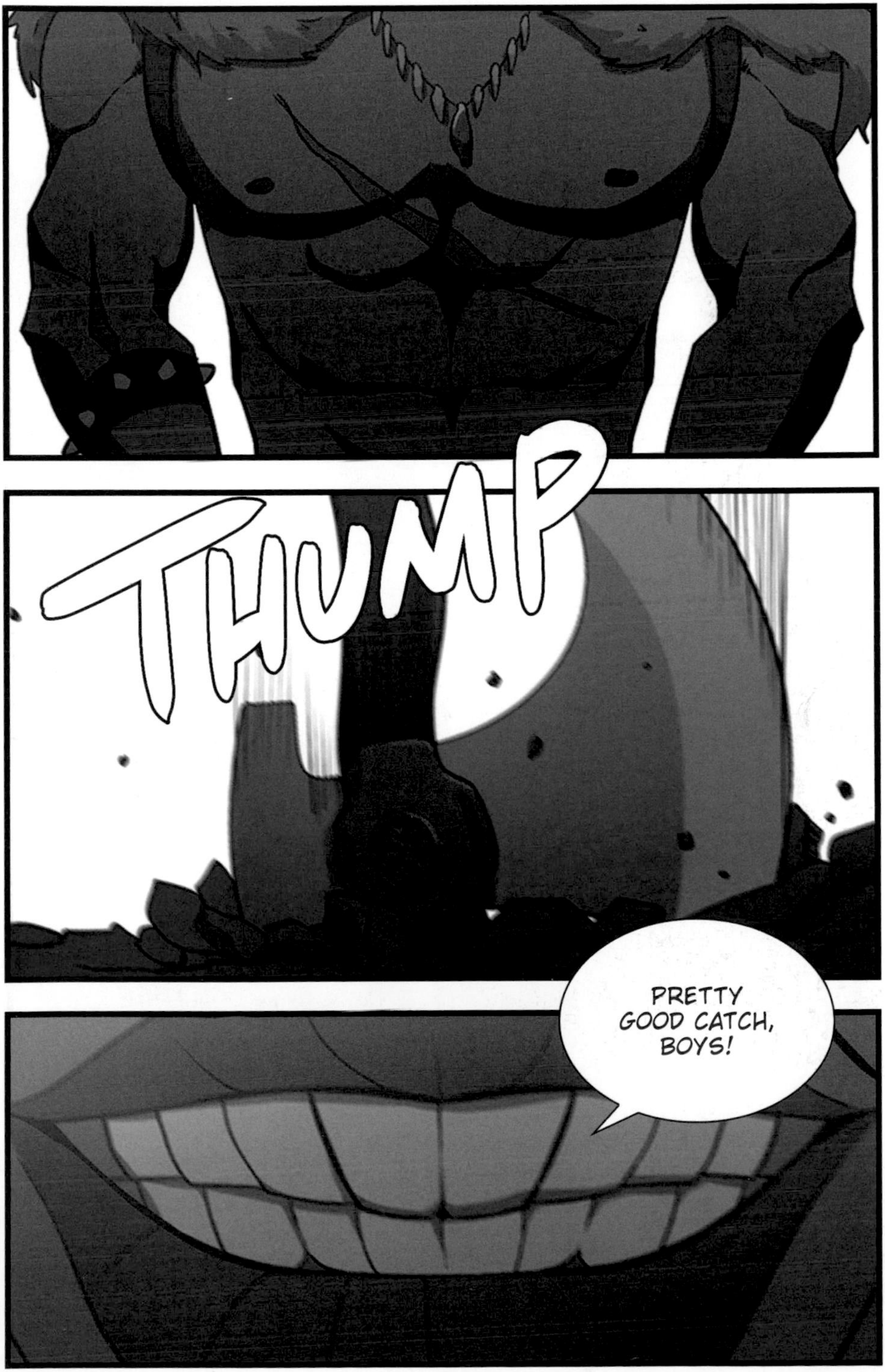
THUMP
PRETTY GOOD CATCH, BOYS!

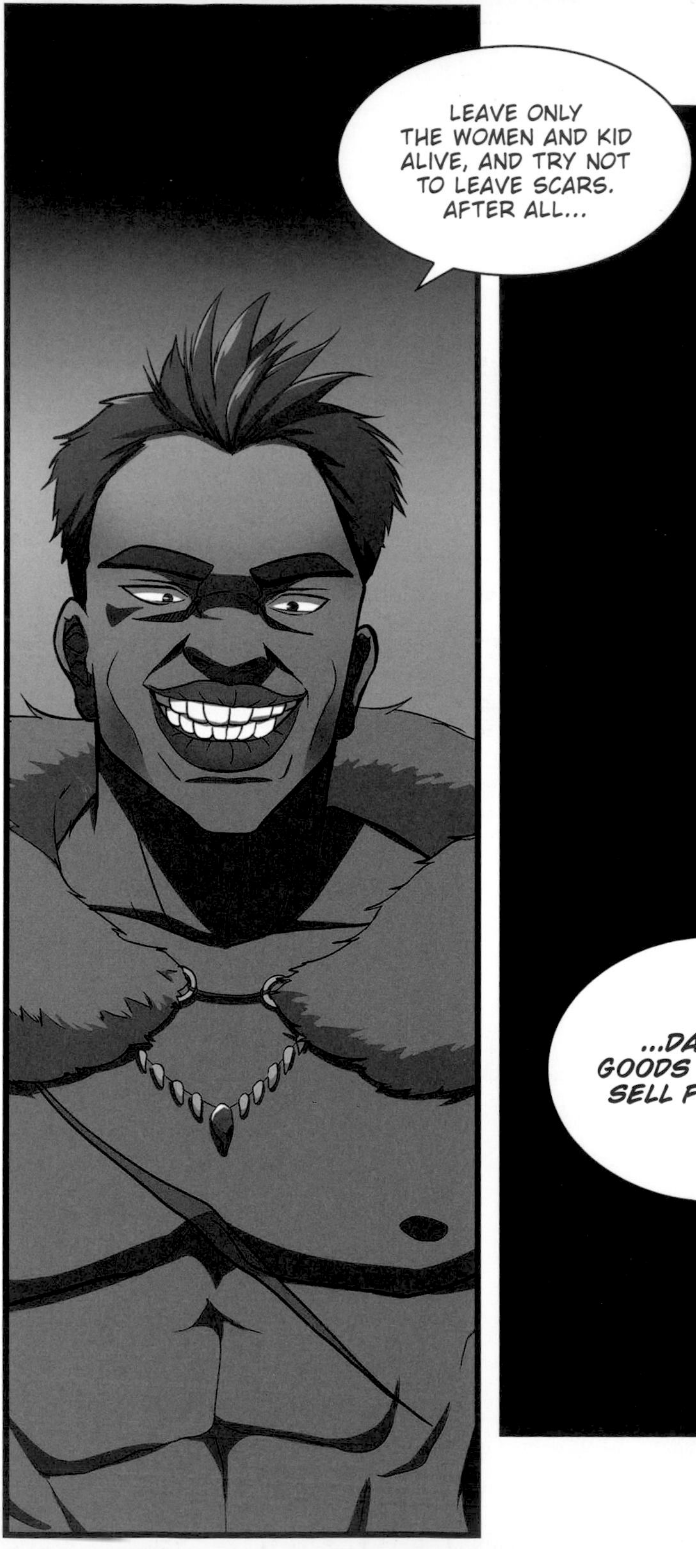
LEAVE ONLY THE WOMEN AND KID ALIVE, AND TRY NOT TO LEAVE SCARS. AFTER ALL...
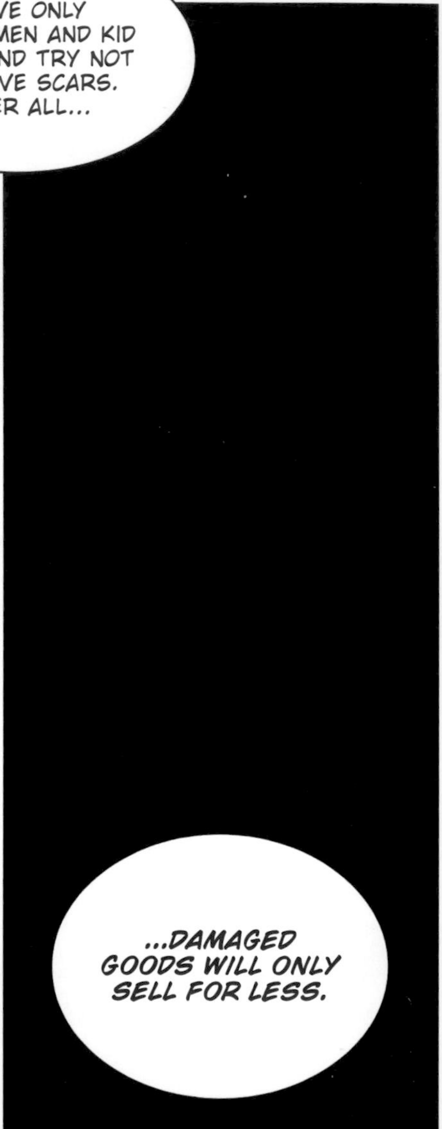
...DAMAGED GOODS WILL ONLY SELL FOR LESS.

THE BEGINNING AFTER THE END

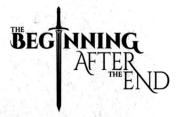

TO BE CONTINUED IN VOLUME 2

THE BEGINNING AFTER THE END 1

21982320482122

Story by TurtleMe
Art by Fuyuki23
Colors by issatsu

© 2015 TurtleMe, LLC
All rights reserved.
Originally published in 2018 and continually updated in serialized form on Tapas (www.tapas.io).
For Tapas Media:
Edited by Gabrielle Luu
Editor in Chief: Michael Son

Yen Press
150 West 30th Street, 19th Floor
New York, NY 10001

Visit us at yenpress.com)(facebook.com/yenpress)(twitter.com/yenpress)(yenpress.tumblr.com)(instagram.com/yenpress

First Yen Press Edition: July 2022
Lettering: Erin Hickman
Art Layout: BonHyung Jeong
Edited by Yen Press Editorial: Liz Marbach, JuYoun Lee
Designed by Yen Press Design: Wendy Chan

Yen Press is an imprint of Yen Press, LLC.
The Yen Press name and logo are trademarks of Yen Press, LLC.

Library of Congress Control Number: 2022935384

ISBN: 978-1-9753-4563-1

10 9 8 7 6 5 4 3 2 1

WOR

Printed in the United States of America